Chapter One
Introduction

Some people believe that gender is intricately linked to most of what we do. I am one of those people. I believe we are like fish, and that gender is the water in which we swim. Fish may not notice the water as they swim along. In much the same way, gender is all around us, moves through us, and serves as the defining force behind some of our social systems – often without us even being aware of it. This book will consider gender to be the water in which we swim. Though it affects some of us more than others, gender remains a largely inescapable designation for most people. Why do you think that is?

Unlike other classes you may take, you already have a connection to this material. You have a gender. Therefore, regardless of your beliefs about the role of gender in this society, you will have to deal with other people's beliefs about gender in general – and your gender in particular. I know a woman who liked to exclaim, "I just want to be known as a director – not a female director." While many of us certainly understand what she was saying, is it even an option? Could you be genderless in this society? What would it mean? What would it look like? Does rejecting masculine activity make you more feminine? Or, vice versa? Is gender a continuum along which we must place ourselves? These are challenging questions that I hope you will be better able to answer at the end of this book.

What Is The Meaning Of Gender?

I enjoy movies, and – every March, like millions of other people across the world – I enjoy watching the Academy Awards (the Oscars). I watch the awards for "Best Actor" and "Best Actress" particularly closely. Have you ever wondered why the Academy uses sex as a primary division when handing out its golden statue? When I've asked my students this question, they often suggest that female actors usually portray different roles than male actors and therefore face different acting challenges. Although I do not disagree with that argument, there are many other valid categorizations that might be more helpful, including young vs. old actors, acting in comedies vs. dramas, and new actors vs. veterans. Should sex should be the primary classification for the Academy to use? What might make more sense?

For most of us, gender is a primary categorizing concept. Research suggests that most individuals notice sex, race, and age first and can quickly sort individuals into categories based on those characteristics (Baudouin & Humphreys, 2006; Ito & Urland, 2003; Zebrowitz, 1997). If you cannot tell what sex someone is, does it bother you? Or, do you just shrug and walk on? See Box 1.1 for a overview of the Saturday Night Live gender ambiguous character "Pat" whose skits involved the lengths to which individuals would go to "discover" his/her gender. Many of us are bothered and look for telltale bulges and clothing cues that may help us. Cognitive research supports the assertion that prototypical (representative) stimuli are actually "easier on the mind" suggesting that individuals who "look" like what we think a man or woman should look like will be cognitively easier and affectively more pleasant to categorize (Winkielman, Halberstadt, Fazendeiro, & Catty, 2006).

Box 1.1 – *Saturday Night Live's* gender ambiguous character "Pat"

Pat was a fictional character created and performed by Julia Sweeney for the American sketch comedy show *Saturday Night Live.* The sketches involved a celebrity guest hosts encountering Pat and then going to great lengths to discover Pat's true gender without being so rude as to actually ask.

How did the sketch keep the gender of Pat unclear? With quotes that start a person thinking one way and then switching:

- **Pat:** Sorry if I'm a little grumpy, I have really bad cramps... I rode my bike over here, and my calf muscles are KILLING me!
- So, what we wanna know is you a brotha or a sista?
- **Pat**: Well, I'm an only child...
- **Pat:** I just want to get a few toiletries. Uh, first of all, I need some protection... from underarm wetness. I'm never one to offend!

Sources: http://www.nbc.com/Saturday_Night_Live/ and http://www.imdb.com/

Writings from western societies in the past several centuries have shown a deep bias toward biological predispositions for gender roles (Fausto-Sterling, 1992). In addition, many of us may overestimate the role that gender plays in a variety of situations.

Consider the child in the following photo:

Figure 1

Try to predict whether or not this child will be good at video games. You get only one guess; however, you can ask any question about the child. What question would you ask? What question would best help you predict this child's video game ability? Do you want to know if the child is a boy or girl? Knowing the sex may tell you something, but not everything. We know, for instance, that boys play more video games than girls (Wright, et al., 2001). But any of the following questions would be more predictive: Does the child have access to video games at home? How much experience does the child have playing video games? Does the child like to play video games? Often, gender or sex will only tell us a small piece of a situation. Gender *may* be related to whether or not children like video games, but the whole picture is more complex. Factors such as amount of free time, whether the child owns a video game, and the child's socioeconomic status all contribute to whether the child will like video games.

The classification of gender into two categories – male and female – oversimplifies the way that gender interacts with a host of other interesting factors and oversimplifies our understanding of gender. Gender is a primary categorization in most cultures (Ortner, 1996), even when it is not necessarily the most logical organizational choice. For these reasons, gender is an important variable for us to understand.

Sex versus Gender

You may have noticed the use of two terms in this chapter – gender and sex. In the social sciences, and in other fields, researchers have begun to use these terms specifically rather than interchangeably. **Sex** refers to the biological occurrence of maleness and femaleness, whereas **gender** refers to the cultural meanings attached to maleness and femaleness (Unger, 1979). "Sex" suggests a nature-oriented state of being, whereas, gender suggests a more nurture-oriented argument of environment shaping the behavior. The vast majority of psychological differences between men and

women are gender-oriented. In other words, these differences can be attributed to environmental influences, or, at the very least, a complex interaction between environment and biology (e.g., Fausto-Sterling, 2001; Litton, 2001). In this book, you will explore explanations for gender differences that arise from biological predispositions, social expectations, and psychological tendencies.

How Is Sex Determined?

We can think about the biology of sex with four different concepts: biological sex, chromosomal sex, hormonal sex, and sexual genitalia. What is your sex? How do you know? What "counts" as the evidence for sex categorization? Fact is, you probably don't "really" know your sex. Unless you have had your chromosomes analyzed for medical reasons or in a biology lab, you probably don't know your chromosomal structure, and chromosomes are the primary determinants of biological sex. If you have XX sex chromosomes (female), you received an X sex

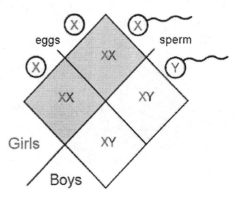

chromosome from your father and an X from your mother. If you have XY sex chromosomes (male), you received a Y sex chromosome from your father and an X from your mother. However, chromosomal anomalies (irregularities) can produce other types of sex chromosome arrangements, such as XO (Turner's Syndrome), XYY, XXX, and others. We will look at these syndromes carefully in Chapter 4, because they teach us much about sexual development in fetuses.

If you do not know your actual chromosomes, then what does that mean for determining sex? Most of us use the clues you would expect. We use external genitalia (do you have a scrotum or labia?), we use internal genitalia (do you have ovaries or testes?), and we use the results of hormones (did your voice deepen during puberty or did you develop breasts?). None of these categories is actually completely separate. Individuals will vary across the categories. For instance, you could be an XY individual whose body does not recognize testosterone, so you resemble a female. Furthermore, knowing someone's sex may not tell you about their gender identification or their behaviors.

Slide Show

Gender: Going Beyond Sex

When psychologists analyze gender, we use additional criteria beyond biological sex. One criterion is **gender identity,** an individual's subjective perception of his or her own gender (Francoeur, 1991). The only way to determine anyone's gender identity is to *ask* him or her. Gender identity helps us to understand why a person with no breasts, short hair, and a penis, could say, "I feel like a woman trapped in man's body." While it may sound like something from a daytime talk show, the implications of these "mismatches" between body and mind are crucial in our understanding of sex and gender. Knowing about these distinctions also helps us from jumping to too many conclusions and reminds us that the simple binary or dichotomous view of sex (or gender) as male/female fails to capture very important information about individuals. Namely, most of our thoughts, feelings, and behaviors cannot be easily slotted into a particular category. In addition, if there are categories, they tend to be overlapping and interlinked. Gender is "socially constructed" -- that is, our gendered thoughts and behaviors come from our social practices. Although it is clear that much of gender is socially constructed, I will provide you with information about biological links whenever the research is available.

What about Sexual Orientation?

Even if you knew someone's gender identity, you may not know anything about that person's **sexual orientation** – that is you may not know to whom this person is sexually attracted. In the past, researchers have also mistakenly treated sexual orientation as a two-category (dichotomous) experience (Mondimore, 1996). As we will see throughout this book and particularly in Chapter 4 on the biological bases of the sexes, it is probably best to think of sexual orientation as similar to gender in that neither one is best conveyed by breaking the concept into only two categories. Although most individuals

would place themselves into one of two categories (either male or female, either homosexual or heterosexual), thinking of these concepts as only two categories keeps us as individuals and as researchers from better understanding the experience of gender and/or sexual orientation. Linda Waters, an artist, songwriter, and self-proclaimed bisexual makes a good argument about the constraints of these labels when she writes about her own experiences as someone living outside categorical gender and sexual orientation experience:

> At this point in my life I am in what some people would call "transition mode." In other words I am living part-time as a woman but many people still perceive me to be a man. My attire tends to be entirely androgynous. In stores and places of business I often get called "ma'am" or "sir" regardless of my attire.... The reason I do this is simple; I do not feel quite capable at this point of "passing" full time as a woman and I absolutely refuse to live as a man. So I choose something which is neither male nor female, nor exactly a hybrid of the two since I think that gender goes a great deal beyond a binary system....

> What about people who have shown sexual interest specifically in me? If a lesbian is interested in a woman who has a penis is she still a lesbian? If a gay male is interested in a woman who wants to exchange her penis for a vagina is he still a gay male? Are we interested in the person behind the sex organs or are the sex organs our primary motivating force in determining to whom we are attracted? ... Is sexual orientation constructed in a manner which even allows for such perspectives as my own? ... Am I bisexual because I am interested both in men and women or am I bisexual because I am interested in the person behind the gender? Or is it some combination of the two? Does gender play a role but not one to the point where I would not be attracted to someone based specifically on their gender? (Waters, 1992, ¶ 1, ¶7, ¶ 8).

"Exploring Sexual Orientation Part 1/2"
"Exploring Sexual Orientation Part 2/2"

Is Gender Fluid?

Throughout this book, I urge you to think of sex, gender, and sexual orientation as fluid categories. They are less separate and more easily changed than most people think. While it might be cognitively easier to think of only two categories that don't overlap, most people don't fit into any categories very easily and gender is certainly a fluid category because it is socially constructed. Individuals and groups in societies construct the meaning of being female or male, or heterosexual and homosexual. Madson (2001) developed a classroom activity where students are asked to choose a one category (lesbian, gay, heterosexual, or bisexual) for a variety of individuals described in short vignettes. The activity helps those involved to come to understand what kinds of dimensions are important to us as we categorize people according to sexuality. Madson designed descriptions that mixed important dimensions such as current relationship status, psychological attachments, self-identification, and current and past behavior.

Try a couple of these categorizations yourself and see what it yields about your own concepts about what is important in determining sexual orientation.

1. A recently divorced woman who had been married to man for 19 years is now living with her female partner.
2. A man who has had several intimate sexual relationships with both women and men, though he generally prefers the company of men.
3. A man who has self-identified as gay since his teens, who has had two brief sexual relationships with women, and who has been involved with his current (male) partner for 3 years (Madson, 2001, p. 35).

Gender Roles

Psychologists speak often about "gender roles." In fact, gender roles are the crux of this book. **Gender roles** are the thoughts, feelings, and behaviors that individuals or societies associate with a particular gender. Gender role differences are the material in much gender-related comedy. Box 1.2 shows an exaggerated view of women from the movie *How To Lose A Guy In 10 Days* and Box 1.3 shows an exaggerated view of men from the television show "*The Man Show.*" Neither the role of a "hyper-feminine" Andie or the one-dimensional men as shown on the "The Man Show" seem to reflect the complexities in the men and women I know. It is important to note that most comedies about gender rest on commonly accepted and exaggerated stereotypes about the genders. If audiences did not have a common knowledge of the stereotypes, the entertainment results would likely not be very funny. So, analyses of popular culture help us understand commonly recognized gender stereotypes. We will discuss how stereotypes are maintained and utilized in Chapter 5 on the "Gender Expectations."

BOX 1.2: Exaggerated Portrayals of Gender in Popular Culture:
How to Lose a Guy in 10 Days

How to Lose a Guy in 10 Days (2003) by Paramount Home Video

Summary: Andie Anderson is a female writer for a woman's magazine. As part of an article for the magazine Andie tries to get "Ben" to break up with her. In less than one week, Andie does all of the following:

- Helps him miss several basketball play-off games. Once they are actually attending, and she asks him go and get her a soda during the exciting last minutes of the game.
- Calls him cutesy nicknames such as "Benny Boop-Boop," "Benny Wenny," and "Benji"
- Takes him to the "chick flick" *Sleepless in Seattle*, during which she tries to talk to him during the movie about "feelings," acts jealous, and gets him into a fist fight.
- Decorates his apartment with a pink quilt, pink towels and toilet seat cover, stuffed animals.
- Names his penis "Princess Sophia."

- Gets them a yappy small dog and then clothes that match each other and the dog.
- Talks about being a "family" by the second date and creates a family album from photos including what their wedding and children will look like.
- Leaves him 17 phone messages in one day.
- Fills his medicine cabinet with women's products such as vaginal cream and tampons.
- Takes him to a Celine Dion concert and buys them matching t-shirts from the concert.
- Crashes his men's poker night and makes them stop smoking and start eating healthy snacks.
- When he still won't break up with her... her friends do the "checklist" and ask if she's been "clingy, needy, whining, talking baby talk, obsessing over his old girlfriends, and talking about her old boyfriends."

Swap the characters and think about what Ben would have done to get her to break up with him. What are the stereotypic "male behaviors" that drive women crazy?

Box 1.3 Exaggerated Portrayals of Gender in Popular Culture: *The Man Show*

The Man Show is "An unapologetic look at things men like, do and think." (Comedy Central, 1999).

What are men like according to the show?
- Fat
- Hairy
- Beer swilling
- Woman ogling
- Football obsessed
- Mother-in-law hating

What do men like/want according to the show?
- Women in bikinis bouncing on trampolines (aka the "Juggies")
- Reducing the "Oprah-ization" of America
- Porn
- Farting – and lighting farts
- Masturbating
- Watch tapes of "Baywatch" in super slo-mo

Imagine "The Woman Show" what would women be like according to the show? What would they like and want?

Gender roles represent our beliefs about men and women. Who is supposed to sit with their legs together? Who is allowed to scratch their private parts in public? In Chapter 3 we will look at theories that help explain how little boys and girls come to understand their own genders and the behaviors expected of them. Chapter 6 will explore the sources of socialization that shape all of our understandings and beliefs about gender.

Why A Psychology Of Gender?

Earlier, I suggested that psychology was just one way to think about gender. Psychology as an academic discipline distinguishes itself from other social science disciplines by focusing on the individual. As psychologists, we try to predict and explain individual's behavior based on our knowledge about their attributes and the situation. Other social sciences offer a wider picture of human behavior. For instance, sociology and political science focus more on groups, and history focuses more on large-scale human behavior over time. The differences among the social sciences are a matter of focus and the research methods best suited to that focus. Psychology has a tapered focus on the individual whereas the focus of the other disciplines is wider. Each discipline can tell us much about gender. No analysis of gender would be complete without the perspectives of history, sociology, economics, and the natural sciences.

In this book, I will focus primarily on psychological research on humans for two major reasons. First, many of you may take other gender courses, and I think it is important to reduce overlap. As an undergraduate, I was a psychology and women's studies major. In women's studies, I enjoyed learning about gender through the variety of lens offered by disciplines other than psychology. It helped to have courses focused within their own disciplines with links to other disciplines to understand the differences and similarities. Second, many of you are likely taking this course for psychology credit, and I like students to get a solid sense of the methods and findings appropriate to particular disciplines. Therefore, my focus on psychological research is, in part, to help you get a better sense of psychology as a discipline. Chapter 2 regarding studying gender will provide the methodological and statistical underpinnings of comparing men and women.

Psychology, with its focus on individuals, often breaks down human functioning into three categories: thoughts, feelings, and behaviors (e.g., Myers, 2004). I have used these three categories to explore the gender differences that psychologists have studied. As you read these chapters be mindful that thoughts, feelings and behaviors are not separate categories, each informs the other and some experiences fall in between the dualisms. I have used these categories as a convenient and traditional way to think about human experience through a psychological lens. Chapter 7 will explore differences in thought, Chapter 8 will explore differences in feelings, and Chapters 9, 10, and 11 will delve into the behavioral differences between men and women. When you measure thoughts, feelings, and behaviors, there are more similarities and fewer differences between men and women than you may think (Hyde, 2005). But despite few differences, men and women can end up experiencing the world very differently. In fact, a central question behind this book is, "Why do men and women experience the world so differently if there are so few sex differences in basic functioning?" Consequently, the two of the last chapters of this book focus on gendered experiences: Chapter 12 explores psychological investigations regarding gender and life stages, so we will focus on relationships, parenting, and aging, and Chapter 13 looks at the experience of work. Finally, in Chapter 14 we will step back to take a look at what we have learned and any conclusions we may be able to draw.

Race, Ethnicity, And Class In The Study Of Gender

Gender is interconnected to many other important aspects of human experience. However, gender's connection to race, ethnicity, culture, and social class is so primary that, as psychologists and students, we should not artificially separate them from each other. Two primary arguments exist for the analyzing gender as associated with race, ethnicity, culture and class. First, just as most early researchers assumed that gender was biologically driven, they also assumed that race and class were biologically driven. Scholars now have ample evidence that gender, race, and class are predominantly socio-cultural constructions (e.g., Gergen, 1999). Secondly, although the patterns are not straightforward, gender, race, and class are too interlinked to parse them into separate categories. For instance, my experience as a woman is further defined by the fact that I am European American and was raised upper middle class.

"Red Eye: Half-Time Report and Unique Gender Study"

Defining Race, Ethnicity, And Culture

For race, ethnicity, and culture I have chosen definitions accepted by the Department of Health and Human Services (2001). I have chosen these definitions because I think it is important for you to see an example of the U.S. government's use of these categories. Given the high level of visibility and usage of government documents, a government definition will represent considerable consensus among scholars as well as a widely reviewed source of information. The Department of Health and Human Services provided these particular definitions in order to help make meaning of the differences in mental health statuses that are seen across ethnic and racial groups.

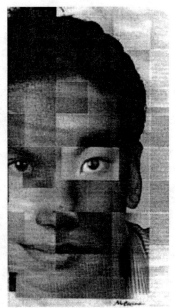

Race: Race is not a biological category, but it does have meaning as a social category. Different cultures classify people into racial groups according to a set of characteristics that are *socially* significant. The concept of race is especially potent when certain social groups are separated, treated as inferior or superior, and given differential access to power and other valued resources.

Ethnicity: Ethnicity refers to a common heritage shared by a particular group. Heritage includes similar history, language, rituals, and preferences for music and foods. The term "race," when defined as a social category may overlap with ethnicity but each has a different social meaning. For example, in many national surveys and in the 1990 U.S. census, Native Hawaiians and Vietnamese Americans are classified together in the racial category of "Asian and Pacific Islander Americans." Native Hawaiians, however, have very little in common with Vietnamese Americans in terms of their heritage. Similarly, Caribbean blacks and Pacific Northwest Indians have different ethnicities than others within their same racial category. And, as noted earlier, because Hispanics are an ethnicity, not a race, the different Latino American ethnic subgroups such as Cubans, Dominicans, Mexicans, Puerto Ricans, and Peruvians include individuals of all races.

Culture: Culture is broadly defined as a common heritage or set of beliefs, norms, and values. It refers to the shared, and largely learned, attributes of a group of people. Anthropologists often describe culture as a system of shared meanings. People who are placed, either by census categories or through self-identification, into the same racial or ethnic group are often assumed to share the same culture. Yet this assumption is an over-generalization because not all members grouped together in a given category will share the same culture. Many may identify with other social groups to which they feel a stronger cultural tie such as being Catholic, Texan, teenaged, or gay. A key aspect of any culture is that it is dynamic: Culture continually changes and is influenced both by people's beliefs and the demands of their environment. (U.S. Department of Health and Human Services, 2001, p. 22, 24).

Social class does not have a standardized definition, as it is not synonymous with income. **Social class** is much closer to the concept of culture defined above than it is to a cut-and-dried notion of how much money one makes. When asked what factors should be considered when decided what class someone is in, respondents answered categories such as the way they speak, where they live, their family background and appearance and behavior (Reid, 1989). Overall, these "way of life" categories were seen as more important than job and income. Interestingly, because the United States purports to be a "classless society" psychologists have largely ignored subjective measurements of class (Argyle, 1994).

Most psychological and sociological studies measure a construct called **socio-economic status (SES)**. Although researchers measure SES in slightly different ways, most use a measure constructed out of one's education, income, and occupational status. Survey researchers have also developed clever indices where they assign an occupation a ranking that combines its earning power with its perceived prestige. A CEO of a corporate has high prestige and high earnings; a car wash employee has low income and low prestige. A real estate agent is a high pay, low prestige job and a minister is a low pay, high prestige job. No matter how it is measured, the experience of social class plays a major role in the experience of gender (e.g., Roschelle, 1997). For instance, despite the fact that researchers get very excited over the large increase in working mothers, we know that poor women have always worked. The largest change has been in the percentage of middle class and upper middle class women who are employed. Consequently, in this case, social class directly affects how a woman might experience society's reaction to her working.

As a caveat, you should be aware that much psychological research tends to report racial differences rather than ethnic differences. As you can tell from the definitions, ethnic differences are harder to measure with standard methods. So, racial categories are more often measured than ethnic categories, and, therefore, racial differences are more likely to be reported than ethnic differences. Fortunately, the most current research in psychology appears to be assessing more ethnic variation than before.

Whenever possible, I will include research on racial, ethnic, and class experiences in this textbook. When the research is not available, I urge you to think about why the research is not available, and what might be learned when researchers start to look.

Looking At Race, Ethnicity, Social Class, And Gender Visually

In the next several figures, I have diagramed ways to think about the potentially complex and different ways that race and gender *could* relate to one another depending on the human behavior of interest. It is important to note that these are not statistical models; these are conceptual models to help you think about these complex issues. In these examples, I refer to the effects as "race" effects, because the research has used racial categories. Of course, these effects are likely to be ethnic effects; however, research would need to determine the specific cultural or ethnic components or variations.

Figure 1.2

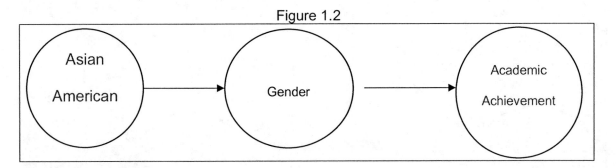

In Figure 1.2, a diagram is shown where academic achievement is the outcome variable of interest. In this model, being Asian American affects the experience of one's gender, which, in turn, affects one's academic achievement. In other words, being Asian American "supersedes" gender and affects gender before gender affects academic achievement. There is a high emphasis on academic achievement in most Asian American cultures. Males and females are expected to do well academically (Julian, et al., 1994; Wong, Lai, Nagasawa, & Lin, 1998). Gender could affect Asian Americans' academic achievement, but for this particular domain, race is the most influential effect.

Figure 1.3

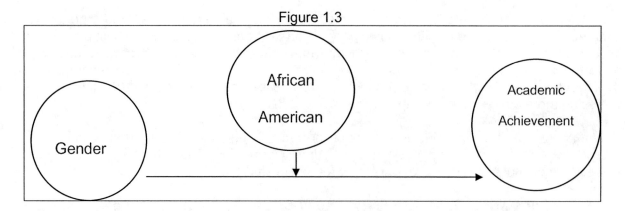

In Figure 1.3, another racial-gender relationship is shown. In this situation, gender has a direct relationship to academic achievement, particularly if one is African American. In many African American subcultures, there is more emphasis on academic achievement for African American women than for African American men (Chavous, Harris, Rivas, Helaire, & Green, 2004) Thus, both gender and race interact to create the outcome.

Figure 1.4

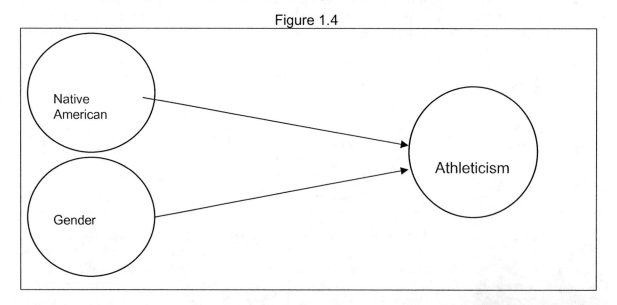

Figure 1.4 shows a situation where there is no direct relationship between gender and ethnicity known for the outcome variable of interest. In this case, gender may affect athleticism because western society may value athleticism more in men than women, and, being Native American may affect athleticism because athleticism is not a highly prized attribute in many tribal cultures (Lewko & Ewing, 1980; Mechikoff & Estes, 1998). But, in this scenario there may be no research that indicates that being Native American or male or female *interact* to influence athleticism.

Overall, these three models to help us think about the potentially complex and different ways that race and gender *could* relate to one another depending on the human behavior of interest. I hope these models spur you to think more fully about the connections, the depth and quality of research required, and, depending on the type of model implied by the research, the practical and policy implications of the findings.

Why A U.S. Focus Rather Than A More Global Focus?

Newer academic work on multiculturalism links cultures across country borders (Gordon, 2005; Wurzel, 2004). This book focuses on gender experiences in the U.S. with resources that will allow interested students to pursue more global understandings of gender. Several factors drove the choice to focus this book on the U.S. First, research indicates that all of us learn best when we study a subject about which we feel a personal connection (Huba & Freed, 2000; Sternberg & Zhang, 2001), and most of the readers of this book will be from a variety of ethnic backgrounds living in the U.S. Second, American colleges have actively pursued the need for more focus on U.S. ethnic minorities in college curricula (e.g., Ackerman, 2002) and sometimes a focus on international cultures can obscure the study of the unique experiences of U.S. - born

 ethnic minorities (Rodriquez, 1996), just as globalization can lead to a form of "homogenization" where cultures and people become more alike (O'Hara & Biesecker, 2003). In fact, the experiences of an African American woman will likely vary significantly from those of a black woman in Africa, or a black African woman immigrant to the U.S. Trying to understand the cultural context of each of these three women requires a deep understanding of the history and psychological variables associated with each culture. Third, I have designed this book to be a concise length, a global perspective would require broader brush strokes, and I wanted to provide some level of depth on the topics that we do cover. At the conclusion of each chapter, I have included website URLs and other resources that will allow interested students to explore gender internationally.

Why Should We Care About The Study Of Gender Psychology?

Throughout this book, I will be urging you to ask a question that is natural for most of us: why should we care about studying gender and its relationship to human functioning? As with all academic topics there are at least three sets of questions and answers. One set is really the answer to "why should *I* care?" and that is more idiosyncratic to your own lives and perspectives. The other set of answers we should be able to answer more uniformly by reframing the question to "Why do *gender psychologists* care?" This book addresses this latter question often, and I hope that you will join "us" in this quest to find more answers. Research is the tool that psychologists use to answer questions, and we will take it seriously throughout this text. Look for the series called, "A closer look at an interesting study." These summaries help you see what kinds of questions can be asked of research papers – primary sources of information, in psychology – and to help you see how interesting research can really be. Finally, there is a third question that asks "why should we as a *society* care?" This question addresses the policy implications of gender psychology findings. Although we will spend less time on this final question, you will see that the conclusions drawn on many of the topics will have direct implications for policy.

Brush Strokes Versus Intricate Detail?

The theories and findings regarding gender psychology are complex. As with most areas within psychology, sets of findings are often qualified with "ifs," "ands," "buts," and under specific conditions. In order to provide a portrait of gender without writing an encyclopedia, I have often painted some of the areas and theories with large brush strokes. Inevitably, it will leave some of you wanting more detail on certain components of the picture. My intent is to make this topic approachable without oversimplifying its implications. Gender psychology is "the psychology of

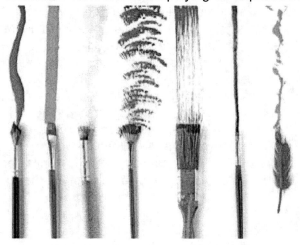

life" with gender as the lens. The psychology of life is an enormous topic, and no book could capture the intricacies and nuances involved in how it is experienced. Brush strokes are problematic when exploring research on gender differences. The overwhelming conclusion regarding men and women is that we are more similar than different. However, we examine differences because it helps us understand the role of research methodology in understanding both similarities and differences. And, we explore differences because we are often called upon to debunk "accepted" beliefs from the past such as men are smarter than women. Most importantly, gender, especially gender behavior is about context. When we study gender, what we really learn about is the role of culture, perceptions, expectations, and situational influences in eliciting gendered behavior. And, one of the key contexts that helps us understand variation in gender behavior is access to, perception of, and use of power. So, while sometimes it may appear that we are focusing on difference, what we really need to focus on is the conditions under which similarities and differences emerge.

I hope this whets your appetite to learn more. Indeed, this book is a bit shorter than some other textbooks precisely because there are so many additional interesting resources in the study of gender psychology that you can read, watch, and experience. I hope this is a jumping off point for you to start your journey in the fascinating world of gender psychology.

Additional ways to think about the material in this chapter

- If you were going to try to disguise yourself as someone of a different gender than yours, what would you change about yourself besides your clothing?
- Given the definitions of race, ethnicity and social class, what is your race? Your ethnicity? Your social class? If someone met you for the first time, what would think your gender, race, ethnicity and social class would be? What are the cues they would use?

Global Connection Opportunities (see Box 1.4 below)

- ❖ http://globetrotter.berkeley.edu/GlobalGender/
- ❖ This site features "research and teaching materials meant to facilitate the integration of Women's and Gender Studies into International and Area Studies philosophy and curricula. This site offers general and specific filmographies and bibliographies on issues pertaining to women and gender in Africa, Asia, Latin America, the Middle East and Arab World, and among minority cultures in North America and Europe as well as links to other interesting resources available on the Web."

Box 1.4

Websites vary in their quality. Before you visit these sites and others, please first become a critical consumer of web information.

Here are three sound websites to help you think about how to ask and answer questions about the quality of websites all of which provide checklists for evaluation web sites.

- ❖ http://www.lib.berkeley.edu/TeachingLib/Guides/Internet/Evaluate.html
- ❖ http://www.library.jhu.edu/researchhelp/general/evaluating/
- ❖ http://www.unc.edu/cit/guides/irg-49.html

Generally speaking, you should be considering:

- ❖ Authorship
- ❖ Publishing body or the source
- ❖ Point of view or bias
- ❖ Referral to other sources
- ❖ Verifiability
- ❖ Currency of the materials

Chapter Two
The Meaning of Difference

Men are, on average, taller than women. A sex difference in height is a well established biological fact. How is this information useful? If you are a doctor measuring a male infant's height, it is more accurate to compare his height to the norms for male babies than female babies. If you were designing jeans, you would make male jeans longer than female jeans. Auto designers take into account average heights when determining where side mirrors are placed. However, do they use average human heights, average male, or average female heights? This chapter will explore how psychologists measure and determine difference. This chapter assumes a beginning level of experience with research design and/or statistics. You may have already had this material, or more advanced material, in other courses. If so, as you read this chapter, try to focus on the research design issues that are particularly salient to gender-related studies.

How Do Psychologists Determine Difference?
Describing A Population

If you wanted to tell someone else how tall your class is, what would you say? Most statistics start at this level. "How can I describe this group in a meaningful way?" If there are two people, you could say, there are two people – one is 5'3" and the other is 5'6". If there are more people, it starts to get messy. What is the easiest statistic with which to describe a group of people's heights? Let's say we have 30 people, 15 men, and 15 women. What can you tell me? You are likely to compute an average – more properly described as a **mean**. You'd take each height, add them all up, and divide by 30. You would say the average height of the group is 5'5". However, that could mean that all 30 people are 5'5". A group of people who are all the same height would be unusual. Even the Rockettes, who have to be similar in height to make the line look even and the dance moves more precise, can be between the heights of 5'9" and 5'11" (Moos, 1997). So, besides the average you may give the **range**. Of the 30 people, the heights range from 4'10" to 6'0".

How To Think About Variance And Overlap

The range will help us understand the high and low ends, but it doesn't tell us the distribution of the individuals according to height. Statisticians call this idea "**variance**." Variance refers to how each individual height varies (moves) from the mean. In statistics, the number most often reported after the mean is the **standard deviation** which is the square root of the variance number. For this book, you'll need a conceptual idea of what these terms mean rather than knowledge of how they are computed.

Figure 2.1

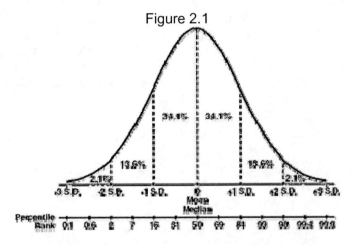

Figure 2.1 shows a traditional standardized **normal curve**. A standardized normal curve means that the mean is zero and the standard deviation is one. The beauty of a normal curve is that by knowing the mean and standard deviation you will know what percent of the population falls within a specified range. As you can see from the chart, information from one standard deviation above the mean and one standard deviation below the mean represents 68% of the population. By adding and additional standard deviation either way (2 standard deviations away from the mean), the data will represent approximately 96% of the population. As we explore some more statistical concepts, we are going to continue to work with height data because height is fairly normally distributed.

If we were to plot out the height of the U.S. adult population (both sexes and all races included), it would look very much like the normal distribution curve shown in Figure 2.1. Currently, for the population of the U.S. (regardless of race), the mean height is 67" (5'7") and the standard deviation is 2" (NHANES III Survey, 1996). If you include the heights that are 1 standard deviation above the mean and 1 standard deviation above the mean 5'5 to 5'9" (or 5'7" + 2" = 5'9" and 5'7" – 2" = 5'5") you will capture 68% of the population. So, 68% of the population of the U.S. is between the heights of 5'5" and 5'9"). Another standard deviation above and below (5'7" + 2" + 2" = 5'11" and 5'7" – 2" – 2" = 5'3") 5'3" to 5'9" picks up 96% of the population. Therefore, an adult's height is 4'7" (or any height below 5'3"), he/she would represent less than 2% of the U.S. population. The same is true if someone was 7'1 or any height above 5'11". Some of us may overestimate how many people are above the height of 5'11" because of the media coverage associated with the National Basketball Association.

Let's consider differences between groups. Go back to our class of 30. If I asked you to tell me about the sex difference in height, what would you tell me? You are likely to give me the mean and the standard for each group. I could look at the numbers and pronounce them as different. However, as researchers we need a more systematic way to understand difference. We ask "is there a **statistically significant difference**?" between these two groups. We compute statistical tests to determine the difference and the probability rate of obtaining that difference. In a classic comparison between two groups, I would report the size of the samples, the means, the standard deviations, the test statistic (e.g., a t value for a t-test, or an F value for an ANOVA) and the probability level. In psychology, the standard accepted statistical probability rate (p) is $p < .05$. That is, the likelihood that the difference is due to chance is less than a 5%. Put another way, if a researcher redid the analysis 100 times, in 95 out of the 100 analyses, she/he would find the difference. So, the phrase, "a difference was found" used in this book means a statistical difference at the .05 level or better was reported by the researcher.

What Does It Mean To Find A Statistical Difference?

To answer this question, let's first go back to the sex differences in height. Figure 2.2 shows the average heights for Hispanic men and women in the U.S.

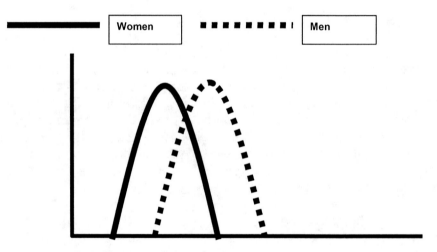

Remember, that a plot of all Hispanics would look like a single normal curve. But, if you plot the two sexes separately, then you see a difference between the curves. If you wanted to convince someone that Hispanic men were taller than Hispanic women, would this chart do it? Probably. However, most people might not notice the more surprising information contained in the chart. First, the difference between the average height of a man and the average height of a woman is 4". Is that a lot? It depends why the information is needed and how it will be used. The second thing to notice is the range in both groups. The difference between a woman in the 5th percentile and the 95th percentile is 8" (4'10" – 5'6") as it is with men (5'3" to 5'11"). This "within group difference" of eight inches is twice the size as the "between group difference" of 4". This is important. When someone describes a difference between two groups, they almost inevitably drop the modifying comment. "Hispanic men are taller than Hispanic women" sounds somewhat different than the "average Hispanic man is taller than the average Hispanic woman."

Throughout this book, I will use the term "on average" or phrases such as "tend to" when discussing difference. It is not about hedging or not wanting to take a stand. It is about correctly conveying the data. Scientists should sound tentative, because most findings are tentative until replicated and generalized.

When thinking about "on average" also remember the "tails" of the curves. The tails are the right and left edges of the curve representing a relatively small percentage of the population. Is it true that for Hispanic Americans the vast majority of people who are 4'10" and shorter are women? Yes. Moreover, are the vast majority of Hispanic Americans over the height of 5'11" male? Yes. Oftentimes, the tails may say something important to us, and we will come back to this question. Overall, the crucial thing to remember about gender and statistical curves is that for almost everything we will study, the curves will overlap. Most individuals (men or women) will fall in the area covered by both curves. So, despite the fact that difference statements such as "men are taller than women" make it sound like the curves look like Figure 2.3 (see below), the curves will usually overlap to a large extent. By the way, while we are discussing height, male professors are taller than the average American of their same age and gender (Hensley, 1993) and a one-inch difference in height has been found to be associated with a $600 difference in starting salary (Frieze, Olson, & Good, 1990). Think about a theory that would help explain those findings - think about social dominance.

Figure 2.3: Gender curves almost never look like this.

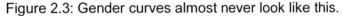

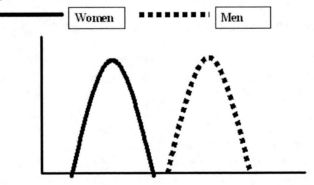

When discussing gender and sex differences, the other important thing to consider is the "shape' of the curve, or rather, the variance of the group. Look at Figure 2.4. In these two curves, the mean would be exactly the same, but the standard deviations would be different. What characteristic might look like this? There is evidence that on some cognitive dimensions, men and women may look like this – we know that men are overrepresented in the category of developmentally disabled and in the genius category (Hedges & Nowell, 1995). But, if you just looked at the means, there would appear to be no gender difference. In addition, many phenomena do not form a perfect bell-shaped normal curve. There are many attributes whose curves are skewed or distorted to the right or left; for instance, the socioeconomic status of college students' families of origin is skewed toward higher incomes. The curves of some attributes

are bi-modal (like a double-humped camel); for instance, women's labor force participation looked like this until recently. The "saddle" represented child-bearing and -rearing years, and fewer women reduce their work outside the home during these years now than they once did.

"Statistics: The Average"

Figure 2.4: Two curves – the men's curve has greater variance than the women's curve

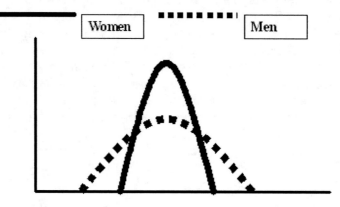

Is A Statistical Difference Always Meaningful?

Recall that the computation of a statistical difference between two groups uses the sample size number. The larger the sample size, the more likely you are to find a statistical difference. Therefore, you could find a difference that is "statistically different" but not meaningfully different. The latter is a subjective. Let's take a look at ACT scores. Who takes the ACT? Every high school student who thinks that he/she might go to college in 25+ states (the rest take the SAT). Approximately, 1.2 million students take the standardized test every year (ACT, 2003). For the English (verbal) test, a perfect score is 36. The average score for women in 2003 was 20.7 and for men 19.8. In math, the average score was 21.2 for men and 20.1 for women. Due to the sample size, the difference is statistically significant. Are these differences meaningful? That depends on how we use them. One way to look at the data is to analyze the percent of men and women who achieve a score considered high enough for a selection of careers. ACT reports that 61% of men are considered qualified as compared to 56% of women. Despite the fact we may find the gap interesting and worth exploring, when do we start to think it is meaningful?

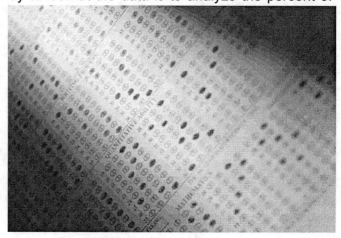

A better example of direct policy implications is the PSAT. The PSAT is the Preliminary SAT, and it is the test used to qualify for National Merit Scholarships. In 2007, 54% of the students taking the

PSAT were female, 56% male (College Entrance Examination Board, 2007); however, the majority of scholarships went to male students (Burdman, 2005). Is that gender difference in finalist status meaningful? Apparently, the PSAT group and their critics both thought so. After a federal gender bias lawsuit in 1994 brought by political watchdog group Fairtest, PSAT added multiple choice writing skill items to be included in the total score (Burdman, 2005). Girls tend to do better on writing skill exams and the inclusion of these items has decreased, but not eliminated, the gender gap (Fairtest, 1998).

We will come back to the discussion of the meaning of gender differences on standardized tests in Chapter 7 on cognition. "Statistically different" and "meaningful" may or may not be the same thing. And, the politics and policy will both affect the interpretation and use of findings.

Methods In Gender Psychology

Gender psychology methods represent standard social science methods. Let's look at a few measurements of interest to this field, and then review some of the standard research design distinctions. Finally, we will take a close look at a procedure called meta-analysis that has significantly and meaningfully impacted the study of gender differences.

Design Vocabulary

Research design in the social sciences uses some very specific terms. Below I have outlined a few that I think you need to know to understand gender psychology research.

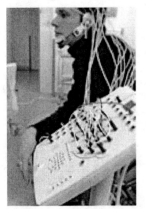

Empirical. Empirical refers to something that is observable and/or measurable. Therefore, empirical research is research that directly observes or measures an occurrence. For instance, empirical research on the unconscious is nearly impossible; however, researchers can conduct empirical studies on proxies of internal states (e.g. measuring brain waves to assess levels of relaxation). Most often in psychology, we *quantify* our results, meaning we convert our observations into numbers and apply statistical tests.

Constructs and *operationalization.* Researchers explore particular areas of interest – we refer to these abstract or general ideas or areas as constructs. When a researcher decides to measure a construct such as aggression, he/she must decide on how to do so. Operationalization is the term that describes how the concept of interest will be measured. If you wanted to measure aggression, could you measure it in more than one way? If you operationalized aggression as *physical acts* with the intent to harm, you will probably get very different results than someone who operationalized it as *verbal acts* with the intent to harm (e.g., Bjorkqvist, Lagerspetz, & Kaukiainen, 1992).

Variable. Once a construct has been operationalized, we refer to the attribute or response that is measured as a variable. The term variable reflects researchers' interest in variation – difference, change, or movement in an area of interest.

Research questions vs. *hypotheses.* Another useful term distinction is the difference between research questions and hypotheses. Research questions frame the area of interest (e.g., Are there gender differences in cognitive functioning?). Hypotheses are researcher predictions about the outcomes of his/her study based on a review of the literature. A hypothesis might read "College men will score better on spatial skills tasks than will college women. " A good hypothesis will state the direction of the expected difference and convey what variables will be measured. In other words, unless the literature cannot support a direction, you don't want to see a hypothesis that says "gender differences will be found." It is neither specific nor theoretical enough!

Cohort. Researchers also like to follow groups across time (panel longitudinal studies) or compare age groups (cross-sectional studies). In either situation, "cohort effects" are likely to affect the results. Cohort effects refer to the fact that individuals may be responding differently depending on the time in which they lived. Cohort effects can happen in very short time contexts. For instance, if your college or university changed its general education plan after you went through it, the experiencing of that program by the cohort who started after you by 5 years may be very different than those who started with you. Societal expectations for men and women have changed so rapidly that cohort effects in gender psychology are of great interest.

Types of research design. We can categorize most studies in the field of psychology into one of three designs. Although case studies (analysis of single person) and observational techniques are viable methods for some areas. Case studies involve the analysis of a single individual (e.g., following an autistic child's response to a treatment plan). Observational techniques involve recording factual events without directly asking questions. For example, a researcher could use observational research to record traffic volume at a particular intersection in order to create a model to help areas of congestion.

1. ***Experimental design***. Experimental design allows a researcher to make cause-and-effect statements. Experiments typically involve one or more variables that are controlled or manipulated by the researcher (**independent variables**) and one or more variables in which a researcher watches for change (**dependent variables** or outcome variables). Often, experimental research assigns respondents to different "conditions." As a term condition merely refers to which experience a respondent had. Let's say we were interested in emotional reactions to movies. We may design one condition where respondents watch violent movies, one condition where respondents watch comedies, and another condition where respondents just sit quietly in a room (the control condition). Experiments rely on random assignment to conditions because any participant attribute that might affect the outcome variable should be evenly distributed across the groups . An example of an experimental design in psychology is a study where children are randomly assigned to a condition where they either watch a violent video or a prosocial video and are then allowed to play with dolls. The level of violent

play with the doll would be the outcome or dependent variable.

2. ***Quasi-Experimental Design***. Many interesting variables cannot be studied with random assignment. Gender is one such independent variable. Researchers cannot randomly assign individuals to male and female categories. However, we can compare men and women. If gender is our

independent variable, we will need a quasi-experimental design. A quasi-experimental design does not allow you to make cause-and-effect statements; however, one can look at the impact of variables upon each other. Many researchers, including me, prefer a distinction between **active** independent variables (those a study can hold constant or manipulate) and **attribute** independent variables (groups that cannot be randomly assigned such as gender, age, race, ethnicity, and social class). An interesting type of quasi-experimental study is educational research. Because classrooms are not created through random assignment, a comparison of a method used in two different classrooms would be quasi-experimental. Let me give you an example. If I wanted to compare types of testing with information retention, how could I do it? Let's say I tested my students in my 7:45 AM Social Psychology course with multiple-choice exams and the students in my 8:50 AM Social Psychology course with essay exams and found that the 8:50 students performed better on an information retention exam at the end. Can I conclude that essay exams better prepare students for retaining information? Not really. Can you think of a difference between the two groups that might be driving the finding? The groups were not randomly assigned. Students pick their course times at my university. Guess what? Students who register first pick the time that is later in the day. So, my 8:50 section is almost always filled with juniors whereas my 7:45 is filled with sophomores. What if the difference were due to college experience? Perhaps juniors, in general, are better at information retention than sophomores because they've had more practice. Although experimental design is more powerful because you can be more sure of the cause and effect, quasi-experimental design is the next-best thing when you have attribute independent variables. Quasi-experimental studies are very common in psychology.

3. **Correlational Studies**. The final type of study examines the relationship between two variables. Since correlation is a type of statistical analysis, sometimes the name of this group of studies confuses students. However, correlational studies refer to any study where researchers explore the strength of the relationship between 2 or more already-existing variables. Determining cause and effect is impossible because you cannot isolate what causes the effect or the timing of the effect. There is a famous saying that "correlation is not causation." (And, if you are a psychology major, I suggest you have it tattooed on your body somewhere). In other words, if you find a relationship between two things, it does not mean one is causing the other one. For instance, if I measure grade point average (GPA) and achievement motivation, I am likely to find a correlation. I hope you can see how high achievement motivation could lead to higher GPAs; but I also hope that you see how a high GPA could enhance motivation. In addition, both relationships could be happening at the same time – each enhancing each other. Finally, with correlational research, it could be that a "third variable" is driving a relationship between two others. Can you think of a variable that may be related to both GPA and motivation? How about intelligence? Perhaps including intelligence, or statistically "controlling for" intelligence, would reduce the correlation or make it go away altogether. One correlation from gender psychology that we will look at

later on is the relationship between testosterone and aggression. R researchers have established that increased testosterone is associated with increased aggression (e.g., mice get more aggressive after being injected with testosterone). However, it also appears that football players have higher levels of testosterone *after* a game than before a game. Consequently, correlations usually only explain one part of a picture. The terms independent and dependent variables are often used only for experimental studies. However, sometimes they are used for correlational studies where the independent variable is the "predictor" variable and the dependent variable is the "predicted" variable.

Assessing A Large Number Of Studies: Tally Method And Meta-Analysis

Conducting good research is difficult. Any particular study involves many hours of work. Unless horribly flawed by design problems, each study has something to offer to science. However, at regular intervals, researchers need to step back and ask "what have we learned?" Most fields have some version of review papers that look at the body of research on a particular topic. In the field of gender psychology (and many other areas), scholars have pursued two specific types of reviews: the **tally method** and **meta-analysis**.

The tally method involves gathering up all the studies that have to do with a particular topic. If a researcher wants to track trends in the research on gender and impulsivity. Impulsivity refers to individuals' responses to stimuli. The more non-systematic someone is, and the less thought used, the more impulsive they are. The reviewer would gather all the studies he/she could find and then sort the studies into one of three categories: 1) men scored higher than women, 2)

women scored higher than men, or 3) no gender difference was found. Methodologists call it the tally method because the researcher is tallying up or counting the number of studies in each category. The results of a tally review give a good sense of the overall picture. For instance, in the 37 studies of impulsivity 8 studies found boys to be more impulsive, 3 studies found girls to be more impulsive and 26 studies found no difference (Maccoby & Jacklin, 1974). The most famous example of the tally method is the impressive work by Maccoby and Jacklin in 1974 that systematically tallied up studies for 6 different domains: 1) Perception, Learning and Memory; 2) Intellectual Abilities and Cognitive Styles; 3) Achievement Motivation and Self Concept; 4) Temperament; 5) Approach-Avoidance and 6) Power Relationships. Each domain represented several subdomains. Table 2.1 shows Maccoby and Jacklin's conclusions. You may want to come back to this chart at the end of the book and see what has held up. After all, most of the studies they were tallying were conducted in the 1960s. One more word about Maccoby and Jacklin. One of the reasons they wrote the book was to directly challenge prominent beliefs about gender differences. The very fact that research existed on these topics suggested the beliefs of the scientific community at that time. If you allow me a political comment, I think that 1974 is still relatively late to be putting some of these ideas to bed! Indeed, as you look at Table 2.1 note the direction and the phrasing of beliefs – they reveal much about the social context of the time including the use of the term sex differences rather than gender differences.

Table 2.1

Unfounded beliefs about sex differences	Sex differences that are fairly well established	Too little evidence or ambiguous findings
1. Girls are more social than boys. 2. Girls are more suggestible than boys. 3. Girls have lower self-esteem. 4. Girls are better at rote learning and simple tasks and boys at tasks that require a higher level of cognitive processing. 5. Boys are more analytic 6. Girls are more affected by heredity, boys by environment. 7. Girls lack achievement motivation. 8. Girls are auditory, boys visual.	1. Girls have greater verbal ability than boys. 2. Boys excel in visual (spatial) ability 3. Boys excel in mathematical ability 4. Males are more aggressive.	1. Tactile sensitivity 2. Fear & anxiety 3. Activity level 4. Competitiveness 5. Dominance 6. Compliance 7. Nurturance and maternal behavior

The tally method is limited, of course. Can you think of problems with "just" counting up the studies? First, the tally method assumes that all the studies are equally valid. In other words, what if Cho found no difference between men and women on verbal aggression and Sanchez found a huge difference – but, Cho's research was better designed? Second, most research journals only publish statistically significant results. Therefore, the tally is more likely to be biased toward studies showing difference. Reviewers diminish this problem by looking for studies that have been conducted but not published (traditionally, conference presentations and dissertation theses). Third, the way that the researchers operationalized the variable of interest can vary widely. Consequently, most current reviews separate the studies by the type of measurement/operationalization used.

Finally, one of the primary concerns about the tally method is that the size of the difference is not considered. In other words, if Harrington found that men outscored women by a huge degree, whereas Fields found that women outscored men by a small degree, it would appear that they "cancelled each other out" because each one would count in a category. In fact, one finding may be larger and/or more reliable.

Although the tally method can provide good summaries, more recently researchers have turned to a newer statistical method for summarizing across research domains. Meta-analysis is the process of converting the statistical results from a single study into a single score which is a measure of the "**effect size**." The larger the difference found, the larger the effect size score will be (on a scale from -1 to +1). Then, because effect size scores are all comparable, a single score can be computed for a particular area of interest. One of the most common effect size formulas is Cohen's d (Cohen, 1988) is obtained by computing the difference between the means of the two groups, divided by a sample-size weighted average of the standard deviations of the scores in the two groups. In Figure 2.6 you will see a series of d scores drawn from a variety of meta-analyses on gender. Cohen (1988) categorized d scores into three sets. He referred to d scores around .20 as "small," around .50 as "medium" and around .80 as "large." I did not include a meta-analyses suggesting that men are more likely to "channel surf" with the television remotes than are women (d = .4) because although it amuses me, the implications do not seem particularly important (d = .4) (Frisby, 1999). You need to know that Cohen was speaking to the levels of difference found in social science rather than, say, chemistry. Because so many variables influence human behavior, most the effect sizes found tend to be smaller than expected. Some fields may scoff at .50 being called medium – but they are probably better able to isolate the variables in which they are interested.

Figure 2.6 Effect Size Chart
Note: Citations from left to right: 1. (Hyde, Fennema & Lamon, 1990); 2. (Hyde, Fennema, & Ryan, 1990); 3. (Signorella, Bigler, & Liben, 1997); 4. (Tamres, Janicki, & Helgeson, 2002); 5. (Kling, Hyde, Showers, & Buswell, 1999); 6. (Hyde, 1981); 7. (Hyde, 1984); 8. (Archer, 2000); 9. (Murnen & Stockton, 1997); 10. (Eagly & Carli,1981); 11. (Eagly & Crowley, 1986); 12. (Archer, 2000); 13. (Eaton & Enns, 1986); 14. (Hall, 1984); 15. (Rosenthal & Rubin, 1982). 16. (Feingold, 1988); 17. (Hyde, 1984); 18. (Hall, 1984); 19. (Hall, 1984); 20. (Hall, 1984);

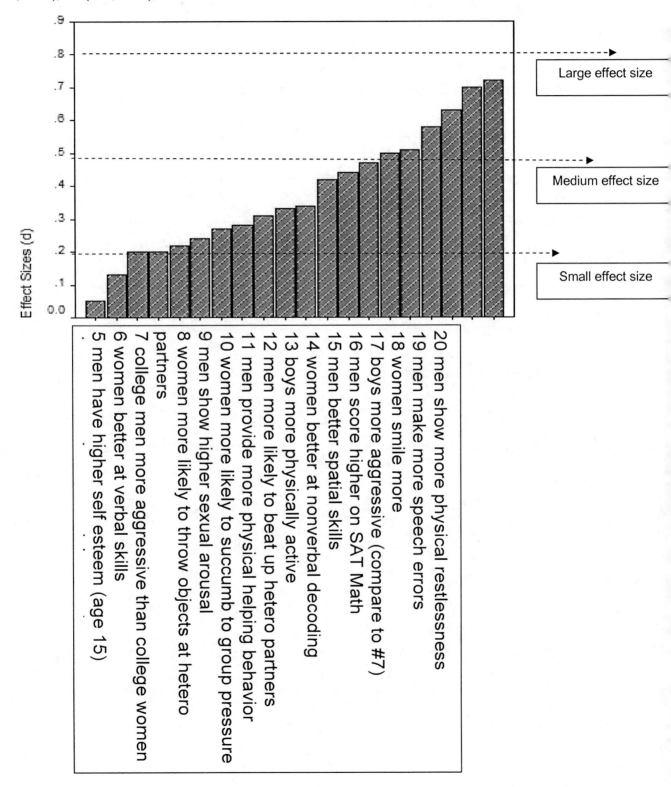

Is meta-analysis the perfect solution? Meta-analysis provided a substantial improvement over the tally method. It solves two of the larger problems: it can quantify the effect size, and a researcher can differentially weight studies that they deem to be of higher quality and worthy of more influence over the final *d* statistic. However, meta-analysis does not solve the other two problems. Researchers must still carefully sort studies by how the variable of interest was operationalized, and researchers must also make sure to secure unpublished data sets in order to correct for publication bias toward statistically significant results. See Box 2.1 for "An interesting study" involving a meta-analysis.

Box 2.1: A closer look at an interesting study…

Who did the study?

Twenge & Nolen-Hoeksema (2002)

What did they study?

This study was a meta-analysis on depression. The researchers were able to look at race, SES, and gender.

Who did they study?

Over 6,000 children ages 8-16, all living in the U.S.

How did they do the study?

They computed difference scores for 310 different samples of children, all of which had completed the same depression scale - the Children's Depression Inventory. Some articles report more than one sample of respondents, so the researchers report number of samples rather than number of articles reviewed.

What did they find?

Girl's depression scores were steady in the 8-11 age range and rose in the 12 to 16 age range. Boy's depression scores were steady from 8-16 (with a high blip at 12). Girls' scores were slightly lower than boys before age 12 and then higher. For instance, at age 15 the *d* score was .22. No racial differences between African Americans and European Americans appeared; however, Hispanic samples showed higher levels of depression. No SES differences found.

What is so interesting about it?

This study is interesting because it corrects for some of the meta-analysis concerns raised in the text. A huge volume of literature exists on the depression measure they studied, allowing them to hold their analysis to one operationalization of depression. The results are highly generalizable to research with that measure. In addition, they were able to test for racial and social class differences.

Scholars have raised some challenging questions as meta-analysis has expanded as a research tool (see Eagly, 1995; and Hyde & Plant; 1995 for an excellent discussion of the use of meta-analysis in gender studies). One of the questions examines whether or not a researcher "should" include gender analyses in their articles. Some scholars argue that the gender analyses should be included where others argue that gender analyses should only be included if they are part of the article's foci. The argument hinges on the role of theory in science. Scientific method rests on several key standards including replication, generalization, and theoretical support. When researchers conduct studies, they are supposed to write them such that any other researcher could enact the same methods (replication). Any other researcher should be able to conduct the same study with different populations or in different environments to check the generalizability of the conclusions. Theory asks how and why things happen. Therefore, theory plays a crucial role in the development of the study as well as the interpretation of the results. Kurt Lewin (1951) is famous for a quote often embraced by social psychologists: "there is nothing so practical as a good theory (p. 169)."

All good research reflects a review of the literature on the topic. A researcher must consider the work that has come before. Not only is a literature review a summary of findings (e.g., Espinosa found X, and Smith found Y), it is a summary of the theoretical framework and the evidence for this framework. The theory that the earth is flat had data that supported it at the time. When scientists generated enough data to make the theory nonviable, a new theory was born. Accumulating data without a theory leads to a set of meaningless findings. So, let's go back to the argument about meta-analysis. If, as a researcher, I have conducted a literature review and found evidence (even mixed evidence) that gender differences might exist, than I have a reason to look for them. However, I should be stating a theory about why they would exist before I conduct my study and, in the perfect world, be measuring something that will help discern a component of a theory. If I am studying diaper-changing skill, and I've hypothesized that women will be faster than men, and I've used the theory that evolution has favored mothers with good caretaking skills, then I would measure the diaper-changing skills of men and women. However, let's say that in order to explore the concept of environmental learning, I add the variable of experience. Now, I compare four groups, women without children, women with children, men without children, and men with children. If I find no overall difference between the diaper-changing skills of men and women, but find that both men and women parents better than non-parents, it would take away some of the credence for the evolutionary theory for this one topic. Or, at the very least, it would argue that regardless of "predisposition," the skills can be learned. Perhaps in a future study, I can train men and women to diaper and see who learns it faster.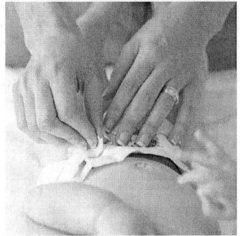

On the other hand, what if I'm conducting a study about taste preference for cilantro versus parsley? I have both secured both men and women participants, but there is no theory to support a gender difference. In fact, I'm using the theory that the geographic region in which one was raised drives the taste preference. In this scenario, I have no reason to suspect a gender difference, no reason to analyze the data for a difference, and no theory to make sense of the data if I found a difference. Should I still report the gender findings (significantly different or not), just in case a researcher down the line wants to conduct a meta-analysis on gender differences in taste? It would make for a stronger meta-analysis if all researchers included the data and effect size on gender. You can see that this is a tricky question. In general, I think psychology is leaning toward more reporting of gender findings (and ethnic and racial findings) but I hope you can see the scientific dilemma.

Gender Bias In Research

Before we leave the topic of research design, I want to explore how **gender bias** can slip into research in several ways. Below, I've outlined four major stages of research and given examples of how bias can be involved. I recommend Lips' (2000) book for an excellent overview of bias in gender research.

Idea formation. In the idea formation stage of research, bias tends to affect the overall choice of the research question. As I mentioned, most early gender research was on stereotypical differences. This may not be a big problem depending on what we do with the study's results, but it may limit our thinking about a subject. In addition, we know that gender may be a variable that is too simplistic to measure without additional variables of interest. So, are we making sure to measure other factors that may influence our understanding of the research question? As most of you are probably acutely aware, young male drivers pay more for car insurance than young female drivers. Why? Young male drivers have higher accident rates. Is gender the primary variable here? No, speed is the actual problem, and male drivers tend to drive faster than female drivers. If insurance companies could do it practically, they should base rates on whether or not drivers speed instead of on gender. Of course, insurance companies are just using gender as a convenient proxy for speeding. By the way, if you are a young male and want to reduce your insurance rates all you have to do is get married. Apparently, marriage slows down your cars!

"Gender Bias"

Research design. Bias can slip into research design in overt and subtle ways. One of the more overt mechanisms for bias revolves around choosing the sample. For instance, is the sample chosen for a given study generalizable? One common problem is to generalize from a clinical population to a general population. For instance, if you wanted to understand menopause symptoms, and you chose a sample of women who have come to their physicians for help with menopause, you would have potential bias. Your study is more likely to "find" troublesome menopausal symptoms in women because you have already selected a sample more likely to be experiencing problems sufficient to present to a physician. So if you concluded that "40% of women experience severe hot flashes," that number would probably be much lower in a general population. It would be like going to a sports bar to measure general attitudes towards professional sports.

It is easy for bias to slip in to studies due to sampling. One of my favorite examples is from 1995, when the Miss America contest was trying to decide whether to keep the swimsuit component of the competition. They conducted the study in the middle of the show, giving a toll-free number for respondents to call. Surprise! 80% of the one million calls supported keeping

the swimsuit component ("Miss America," 1995). Now, who is most likely to call? And, for whom is that sample representative? In fact, that might have been the perfect group to poll; it would only be a problem if the pollster then claimed it represented "American's opinions" about the swimsuit competition or some other unsupportable claim. Be especially wary of surveys where the respondents have to show high initiative to respond (like those "surveys" where you have to call a 1-900 number and pay to give your opinion or advice columns that ask you to share your opinions), as they immediately bias the sample toward those with especially strong opinions.

Subtle bias in research design often produces unexpected gender effects. It turns out that a researcher can provoke gender differences in the outcome variables (e.g., productivity) just by having a male experimenter (or vice versa) administer the test (for a current example where gender of experimenter is purposefully manipulated see Green, Sandall, & Phelps, 2005). In some early memory studies, it appeared that men had better recall memory until researchers discovered that both men and women remember gender-linked ideas and items better and the early studies were unknowingly using "male-linked" topics (again, for a current example of purposeful manipulation see McGivern, Huston, Byrd, King, Siegle, & Reilly, 1997). All studies also have trouble with social desirability bias where respondents answer the way they think they "should" based on society's or the experimenter's expectations. Social desirability can appear in gender-specific ways.

Finally, researchers must assess gender differences with comparable measures. One of my pet peeves is research on one gender that is then "assumed" to be different from or similar to the other gender without any actual assessment. For instance, most of the research on heart disease was conducted on men and "generalized" to women. Current research now shows that heart disease may present differently for women. Another example is Carol Gilligan's work on moral development. Gilligan (1982) wrote some fascinating material on women faced with abortion decisions. However, when the she links her findings to men's moral development assessed in other studies, the design starts to fail. Think about it, what decision for men is equivalent to an abortion decision? It is just not comparable to anything in men's lives. In order to make the gender distinction, the construct must be assessed with comparable measures.

Data discussion and implications. Researchers have to explain both what they found and what they think it means. Gender research can reflect a few systematic biases – most of which researchers have vastly improved in recent years. First, the labels researchers use to describe phenomena can be somewhat loaded. For instance, think about the phrases "men's inability to communicate" or "women's lack of ambition." Whose standards are being reflected in those phrases? Another common problem is to presume that something is due to biology because we lack information about another cause. In fact, to suggest a biological cause means that a

researcher should be able to propose a specific biological mechanism. So, for instance, if someone argues that women are more nurturing because they give birth (not due to the experience of childrearing – but due to childbearing), they should be able to propose what hormones or other biological changes can be traced to behavioral changes. In a similar vein, some researchers have shied away from theories of biological causation for equally political reasons. Succinctly put, we need solid theories with strong empirical support, no matter "where" they come from.

Dissemination. After a researcher conducts a study, what happens to it? Most researchers submit their studies to peer-reviewed professional journals. If similarly-trained individuals deem that it adds something to the field, then the journal will publish it. However, we know that journals and reviewers produce a bias toward positive results (in gender, a bias toward finding gender differences). We also know that less diligent publications may publish some poorly-designed studies. Finally, we know that popular press is a very different medium than professional journals. If the popular press picks up a study in a professional journal it is often unrecognizable by the end. I call this the "Bozo Factor."

Let's take a study from several years ago, where researchers found that menstrual cycle fluctuations correlate with women's verbal alacrity. Two researchers presented their findings at the meeting of the Society of Neuroscience in 1988, Kimura and her graduate student, Hampson, who was presenting on her dissertation findings. The work each presented was similar as they worked together in the same laboratory. The actual research that was presented was very interesting, although, like all research, it needed to be borne out with additional research and additional measures of the construct. For instance, Kimura measured verbal alacrity by how quickly respondents could say "a box of mixed biscuits in a biscuit mixer." The measure was how quickly they could say it 5 times. At the beginning of the menstrual cycle, when estrogen was low, the average time was 17 seconds, when ovulating, 15 seconds. The researchers in question did not make outrageous claims. When Hampson's study made it to print in a respected journal, a process that often takes a couple of years due to peer review and publishing lag times, the author wrote that "it should be noted that although the present findings may have some theoretical importance, their practical significance should not be overestimated (Hampson, 1990, p. 40). However, before any of that happened, the Bozos got involved. The very next week after the neuroscience conference, the *New York Times* ran a front page story and *Newsweek ran* a one-page story about it (Clark, 1988). Not only were the researchers misquoted, their quotes were mixed up such that Kimura was quoted on Hampson's research and vice versa (Hampson, personal communication, October 2, 2003). Professional writers searched out individuals to comment on the findings. Keep in mind that unless they attended the conference, these commentators only had the media's version of the findings. *Newsweek* asked non-scientist, politically active individuals to respond, such as the president of the New York chapter of the National Organization for Women. Then, they cited an individual from the Women's Health Network, without listing her credentials, whose comments they paraphrased as she "worries that the report could encourage youngsters to take estrogen in order to raise their SAT scores" (Clark, 1988, p. 61). In another popular-press article, another commenter says "this could change the timing of SATs in America." Halt. Rewind. How did we get from "a box of mixed biscuits in a biscuit mixer" to "excuse me, I'm menstruating, can I take this test in 2 weeks when I'm ovulating?" Nowhere in the original article did the researchers make any link from their results to something like the timing of national exams.

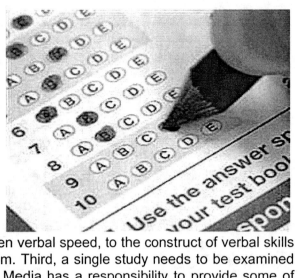

The example above about menstruation and verbal skills illustrates several of the important messages from this chapter. First, although the researchers found a statistically significant difference, the difference between 15 and 17 seconds may not be "meaningful" when it comes to the policy implications that others suggested. Second, it is a big leap from the construct of verbal skills operationalized as spoken verbal speed, to the construct of verbal skills measured by a pen-and-paper standardized exam. Third, a single study needs to be examined in the context of the other research in the field. Media has a responsibility to provide some of that context, and the quickness with which material is disseminated reduces the changes of this happening. Fourth, the media should allow other researchers to provide the critical commentary on the study. Although anyone has a right to comment on the study, research design concerns and policy implications should really be discussed by the peers of Kimura who have the training to do so. For instance, Sommer (1992) outlines several problems with research on hormone fluctuations and skill assessments, including the lack of control groups, the failure to keep examiners "blind" to the purpose of the study or the status of the respondents, and variation in the operationalization of verbal skills. Fifth, many stories that make a big splash in the media do not receive follow-up by the media. In this case, follow-up would have shown limited support for the original findings and additional studies that add to the complexity of the picture (such as men's testosterone being lower in the spring and related to better spatial ability than men in the Fall; Kimura, 2002).

Overall, I tell you this story as a cautionary tale about the role of the media in choosing "juicy" gender studies for the public and to encourage you to be a careful consumer of gender research.

Should Psychologists Study Gender Differences?

The accumulation of research regarding gender in the past 30 years has now allowed scholars to reflect more fully on the endeavor. Overall, it appears that gender research will continue and that it has produced some fascinating questions and answers. Scholars who debate the study of gender have outlined several key issues – many of which may conflict with one another (see Anselmi & Law, 1998, for a collection of articles from some well-known gender psychologists).

1. Gender differences attract attention. The public is interested in them.

2. Scientific research is the only way to dispel myths and break stereotypes.

3. Research suggests that there are some "truths" to the stereotypes that people hold about sex and gender. However, most people do not really over-exaggerate the differences.

4. Too much focus on similarity can create norms based on one gender or one way of doing things.

5. Small differences can be overblown. Journals overemphasize difference by being more likely to publish studies that find difference.

6. Study of differences assumes some stable, underlying difference between men and women.

7. Descriptions of stereotypes can become prescriptions – that is, if men are supposed to like sports, does a man have to like sports to be a real man?

8. Gender research has revealed that gender is much more complex than expected, and complexity suggests a need for more research and fewer global differences statements.

In the concluding chapter of this book, I will reintroduce these assertions. Take a moment to form your own opinion right now. Preferably – write it down. Let's see if you have different opinions at the conclusion of this book.

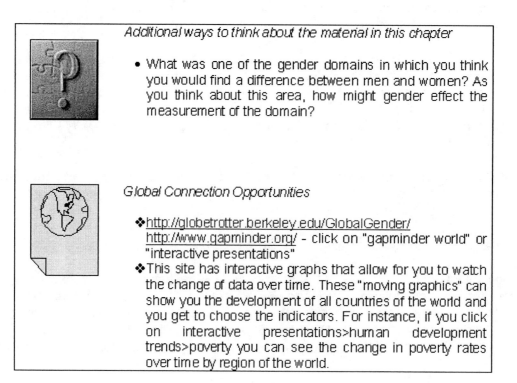

Additional ways to think about the material in this chapter

- What was one of the gender domains in which you think you would find a difference between men and women? As you think about this area, how might gender effect the measurement of the domain?

Global Connection Opportunities

- ❖ http://globetrotter.berkeley.edu/GlobalGender/ http://www.gapminder.org/ - click on "gapminder world" or "interactive presentations"
- ❖ This site has interactive graphs that allow for you to watch the change of data over time. These "moving graphics" can show you the development of all countries of the world and you get to choose the indicators. For instance, if you click on interactive presentations>human development trends>poverty you can see the change in poverty rates over time by region of the world.

Chapter Three
The Development of Gender Understanding

A. *Why do psychologists study theory?*
B. *Psychodynamic Theories*
C. *Social Learning Theories*
D. *Cognitive Theories*
E. *Blended and Expanded Theories*
F. *Measuring Femininity and Masculinity*

Josie, my daughter, recently watched a young male friend's diaper change, opining, "What a great penis! I wish I had one just like it!" I choose to think she meant this in an inclusive, everything-is-possible-and-I-also-love-my-vagina way, as opposed to some old-school penis envy kind of way.

Ingall (2004)

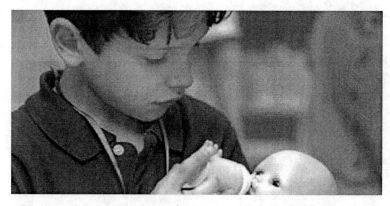

Parents often have stories, such as the one above, pertaining to their toddlers making funny comments in regards to biological sex differences. In addition, children make comments that reflect beliefs that might be seen as reflecting gender confusion. For instance, a little boy might say, "When I grow up I want to be a mother," or "Girls with short hair are boys." How does a child come to know he/she is male/female? When? Or, that men have penises and women have vaginas? How and when do they come to understand that boys grow into men and girls grow into women? How do they come to associate various behaviors and attitudes with a gender?

This chapter considers the fascinating topic of gender identity. When and why do children come to recognize themselves as boys or girls? This chapter also considers the question of gender-linked behaviors. When and how do children come to link various behaviors to a gender? We will look at three major theories. If you have had a psychology course, they should sound familiar. If you are new to psychology, please remember that I'm only giving you enough background in the theory for you to be able to understand the gender aspect – each theory actually addresses much larger issues.

Before we start, I want you to reconsider why scientists have theories. In Chapter 2, we discussed the role of theories in research and suggested that they help us guide research and answer the "why?" questions associated with research. It will be important to remember the role of theory as we look at gender identity and acquisition, because each theory has its own explanatory power and its own drawbacks.

Freudian Psychoanalytic Theory

Gender is crucial to Sigmund Freud's theories of child development, especially for boys and men. Freud postulated that there are three components to the psychological structure of each individual: the id (primal and animalistic; namely, sexual and aggressive instincts); the ego (a rational system that runs interference between the id and the superego); and the superego (perfectionist and moralistic) (Freud, 1924/1960). These three structures are largely unconscious or nonconscious only a small part of our conscious selves are away of these personality structures. Freud believed that gender identification occurred between the ages of 3-6, a stage he referred to as the "phallic stage" (preceded by oral, anal, and followed by latency). Freud also speaks of "complexes" which in **psychoanalytic theory** refers to a combination of emotions and impulses that have been rejected from awareness but still influence a person's behavior.

"Summary of Freud's Psychoanalytic Theory"

As we look at his theories separately for boys and girls, it is helpful to think about a child's love object and a child's identification with a parent. In short, in Freudian theory, a boy's task is to identify with his father rather his mother, and a girl's task is to shift her love object from her mother to her father. Both boys and girls start out with their mothers as both their love objects and their identification objects. One of the things you might particularly like about these theories is that you may finally understand where some famous phrases came from!

The Oedipus and Elektra Complexes

The Oedipus Complex – *boys' development.* <u>Oedipus Rex</u> is a Greek tragedy written by Sophocles in the years around 400 BC (Knox, 1994). Like many Greek tragedies, the plot implies that no one should attempt to escape fate. In Oedipus, the play, a seer prophesizes to a king that his newborn son will rise up to kill him one day and will sleep with the king's wife (the boys' mother). To escape this fate, the king sends a servant to kill the boy, named Oedipus. The servant is unable to do the deed, and sheepherders raise the boy. Years later, the boy is now a young man and knows nothing

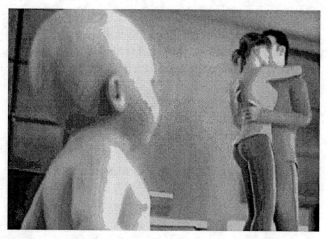

of his heritage. He travels toward his town of birth, and along the way gets into an altercation with the king and his men. He ends up killing the king, traveling into town, and marrying the queen (his mother). Finally the prophecy and its results are revealed, and Oedipus plucks his eyes out.

In this play, Freud saw parallels to his theory regarding boys' gender development. Freud outlined most of his Oedipus complex in his book *Interpretation of Dreams* (1899/1980). Recall that a boy needs to shift his identification from his mother to his father. A boy has an unconscious (id-driven) desire to sleep with mom, and he sees his father as the rival for his mother's affection. He projects these rivalry feelings onto his father and thinks that his father sees him as a rival. Then, the boy views a naked woman (often a sister) and concludes that her penis has been removed. Oftentimes, if the woman he sees is a sister, he concludes that Dad has removed her penis, and he begins to fear that this will happen to him too. Freud called this fear "castration anxiety" and theorized that it leads the boy to be motivated to appease his father so that he won't be castrated too. The boy starts to identify with his father and starts to act like him to prove his allegiance. Freud describes "successful resolutions" to Oedipal complexes, where boys develop strong superegos due to the conflict while also tending either to fear women or have contempt for them.

Think about the theory we just covered. Can you come up with any anecdotal evidence to support it? Well, many of you may have heard little boys say, "When I grow up I'm going to marry Mommy." Boys will often try to understand girls' anatomy by referring to the "loss" of her penis. However, Freud's theory is about the unconscious. The unconscious is almost impossible to study and has yet to be proved or disproved.

The Elektra Complex – girls' development. Freud struggled in understanding girls' development (Freud, 1925/1974; Young-Bruehl, 1990). Eventually, he lighted on the Greek myth of Elektra. Elektra is a woman who urges her brother to kill their mother because the mother has murdered their father and taken a lover. Frankly, the myth does not fit nearly as well with his theory as the Oedipus story. In Freudian theory, a girls' love object must switch to her father; however, her identification should stay with her mother. So Freud theorized that a girl loves her mother, but one day she notes that dad has a penis. She sees that the father gets to be with mom because of his penis, and the girl develops "penis envy." Later, this penis envy is converted into a wish for a child (particularly a boy child). She also blames mom for her lack of a penis. In order to resolve this conflict, she switches her love object to her father. Freud believed that girls' complexes were not as intense as boys', and that girls had less solid superegos as a result.

Interestingly, several theorists have expanded on this theory. One of Freud's students, Karen Horney (1942), suggested that penis envy may be less biological and more a recognition of the power that comes with having a penis. Others have written about women's ego boundaries, and how they may be related to the mother-child relationship and women's interest in sustaining relationships with others (e.g., Chodorow, 1978). These elaborations came from individuals who were not challenging Freud's overall theory. Many, of course, challenge his entire theory.

What Is Wrong With Freud?

Psychologists have many serious concerns about Freudian theories, especially as they pertain to gender (e.g., Crews, 1995; Ellenberger, 1981; Kagan, 1989; Mitchell, 2000; Webster, 1996). First, as mentioned above, due to their dependence on unconscious motives and desires, these theories cannot be tested with empirical evidence; they therefore make poor scientific theories. Secondly, Freud's theories are incredibly context-bound. His theories reflect the social and cultural mores of Vienna, Austria, at the turn of the century. Students like you very quickly start to ask salient questions such as "What if there aren't two parents?" "What if there is no sister?" etc. Third, Freud was generally uncomfortable about women and women's development. He asked "What does a woman want?" He viewed women's development as somehow lesser than men's, and he viewed homosexuality as an Oedipal or Elektra complex gone bad (Freud, 1925/1974). He didn't really fully "get it." Fourth, there is no doubt that his gender development theories are extremely phallocentric – that is, they rely on the notion that development occurs around the fear of losing ones penis or the anger over not having one. Women, then, are defined "in the absence of" as opposed to an emphasis on what they might have.

Fifth, there is growing evidence that Freud made a serious error when analyzing young women. In particular, many of the women Freud saw privately in his practice discussed incest experiences with him. According to Masson (1984), Freud originally presented his case to his colleagues with the implication that girls were being either harassed or molested by their fathers and other male relatives. However, he received such severe criticism for his stance that he backed off it. He chose instead to reanalyze cases to say that the sexual "fantasies" were all part of  women's unconscious motives as related to the Elektra complex. Sixth, Freud basically believed that all humans are psychologically challenged to some extent – we vary in our level of neuroses, but we all have them due to our unconscious personality structures. On a bad day, I tend to agree with him. However, it is appropriate to ask whether a theory essentially based on an illness model holds good explanatory power as a developmental theory.

Why Do Psychologists Still Study Freud?

Psychologists still study Freud for several good reasons. As one of the first people to write about these types of issues, Freud's theories set the discourse about these topics. Much of what was written for a long time was a rebuttal or support of his theory; consequently, understanding his theories is key to understanding the state of gender theory today. Secondly, Freud's attention to the influence of early childhood experiences revolutionized psychologists' understanding of human development, even if one does not agree with his theories. Third, Freud's attention to sexuality and sexual impulses also broke down a door and allowed for discussions of this nature. Indeed, his insistence that both men and women have sexual urges spurred much of the early sexual revolution (1920s) in the U.S. as well as the development of academic and cultural discussions of sexuality. Finally, there are a large number of individuals who still believe very strongly in Freudian theory and the psychoanalytic theories it spurred. Interestingly enough, the field of literary criticism seems to discuss his theories more than most psychologists, but there are still many therapists who study and use his theories. Overall, Freud's theories prompted discussion of many important and previously taboo topics in both scientific arenas and in popular culture. Indeed, Freudian scholars like Westen (1988) argue that "Freud's scientific legacy has implications for a wide range of domains in psychology (p. 333)."

Social Learning Theory

The American empirical tradition in psychology was in many ways a direct response to the murkiness of Freud's theories about the unconscious. In particular, learning theorists focused on observable behavior. Famous learning theorists include B. F. Skinner and John B. Watson. When applied to gender, traditional learning theory argues that we learn gender identity and roles through direct teaching and observation – what happens to an individual. In general, learning theory focuses on the acquisition and extinguishing of behavior in animals and humans. In the late 1970s, Albert Bandura (1977) introduced "**social learning theory**." Bandura's expansion of traditional learning theory included some key additions allowing for indirect influences – what happens around an individual. Bandura discussed learning through observation and modeling, and generalization.

"Social Learning Theory"

Reinforcement

In traditional learning theory, individuals who are rewarded for their behaviors will be more likely to repeat them just as those who are punished for their behaviors will be less likely to repeat them. The underlying assumption of learning theory is that we are motivated to get rewards and avoid punishment. Taken to another level, learning theory has also studied "shaping," where a progressive set of reinforcers can "shape" a complex behavior or a set of behaviors. Gender role acquisition is a slow process taking place over many years. My father-in-law is a very gender-role-traditional fellow. One day we were watching his 6-year old granddaughter, and he commented to me "isn't that amazing, she just naturally likes to wear fancy dresses." While I love this man, I cannot go along with "naturally." Since the moment that child put on that dress for church, she had been complimented and remarked upon throughout the day. Clearly, she was being rewarded for her choice of a more traditional dress for girls.

Learning through observation suggests that you need not be directly reinforced or punished to influence your behavior. A child who sees another child lose TV privileges for stealing a cookie will "learn" that stealing a cookie comes with negative consequences. Modeling suggests we can learn through observing models. They can be real models (like dad or a favorite uncle) or symbolic models (such as a cartoon character). A child then imitates the behavior of the model. In addition, he or she can admire the model and take on particular behaviors as a form of imitation without any direct reinforcement for that particular behavior. To model, children must pay attention, remember, and replicate the behavior and be motivated to perform it. Generalization refers to the idea that we can expand (or generalize) from a specific to a global.

In this case, a little girl who is rewarded for having a clean room may come to believe that neatness in other areas is important.

Bandura also suggested that while environment influences behavior, behavior can also influence the environment as well (a concept called reciprocal determinism). If you think of a parent as the environment and the child as the behaver, this will make more sense. It rarely takes my students long to think of a time when they've seen a child who has his or her parents well trained!

Overall, social learning theory is fairly straightforward in its application to gender role acquisition. It argues that boys and girls are differentially rewarded and punished for gender-appropriate and gender-inappropriate behaviors. This learning takes place over a long time and involves many occurrences of rewards and punishment. It should be easy for you to think of examples. For instance, know that many little boys are directly punished or shunned for doing gender-inappropriate activities like crying or playing with dolls? More widely, there is evidence that parents react more negatively to cross-gender-typed behavior than to gender-typed play. For instance, Leaper, Leve, Strasser, & Schwartz (1995) analyzed mothers' 8-minute interactions with their children playing with a toy dish set or toy car and track set. They found that mothers used more controlling statements ("don't put the car on that track yet") when their children were involved in cross-gender play (e.g., boys with the dishes and girls with the cars). Controlling statements are contrasted to supportive ("yes, that's right") or collaborative ("let's pretend to eat lunch"). Mothers also made more supportive statements when playing dishes with their daughters than they used in any of the other situations.

The types of **reinforcement** and perceptions of that reinforcement may also vary. Sport teams provide an interesting area to measure some of these variables. For instance, Millard (1996) found that male soccer coaches provided more frequent technical instruction than did female coaches, whereas female coaches provided more general encouragement than male coaches. In addition, although Millard only assessed female athletes, those with high ability perceived themselves as more competent if they received more frequent praise and less corrective information (Allen & Howe, 1998). In Chapter 6 "sources of socialization," we will learn that society appears to be more accepting of women pushing gender boundaries than we are of little boys doing so. If you don't believe me, let me sum it up with a simple question – would you rather be called a tomboy or a sissy?

Finally, evidence exists for modeling as suggested by social learning theory. In the Leaper (2000) study highlighted in the "A closer look at an interesting study…" you will see that mothers and fathers modeled different play behavior from one another even with the same set of toys.

A closer look at an interesting study…

Who did the study?

> Leaper (2000)

What did he study?

> The type of behavior exhibited by parents when playing with their children. He explored how that play behavior varied according to the type of play toy, the gender of the child, the gender of the parent, and the ethnic background of the families.

Who did he study?

> 98 two-parent families with a preschool-aged child (49 with a son, 49 with a daughter). 34% of the sample was Latino American. The European American families had a much higher socioeconomic status than did the Latino American families.

How did he do the study?

> He video recorded mother-child interactions and father-child interactions. Each parent-child dyad was recorded playing for 8 minutes with three different sets of toys (a zoo set as a gender-neutral toy, a plastic food and place settings set for a feminine toy, and a toy car with track set for a masculine toy). Later, raters assessed the play activity on the tape for two major behaviors, "affiliation" and "assertion." Affiliation referred to the closeness of the interaction and was coded on a range from distant to engaged. Assertion referred to the amount of direction provided by the parent, ranging from non-direct to direct.

What did he find?

> Parents appear to provide different role models for behavior with the toys. Fathers were more assertive (directive) than mothers. Mothers tended to show more affiliation (but only with the toy track set). The highest level of assertion and affiliation was seen with the dish set — for all combinations of boys and girls and mothers and fathers. However, most of the variation in the ratings was accounted for by the type of toy not the gender of the child or parent — meaning the activity type was guiding the level of affiliation and assertion. In general, the Latino families tended to be higher on both assertion and affiliation suggesting a family closeness that is often seen in Hispanic cultures.

What is so interesting about it?

> This study is interesting because it provides support for two important theories. First, the parents were engaged in different behaviors exemplifying the type of modeling suggested by social learning theory. Second, the type of toy directed much of the parenting behavior, suggesting the kind of context variables emphasized by sociocultural or

Beyond Reinforcement

The research literature provides clear support for learning theory. However, it does not tell the whole story. For instance, it does not explain children who persist in "gender-inappropriate" behavior. In addition, it turns out that parents don't treat children *that* differently according to gender (e.g., Lytton & Romney, 1991). They do treat them differently, but not enough to statistically account for the large differences in gendered behavior. Finally, children are active players in their own development and social learning does not adequately capture the nature of children's own role in their behaviors.

Cognitive Development Theories

Traditional learning theory has been criticized for its portrayal of individuals as clay-like lumps just waiting to be shaped by reinforcers. Even social learning theory undercounts the role of the individual in creating his or her own environment and behavior. **Cognitive development theories** more fully recognize the role of the individual by focusing on the stages of thought and reasoning children go through as they mature. Theories that stress problem-solving and memory (often referred to as information processing theories) and theories that stress qualitative changes in cognitive abilities (thought, learning and memory) (e.g., Piaget, 1929) focus on cognitive development. In general, theorists agree that children's cognitive abilities change as they age. However, theorists debate whether these changes are gradual or involve more substantive shifts. When applied to gender role development, cognitive development theory suggests that as children become more sophisticated in their thought, they become more complex their gender understanding.

Kohlberg's Three Stage Theory

Stage 1. Lawrence Kohlberg (1966) a Harvard developmental psychologist who studied with Piaget outlined gender stages where a child grows from his or her understanding of gender identity to larger understandings of the connection of gender to attitudes and behavior . In the 1st stage, children become aware of their gender label – "I'm a boy" or "I'm a girl." Children know that there are two categories and which one they are in by ages 2 or 3.

Stage 2. The 2nd stage is the egocentric stage. A child has a thought pattern such as "I'm a girl and it's best." Boys and girls prefer and value their gender over the other gender. The motive is to feel masterful and competent. Related to this need for mastery, they then tend to show preference for "girl-type" or "boy-type" things. This stage tends to develop around 4 or 5. This is also the stage where children will identify with and imitate the same-sex parent.

Stage 3. In the 3rd stage (ages 5-7), children begin learning there can be exceptions to the rules. In one study researchers described a situation where George is playing with dolls and is told not to by children in the 5-7 age range (Lamb & Roopnarine, 1979). Generally, children under the age of 6 will say that it is wrong of George, and he should be punished. Children over 6 tend to answer that George has the right to do what he wants.

"Kohlberg's Theory of Moral Development"

42

Comments on Stage Theory

In stages 1 and 2, children tend to be very rigid about gender roles. I have a friend who is a female physician. She was amused by her 3-year-old's unbendable assertion that "girls cannot be doctors." I also have a friend in my water aerobics class who said to me "you can't tell me

there aren't many gender differences; I work with four-year-olds in a daycare center." She went on to talk about their differences in play patterns. If I had rebutted, I would have said, "Of course you would notice these differences more than others would because you work with four-year-olds who are in the prime age to make rigid cognitive distinctions between boys and girls and acquire the behavior that promotes their own category. Both gender segregation and play pattern differences are consistently seen at this age." However, I did not rebut her, because it was time to workout our stomach muscles not the muscles in our faces.

As with all stage theories, although most theorists argue that children go through them in a fixed way (that is, all children go through stages 1, 2, and 3, in that order), individual children may go through these stages at very different rates. As children mature past the ages of 5-7, they tend to show a greater knowledge of stereotypes, a greater flexibility toward categories, and greater sex-typed personal preferences. In addition, although there is evidence of social environmental factors, the cognitive elements such as stereotypes and flexibility are clearly linked to cognitive maturity (Serbin, Powlishta, & Gulko, 1993). Finally, stage theories of children's development elicit some standard criticism that should be seriously considered (Lerner, 2002). First, these theories are based on estimates of children's cognitive abilities, and they may be more or less developed than estimated. Second, stage theories have difficultly accounting for children who show "mixed" forms of thinking – thinking that reflects more than one stage. What does it mean for the theory if children cross more than one stage? Finally, the sequence and or timing of the stages may be culturally determined so the original theories may be "too" Western in the specifics.

Development of Gender Identity, Constancy, & Stability

The stages of gender acquisition parallel the development of the understanding of gender over time. Developmental researchers distinguish among three types of stages that comprise **gender constancy** (Slaby & Frey, 1975). The overall acquisition of each of these understandings is often referred to as gender constancy. The 1st stage is **gender identity.** As noted, most children know their gender identity by age 3. Between the ages of 3-5, children generally show an increase in gender stereotype knowledge, an increase in a positive evaluation of their own gender category, and rigidity of beliefs (Ruble, Taylor, Cyphers, Greulich, Lurye, & Shrout, 2007). **Gender stability is** the 2nd stage and refers to the understanding that boys grow into men and that girls grow into women. Children usually acquire gender stability by age 5. You may have heard

children who don't yet have gender stability. I know a little girl who told her mother that "when I grow up and become a man, I will marry you." Freudian analysis aside (!), here is an example of a child who does not yet have the concept of gender stability. Lastly, children reach the 3rd stage, gender consistency. **Gender consistency** refers to the idea that gender is constant regardless of external changes. For instance, Pablo is still a boy even if he has long hair. Children acquire this between the ages of 5-7. In one study, 40% of 3-5 year olds had gender consistency already (Bem, 1989).

Table 3.1 provides a sampling of the types of questions that a researcher might ask a little girl named Monica to establish whether she has acquired each stage. Just flip the gender to try the questions on a boy. You might want to change the name too.

Table 3.1

Gender Identity   • *Are you a girl or a boy?*

Gender Stability
  • *When you were a little baby, were you a little girl or a little boy?*
  • *Could you ever be a boy?*

Gender Consistency
  • *If you wore boy's clothes, Monica, would you be a boy or a girl?*
  • *If you, Monica, played boy games, would you be a boy or a girl?*
  • *Could you be a boy if you wanted to be?*
 	
Note: My students often giggle at the last question, but remember that these are children answering the questions.
 	
Adapted from Coker (1984) and Slaby and Frey (1975).

Although some gender development questions remain unanswered, cognitive developmentalists have amassed strong empirical support for the theory (Martin, Ruble, & Szkrybalo, 2002). Research that supports cognitive developmental theory includes a study in which 90% of 3-6 year old children were able to sort "correctly" 18 gender-stereotypical toys into feminine or masculine categories (Martin, Wood, & Little, 1990). Table 3.2 shows the stereotypical toys used in the study.

Table 3.2

Stereotypical Masculine Toys	Stereotypical Feminine Toys
Truck	Doll Clothes
Army Tank	Purse and Comb Set
Train Engine	Sewing Machine
Cars	Dolls
Motor Bike	Makeup Kit
Airplane	Tea Set with Tray
GI Joe Soldier	Baby Doll and Crib
Tool Kit	Iron and Ironing Board
Baseball	Dollhouse

Young children who are able to label and identify their own sex also spend more time with same-sex playmates (Fagot, 1985) and spend more time playing with same-sex-typed toys (Caldera, Huston, & O'Brien, 1989). In longitudinal research, Fagot & Leinbach (1989) found that children who were earlier than others at gender labeling were also more likely to engage in gender-typed play earlier.

In addition, some fascinating infant research supports very early cognitive comfort with stereotypical information. Toddlers will stare at pictures of gender-atypical behavior (e.g. a man putting on lipstick) longer than pictures of gender-typical behavior (Serbin, Poulin-Dubois, & Eichstein, 2002). In general, babies stare at novel or unusual stimuli longer, indicating that the gender atypical was "unusual" to the babies. Sex-typed play activities and interests emerge in the first few years of life (Huston, 1985), and these interests are stronger for children with consistent gender identity and awareness of gender stability. At 24 months girls will choose a male doll to do stereotypically masculine activities (fixing a car, shaving), and boys will do so at 31 months (Poulin-Dubois, Serbin, Eichstedt, Sen, & Bissel, 2002). The gender difference seen in the study is most likely due to girls' overall faster cognitive development (e.g., Martin & Dinella, 2002).

Overall, cognitive development theory helps explain when and why children might acquire gender-role specific behavior and allows for the fact that the child is active in the process. Used together, social learning and cognitive development theory are powerful explanatory theories of gender-role acquisition.

Gender Schema Theory

Gender schema theory, postulated by Sandra Bem (1981), is a cognitive development theory that is more specific to gender. Schemas are cognitive structures that help us make sense of the world. Psychological research clearly supports the concept of schemas forming, existing, and influencing our acquisition of new knowledge. In Bem's theory, an individual with strong gender schemas would be quick to sort people and things into masculine and feminine categories. Indeed, individuals with strong gender schemas would organize information more readily by gender than by other salient categories (e.g., age or race). Someone who is gender aschematic will see gender as less important and perpetuate fewer stereotypes. Bem argues that culture drives the extent of an individual's or group of individuals' reliance on schemas and the extent to which things are sorted by gender (e.g., hair styling is feminine, barbecuing is masculine).

One of the appeals of Bem's theory is that she speaks directly to the concept of raising children. Indeed, my students have often asked me to cover more material on raising less-gender-rigid children. Bem (1983) argues that children need to learn to break their schemas. If you were a parent, how would you respond to your daughter's assertion that "girls don't like to play baseball?" As you might suspect, Bem recommends that the parent try to break the schema by giving a concrete example that doesn't fit the schema, "Your Aunt Deb likes to play baseball." Bem goes on to comment that there really are two schemas to break -- "girls don't like baseball" AND "boys like baseball." Therefore, a parent might want to follow up with, "And your Uncle Dean hates to play baseball."

Bem also suggests that we should teach children that biology is the only difference – thereby reducing the number of gender associations. Bem records one of the funniest stories from this area of biology and gender associations. As you read it, keep in mind that this is also a story about gender constancy. Bem's own son wanted to wear barrettes to kindergarten, and this is the story the teacher told about the experience.

> Several times that day, another little boy had asserted that Jeremy must be a girl, not a boy, because "only girls wear barrettes." After repeatedly insisting that "Wearing barrettes doesn't matter; I have a penis and testicles," Jeremy finally pulled down his pants to make his point more convincingly. The other boy was not impressed. He simply said, "Everybody has a penis; only girls wear barrettes." (Bem, 1998, p. 109)

Research support for gender schema theory is mixed. Although there is support for the idea that children develop information about gender in line with their cognitive capacities, there is no strong empirical support for the idea that these schemas directly shape children's beliefs and behaviors (Fagot, 1995). Martin, who advanced a similar cognitive theory (Martin & Halverson, 1981) to Bem's, now suggests that children's organization of gender knowledge is probably less hierarchical than first expected (Martin, 1993). Instead, information is organized into components (e.g., occupations, clothing) that can overlap with categories like men and women. Research then needs to turn from looking at how children sort traditional stimuli (such as fire trucks) to see whether and how children start to associate specific items with a gender. For instance, Leinbach, Hort, & Fagot (1997) found that 4-year-olds have started to associate butterflies and hearts with girls, and bears and fire with boys. Fagot makes a nice link between the research and children's ability to understand these concepts when she comments: "It is plausible that these youngsters have begun to associate qualities such as strength or dangerousness with males, and gentler qualities with females, whether or not they can name the attributes involved (1995, p. 23)."

Overall, cognitive developmental theories' focus on the active role of the child and cognitive maturation has revolutionized much of developmental theory in psychology. When applied to gender, the research on these theories supports several key ideas. First, children learn gender stereotypes and gender labeling early in their childhoods. Second, increased cognitive maturity is related to more complex understandings of gender categories. Third, children are active participants in the process of acquiring and sorting knowledge and experience. One criticism of the theories is that they have yet to elaborate a clear process of how children acquire gender-related behavior as related to their cognitive understandings. Another criticism is that children show gender-typed behaviors before they have full gender understanding (Bussey & Bandura; 1992; Bussey & Bandura; 1999). However, there are methodological and interpretative debates that leave this an interesting area of study.

Blended and Expanded Theories

As you might expect, the combination of social learning and cognitive developmental theories provides the most powerful explanation of children's gender identity and behavior acquisition. Indeed, Bussey and Bandura (1999) essentially argue that their "social cognitive theory" provides all the explanatory power needed. But Martin, Ruble, and Szkrybalo (2002), in a fascinating review of the theoretical and methodological differences leading to the current debates, provide a great reason why we shouldn't conclude that the blended theory ends the theories debate. They write "joint considerations of multiple perspectives raises interesting and important questions about gender development that would not be considered by the social cognitive theory view alone" (p. 927). Indeed, the debate adds richness to our understanding of gender development, and researchers still have many interesting studies to conduct. For instance, Martin et al. note that we still don't know how external standards of gender role conduct become internalized into personal standards.

Finally, it is important to understand that gender acquisition does not stop after age 7 (an argument made especially well by the social learning theorists Bussey & Bandura, 1999). We know that in young childhood there is great pressure on boys to conform to stereotypical gender roles and that adolescence is the time of great pressure on girls. College students tend to have flexible, less rigid notions, and new parents tend to resort to more traditional roles. Finally, senior citizens tend to show a liberalization of attitudes and behaviors (see Bee, 2001 for a good review of gender roles over the lifespan). We will cover all of this more in-depth later in the book, but I don't want you to get the idea that the development stops.

As we close out this section on theories of gender role development, let me remind you that this is a psychology book. To truly understand the context of gender roles in any particular society, you would need to understand some additional layers of analysis. Sociology and anthropology offer a more macro view of gender. Sociology offers an analysis of "gender stratification" focusing on the unequal distribution of wealth, power, and privilege between men and women who are then "stratified" into different social groups or experiences. Aggregate data show that societies vary in how influential various subgroups are in organizing a society. Gender would be one subgroup for which you could analyze differences in wealth, power, and access to opportunity for social stratification. Institutions such as government and schools play a role in perpetuating or breaking gender stratification. Anthropology analyzes differences among cultures to look for common and unique themes in cultural organization around sex and asks questions such as "How do we explain the differing status of women among societies?" Overall, there is general agreement that equality will only be reached when women's work receives as many rewards (economic and psychological) from society as men's work does. All of this is to give you a flavor of additional levels of analysis that help scholars understand gender. I encourage you to look into them and/or into women's studies courses and they will give you a better understanding of gender and gender psychology. In the conclusion chapter of this book, I will suggest some additional readings that may be of interest to someone who wants to delve into these topics.

Measuring Femininity and Masculinity

Although throughout this book I suggest that there are few measured gender differences, most of us have fairly well-developed notions of what it means to be feminine or masculine in this society. We have just covered the theories that help us understand how a child comes to recognize his or her gender and the behaviors associated with them. However, we also know that individuals vary considerably on almost all psychological dimensions. Needless to say, researchers are interested in measuring the extent to which an individual man or woman is masculine or feminine. The early researchers assumed that if one is masculine, he or she is less feminine and vice versa. Psychologists refer to this as a unidimensional attribute. A classic unidimensional attribute is extraversion and introversion – because if you are more of one, you must be less of the other. Look at the figure below (Figure 3.1). If I asked you to place yourself on that continuum, could you do it?

Figure 3.1

Masculine ←————————————————————→ Feminine

Do you sense any problems with this? Bem (1974) and other researchers began to realize that a single continuum did not fully capture human experience as masculine or feminine. The **Bem Sex Role Identity** scale (BSRI) seeks to measure the extent to which an individual sees him or herself in gender-role stereotypical ways. The BSRI conceptualizes masculinity and femininity as two separate dimensions – masculinity and femininity. Consequently, an individual could score high on both, or low on both, or some other mix of scores. The BSRI is a simple measure consisting of 60 personality characteristics. The respondent describes the extent to which each characteristic describes him- or herself on a scale from 1 (never or almost never true) to 7 (always or almost always true). Bem selected the characteristics according to research with the general population that suggested that 20 of the characteristics are seen as "masculine" (such as self reliant and ambitious), 20 as "feminine" (such as gullible and compassionate), and 20 as "neutral" (such as happy and conceited).

When my students discuss the BSRI, there is inevitably a conversation akin to "Who says ambition is a male characteristic?" It is an excellent question and the key to understanding the measure. The characteristics used for the BSRI represent stereotypical and public versions of masculine and feminine characteristics. Not everyone involved in the pilot work rated "ambition" as masculine – but, overall, people rated it as being more masculine than other characteristics. Consequently, the BSRI is a good measure of the extent to which an individual rates himself or herself in a way that is stereotypically feminine or masculine.

Individuals gain a masculinity score and a femininity score and are sorted into one of four categories. Look at Figure 3.2.

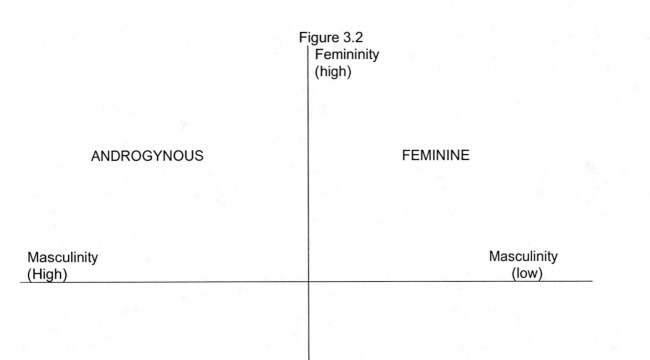

Figure 3.2

Femininity (high)

ANDROGYNOUS   FEMININE

Masculinity (High)   Masculinity (low)

MASCULINE   UNDIFFERENTIATED

Femininity (low)

Others have argued that androgyny may be best represented by balance between masculinity and femininity rather than high scores on both. Although we need more studies on this topic, several current studies indicate that undifferentiated and androgynous individuals are often similar to one another on outcomes such as personality and behavioral measures (e.g., Das, 2001). More recently, the masculinity and femininity scales of the BSRI have been used simply as two scales, although a majority of researchers still use the classifications (Hoffman & Borders, 2001). The classification appears to be less methodologically sound despite its popularity. And, popular it is. If you request all the articles in PsychLit that have used this measure, approximately 1500+ articles show up. An additional 530+ articles use a similar measure, the Personal Attributes Questionnaire discussed below.

The concept of **androgyny** gained a large amount of popular press as well as continued empirical attention. The concept captured the public's growing interest in gender equality that paralleled the women's movement of the mid-1970s. Consequently, the idea that the "ideal" person was high on both masculine and feminine qualities had its own appeal at the time. Indeed, people appear to see both androgynous men and women as being better adjusted and more likeable (Jackson, 1983). Paralleling the popular appeal of the concept was research suggesting that androgyny was correlated with a host of positive attributes and experiences, such as psychological well-being, adaptability to new situations, and higher self-

esteem (as reviewed by Pyke, 1985). To give you a flavor of this type of research, Rose & Montemayor (1994) found that, when sorted according to Bem's categories, androgynous adolescents had the highest perceived scholastic competency, close friendship competency, and global self-worth. Furthermore, when the scales were used as single dimension scales, masculinity predicted perceived scholastic competency and close friendship competency in both girls and boys, and perceived global self-worth in girls. Femininity predicted perceived scholastic competency in boys. Look back over those findings. Why might those relationships exist?

Methodological concerns with gender-role-identity scales exist. One major critique of the BRSI was that it may be a better measure of instrumental and expressive traits than of masculinity and femininity. Instrumental refers to traits that facilitate goal achievement. Expressive refers to traits that facilitate good relationships. Considerable evidence supports the idea that most stereotypical views of men and women can be categorized using these terms. Consequently, a similar measure developed by Spence and Helmreich (1978), the Personal Attributes Questionnaire (PAQ), uses the labels of expressive and instrumental to categorize the attributes. This distinction between the terms will make more sense after you hear the next critique.

Although the research did support a relationship between androgyny and higher self-esteem, it appears that that it was the high masculinity scores driving the relationship, rather than the fact that an individual was high on both masculinity and femininity. This was particularly true for women. If you think about instrumental traits being those that are goal-oriented, then it makes sense that those types of traits may be related to positive mental outcomes. It is difficult to disentangle the gender from the agency of the traits. Think back to those findings by Rose and Montemayor (1994). Does the instrumental and expressive difference help make sense of those findings?

No matter what the label is for the gender-role attributes, it is important to recognize that the traits are differentially valued by society. Indeed, the context of the traits is key to understanding how people might value them. So, for instance, if you are thinking about a leader for your group, do you want someone who is "yielding" (a feminine or expressive trait) or "self-reliant" (a masculine or instrumental trait). If you were looking for a caretaker for your ailing father, would you change your mind? Indeed, one area of research that continues to find strong relationships between androgyny and behavior are studies of leadership. For instance, Kent and Moss (1994) found that androgynous and masculine undergraduates (men and women) were more likely to emerge as leaders in classroom situations.

In addition, current research using the PAQ suggests that the stereotypical notions of maleness are more narrow than are the stereotypical notions of femaleness. Again, this narrow view of masculinity may be why women "pick up" an advantage with masculine qualities but men do not appear to pick up a psychological well-being advantage with higher feminine qualities. Finally, perceptions of other people's masculinity and femininity are often biased by our own traits and expectations. For instance, in a study done with male respondents, men who scored high on masculine scales were the most prone to see most women as high in femininity and low on masculinity. Androgynous men were more likely to perceive women as having androgynous characteristics (Hudak, 1993). Male professors with low femininity scores (but not necessarily high masculinity scores), and female professors who are gender-neutral (i.e., androgynous or undifferentiated) were more often chosen by students as their best professors (Das, 2001).

Will These Measures Carry Into The Future?

Many of you reading this textbook were probably not born when the BSRI and the PAQ were published. Even if you were, you can join us in wondering if these measures are still useful. After all, haven't individuals' views of what is masculine and feminine changed? Interestingly, the jury is still out on this one. Some researchers suggest that the BSRI can no longer tap stereotypical masculinity and femininity because there is less overall agreement on whether a particular item squarely "fits" into a category of masculine or feminine (Hoffman & Borders, 2001). However, others have found a continued viability to the measure. Holt and Ellis (1998) found that college students still ranked each of the masculine traits as being "more desirable in a male" and each of the femininity traits as being "more desirable in a female." Think about this. Would you expect current college students to be good "representatives" of the public view on gender stereotypes? Why or why not? Even Holt and Ellis wonder whether their sample was more stereotypical because they were rural southern college students and much of the other research is with more urban northeastern college populations. Researchers in this field will not just sit back and wonder if these measures still work. They will be actively tracking societal shifts in personal and stereotypical views of what constitutes masculine and feminine behavior. Measures will follow that will be able to assess whatever these new beliefs will be.

"Masculinity vs. Femininity"

Overall, in this chapter we have attended to theories that attempt to explain how children come to associate specific behaviors with particular genders. We examined theories with very different concepts of the motivation behind gender role acquisition. The combination of social learning and cognitive-developmental theories currently provides the most viable arguments about the process; however, it is important to understand the historical perspectives on these issues. Finally, we examined the measurement of gender-linked attributes with traditional masculinity and femininity scales in order to start exploring the interchanges between gender and gender roles. In Chapter 6, we will look more closely at factors that influence children's perceptions of gender including, parents, peers, and schools. However, before we discuss "gender socializers" more fully, in the next chapter we are going to explore factors that influence gender with an eye to the nature/nurture debate.

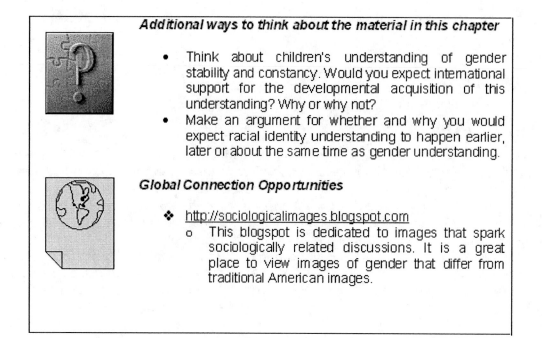

Additional ways to think about the material in this chapter

- Think about children's understanding of gender stability and constancy. Would you expect international support for the developmental acquisition of this understanding? Why or why not?
- Make an argument for whether and why you would expect racial identity understanding to happen earlier, later or about the same time as gender understanding.

Global Connection Opportunities

- ❖ http://sociologicalimages.blogspot.com
  - o This blogspot is dedicated to images that spark sociologically related discussions. It is a great place to view images of gender that differ from traditional American images.

Chapter 4
Biological Bases of Sex

A. Sexual Reproduction: Why do we have men and women?
B. Sexual Dimorphism: "How come we look different?"
C. Typical Sexual Development: How do we come to look different?
D. Atypical Sexual Development: What can we learn from anomalies?
E. Evolutionary Theory: What is the relationship between genetic encoding and complex behaviors?
F. Nature/Nurture Interaction: How do biology and environment interact?

Two children approach a sand box. They play for a while. The girl has a truck that the boy wants. He bonks her over the head with a shovel to obtain the truck. She responds by yelling "you stupid jerk!"

How did this happen? What made this boy act like a boy? And, this girl act like a girl? Was there something in his hard-wiring that made him more likely to bonk? Was she predisposed to responding verbally rather than physically? Would they respond differently if they were older? Younger? Would we, as observers, respond differently, if they were older? Or we were? What are the expectations for their behavior from the important others around them?

The answers to these and other important questions lurk in the chapter below.

The last chapter discussed psychological theories about how children come to acquire gender-typed behavior. This chapter focuses on the causes and correlates of gender and sex differences – the etiology of gender differences. First, we will explore the biological differences between men and women, an exploration which requires a good sense of sexual differentiation. We will examine biological anomalies that help us understand "normal" development. We will also consider another major component of biologically-based theory by looking at evolutionary theories of gender differences. The biological theories represent "**nature**" perspectives on gender and sex. Nature theories indicate that gender is something biological or predisposed in children. Then, we will make a rather abrupt shift to explore the "**nurture**" side of gender differences. Here we analyze the role of gender stereotypes in shaping the environment in which boys and girls are raised. The next chapter examines "sources of socialization," so in this chapter we will look more at the expectations regarding gender rather than the specific shapers of gender. Finally, we will take a look at the way that nature and nurture interact to create gendered behavior.

This chapter explores the tension between nature and nurture theories and the evidence that nature and nurture causes tend to interact. So, for instance, in reference to the sand box scenario above, a nature theory might argue that the boy is hardwired to act more aggressively whereas a nurture theory may argue that responding with physical aggression is a social expectation for boys. In truth, the answer probably lies in the interaction between the two. The boy may be predisposed (that is, a biological tendency or "readiness" to act in certain ways) to be physically aggressive and then placed in situations where that physical aggression is rewarded or assumed to be normal. This chapter also serves to set up the kinds of questions we will be asking when we explore the "why?" of the gender difference domains we will analyze in the rest of the book.

Sexual Reproduction: Why Do We Have Men And Women?

As you are most likely aware, human reproduce through "**sexual reproduction**." Sexual reproduction means the combination of genetic material from two sources. Scientists contrast sexual reproduction to asexual reproduction which involves the replication of the same genetic material (e.g., amoebas). What is the benefit of sexual reproduction? After my students answer "it's fun," we usually remember that the major benefit of sexual reproduction is to provide genetic variation. Genetic variation provides for the substantial within species variation that we see (for instance, the variation in height in humans). Genetic variation will also result in mutations. Mutations can prove useful or harmful. Here is your quick reminder course on evolution. Evolution is essentially the name of the process for the change in the genetic constitution of a population over generations. Scientists used to believe that change in a species came about through direct behavior (e.g., giraffes' necks got longer because they needed to stretch to eat). However, Darwin (1859; 1871) proposed a different theory. He argued that the **random mutations** that occurred through sexual reproduction would occasionally result in a useful characteristic. For instance, giraffes that happened to be born with longer necks would eat better

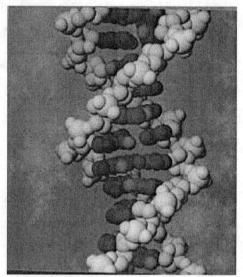

than those with shorter necks. If the mutation was useful or adaptive, those individuals would be more likely to survive ("survival of the fittest"). These surviving individuals would reproduce with one another and be more likely to produce offspring with this special characteristic. This is a form of "**natural selection**" where adaptive characteristics are "selected for" by the environment. Current work on evolution suggests a few caveats to the theory (Futuyma, 1998). First, natural selection can occur for any adaptive characteristic, although a mutation may lead to quicker change. Second, there can be random evolution, "genetic drift" (random variation creating a generation different from its predecessor), or new combinations of genes through migration of species and/or cross breeding. Finally, natural selection may not lead to evolution; it can serve to maintain the status quo.

"Natural Selection Made Easy"

In humans, the genetic material for new life is provided by a man and a woman. The woman gestates and births the offspring. A female human provides 23 chromosomes, of which one will be her **sex chromosome**, an "X." A male human provides 23 chromosomes, of which one will be either an X sex chromosome or a Y sex chromosome. The chromosomes pair up – see Figures 4.1 and 4.2 for a karyotype (depiction of the chromosomes in a cell) of a male (XY) and a female (XX). By the way, you may find it interesting that the male does not determine the sex of the offspring in all species.

Male   **Female**

Sexual Dimorphism: "How Come We Look Different?"

Although male and female humans look different, compared to other sexual reproducers we actually look very similar. Scientists call physical differences in males and females "**sexual dimorphism**," and they have discovered evidence of this difference existing over 260 million years ago (Mayell, 2003)! Sexual dimorphism is greatest in species where the males have to compete for reproducing with the females – hence, brightly colored males and subtly-colored females in some bird families and various male animals with horns and females without. These physical characteristics appear to attract the females' attention (color) and/or facilitate competition with other males (horns). The sexes in animals who mate for life (like mourning doves) or have simple mating systems (bass, walleye, and carp) generally look quite similar. For those of you who like the Animal Channel, you'll be interested to know that some fish become

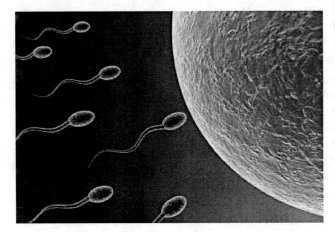

more sexually dimorphic at breeding season (such as male bluegills that develop more color, Stanley, 1988).

Another interesting "difference question" centers on why men and women have different size **gametes**. In other words, why are sperm small and eggs large? Small gametes such as sperm increase the chance of fertilization because more of them can be produced. An average ejaculation includes approximately 200-600 million sperm! However, one of the gametes needs to be able to store food for a longer life. Females are born with 300,000-400,000 eggs and will eventually "use" 300-400 of them through ovulation. In humans, the egg has a food store that increases its chance of survival. Sperm live about 24 hours but can survive up to six days. Eggs live 24 to 48 hours and must be fertilized within that time. If fertilized, the egg provides nourishment until implantation approximately seven days after fertilization (Lewis, 2003). Men and women could produce both types of gametes (testes and ovaries) as some animals do; however, it appears that it is more efficient to have one sex specialize in one type of gamete.

"How the Body Works: Gamete Cells"

Several years ago an anthropologist named Emily Martin (1991) examined the portrayal of sperm and eggs in college biology textbooks. She found that textbooks portray sperm in stereotypically masculine ways and eggs in stereotypically feminine ways. Authors portrayed sperm as active and strong. Authors portrayed eggs (often colored pink in photos) as large and passive. They "drifted" down the fallopian tubes "waiting" to be inseminated. Martin argued that the imagery connoted a Sleeping Beauty/Prince Charming scenario where sperm are warriors and eggs are damsels-in-distress. In reality, eggs are not female and sperm are not male – they are not "gendered." nor is the imagery accurate for what really happens. In fact, insemination is a collaborative activity between the egg and sperm, it is not a competition between bounding sperm to see who gets the prize first. Freedman (1992) writes a delightful "correction" to the traditional view.

> First, a wastefully huge swarm of sperm weakly flops along, its members bumping into walls and flailing aimlessly through thick strands of mucus. Eventually, through sheer odds of pinball–like bouncing more than anything else, a few sperm end up close to an egg, as they mill around, the egg selects one and reels it in, pinning it down in spite of its efforts to escape. It's no contest, really, the gigantic hardy egg yanks this tiny sperm inside, distills out the chromosomes, and sets out to become an embryo. (p. 61).

Freedman and Martin approach this topic of gendering sperm and eggs with good humor, but both note that the imagery perpetuates gender stereotypes and inaccurate biological knowledge. Take a look at a newer human biology textbook – see if things have changed in the past few years!

Typical Sexual Development: How Do We Come To Look Different?

Although we don't look all that different, certainly men and women have different physical traits. How do they come about? The process of developing either male or female internal and external genitalia is called **sexual differentiation**. In humans, all fetuses start out the same and are then differentiated into males or females. Scientists refer to this state of pre-differentiation as "**bi-potential**" – meaning it could go either way. Look at Figure 4.3. It shows which of the internal and external genitalia come from the same source. For instance, the gonads either form into ovaries or testes. The tubercle forms into a penis or a clitoris. The ducts form the ovarian tubes or the Wolffian ducts. We have come to learn that it is the "Y" chromosome that masculinizes the fetus. In some ways, you can think of "female" as the default sex. The fetus will look female unless it is transformed to look male.

Figure 4.3

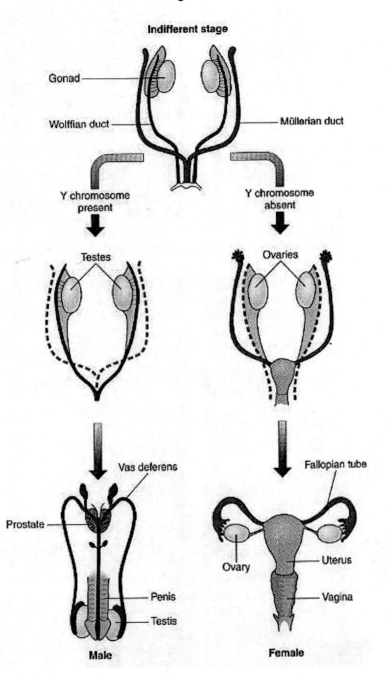

The easiest way to think about sexual differentiation is in terms of stages.

1. Stage 1: **Genetic Differentiation**. The fetus has either an XX sex chromosome structure or an XY chromosome structure.

2. Stage 2: **Gonadal Differentiation**. At approximately the 7th week of pregnancy, the presence of the Y chromosome causes the gonads to develop into testes. The testes start to produce testosterone.
3. Stage 3: **Hormonal Differentiation**. The ovaries produce estrogen; the testes produce androgens such as testosterone.
4. Stage 4: **Genital Differentiation**. Both the internal and external genitalia are formed. By the end of the 1st trimester (12 weeks), you can usually differentiate visually between male and female fetuses – but it is easy to miscall it at that time too.
5. Stage 5: **Brain Differentiation**. In approximately the 17th week of pregnancy, the hormones act to prepare the brain to be ready to recognize the androgens and estrogens produced at puberty. Most hormones work as a type of lock and key, and the brain is prepared to recognize the proper connections. Scientists distinguish between brain "organization" and "activation." This stage organizes the brain such that it can be activated in puberty (Hadley, 1996).

Here are a few important reminders. Both men and women produce estrogens and androgens – the former are higher in women, the latter in men. About one year after birth, if you measured the levels of hormones in the blood of boys and girls, you would find no differences; it is at puberty that you get these differences again. However, many scientists argue that the brain organization itself (not the activation) may lead to some of the detected gender differences. Finally, hormones are, in themselves, examples of nature/nurture interaction. Environments, including behavior, can affect hormones, just as hormones can affect behavior. Chapter 10 on aggression will help make these caveats clearer. By examining a particular set of behaviors (aggression), we will be able to revisit the discussion of organization vs. activation of the brain and the reciprocal relationship between hormones and behavior.

Table 4.1 shows the stages and the weeks of gestation.

		Women	**Men**
	Genes:	XX	XY
6 wk	Undifferentiated		
7-12 wks		Ovaries	testes
12-17 wks		no testosterone	testosterone, Mullerian Inhibiting Substance
		Wolffian ducts degenerate	Mullerian ducts degenerate
		Mullerian ducts differentiate into fallopian tubes, uterus, upper vagina	Wolffian ducts differentiate into epididymis, vas deferens, ejaculatory duct
12-20 wks		Rudimentary Genitals	
		outer vagina, clitoris	penis, testes descend

Tubercle -->		Clitoris	glans penis
Folds -->		labia minora	shaft penis
Swelling -->		labia majora	scrotum
		| | V	| | V
		Women hypothalamus	Men hypothalamus

Atypical Sexual Development: What Can We Learn From Anomalies?

I have just described a typical development – now we will look at unusual occurrences **(anomalies)**. Gender scientists look at anomalies for several reasons. First, anomalies teach us about typical development. Several anomalies have helped rule out alternative hypotheses about what typical development requires. Second, we study anomalies for their own sake – to think about biological and psychological treatments for them that may or may not be helpful. Third, anomalies help us think about difference – in particular when do differences require treatment as compared to being seen as natural variation. And, finally, anomalies often challenge us to think about our most deep-seated beliefs about sex and gender. A variety of biological occurrences can result in anomalous sexual differentiation outcomes. Overall, approximately 1 in 2,000 live births results in some form of **ambiguous genitalia** (American Urological Association, 2003). We will first look at chromosome anomalies and then other sexual differentiation anomalies.

As we look at chromosome anomalies, you should know that the X and Y chromosomes are very different. The number of genes – the basis for hereditary traits – is different between these two sex chromosomes. The X chromosome has over 5,000 genes, of which more than 300 have been mapped. The Y chromosome has 85 genes, half of which have been mapped (Lewis, 2003). Keep in mind that only some of the genes on the X chromosome are sex-related; many are genes that are components of more complex attributes (including face shape and hair color)

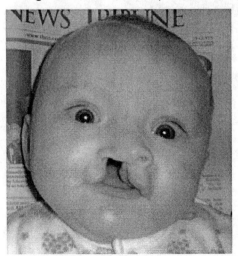

that require information from other genes on other chromosomes to develop. All humans need an X chromosome to survive. Men are more vulnerable to X-linked diseases such as hemophilia and color blindness because the "lack of" two X chromosomes means that a male who inherits an X chromosome with a problem does not have another X chromosome to counteract it.

Finally, as we look at biological occurrences commonly called birth defects, you should know that the vast majority of birth defects have some genetic basis. But most occurrences are not inherited genetic problems; they are random mutations and therefore have low reoccurrence rates. Approximately 20% of birth defects are chromosomal (such as Down's syndrome), and approximately 80% are a specific gene mutation (including spina bifida and cleft lip). We are only going to explore sex-development-oriented anomalies. I have included a fair amount of information on some of these anomalies to give you a good sense of what they can teach us. However, most of the specifics are not crucial to understanding the overall implications.

Chromosome Anomalies (Anomalies Due To Too Few or Too Many Chromosomes)

Turner's Syndrome (X0). **Turner's Syndrome** is the name given to children born with just one X chromosome. In approximately 1 in 2,500 female live births, one chromosome is lost before or after fertilization, usually from the father. Turner's is the syndrome that helped the medical community understand that it is the Y chromosome that masculinizes fetuses. Described in 1938 by a man named Turner, geneticists are fascinated by Turner's because over 97% of fetuses with XO spontaneously abort. Yet, when a child is born with Turner's, the symptoms are relatively mild (Turner Syndrome Society, 2003). Most Turner's Syndrome women share the characteristics of short stature and no ovarian development. Some develop other physical features such as a webbed neck, and arms that turn out at the elbow. They are prone to cardiovascular problems, kidney and thyroid problems, skeletal disorders, and hearing and ear disturbances. Although Turner's was originally thought to be linked with developmental disabilities, it appears now that Turner's individuals mainly have diminished math and spatial skills and good verbal skills. We will return to this latter fact in Chapter 7 on cognitive skills.

Individuals with Turner's do not fully develop ovaries (indicating that it takes two Xs to do so) and therefore do not produce hormones. Individuals with Turner's have female external genitalia when born but will not develop secondary sex characteristics at puberty (like breast development) without hormone supplements. If a Turner's diagnosis is given early, doctors usually treat the symptoms with growth hormones and estrogens. Caught early, with estrogen supplements individuals with Turner's can develop secondary sexual characteristics. Although individuals with Turner's never ovulate, they can carry donor embryos to term. Our "closer look at an interesting study" profiles a recent study on the psychological well-being of women with Turner's Syndrome.

Box 4.1: "A closer look at an interesting study..."

Who did the study?

> Boman, Bryman and Möller

What did they study?

> The psychological well-being of Turner's Syndrome women.

Who did they study?

> They studied 63 women diagnosed with Turner's (mean age = 31.5).

How did they do the study?

> They used data from medial examinations and medical records. They measured well-being with an index comprised of 22 items assessing subscales of anxiety, depressed mood, positive well-being, self-control, general health and vitality. Finally, they interviewed the women to obtain a measure of social functioning.

What did they find?

> Several indicators were related to lower psychological well-being: lack of sex hormones during adult life, presence of hearing impairment, higher age of diagnosis, higher age at menarche or induced bleeding, higher chronological age and difficulty in school. In fact, two factors significantly contributed to poorer well being — late age of diagnosis and school difficulty.

What is so interesting about it?

> A good juxtaposition of psychological and physiological implications. Discussion indicated that hormonal treatment's which could bring on puberty also stunt growth, leaving patients, their families and doctors with difficult choices regarding the relative worth of height vs. potential increased well-being from a more normally timed puberty.
> Article also validates the importance of early diagnosis.

Klinefelter's Syndrome (XXY). Turner's Syndrome and Klinefelter's are the two most common sex anomalies. Many individuals never know they have either syndrome. If they received a diagnosis, it was most likely because they were seeing a physician due to infertility. Nowadays, due to technology and awareness, both syndromes can be diagnosed prenatally (with a karyotype), at birth, or at adolescence.

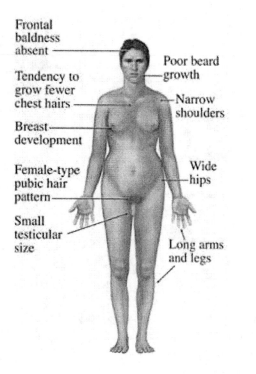

Frontal baldness absent

Tendency to grow fewer chest hairs

Breast development

Female-type pubic hair pattern

Small testicular size

Poor beard growth

Narrow shoulders

Wide hips

Long arms and legs

Klinefelter's Syndrome occurs in approximately 1 in 500 male life births (Block, 1993; Klinefelter Syndrome and Associates, 2003). Klinefelter, a physician, discovered the syndrome in the 1940s. Some individuals today prefer the terminology "XXY males" over "Klinefelter's," so you will see references to both categorizations. The vast majority of individuals with Klinefelter's show a XXY chromosome pattern, but approximately 20% are comprised of XXXY and other combinations. As you might guess, with Klinefelter's individuals develop genital sexual characteristics of both males and females. The presence of the Y chromosome leads to male development during gestation by developing the testes. However, the added X leads to small gonads and weaker levels of testosterone. Individuals with Klinefelter's are sterile. At puberty, many develop female characteristics such as breast development and broad hips and a rounded body frame. They lack facial and body hair. As compared to other males, XXY males are more likely to be overweight, and they tend to be taller than their male relatives.

"Klinefelter's Syndrome"

Individuals with Klinefelter's often show language impairment. They may learn to speak later than other children and to have difficulty learning to speak. This language impairment causes Klinefelter's individuals the greatest psycho-social difficulties. Surgery to reduce breast size can treat that problem in individuals with access to treatment. If diagnosed before or during puberty, individuals with Klinefelter's can receive regular injections of testosterone, which promotes facial hair growth and a muscular body type.

XYY. Although there is no name for this syndrome, **XYY** occurs in approximately 1 in 840 newborn males. The only persistent findings are that XYY individuals are taller than the typical population and have more trouble with motor coordination. But, XYY men are interesting on a cultural level. Some scientists originally put forth the hypothesis that XYY individuals were "hyper masculine." See the cartoon in Figure 4. 5.

Figure 4.5

"That's Dead-Eye Dan, known far and wide for his fast gun, mean temper and extra y chromosome."

Poorly designed studies (single cases, small groups, mental institution and/or prison-only samples), often conducted by researchers who were not "blind" to the diagnoses of those they were interviewing, suggested that XYY individuals were more masculine, more aggressive, and therefore more criminal. The media gobbled up the results and exaggerated the implications (Suzuki & Knudtson, 1990). In the late 1960's, *Newsweek* published an article about XYY individuals entitled "Congenital Criminals." However, when researchers began to identify XYY individuals at birth and then follow them to see if they developed criminal tendencies, the medical community wrote a full-force response and rebuttal to the aggressiveness theories. An organization called Science for the People and two geneticists (Beckwith & King, 1974) challenged the ethics of the studies and their methodological flaws. They stated that the relationship between XYY and criminality was more "casual rather than causal." Several studies were shut down. The XYY controversy was one of the most public debates over ethics and design concerns in genetic studies until more recent cloning debates (Suzuki & Knudtson, 1990).

Finally researchers published a well-designed study where they assessed 4100 Danish respondents comprised of three groups: a sample of tall XY men, a sample of XXY men, and a sample of XYY men (Witkin, Mednick, Schulsinger, Bakkestrom, Christiansen, Goodenough, et al., 1976). After controlling for socioeconomic status, they found that XXY and XYY men tended to have lower IQs. The XYY men had committed more personal property crimes but not crimes against people. In other words, these individuals were probably more likely to be caught, but not more likely to commit. In fact, researchers now think that the only consistent "symptom" of XYY is an extra Y chromosome!

Triple X Syndrome (XXX). **Triple X** occurs in 1.6 per 1000 life female births. Individuals with Triple X tend to have normal fertility and pubertal development. They tend to be taller than XX women and show slightly lower verbal IQ.

In recent research, the overall finding appears to be that any additional chromosome leads to decreased mental abilities including lower IQs.

Hormonal Anomalies (Anomalies Due To Hormonal Problems)

Androgen Insensitivity Syndrome (Testicular Feminizing Syndrome). **Androgen insensitivity** in XY males is the most common of the hormonal problems; however, the incidence of ambiguous genitalia disorders is low overall with 1 per 6,500 live male births ("What is AIS?", 2002). Ambiguous genitalia means that the individual has not fully differentiated as either male or female. Traditionally, at birth the baby's sex cannot be declared on the basis of visual inspection. In this condition, a genetic mutation causes cells NOT to be sensitive to androgens. Consequently, there is limited fetal masculinization. The body produces androgens but cannot recognize them. Newborns look female because their rudimentary testes did not descend. Individuals lack a uterus because the body continues to recognize the hormone that inhibits the Mullerian tubes. In regular sexual

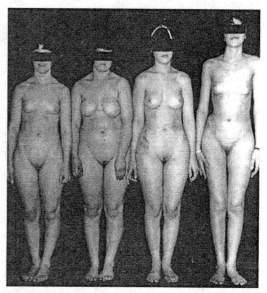

development and in AIS males, Mullerian tubes are inhibited and the Wolfian ducts develop into the epididymis, vas deferens. and ejaculatory duct. Since there is no uterus, there is no menstruation. At puberty, the body responds to estrogen so there is some breast development. However, since hair is developed by androgens, there is no underarm or pubic hair. These individuals are sterile. Evidence suggests that androgen-insensitive males usually identify as female and live their lives without much psychological difficulty."

Congenital Adrenal Hyperplasia (CAH) or Adrenogenital syndrome (AGS). In this syndrome called by either name, the enzymes that are needed to synthesize adrenal hormones are deficient, leading to a large accumulation of androgen. It can affect either XY or XX individuals. The most common form is 21-hydroxylase deficiency which has a severe form and milder forms. Scientists label the severe form Classical CAH (CAH) and it occurs in 1 in 15,000 births. The milder form is called Non-Classical CAH (NCCAH), and is more common, although

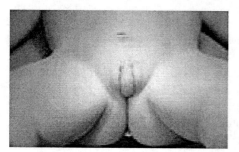

the estimates vary widely. XX individuals show extensive masculinization of external genitalia. Individuals can have internal genitalia such as ovaries but also external genitalia such as a penis and testes. If it is caught early, doctors can administer cortisone to suppress male development. XY individuals can reach puberty (in terms of the level of hormone and the type of development possible in a young child) by age 1 (something called "Infant Hercules Syndrome") and are at high risk for testicular tumors.

Researchers are greatly interested in CAH/AGS girls. CAH/AGS girls are XY individuals who have experienced significant male hormone infusions prenatally. If you were a researcher, in what would you be interested? Researchers have been especially keen to look at these girls' activity levels and interests. As you might suspect, the samples for these kinds of studies are small. Two researchers are especially well known in this field – Anke Ehrhardt and John Money (e.g., Money & Ehrhardt, 1972). They have spent their careers studying the outcomes of individuals who used to be called "hermaphrodites." For instance, in one study, they compared 15 girls with early-treated AGS, and 10 girls with progestin-induced hermaphrodism (a syndrome similar to AGS), to 25 girls without AGS, with a median age for all the girls of 12 ½ years old (reported in Money & Ehrhardt, 1972). Reflecting good design practices, they "matched" these girls on IQ, age, socioeconomic status, and race. In other words, the researchers constructed a control group by finding girls as similar to the treatment group as possible on important characteristics. Matching reduces the chance that any differences seen are due to the demographic or attribute factors. They found that the girls who had early experiences with male hormones were more likely to exhibit tomboy behavior, less maternal behavior, and more high-energy behavior. For example, the girls without AGS were more likely to play with dolls as compared to guns and more likely to have daydreams about pregnancy and motherhood. However, other studies find no differences and there were significant methodological problems with the study. For instance, the study relied on the self report by the parents and the parents of the male-hormone-exposed girls, of course, knew the children's biological backgrounds. Even Ehrhardt (1984) indicates that she thinks that the data support only subtle effects of prenatal hormone factors and the current evidence appears in to be in a similar vein.

Dihydrotestosterone deficiency (DHT). DHT is another enzyme deficiency, and it is inherited. Although there are very low rates in the U.S., the rates are high enough in the Dominican Republic that the locals have a name for it. They call it "guevedoces" which translates to "penis at 12." These XY individuals look female at birth. However, at puberty, their voices deepen, their testes descend, and their penises develop. Imperato-McGinley, Guerrero, Gautier, and Peterson (1974) studied 38 individuals who had this condition. Their provocative conclusion was that the islander's label for the disorder and their behavior toward affected individuals indicated flexibility in their conception of gender. Eighteen of the DHT-deficient children successfully assumed a male role, marrying and fathering children. Imperato-McGinley's findings challenge us to think about more flexible notions of gender. What would it take for mainstream culture in the U.S. to be as accepting of someone changing genders in adolescence?

What Do Sexual Anomalies Teach Us About The Meaning Of Gender?

Many of these chromosomes and hormonal problems can lead to some form of "hermophadism" or some combination of male and female sexual attributes. Most current literature refers to individuals with some form of ambiguity as "intersexed," and I direct you to the website of the Intersex Society of North America (ISNA, 2003). The

intersex movement seeks to reduce what advocates view as unnecessary surgeries, especially those performed at birth, because genital alteration can cause significant nerve damage that reduces or eliminates sexual pleasure. ISNA's motto is "building a world free of shame, secrecy, and unwanted sexual surgeries." Organizations such as the one above argue that these surgeries mostly serve to make the parents feel better but may or may not be in the best interest of the child. The popular press has covered much of this debate, including a high-profile book entitled *As Nature Made Him: The Boy Who Was Raised as a Girl* in which Colapinto (2000) details the life of David Reimer, who was born one of twin boys. Reimer received a botched circumcision and was raised as a girl named Brenda. At age 14, Brenda decided to live as a man. One of the more interesting aspects of the story is Reimer's and the current intersex movement's anger at the physicians who argued that gender can be established with sex-hormone treatments and the will to do so by the individual and those around him/her. Overall, the collaboration developing between scientists and intersex individuals indicates how little we know about the scientific, personal, and political implications of these sex variations.

As I've noted through this book, gender has a great deal of meaning to most people. Sometimes it is difficult to know how deep our feelings go. For many years, I've used the

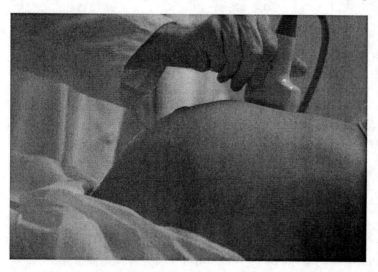

following piece to help students identify their own feelings. It comes from a genetics counseling professional newsletter and is presented as an ethical dilemma over what the counselor should tell the clients about a mistake in identifying the sex of premature fetuses. At 22 weeks gestational age it would be difficult to visually distinguish between a penis and a clitoris. I urge you to think about your own reactions to the mistake, not the bioethical or right-to-know dilemma the counselor faces. *Why* would it matter to you to know?

Two infants were born at 22 weeks gestation to a 29-year-old Caucasian woman. Physical exam of the infants at birth concluded that the infants were consistent with 22 weeks, birth weights were 370 grams and 248 grams, and the assessment of the attending physician in the delivery room was that both infants were live born, non-viable male infants. The infants were admitted to the intensive care nursery and provided comfort care. Both died within one hour of birth. The parents had very much wanted these infants and had named them James and Andrew at birth. The father held the infants, and a memorial service was held for them following death. The death certificates were made out in the names of James and Andrew. Chromosomes were drawn in the intensive care nursery as part of the work-up of premature birth to aid in the counseling and medical care direction of the couples' future pregnancies. Six weeks after the death of the infants, the chromosome report returned showing both infants with a karyotype of 46 XX. What should the parents be told? (Peabody, p. 10)

This material challenges many of us on both personal and professional levels as it prompt us to think about the meaning of gender at the very heart of the matter.

In the previous section of this chapter, we have looked at sexual differentiation and anomalies. Besides the intrinsic interest in knowing about typical sexual differentiation, it is also crucial that students of gender psychology know about the biology of sex. For many sex or gender differences, theories will propose biological explanations often based on arguments about biologically based predispositions, brain functioning, and/or hormones. Most of the biologically-based arguments are empirical questions and need to be explored by trained researchers. Fortunately, a growing number of psychologists and other scientists are training in **neuropsychology** and are bringing a fuller sense of nature and nurture into the discussion of human behavior. I hope that this chapter has already given you a glimpse into the complexities of research on the biology of sex and gender. Before we turn to environmental or nurture arguments, let's turn briefly to another set of "nature" theories. Evolutionary theories have received much attention in the field of psychology in the past several years and are playing a rising role in debates regarding the nature/nurture components of gender behavior (Angier, 1999; Buss, 2005; Gould, 2002; Laland & Brown, 2002, Myers, 2001).

Evolutionary Theory: What Is The Relationship Between Genetic Encoding And Complex Behaviors?

Related to the basic premises of Darwinian theory, **evolutionary theory** argues that men and women have developed certain cognitive and behavioral predispositions based in genetics and human experience (e.g., Buss, 1998). To help illustrate some of the key aspects of evolutionary theory, let's consider men's and women's spatial context aptitude. We will cover several theories regarding this spatial skill difference and other related spatial abilities in Chapter 7 on cognition. In order to explore an evolutionary argument for this chapter, the "sex difference" finding under discussion is the consistent but small-medium effect size associated with men's greater ability in "spatial skills" – namely rotating 3-D objects Several theorists argue that hunting and gathering over thousands of years of human history have led to this difference (e.g., Ecuyer-Dab & Robert, 2004). Men were assumed to be the hunters. Spatial skills enable hunting and the best hunters were more likely to gain food, attract women and reproduce. The question regarding why men hunt and women gather tends to be explained by the fact that childbearing and rearing required women to stay close to the village and to each other and made them less mobile for hunts (Panter-Brick, Layton, & Rowley-Conwy, 2001). Others have argued that men with better spatial skills are better at roving around in order to distribute their genetic seed. As with many sociobiological or evolutionary theories other animal species besides humans are used as an example. For instance, male voles (small mammals) show increase spatial abilities (measured by mazes) during mating season (Gaulin, FitzGerald & Wartell, 1990).

"Some Basics – Evolutionary Theory"

It is beyond the scope of this text to grabble with the full complexity of evolutionary theory as an explanatory device for human behavior. However, any serious psychology student must be mindful of the parameters of the debate. Psychologist Nora Newcombe (2006) provides a useful framework for assessing the role of evolutionary psychological theory to psychology. Newcombe argues that several aspects regarding evolutionary theory are *not* under dispute or debate by psychologist for instance the theory itself, the reliance on reproductive success as criterion and the idea that there are evolutionary pressures on cognition and social behavior in all species including humans. Newcombe questions the role of large scale theory in explaining smaller behaviors and the lack of empirical evidence for many of the pieces that are supposed to add up to the picture. For instance, in terms of spatial ability, does hunting require greater spatial skills than gathering? Does 3-D ability enable aiming? Anthropological evidence exists to indicate both men and women made tools – although they may have served different purposes (e.g., weapons as compared to baskets). She further questions why there would be a sex-specific evolutionary benefit to spatial skills. Finally, we and others question the usefulness of species-to-species comparisons. For most human behaviors it is possible to find examples of other species that explain one form of the behavior or another. Or, there is an important difference between the species and humans. For instance, voles are territory animals whereas humans are social animals and live in groups. Another excellent example of this problem is monogamy as a human behavior – it is relatively easy to find species who mate for life (e.g., otters) and those who are active in genetic distribution (rodents). How are these other species like humans in genetic and social ways?

Evolutionary theory as applied to human behavior tends to explain small level behaviors (such as visual spatial skills) with genome level explanations – that is, the theory and the behavior are not matched on level of scope (e.g., Nanay, 2002). When articulated at its most sweeping, speculative version, evolutionary theory tends to be "innatist" assuming that humans are not shaped but are rather born with the innate behaviors and information they need. Perhaps most challenging to theories and researchers is the fact that the human mind has more plasticity than many theories imply. Humans are not "coded" to be able to live in only one environment.

As also argued in Chapter 2, media attention to theories that result in sweeping generalizations are disruptive to scientific method and the public's understanding. Evolutionary theories expressed in the popular press tend to appear deterministic and portray humans as hapless inheritors of good and bad behavior genes. For instance, out of a book that includes many more nuanced statements (Geary, 1998), a short article about the same book pulls out the quote where Geary suggests that girls playing with dolls more so than do boys has "*nothing to do with Barbie, television ads, or gender stereotypes and has everything to do with human nature and the best interests of women* (APA, 1998, p. 23)." The "best interests of women" (as a group – not as individuals necessarily) lie in practicing to raise children. The term "nothing" is insupportably strong in light of research that shows direct links between socialization and play choices, and humans as active shapers of their environments. The coverage of the statement and the statement itself are not useful to endeavor of the conducting of research and application of its results.

Newcombe (2006) concludes her comments on evolutionary theory by arguing that psychology as a discipline should embrace evolutionary theories in the same way that psychology utilizes other important theories – as a basis for empirical research into topics of interest. Nature, nurture and interaction theories all need to be weighed as useful theories given the criteria set out in Chapter 2. Does the evidence support their hypotheses? No scientist or critically thinking student can run to one and away from another because we don't "like" what they say. However, all theories can be held to stringent criteria and scientific method. Roberts comments that we should focus less on the divisions between biological and environmental theories and more on their "interimplications" (2000, p. 19). It will only be through better research that we can come to more fully understand the implications of the interactions and the specifics of the interactive mechanisms.

Nature/Nurture Interaction:
How Do Biology And Environment Interact?

We will close out this chapter with a brief example of how nature and nurture can interact to produce gender-related behavior. You'll recall that I started the chapter with the following scenario "*Two children approach a sand box. They play for a while. The girl has a truck that the boy wants. He bonks her over the head with a shovel to obtain the truck. She responds by yelling "you stupid jerk!"* After reading this chapter, I hope you have some new ways of looking at this situation. You should be able to describe how he developed into a boy and she into a girl. I suspect you might be able to formulate a theory of how his testosterone makes him more likely to pursue physical aggression and perhaps a theory about how she is "wired" to respond verbally. You might also acknowledge that we have stereotypes about boys being more aggressive and girls more caring. Perhaps these children are responding to these stereotypes

and acting in expected ways? But what if it is even more complicated than that? What if nature and nurture interact? What if he is born with a slight predisposition to respond to aggravation by bonking? What if this predisposition is aided and expanded by the fact that when he hits, adults around him respond with "well ... he's a boy!"? As much as many of us might want a simple explanatory theory, almost all the evidence points to an interaction between nature and nurture. Interaction is more than a 1 + 1. Interaction suggests that each works to affect the other. So, it is not like a recipe with a measure of this and a measure of that – it is a recipe whose outcome changes when the ingredients react and whose ingredients may even change by being added.

"Nature vs. Nurture"

In the next chapter we will take a look at some key ingredients in children's (and adults') lives as they hear and see images and expectations of men and women.

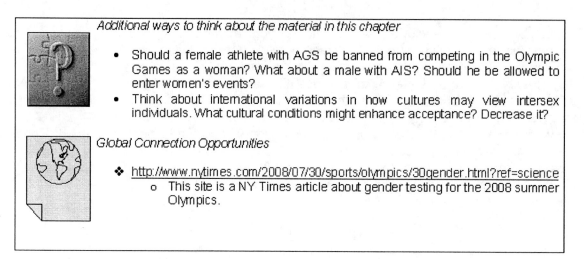

Additional ways to think about the material in this chapter

- Should a female athlete with AGS be banned from competing in the Olympic Games as a woman? What about a male with AIS? Should he be allowed to enter women's events?
- Think about international variations in how cultures may view intersex individuals. What cultural conditions might enhance acceptance? Decrease it?

Global Connection Opportunities

- ❖ http://www.nytimes.com/2008/07/30/sports/olympics/30gender.html?ref=science
  - o This site is a NY Times article about gender testing for the 2008 summer Olympics.

Chapter 5
Gender Expectations

I wrote most of this book in my university's library. One day, just after completing a segment where I argued for the similarities of the sexes, I left the library to meet a friend. On my way, I came upon the university's wrestling team. Teams of two had harnessed themselves to a panel truck and were pulling it 100 meters. I stopped and stared. What would possess them? I passed two young women – both around 5' and small-boned. I said "Girls, let's strap on some harnesses and show them what's what!" They laughed and said "We'll get right on it" and walked on. My friend joined me and we watched. She suggested that at the end of this book, I put a picture of the event with a caption: "I really didn't mean it, men <u>are</u> from Mars!"

I relay this story because none of us are free from our own gender biases. Even though my rational mind could logically argue that men from a wrestling team might be imbedded in a context where they are expected to act in traditionally macho ways, my less-rational mind was saying "What's wrong with these people?"

University of Wisconsin – La Crosse Strongman competition. The truck pull component of the event.
Photo: Travis Erickson (used with permission)

Psychologists often contrast theories regarding the "nature" of human processes with those the focus on the "nurture." Nurture theories reflect the environmental influences on us. As humans, each of us lives in multiple environments even within the same day. Even family studies must reckon with the fact that siblings can each experience a family differently, even identical twins, not only because of their own predispositions, but also because each child has a different sibling affecting their environment. So, environment influences include both people and situations. In this chapter we will examine classic environmental influencers – media. Whereas in Chapter 6, we will examine the role of parents, peers, and schools. For the rest of this chapter, I want you to think about the environment in terms of the expectations society and individuals may hold for gender. In the Chapter 3, we explored how gender could be both constructed and reinforced. Here we consider a more subtle process of how societal expectations can create different environments for different people.

Expectations

Soon after the wrestling experience, I was telling my water aerobic buddies about the book. My water aerobics class consists mainly of women 65 years-old and older. When I told them that the book would emphasize the fact that empirical evidence does not yield large differences between the sexes, they hollered! One of them said, "Are you crazy? Not only are they different, but they get more different from us every year as we age!" I suggested that they could have a chapter at the end of this book entitled "The Water Babes Talk Back." I tried to explain that behavior differences are a different beast than attribute differences, and that a lifetime of experience forms who we are when we are older. Even then, I heard one woman say "Men are so pessimistic" while another woman retorted "No, it's women who are so pessimistic." This experience at water aerobics nicely represents a few key issues that we will examine in this chapter: that we all bring cognitive bias to the way we think about and interpret events, that personalities inform behavior just as experiences form personalities, and that stereotypes about gender are a strong component of our society. The chapter concludes with a discussion of media. Media directly affects the formation and perpetuation of stereotypes and gender expectations.

Stereotypes

Researchers exploring **stereotypes** about men and women find fairly consistent results. Respondents can generate lists of words that they think better represent men and/or women. People can tell you what the stereotypes are, even if they claim not to use them. So, why do researchers care about stereotypes? Overall, researchers care about stereotypes because we've collected good evidence that individuals fall back on stereotypes (especially in the absence of other information) and that they act on those stereotypes.

"Gender Stereotypes in Media"

How Do We Form Stereotypes?

Stereotypes are "a set of beliefs about the personal attributes of a group of people" (Ashmore & Del Boca, 1981). Women are emotional. Men are unfaithful. Most stereotypes are formed in our childhood, aided by our family's values and those of our peer groups. Can you think of particular overgeneralizations that the folks you hung out as a kid with had? I can. Now, I can tell you about overgeneralizations that faculty make about students and vice-versa. Although some people form stereotypes through direct experience, experience is not a prerequisite to holding the view. Research firmly supports the idea that stereotypes form, in part, as a by-product of the way we think. Our propensity to categorize in order to deal efficiently with large amounts of incoming information leads us to make categories about people and then generalize from them. All it takes to create a stereotype is for someone to believe that a certain attribute is more likely for a certain group of people. Often individuals come to believe erroneously that an attribute corresponds to a group or they overestimate a weak relationship. Social psychologists call this an "**illusory correlation**" (Hamilton & Rose, 1980).

Why Do We Worry About Stereotypes?

Assuming that we could label the attributes associated with any given stereotype as negative, positive, and/or neutral, why do we care if people hold them? One of the major reasons we care is that there is a direct link between stereotypes and prejudice, and a link exists between prejudice and discriminatory behaviors, including hate crimes (Nelson, 2002). Another reason we care about stereotypes is that they are really hard to break. I had a college professor who described them as "universal, ineradicable, functional and harmful" (Crawford, 1991, personal communication). Stereotypes persist even in the face of discrediting information. Social psychologists have identified several disturbing patterns associated with the fact that most of us are really stubborn about letting our beliefs go after we have come to believe them.

Let's examine the old stereotype that "blondes are dumb" reflected in "dumb blond" jokes. "Dumb blonde" jokes are, of course, directed toward women despite their gender neutral name. I use this example because it is a real stereotype but I do not believe its perpetuation is as potentially harmful as other real stereotypes such as racial stereotypes. Dolly Parton responded to the dumb blonde stereotype with a great joke of her own: "I don't' mind dumb blonde jokes, 'cus I know I'm not dumb and I know I'm not blonde." Let's say that a woman has the belief that "dumbness" is related to "blondeness" (in this case an illusory correlation). Like other humans, she will promote and protect this belief. She will actively select for information that fits that category of "dumb blonde." When this person meets a dumb blonde female, she will think "See? I told you blondes were dumb." If she meets a dumb brunette female, she is likely not to think about her in reference to her category. She probably does not have a "dumb brunette: category. If she is forced to think about the dumb brunette, she is likely to rely on explanation such as "She's the exception that proves the rule" or "She's really a blonde who dyes her hair darker." In addition, if she meets a dumb man, she is not likely to think about his hair color because she is not likely to have a category for dumb men based on hair. She is selecting "data" that fit the hypothesis and ignoring the data that don't. Social psychologists call this process "selective attention to stereotype-relevant information" (e.g., Bodenhauser, 1988). People will also actively look for information that confirms their preconceptions, called "**confirmation bias**" (e.g., Snyder & Swann, 1984). In addition, people will hold tight to their preconceptions even when faced with directly discrediting information, called "**belief perseverance**" (e.g. Slusher & Anderson, 1989). It is easy to do, is it not? When we don't like information we receive, we are likely to be good at thinking of reasons why that information isn't valid.

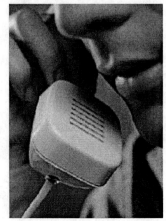

In addition to the all of the cognitive machinations associated with protecting our beliefs, stereotypes affect our behavior? We tend to act on our beliefs in such a way that our actions bring about the expected behavior. Researchers call this process "**self fulfilling prophecy**." It requires two phases. First, a person must have a belief and act on it. Then, the person's actions must elicit the expected response. One classic self-fulfilling prophecy study led undergraduate males to believe that they were talking to either an attractive woman or an unattractive woman on the phone by showing them a picture before they had the conversation (Snyder, Tanke, & Berscheid, 1977). Like most of us, these men held the belief that attractive women have better social skills. When led to believe they were talking to an attractive woman, their own behaviors changed – for instance, they asked more open-ended questions allowing for more interesting answers. Afterwards, those men who thought they were talking to an attractive woman reported the conversation as better than those who thought they were talking to an unattractive woman. Although that finding represents a certain level of stereotypic-relevant information-processing, this is not self-fulfilling prophecy. It turns out that the real women to whom they were talking actually **did** respond with more social skills when the men they were talking to thought they were attractive as assessed by independent raters who listened to the tapes afterwards without knowing the study design. Self-fulfilling prophecy studies help us understand how insidiously stereotypes can creep into our behaviors.

Finally, along with the evidence that we have **explicit** stereotypes and act on them, researchers have now shown that we also have **implicit** stereotypes (those below the consciousness level) that appear to "awaken" when primed (e.g. Bargh, Chen & Burrows, 1996; Greenwald & Banaji, 1995; Macrae, Bodenhausen, Milne, Thorn, and Castelli, 1997). For instance, respondents will more quickly associate the adjective "good" with young than they will with old (also more readily with European American than with African American).

Research on implicit stereotypes helps us understand why there is a difference between "knowing" a stereotype and "acting" on a stereotype. However, because they are so easily activated, the research also implicates stereotypes in biased thoughts and behaviors. Our "A closer look at an interesting study" for this chapter is on behavioral outcomes of implicit stereotypes. Finally, given the strong cognitive basis to stereotypes, what does it suggest about countering them? If you ask people "not" to think about their stereotypes, it tends to make them more prominent (less implicit, more explicit); however, it does appear that if you ask people to think in an egalitarian (equal) manner, that process reduces stereotyping (Nelson, 2002).

Box 5.1: A closer look at an interesting study...

Who did the study?

> Shih, Pittinsky & Ambady (1999)

What did they study?

> They assessed the mathematical skills of Asian American women after they had either had their "ethnic identity" activated or their "gender identity." The stereotype of Asian Americans is that they have superior quantitative skills as compared to European Americans, and, as we have noted, the stereotype of women is that they have inferior quantitative skills as compared to men.

Who did they study?

> Forty-six U.S. female undergraduates and 19 Canadian female high school students from Vancouver. The authors chose Canadian women because Vancouver has a higher number of recent Asian immigrants.

How did they do the study?

> Asian American women respondents were randomly assigned to a condition where they had their ethnic identity activated (via a series of background questions regarding their heritage) or they had their gender identity activated (via background questions about their sex and whether they lived in single-sex halls) or a control condition. Respondents then completed a math test.

What did they find?

> As compared to the control condition In which no aspect of identity was activated, scores were higher in the ethnic identity condition and lower in the gender identity condition.

What is so interesting about it?

> This study illuminates the role that implicit stereotypes can have on actual behavior. Although they could not evaluate? it in this study, the authors point out that they would be interested to see what happens if both identities are activated. The study exemplifies the type of research occurring on stereotypes currently.

What Are The Stereotypes Of Men And Women?

As suggested earlier, survey respondents generate consistent stereotypes about men and women. In general, researchers classify gender stereotypes into two categories where men's characteristics represent active, agentic or instrumental qualities associated with leadership and accomplishment, and women's characteristics represent instrumental or expressive qualities associated with orientation toward emotion and relationships (Kite & Deaux, 1987). Table 5.1 shows a list of classic gender stereotypes in the United States. In addition, researchers have detected some fascinating international agreement toward the stereotypes

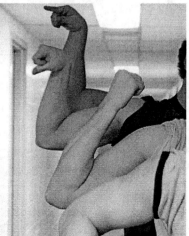

with six male characteristics mentioned by all 30 countries studied (adventurous, dominant, forceful, independent, masculine, and strong) and three items for women (sentimental, submissive, and superstitious) (Williams & Best, 1982). Although, both negative and positive stereotypes are known for both men and women, the stereotypes for women tend to be less desirable than stereotypes for men (Kite & Deaux).

Table 5.1
Sample gender stereotypes from Allen (1995)

Men – Positive Stereotypes	Men – Negative Stereotypes
• *Self-confident* • *Makes decisions easily*	• *Egotistical* • *Undisciplined*
Women – Positive Stereotypes	Women – Negative Stereotypes
• *Aware of others' feelings* • *Emotional*	• *Gullible* • *Complaining*

Several key issues regarding individuals' use of gender stereotypes should be highlighted here. First, individuals exaggerate stereotypes. Respondents see the differences between men and women as larger than they actually are and larger than they rate themselves as men and women (Allen, 1995; Martin; 1987). Second, research suggests that individuals tend to "default" to gender stereotypes. If a perceiver has access to other important individuating information, stereotypes are "swamped" by the more important information. However, in the absence of individuating information such as age and occupation, individual perceivers will default to stereotypes to judge others' behaviors. In fact, they appear especially to use the information to predict future behavior (as in, "Who will bake the brownies?") (Biernat & Kobrynowicz, 1999). Third, individuals use gender stereotypes more heavily in stereotypic situations. So, for instance, respondents used stereotypic information when choosing candidates for a traditionally masculine or feminine job – but not for a traditionally gender-neutral job (Biernat & Kobrynowicz, 1999).

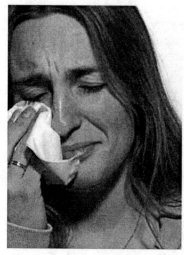

Fourth, perceptions of an individual from a group tend to be "normed" to that group. For instance, a tall man is guessed to be taller than a tall woman. Of course this last example makes sense, but what if the group norming characteristic were something like emotionality? Then, an emotional man would probably be perceived as much less emotional than an emotional woman, because women are seen to be more generally more emotion (Biernat & Kobrynowicz, 1999). In a related set of findings, gay men are seen in predominantly feminine terms, whereas lesbians are seen in masculine terms (Kite & Deaux, 1987). In this case, sexual orientation "trumps" gender but also realigns the stereotypes. Fifth, stereotypes appear to be triggered by stereotypic visual cues such as a briefcase for a man or a bikini for a woman (Deaux & Kite, 1993).

Sixth, although described as pertaining to approximately 50% of the population, in fact, gender stereotypes are both race- and class-bound. For instance, Landrine (1985) found that respondents rated all women as stereotypically feminine, respondents rated European American women as more dependent, passive, and emotional than African American women. In addition, respondents rated lower-class women as more confused, dirty, hostile, inconsiderate, and irresponsible than middle-class women. Finally, what racial and class groupings do you think fit the most stereotypic view of women? Respondents saw European American women and middle-class women as most similar to traditional stereotypes of women. Respondents also appear to see lower-class men as more defiant and aggressive than middle-class men. In addition, traditional racial stereotypes are visible in patterns such as Hispanic men seen as more "machismo" and African American men seen as more violent than European American men (reviewed by Lips, 2000).

Seventh, within the categories of men and women, researchers have identified some standard subtype stereotypes (Deaux, Winton, & Crowley, 1985). We tend to categorize men into business man, blue-collar working man, macho man, and athletic man. We tend to categorize women into sex object, career woman, housewife, and athletic woman. For several years, I've assigned my students the task of finding a print ad image of a woman or man that they like and dislike. Most of the time, students like the ads best where it is difficult to pigeonhole the model into one of the subcategories. So, for instance, students will tend to select a photo of a woman holding a briefcase and a baby. Try it. I think you'll find it interesting.

What If The Stereotypes Are True?

Social psychologists often debate the idea that there is a "kernel of truth" behind many stereotypes. Given social stratification by gender, it is not surprising that men's and women's experiences can differ greatly. So, for instance, women do more childcare than men. And, men are more likely to be mechanics than women. The trouble comes in the translation of the action to the idea that the whole group is more likely to be a certain way. Are women more nurturing? Are men more mechanical? Furthermore, even if a characteristic is slightly more true for one group than another, it is inappropriate to expect that characteristic in any one individual.

Overall, I have focused on how we use stereotypes as a way for you to see that "environment" is a much larger and more complex concept than just "what's not biological." Box 5.2 that shows a media awareness group's suggestions for discussing media stereotypes with kids.

Media

When all else fails, we can always blame the media! Unfortunately, when it comes to systematically stereotypic portrayals of men and women, the media deserves to shoulder much of the blame for perpetuating stereotypes. They may even need to take some heat for creating some stereotypes! Who is the "they"? Media is the name we give to all forms of communication used to provide information. Therefore, media involves all individuals and organizations whose business it is to communicate information for commercial or non-commercial reasons (including entertainment!). Below, we will review research on several forms of media and see that a consistent pattern of stereotypic portrayals of men and women emerges.

Box 5.2:

Talking to Kids about Gender Stereotypes

Images of men and women in the media are often based on stereotypical roles of males and females in our society. Because stereotyping can affect how children feel about themselves and how they relate to others, it's important that they learn to recognize and understand gender stereotypes in different media.

Here are some tips to help kids understand how boys and girls and men and women are stereotyped in the media.

Start talking about gender stereotyping early on. Familiarize young children with the concept of stereotyping (simple, one-dimensional portrayals of people, based on generalizations based on gender, race, age, etc.) and help them understand the role gender stereotypes play in the storybooks and cartoons they enjoy. Point out non-traditional heroes and heroines in children's media.

Look at how boys and girls are stereotyped in advertisements and in movies and TV programs. Talk about how these images are limiting for children, who may feel they aren't "normal" because they don't fit the mould, for example, a girl who plays sports aggressively or a boy who likes reading and drawing.

Ask kids to think about how realistically males and females are portrayed in the media. Ask them to compare the images of men and women they see on TV with people they know in real life. Are the standards for attractiveness the same for men and women? Are females generally more concerned about personal relationships, while men are more concerned about their careers?

Examine advertising for a stereotypical male (someone who is confident, physically active, aggressive, in control) and a stereotypical female (someone who is beautiful, helpless, domestic, sexually attractive). Discuss how such images can influence how we perceive sex roles.

Talk about the differences in video games designed for boys and girls. Look at the images of men and women in games designed for boys. Who are the aggressors and who are the victims? What about games where the women are the "shooters"? Is this a step forward for women? Why do so many girl-specific games promote stereotypical interests such as make-up and fashion?

Look at gender portrayal in popular music. Discuss the marketing of male and female musical artists: how does it differ? What role does attractiveness play in the promotion of female artists: is it the same for male artists? Talk about the sexism and

---

violence directed at women in some music lyrics and videos.

Look for strong, realistic portrayals of men and women. The media can provide engaging, positive and non-traditional role models for boys and girls. Counter the many stereotypical gender portrayals kids are exposed to with media portrayals of sensitive men and strong women.

Media Awareness Network (2003)

Books and Television. Books that children read show some consistent patterns, namely, under-representation of women, stereotypic attributes and activities for women, and the portrayal of white and middle class as normative. Several studies analyzing Caldecott Award-winning books for 3 to 5 year-olds over the years between 1937-1991, note some of these patterns (Crabb & Bielawski, 1994; Kolbe & LaVoie, 1981; Oskamp, Kaufman, & Wolterbeek,

1996). First, male characters outnumber female characters three to one. Second, authors portray men and women in traditional settings and with stereotypic attributes (for instance, an emotional mother in a kitchen or a standoffish Dad going to work in a tie). Third, current books show better numerical ratios than older books and a wider range of attributes and activities for both sexes. School books and comics show similar patterns to those found in children's books. For instance, Witt (1996) found a three to two ratio in biographies, and illustrations featuring boys and men outnumbering those of women and girls two to one in textbooks. In newspaper comics, images are improving, yet illustrators are still more likely to show women as passive (Brabant & Mooney, 1997).

Finally, the primary characters in most novels are male. Publishers are interested in doing "what sells" and are afraid of losing the male audience. We can link this issue of books and marketing to the narrower latitude given to boys and maintained by boys. Girls can read books written by both men and women, whereas boys will be more apt to read books only by men. *Harry Potter* author Jo Kathleen Rowling's publisher asked her to use her initials in order to mask the fact that she was a woman (Bradley & Stahl, 1999).

Interestingly, surveys of television shows yield gender ratios and stereotyping problems similar to those in books, along with similar slow improvement. For instance, sitcoms show the same trend as books by beginning to show a wider range of family forms and functions, and

more egalitarian roles (Olson & Douglas, 1997). However, television is notable for having more explicit sexual content and therefore, teaches more messages about sexuality as compared to other media sources such as books (Ward, 1995). One of my favorite summaries of this material says that TV teaches girls how to be sexy, not how to be sexual. Sex-related talk appears in over 50% of television programming and shows the risks and responsibilities of sexual activity in less than 10% (Kunkel, 1999). Three forms of television remain widely gender specific. Men watch more sporting events than women, and women watch more soap operas and daytime talk shows than men (Gerbner, et al. 1994). Finally, in an odd development, sitcoms and television ads appear to be featuring "dumb and proud of it" white males. This trend of portraying men as dumb is difficult to understand and has raised some ire in many Internet discussion rooms. One person wrote in, "Somehow I don't think any other race could have been portrayed [this way] without eliciting major protests" (Adahere, 2003). It is an interesting phenomenon even in light of the fact that most European Americans do not see "white" as a race. In fact, individuals in dominant social groups are much less likely to see their social groups as salient to their self concept than are individuals from less dominant groups (see nice review in Tatum, 1997). So, a African American is more likely to mention being African American than a European is to mention being European American, a woman is more likely to mention being female than is a man to mention being male.

Music and Music Videos. Over the past several decades, music videos have garnered the attention of many gender researchers. In general, music lyrics have become more sexually explicit and so have the visual images in the videos. In addition, music videos are one of the primary programming categories watched by adolescents. Music videos are viewed in over 55 million U.S. homes and the numbers continue to grow (Strouse, Buerkel-Rothfuss, & Long, 1995). Sexuality in music, per se, does not have to be a gender issue; however, the sexuality in music videos and lyrics is gendered. Men and women are portrayed in very narrow ways. Rap lyrics and images receive much criticism for excessively violent and sexual content; however, many rock groups show similar patterns. See Table 5.2 for some rap and rock lyrics from top-selling groups.

Table 5.2

Magic Stick (Lil' Kim with 50 cent) Lil' Kim not a whore But I sex a nigga so good, he gotta tell his boys When it, come to sex don't test my skills Cause my head game have you HEAD over heels Give a nigga the chills, have him pay my bills **Used to Love Her (Guns 'n' Roses)** I used to love her But I had to kill her I had to put her six feet under And I can still hear her complain

A set of documentaries now exist that explore the images of women in rock videos. "Dreamworlds I, II, & III: Desire, Sex, Power in Music Video" (1990, 1997, 2006) showcase the images of videos, often without the soundtracks. The commentator, Sut Jhally, argues that music videos portray adolescent male "dreamworlds" where women are nymphomaniacs and subservient to men. Women outnumber men in most of these videos, and sex is portrayed as easily obtainable by men without the "bother" of courtship. Jhally makes the argument that the videos imply that all men could live in this dreamworld (Media Education Foundation, 1997). Empirical research on music videos on MTV finds that videos portray women primarily as sex objects or as sexual predators and that semi-nudity is the norm (Signorella, Bigler, & Liben, 1994). Country music, one of the top radio formats in the U.S., portrays male artists more stereotypically than female artists. Country music videos are fairly egalitarian, although scanty dress for women and suggestive poses for women are common (Andsager & Roe, 1999). In all forms of popular music, the ratio of male to female artists runs at approximately 3 to 1.

Pornography. Another source of very stereotypic portrayals of men and women is pornography (generally speaking, material that is primarily used to, or intended to, sexually arouse or excite sexual desire in people). We will cover pornographic images in the chapter on aggression (Chapter 10) and the chapter on sexuality (Chapter 9). However, in this chapter it should be noted that pornography is a 100 billion dollar business with a growing number of female consumers. A survey of adult video customers found that approximately 90% were heterosexual men (20% of whom were renting or buying the movie to watch with their female partners) (Adult Video News, 1998).

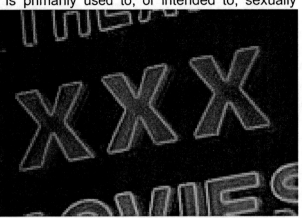

Advertising. Advertising is designed to sell products. However, along the way to selling products, advertising also sells dreams, perfection, forms of reality, views, cultural myths, and values (e.g., Kilbourne, 1999). Advertising is not particularly subtle and it is relatively easy to empirically show trends in sexualized, racist, and sexist images.

Advertising over time. Advertising is not new. Advertising in some form goes back centuries. However, advertising is currently much more pervasive than it used to be and qualitatively different. We are all bombarded by messages everywhere we look and listen. Twitchell (1996) coined the phrase "adcult" to refer to a culture completed infiltrated by advertising. In some ways, due to the high volume of messages, all of us learn to tune out some of the advertising. We live in a "message dense" society, meaning we have much to which we can attend. So, advertisers must first get our attention. However, it is also true that the sheer number of advertisements creates this pervasive view of a reality that is not attainable by any person. Furthermore, advertisers are in the business of trying to sell consumers a reality we are supposed to want. Research on the media provides solid evidence that media images tend to be very narrow and convey a particular ideal over and over. By selling ideals and values media plays a direct role in conveying stereotypic, often negative images of individuals, subgroups, and the larger society. In the past, advertising images of ethnic and racial groups were almost always reinforcing stereotypes about that group because the ads were directed at white, middle-class buyers. For instance, Latinos were presented as

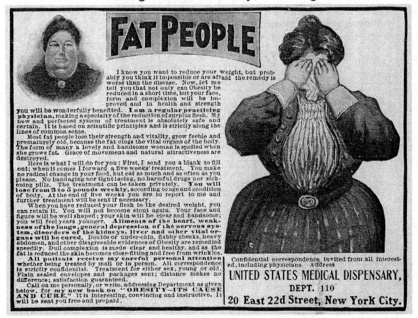

"spitfires," African American women like Mammy-type characters, Native American men like noble savages, and Asians, especially Asian women, as subservient (Wilson & Gutierrez, 2003). Recent research provides convincing evidence that advertising is become more attentive to consumers who are not white, middle-class or rich, and male (Reichert & Lambaise, 2003). In part due to industry changes that allow advertisers to hone in on the demographic of their choice (e.g., Asian American women ages 18-24), advertisers now prepare ads aimed at a wider segment of society. Consequently, although still overly sexual and perfect, there are notable examples of advertising intended to appeal to gay and lesbian populations, African Americans, Hispanics, Asian Americans, and individuals with disabilities – anyone with buying power. So, for instance, advertisers in a survey of gay and phone books were slightly more likely to use male photographic images than were advertisers in the more mainstream phone book (Waugh & Rienzi, 1998). However, despite improvement, images of people of color still lean toward old stereotypes (see Box 5.1 for this chapter's "*A closer look at an interesting study*").

Box 5.1: "A closer look at an interesting study…"

Who did the study?

Plous & Neptune (1999)

What did they study?

The depictions of African and European American men and women in fashion advertising.

How did they do the study?

The did a content analysis of ten years of fashion advertisements: two magazines with a predominantly female European readership (*Cosmopolitan & Glamour*), two magazines with a predominantly female African American readership (*Ebony & Essence*), and two with a predominantly male European American readership (*Gentlemen's Quarterly & Esquire*). They did not look at African American male magazines because there are no mainstream ones to assess. They identified 12,472 advertisements and then randomly selected five from each issue resulting in a sample of 1,800 advertisements. They coded each ad for four dimensions: racial/gender composition (who is in the ad?), body exposure (how much body are as exposed), body position (low status or animal-like if crouching or on all fours), clothing (two categories – sexual attire and animal prints).

What did they find?

Women's body exposure was higher than men's. African Americans were significantly underrepresented in European American magazines (except for African American women in European American women's magazines). European American women's body exposure increased over the ten years. European American women were the most likely to be shown in low-status positions and African American women wore the majority of animal prints – usually shown as predatory animals.

What is so interesting about it?

Research that analyzes the number and type of images or concepts in a media form is called "content analysis." Content analysis provides a good way to see large-scale patterns and trends over time. This study shows both the pattern of women in submissive and sexual roles as well as the racism that runs through mainstream advertising. The other reason this study is interesting is that its methodology is approachable and any of you who wish to replicate a component of it would be easily able to do so. Recently, my students have analyzed *Maxim* and *FHM* and found similar

"Killing Us Softly"

Ideal men and women. Advertisements sell an ideal of masculinity and femininity. Research consistently finds that men are shown as work-oriented and authoritative. In addition, the image of men must convey this authoritativeness and a physical ideal. Stern (2003) offers this portrayal of the ideal man:

> Men 'should' be powerful, strong, effective, and even domineering or destructive when necessary...the ideal body type is the "muscular mesomorph" a man with an average but well-proportioned build,...an ideal man is in "good shape" displaying a high energy level, flat stomach, stamina and the "right " weight in proportion to height. .. the aesthetic of handsomeness requires clear tanned skin, abundant healthy hair, a sculptured nose, and non-prominent ears... all told, the manly man can be satisfied with his body when it conforms to the ideal, signifying power, grace and potency. (p. 222)

Makes me feel glad to be a woman where I just have to be young, skinny, dumb, passive and ready to go to bed at any minute!

Research consistently finds that women are shown as passive, dependent, sex-objects, and domestic. Kilbourne (2003) offers this summary of passively sexualized women as "young, thin, carefully polished and groomed, made up, depilated, sprayed and scented (p. 174)." Needless to say, rarely is anyone in advertising middle-aged, old, unattractive, or somehow imperfect (e.g., homosexual or disabled).

One advertising phenomenon that reflects the stereotypes of active male and sex-object woman is called "faceism" (Archer, Iritani, Kimes, & Barios, 1983). Faceism refers to the phenomena in advertisements and news pictures in which men are more likely to be represented by their faces (a headshot) whereas women are more likely to be represented by their whole bodies or isolated body parts (just the legs is a common sight). Figure 5.3 shows a subtle but noticeable faceism. Overall, advertising provides a consistent, stereotypical, unreachable image to both men and women.

Figure 5.3

Language. Before we leave the topic of media, it is worth taking a minute to discuss language. Three major ideas regarding language appear to be strong and reliable findings.

1. The generic male "he" which is supposed to be read as "he or she" is, in fact, not read in that way. Both men and women and boys and girls tend to read "he" to mean "he." More inclusive language does appear to make a difference (Foertsch & Gernsbacher, 1997; Khosroshahi, 1989).

2. Language connotes power. The ability to name concepts, ideas, and people is most often in the hands of those with the power to name (Cameron, 1990; Hall & Bucholtz, 1995). If one looks at the history of many political movements, naming is an important component of gaining power (e.g., choosing a name for ones' group vs. accepting a name; "colored" vs. "African American").

3. The feminist movement's attention to language has resulted in important changes in both #1 and #2 above. "Gender-free" references commonly appear in most major publications now. For instance, the American Psychological Association's publication guidelines insist on gender-free language (APA, 2001). Second, the feminist movement has named several key experiences that previously lacked a name by which they could be discussed (e.g., "domestic violence").

The Context of Behaviors – The Leadership Example

Throughout this book when we examine gender differences and similarities, the vast majority of studies find that human behaviors differ strongly depending on the expectations of the actor and the expectations of the perceiver of the action. In chapter 13, we will explore work and work/life balance for men and women. However, in the current chapter, we will explore findings regarding gender and leadership. Perceptions of leaders and leadership ability are strongly influenced by expectations and stereotypes and therefore leadership is an excellent behavioral domain in which to explore the role of gender.

Leadership research addresses two primary areas. First, do men and women behave differently as leaders? Secondly, do male and female employees perceive male and female leaders differently? The research on leadership behaviors indicates a consistent gender differences. Meta-analyses confirm two differences in orientation (Eagly, Johannesen-Schmidt, van Engen, 2003; Eagly & Johnson, 1990; Lauterbach & Weiner, 1996). First, female managers tend to focus more fully on the interpersonal dimensions of their roles than do male managers. For instance, when influencing superiors, women managers reported acting in ways more consistent with the organization's interests and considered the interpersonal implications and other's views; whereas men report acting in ways more consistent with self-interest (Lauterbach & Weiner, 1996). In a meta-analysis of 162 studies comparing the leadership styles of women and men, Eagly and Johnson (1990) found a tendency for women to lead in a more **democratic** and participative style than men(as compared to **authoritarian** or **laissez faire** styles). Second, meta-analyses have confirmed that women leaders appear to more consistently use a leadership style correlated with productive and satisfying work environments (Eagley, Johannesen-Schmidt, van Engen, 2003; Eagley & Carli, 2007). Women are more likely to be "transformational" leaders who try to inspire others and promote others' skills and creativity. In particular, women are more likely to reward employees for good performance. Other forms of leadership are laissez faire (which is "hands-off") and transactional which focuses more on tit-for-tat punishments and rewards.

How do employees respond to male and female managers? In general, as we have seen several times in this book, employees are disapproving of managers who act in ways that are inconsistent with their gender role. In fact, Eagly and Karau (2003) suggest that female managers may use more communal or interpersonal democratic styles precisely because employees respond poorly (uncooperative or disapproving) to a more assertive and direct style. However, overall, female leaders will need to show both traditional leadership qualities (agentic qualities such as assertiveness) and the more traditional feminine qualities of caring for others. In addition, the same behavior displayed by a female leader and a male leader is likely to be perceived differently by those on the receiving end. Women displaying traditionally male behaviors (such as self-promotion) will be judged much more harshly than men (meta-analyses by Eagly, & Karau, 1991; Eagly, Karau, & Makhijani, 1995; Eagly, Makhijani, & Klonsky, 1992). In addition, men appear to react more negatively to female leaders using solely "masculine" traits than do women. Overall, perceivers see men as meeting high standards for competence and more suitable to leadership (Eagly & Karau, 2003). Men are also more likely to emerge as leaders, an occurrence that appears to be linked to both their behavior as well as perceptions of others. As you might suspect, all of these situations are more likely in situations where masculine traits are particularly expected or demanded (Ridgeway, 2001). Although this leadership advantage for men has declined, men still predominate in real leadership positions as well as laboratory simulations of leadership (Eagly & Karau). In addition, both men and women show a preference for male bosses (Carroll, 2006; a finding that has cross-cultural support, e.g., The Financial Express, 2008). Findings regarding preferences for male bosses need to be considered against the backdrop of research that suggests that on average women manifest leadership styles more consistently associated with positive outcomes in performance (Eagly, 2007).

The presidential election of 2008 provided a fascinating large scale backdrop for a discussion of ethnicity, gender and leadership. In the democratic primary, Hillary Clinton was largely criticized when she crossed the gender line and came across as "not feminine enough", whereas Barrack Obama was criticized if he came across as "too black." The evidence suggests that both candidates were more fully scrutinized as to whether or not they could be effective leaders more so than a white male would have been – race, ethnicity, and gender mattered in these conversations (Duerst-Lahti, 2007; McIlwain, 2007). The addition of Sarah Palin to the Republican ticket further fanned the heated debate over women and leadership and the types of qualities/experience needed. In terms of ethnic and/or racial patterns, as the United States continues to become more ethnically diverse and more candidates of color are elected, it will be interesting to analyze the trends. Hajnal's (2007) book analyzing white votes and black candidates indicates that whites tend to rely on their racial attitudes when a candidate is new to politics but use more conventional factors (such as experience) when evaluating black candidates in subsequent races. The pattern Hajnal notes fits with the cognitive psychology research on stereotypes which would suggest that voters will be "forced" to expand their category of leadership when those in leadership positions represent a more diverse United States. However, in order to conduct "real world" research on the interplay of race, ethnicity, and gender in election outcomes and perceptions of political candidates, the U.S. will need to experience many more elections with candidates representing a larger spectrum of diverse backgrounds. Figure 5.1 depicts the suspected relationship between race and gender and perceptions of leadership ability. In this situation, gender has a direct relationship to perceptions of leadership ability and it directed affected by ethnic minority status where white women are more likely to be perceived as having leadership qualities.

"Will the Presence of Sarah Palin and Hillary Clinton Translate into a Larger Role For Women in Politics?"

Figure 5.1

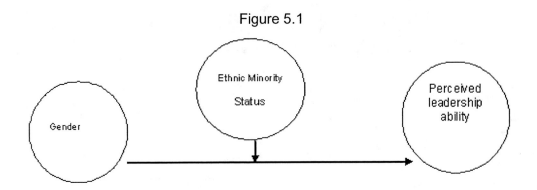

Overall the research on leadership indicates individuals' expectations for and experiencing of leaders' styles link back to the perceivers' individual and societal values. One of the big challenges in terms of gender and leadership, is that the "ideal woman" (nurturing and caring) appears to be at odds with the "ideal leader" (decisive and action oriented). Consequently, the expectations for women leaders lead directly to a double bind. Overall, the leadership research provides an excellent example of how an individual man or woman's behaviors may be affected by their own beliefs about what is appropriate and desired and it is, in turn, interpreted by others' beliefs about idealized behaviors for people in specific roles. In the next chapter, we will delve more fully into "sources of socialization" – the individuals and societal instructions that influence our expectations regarding gender.

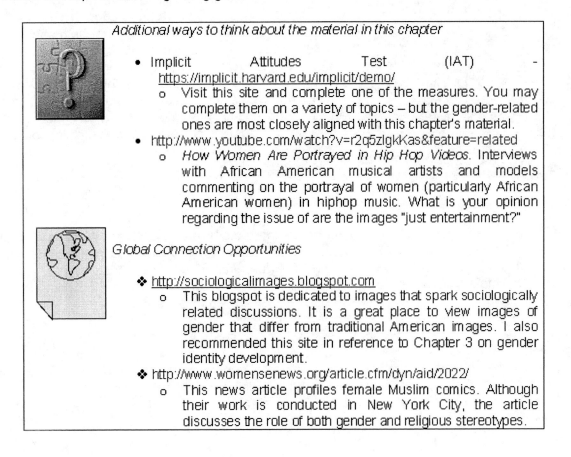

Additional ways to think about the material in this chapter

- Implicit Attitudes Test (IAT) - https://implicit.harvard.edu/implicit/demo/
  - Visit this site and complete one of the measures. You may complete them on a variety of topics – but the gender-related ones are most closely aligned with this chapter's material.
- http://www.youtube.com/watch?v=r2q5zlgkKas&feature=related
  - *How Women Are Portrayed in Hip Hop Videos.* Interviews with African American musical artists and models commenting on the portrayal of women (particularly African American women) in hiphop music. What is your opinion regarding the issue of are the images "just entertainment?"

Global Connection Opportunities

- ❖ http://sociologicalimages.blogspot.com
  - This blogspot is dedicated to images that spark sociologically related discussions. It is a great place to view images of gender that differ from traditional American images. I also recommended this site in reference to Chapter 3 on gender identity development.
- ❖ http://www.womensenews.org/article.cfm/dyn/aid/2022/
  - This news article profiles female Muslim comics. Although their work is conducted in New York City, the article discusses the role of both gender and religious stereotypes.

Chapter 6
Sources of Socialization

A. *Parents*
B. *Peer and Play*
C. *Schools*
D. *Religion*
E. *Politics*

> I have a brother two years older than I am. Until he went away to college, it was his job to mow the lawn. It wasn't an odd situation except that he had horrible hay fever. Sneezed and wheezed his way through it. Me? Allergy free.
>
> Fast forward. I am the mother of two boys who are five-years-old one Halloween. Proudly, they announce "We want to be brides or witches for trick-or-treating." Less proudly, I quickly respond "Witches is a wonderful idea!"

Were my parents wrong to have my brother mow when I could have? Was I wrong to edge my boys away from dressing as brides? Who and what help shape our gender attitudes and behaviors? How do these sources of socialization create, reinforce, and reflect gender stereotypes? This chapter surveys the research on the major sources of socialization. Although we influence and are influenced throughout our lives, much of the research focuses on children because childhood and adolescence is the most active time for shaping and responding.

Parents

We will use the term parents to include adults involved in raising children; these individuals can be biological, adoptive, foster, extended family and/or any combination of the aforementioned. One strongly believed myth about parents in the U.S. is that there is a huge preference for male children. In fact, the research overwhelmingly indicates that most parents want two children, one boy and one girl (Buss, Shackelford, & LeBlanc, 2000; Marleau & Saucier, 2002). However, it is true that people prefer their first child to be a boy, and that couples will have more children trying for a boy than for a girl. Each semester I usually have a young woman in my class who is the third, fourth or fifth girl in a family trying for a boy. She almost always has a younger brother or sister! Once a friend of mine was standing in a line at a mall with her son, when a neighboring man with three girls leaned over and said, "Trade you my three girls for your son." Some of us could have similar stories on the flip side, but they're probably a little less likely.

"Parents R Us"

Internationally, gender preference for children manifests in a much more striking manner. Many cultures have strong preferences for male children. India and China are most often in the news. China's one-child policy, enacted in 1979 to reduce overpopulation, results in financial fines for those who have more than one child and in more extreme cases may lead to pressures to abort a pregnancy or forced sterilization (Fong, 2004). One clear result of the policy is a growing sex ratio problem. Typically, for every 100 baby girls born, 105 baby boys are born.

However, in China, the ratio is 117 males to 100 females overall, and up to 140 to 100 in the countryside where males are wanted for field work (Pomfret, 2001). In India, the ratio is as high as 125 males to 100 females in the rural areas. In both countries the sex ratio is being altered by the termination of fetuses known to be female or the murder of female children at birth "infanticide." Although couples in India are not constrained to one child by policy, financial and social considerations increase the pressure to have boys. Interestingly, many Indian couples have fuller access to modern technology, so a large number of couples are using prenatal chromosome analysis (chorionic villus sampling or amniocentesis) to determine sex and terminating pregnancies if the sex is not "right" (Rohde, 2003). Even in China, ultrasound machines are being produced cheaply and at high volume. In both countries, not only are there social reasons to prefer boys (to serve family and ritual roles, for example), there are economic reasons as well. Most families will "lose" a daughter to the family into which she marries, whereas a son stays. In addition, property inheritance is strongly sex-linked to boys. There are serious implications to the sex ratio imbalance. Older, more financially established men are more apt to secure a wife; whereas, younger, poorer men have many fewer options. In China, there has been a huge increase in kidnappings of women and in a slave trade selling Vietnamese and North Korean women to Chinese men. Patterns of the trafficking of women argue for the idea that a sex ratio imbalance will coincide with an increase in the view of women as "commodities" (Zhao, 2003).

What is to be done about the welfare of girls and women in these countries? How far of a leap it is for a society to go from a "slight preference for male children" to these types of sex ratio imbalances?. While we may laugh off a father-to-be buying a little baseball glove hoping that the child will be male, China and India are demonstrating the very serious consequences to any societal pattern that leads to a systematic devaluing of one group of people over another.

In the United States, research indicates a strong pattern of gender expectations among new and expectant parents for their children. In a now-classic study, Rubin, Provenzano, and Luria (1974) interviewed parents within 24 hours of the birth of their first child and found that the parents had already begun to see their infants based on gender. New parents described their daughters as softer, finer featured, and more delicate than boys, and described sons as firmer,

 stronger, more coordinated, hardier, and more alert than girls. Fathers appeared to exaggerate these differences more than mothers did, and the researchers found no objective differences among the infants. More current research found a similar pattern based on the results of ultrasound pictures (Sweeney & Bradbard, 1988). Once babies are born, parents and other well-intentioned individuals bombard them with gender-specific items. Hospital personnel wrap them in pink or blue blankets; they receive color-coded clothes, gender-specific toys, and even gender-specific greeting cards (Bridges, 1993). One study of infants 1-12 months old found that 90% of them were dressed in gender-typed clothing (Shakin & Sternglanz, 1985).

Of course, once parents get to know the individual attributes of their children, their behaviors and expectations become more individualized to the child. Consequently, although researchers have found differences in parents' behavior with their sons and daughters, they tend to be smaller than one would expect upon seeing the gender differences in children's preferences and behavior. Leaper's (2002) review of the literature on parenting and gender indicates several categories of parenting behaviors that reveal parenting differences based on the sex of the child. Before addressing these categories, let us review three of his caveats. First, Leaper encourages his readers to remember that children's behaviors and temperament can evoke different types of responses by their parents. Second, researchers and consumers of research must consider parent-child interactions in developmental and social contexts. Finally, parent-child interactions depend on both the gender of the child and the parent, so observers can interpret particular behaviors by either a parent or a child differently depending on the gender of the child or parent! We will consider race, ethnic, and social class variation at the end of this section.

1. **Language development.** Parents tend to initiate more verbal interaction with girls than boys (especially at infancy). However, given girls' greater developmental speed and earlier acquisition of verbal skills (which have been established even in the absence of adult prompting), these findings are likely to reflect the interaction of nature and nurture.

2. **Autonomy.** Parents encourage more autonomy in boys than girls and allow more autonomy earlier in childhood. Leaper puts forth two major theories regarding this difference. First, mothers are more verbally directive with girls than boys, giving them more concrete instructions about how to act and be. Second, infant and toddler boys are more likely to display higher levels of negative emotionality which appears to lead to some distancing by parents. The distancing may lead to the development of more independent skills, although more research is needed on this topic. In adolescence, boys appear to receive less monitoring than do girls (especially by fathers).

3. **Affection.** Both fathers and mothers express more physical and verbal affection with daughters than sons.

4. **Emotion talk and emotional expressiveness.** Parents talk to daughters more about emotions, and talk to daughters more about sadness whereas they talk to boys about anger. Parents also talk about emotions differently with boys and girls. Girls are

encouraged to be sensitive and understanding of emotion, whereas boys are taught to be "in control" of their emotions.

5. ***Physicality.*** Parents tend to inflict more physical punishment on boys and stimulate more motor behavior in sons than daughters. Parents may also play differently with their children depending on their gender. In particular, fathers tend to roughhouse with boys more than girls and mothers roughhouse less than fathers. Both parents tend to talk more with daughters. In addition, parents tend to encourage sports participation in boys more than in girls.

6. ***Self Esteem.*** Girls display lower self-esteem than boys do in adolescence. Both boys and girls who are close to their same-sex parent and feel accepted by that parent appear to have higher self-esteem. Boys show negative outcomes when parents do not give them enough independence, girls show negative outcomes when parents do not give them enough emotional support. However, girls also do poorly with overly restrictive control.

Finally, researchers can identify some systematic differences in gender-linked parenting based on social class, ethnicity, and race. Most of the differences appear in the arena of career preparation. For instance, African American parents socialize their daughters more toward economic responsibility than do European American parents (Greene, 1994; Mcdoo, 2002). Hispanic and European American women are encouraged to choose more family-friendly occupations over high-paying occupations (e.g., choosing nursing rather than doctoring (Okamoto & England, 1999). Social class intersects with these findings. For instance, Hill (1999) found that middle-class (as measured by education) African American families conveyed more egalitarian gender ideals and behaviors to their children than did working-class African American families. Hill also indicates that in African American communities, both high religiosity and working class status yielded more traditional gender roles. Findings on social class indicate that poverty affects children's socialization more than other social class variations. Children raised in poverty are more likely to experience an extended kinship network (blood related and not), less likely to have married parents, more likely to have young mothers, and more likely to have siblings (Rank, 2000). Although very little empirical evidence exists on gender role socialization among the poor, it is reasonable to assume that the gender models of home life are less traditional. How those models parlay into behaviors and attitudes remains to be studied. As consumers of research, we need to recognize that images of gender role socialization are overwhelmingly European American and middle class and may not be able to be generalized to other social class, ethnic or race experiences with accuracy.

Some aspects of parenting that may affect gender may not even be addressed in the research that currently focuses on European Americans of the middle class, such as how to interact with the dominant culture, how to preserve heritage in youth (see Glover's 2001 insights on Native American parenting), or promoting family interdependence (see Chao & Tseng's 2002 work on Asian American parenting). We do not have enough research on the intersections among class, ethnic, and race in gender role socialization to make secure claims; however, social group variation in gender is intricately linked to the role of gender in those specific subgroups. In other words, a larger cultural context influences the meaning of gender. Gender is just one way through which parents transmit values to children. Consequently, when it comes to the gender socialization of children, the model most likely looks like Figure 6.1, in which the cultural expectations inform the gender expectations.

Figure 6.1

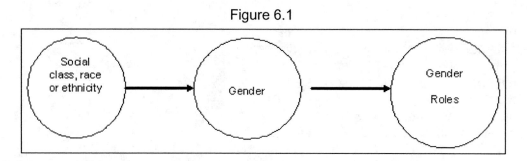

Researchers have begun to address the gender role implications of gay, lesbian and bisexual parents (Savin-Williams & Esterberg, 2000). Large scale projects indicate that lesbian couples have more egalitarian roles than do gay male or heterosexual couples. As parents, lesbian women appear to be more like heterosexual women than gay men. And, gay men were more like heterosexual men than lesbian women. In other words, gender matters. No systematic research assessing the gender role development of children of gay, lesbian, and/or bisexual parents exists, but it will be interesting to watch for results in the next few decades.

Three arenas appear to most strongly shape children's gender-typed activities – chores, toys, and play (e.g., Blakemore, 2005; Bronstein, 2006; Etaugh & Liss, 1992; Van Volkom, 2001). We will consider the evidence in each of these arenas below. It is often tempting to ask "so what?" in reaction to any singular finding regarding gender preferences or patterns. So what if boys play more video games than girls? In order to answer the "so what?" question with critical thinking, we must consider the skills and behaviors children learn from their chores and their play. In addition, we have to think about the cumulative effects of exposures to gender-typed activities.

Chores

Gender differences in chores tend to break down along autonomy and amount of time lines. Boys do more autonomous and less time intensive chores such as mowing the lawn, shoveling snow, taking out the garbage, and doing yard work. Girls do chores which require longer time commitments and which tie them to the home, or the daily work of the home, such as cleaning, washing dishes, cooking, and babysitting (White & Brinkerhofff, 1981). The fact that girls spend more time doing chores than boys is mirrored in most households where women do approximately 75% of household chores Hoelter, 2002). In an interesting comparison, Benin and Edwards (1990) found that sons and daughters do similar types and amounts of chores in households where fathers are employed and mother are not non-employed. Daughters in dual-earner families spend more time doing chores and do more gender-typed chores than sons. The authors suggest that busy dual-earner families may be defaulting to easy arrangements such as daughters doing "girl-type" chores.

Let's return to the original question. What do children learn from gender-typed chores? First, they learn expectations and stereotypes. Recall from Chapter 5 that gender stereotypes are best understood by men's stereotypes being about agency and women's about consideration. Boys are "supposed" to help with the car maintenance; girls are "supposed" to start dinner. Second, they learn the skills to carry out these chores. All of us are more likely to pursue activities we know how to do later in our lives. So, who then is both better at and more likely to do kitchen work? Yard work? Chores play an important role in training us for our future roles. Finally, families with children of the same sex tend to be more egalitarian. So, if families have "only" boys or "only" girls, they will tend to disperse the chores (boy and girl chores) across the available children. Anecdotally, I know that some families appear to choose one child to be the designated "boy-chore" or "girl-chore" child in their families (e.g., in a family with two girls – the older one does the "boy chores"). Rather than evenly spreading chores out evenly among the children, their parents seemed to select one child to take the place of the boys or girls they did not have.

Play

Parents influence children's play in two primary ways. First, when parents play with children they tend to reinforce stereotypic behavior. For instance, in laboratory studies, parents will choose "masculine" toys from a group of toys to play with a male child and "feminine" toys to play with a female child. However, parents show more latitude when picking toys to play with girls (Wood, Desmarais, & Gugula 2002). Second, parents tend to give boys more latitude physically, but expect girls to stay closer to home and be less physically active than boys (Leaper, 2002). Overall, boys are restricted to masculine activities more than girls are. Girls can participate in "boy stuff" and "girl stuff" without receiving too much flack. Boys who participate in "girl stuff" get more grief. In an earlier chapter, I asked you to compare "sissy" to "tomboy." Sissy is a much more serious insult than tomboy, a difference that reflects this rigidity in terms of masculine behavior and definition of masculine as that which is not "feminine." Similarly, boys who are ridiculed with "gay or faggot" and girls who are ridiculed as "dykes" are paying the price for crossing some elusive gender line. Despite a changing culture, girls who are active in sports or other "masculine" activities still run the risk of being branded dyke. For gays and lesbians, this use of sexual orientation accusations to enforce gender boundaries can be especially painful, but the accusations are used to uniformly with children and teenagers to try to enforce societal gender norms.

Our "A closer look at an interesting study" Box 6.1 for this chapter illustrates the relationship between gender, play styles and playmate preference.

Box 6.11: A closer look at an interesting study...

Who did the study?

Alexander & Hines (1994)

What did they study?

They assessed gender labels and play styles role in children's playmate preferences. The robust research finding that boys prefer to play with boys and girls with girls is often attributed to the gender label (e.g., "Chris is a girl") and/or to play styles (e.g., "Chris is drawing."). They designed a method which allowed them to help disentangle gender labels and play styles.

Who did they study?

60 children between the ages of 4 and 8 years recruited from the elementary school associated with the University of California Los Angeles. The sample was primarily European American and middle income.

How did they do the study?

They interviewed the children and showed them a series of cards. Each card included a drawing representing a play style – either a toy (e.g., cosmetics or toy gun) or an activity (e.g., wrestling or party). In addition, the cards showed figures with "obvious" gender cues or lacking gender cues as a measure of a gender label. The image below depicts the card that indicated an obvious girl and an obvious boy with a gun. The main study involved children indicating their preferred playmate across 40 cards that varied the activity and the obviousness of the sex of the child.

What did they find?

As would be expected, boys indicated a preference for high activity play, masculine toys, and to play with boys; whereas girls preferred playing with girls, feminine toys, and non-aggressive play. In addition, regardless of age, they found that for boys play style was more important than gender label. In other words, if forced to choose, boys in this study chose to play with a girl with a masculine play style rather than a boys with a feminine play style. The authors indicate that the finding is in line with the theory that boys are restricted to a narrower range of appropriate play. For girls, gender label was a stronger predictor than play styles for younger girls, but for older girls, play style was more important.

What is so interesting about it?

The study represents a good example of how experimental studies can be done with children in relatively simple manner. In addition, it is the type of study that allows for researchers to explore the implications of cognitive developmental theories and gender schema theories as it provides for both age and sex comparisons. Finally, I chose this study for this chapter because it speaks to play styles, toy selection, and same-sex play preferences.

Toys

Whenever I go into a store with toys, I like to look down the toy aisles and squint my eyes. I get just a blurry sense of camouflage in one aisle and pink in another! Although it is easier to find gender-neutral toys than it used to be, adults and children can still easily classify most toys into "boy toys" or "girl toys" (Blakemore & Centers, 2005). Even when someone orders a child's meal at a fast-food restaurant, the restaurant will often have you indicate whether or not your child is a boy or girl so that they can give you the "appropriate" toy. Table 6.1 shows the top toys that shoppers' indicated were the "hot toys" they were going to purchase for the holiday season of 2008.

Table 6.1 Top "Hot Toys" for Boys and Girls 2008
National Retail Federation (2008)

Top Toys for Boys	Top Toys for Girls
Video Games	Barbie
Nintendo Wii	Disney Hannah Montana
LEGO	Dolls (generic)
Cars (generic)	Bratz
Transformers	Nintendo Wii
Elmo	Video Games
Star Wars	Elmo
Hot Wheels	High School Musical
Remote Controlled Vehicles	Disney Princess
Xbox 360	American Girl

Research clearly indicates that men and women sort toys into gender categories with ease and that children give strong preference to gender-typed toys (e.g., Alexander & Hines, 1994; Blakemore and Centers, 2005). In addition, as argued in Chapter 3 in relationship to cognitive development, as opposed to merely passive recipients, children are actively involved in these choices and preferences. Martin, Eisenbud, and Rose (1995) found that even with very attractive toys, children liked toys less if they were labeled for the other sex and expected other girls and boys to do the same. However, Pennell (1999) found that adults sort toys more strongly on gender than do children who also look at criteria such as fun. In a clever twist on this research, Pennell also analyzed the toys that children requested from Santa and found that boys asked almost exclusively for boy-type toys, that girls showed slightly less rigidity, and that the most stereotypic requests came from children around the age of five. Toy companies have also experienced flops trying to introduce toys with gender-specific variations. Lego unsuccessfully tried to introduce pink and purple blocks without any other changes. More successfully, they now have princess castle sets to build out of Lego blocks. Recently, I noted that video games based on the Nancy Drew mysteries have changed the phrase on their packaging from "for girl sleuths 10 and up" to "for mystery fans 10 and up." As, Kafai (1999) notes, most companies and researchers need to spend more time pursuing interesting questions about the range and versatility of children's play behavior, rather than the simple gender category of the behavior or toy.

What do children learn with toys? Toys tend to suggest to children a certain "way" to play especially if they have a narrow scope. Barbie™ makes a lousy machine-gun, and a gun does not look great in a ball gown. Blocks and art supplies are more versatile. How children play with their toys can also yield differing reinforcing behavior from the people around them. For instance, a boy making a vroooom sound with a toy car and a girl tucking in a doll are likely to receive approving responses from adults. Toys serve to reinforce stereotypes for adults and children alike. In addition, toys teach skills and types of play. Blakemore and Centers (2005) had participants rate toys in their suitability for boys, girls and both and established five categories of toys strongly masculine, moderately masculine, neutral, moderately

feminine, and strongly feminine. In a second study, where participants rated the characteristics of the toys, the characteristics were found to vary by gender category. Participants rated the "girls' toys" as more highly associated with physical attractiveness, nurturance, and domestic skill. In contrast, the boys' toys were rated as violent, competitive, exciting, and somewhat dangerous. Neutral or moderately masculine toys were those most associated with positive educational characteristics.

Toys also convey aspects of the ideal. One of the more famous examples is the debate over Barbie™ dolls and their body dimensions and what that conveys to girls. Simply put, her dimensions are not realistic. Interestingly, neither are the dimensions of G.I. Joe™. Indeed, GI Joe has bulked up over the past few years. Take a careful look at the tables below that compare the average dimensions of women, men, models, Barbies™ and GI Joes™. As a further example of gender categorizing Barbie™ is a "dolls" and GI Joe™ is an "action figure."

Tables 6.2 and 6.3 Doll Dimensions "Translated" to Human Sizes

Females

Measurements	Average Female	Typical Female Model	Barbie™ Doll
Height	5 feet, 4 inches[1]	5 feet, 10 inches[2]	6 feet, 9 inches[3]
Weight	152 pounds[1]	114 pounds[2]	
Clothing Size	Size 14[1]	Size 6/8[2]	
Bust	39 inches[1,2]	34 inches[2]	41 inches[3]
Waist	31 inches[1,2]	24 inches[2]	20 inches[3]

Males

Measurements	Average Male	Typical Male Model	G.I. Joe™ 1960s	G.I. Joe™ Today
Height	5 feet, 9 inches[1]	6 feet[2]	5 feet, 10 inches[4]	5 feet, 10 inches[4]
Weight	180 pounds[1]	155 pounds[2]		
Bicep			12 inches[4]	27 inches[4]
Chest	42 inches[1]	39 inches[2]	44 inches[4]	55 inches[4]
Waist	36 inches[1]	30 inches[2]	32 inches[4]	36 inches[4]

Note: Chart developed for a grade school curriculum developed by the WIN Rockies program (Wardlaw, 2003).

[1] Centers for Disease Control and Prevention (2002)
[2] Kirby (1999)
[3] Holmes (1999)
[4] Pope, Olivardia, Gruber, & Borowiecki (1999).

Overall, the often quoted adage "Children's play is children's work" is reflected in the skills and characteristics associated with children's toys. Children learn about the world through toys and play.

Video Games

Video games' relative newness and established gender differences in use deserve additional attention as "toys." Boys play more video games than girls do (Wright, et al., 2001). In fact, one evening I was reading the article just cited and my eleven-year old son asked me about it. When I explained that it looked at the number of hours that boys and girls play video games, my computer-attached child looked seriously at me and asked "Girls play video games?" Over time, we have seen a drop-off in the amount of TV that boys watch, but the screen time remains the same as boys have moved into more video game-playing (Wright, et al., 2001). Both boys and girls play more video games as they age, and boys play more at each age level.

See Table 6.4 for an interesting comparison of the types of video games and TV programs that show a gender difference in usage. The data used for the table comes from a study notable for surveying almost 3000 children. Video gaming in terms of number of minutes has risen for both boys and girls in the past several years (Marshall, Gorely, & Biddle, 2006). Children play most video games on gaming platforms such as Nintendo™; however, computer game use is rising. More educational software exists for computers than for gaming platforms, and middle-class and upper-middle-class children are much more likely to have computers at home than working-class, or poor children. African American and European American children play more video games than Hispanic children do and African American children play a lower percentage of educational games than European Americans even when controlling for social class variation (Bickham, Vandewater, Huston, Lee, Caplovitz, & Wright, 2003). Regardless of race, children's skills and preferences predicted video game use more than parent and family characteristics did. The authors suggest that parents may not monitor video gaming as much as they do TV viewing and that video gaming is harder to monitor. In addition, in findings that "provoke as many questions as they answer" (p. 133), parental education level predicts educational video game use for European American and Hispanic children, but only income predicts use for African American children.

Table 6.4

Type of programming	Girls Mean number of minutes per week	Boys Mean number of minutes per week
TV – Comedy programs	229.91	179.99
TV – Fantasy Programs	104.11	130.53
TV – Non educational cartoons	261.35	299.37
TV – Sports	53.16	170.90
Video Game Overall Sports video games	264.85 2.33	374.77 24.62

Note 1: *No gender differences were found in 5 other TV categories, including educational, educational cartoons, action, reality-based, and relationship drama programs.*

Note 2: *Larger samples increase the likelihood of statistical significance. These researchers held their data to a stricter standard (.01) rather than the traditional .05. to help offset the large sample size.*

Analysis of the *content* of video games yields some additionally intriguing gender-related facts. First, there are very few female characters. Beasley & Standley (2002) found only 13% of the characters were female in their content analysis of 47 games and 597 characters. Second, the women in the videos are much more likely to be scantily clad than are the men. Women shown in video games rated "mature or teen" had larger breasts than those rated "E" for everyone. Critics raise concerns over the perpetuation of unobtainable ideals especially under the condition of pre-teen and teen boys' steady "diet" of these images with very few more realistic variations.

Of greater concern is the amount of violence in the video game "diet." Dietz (1998), in an analysis of 33 games, found that over 80% of the games have aggressive content. Goldstein (1998) found that Sega's version of "Mortal Kombat" outsold Nintendo's by 7:1. Why? Sega's version included a lot more blood and features like "getting to" behead characters. In games where users can choose "blood on" or "blood off", those who choose "blood on" both perceived greater gore and reported more physically aggressive intentions on an aggression scale (Farrar, Krcmar, & Nowak, 2006).

"Video Games: The Difference in Gender Specific Marketing"

Most of the video games available do not intend to appeal to girls, and games that are marketed directly for girls center around extremely gender-typed topics (Subrahmanyam & Greenfield, 1998). One best-selling video game is "Barbie™ Fashion Designer." Several scholars in this area suggest that early in video game history makers erred by equating action with violence. In fact, girls like action but are less attracted to violence than boys. In research with 9-10 year old boys and girls creating their own games, all of the children preferred adventure over other themes. Boys created more good/evil conflict, and girls created

obstacles but not much evil (Kafai, 1999). Girls also like to participate in reality-based role-play (as compared to fantasy) in familiar settings with familiar characters (Subrahmanyam & Greenfield, 1998). Consequently, developing video games that appeal to girls should not be that difficult. More than 60% of the 50 million+ copies of the "The Sims" video games were sold to women or girls (Carvajal, 2006). Business-related press stories indicate a growing interest in tapping female consumers for gaming products (e.g., Carvajal, 2006; Roth, 2006; Waters, 2006).

Why do we care about the use of, and images in, video games? A couple of factors affect why we should care about girls' lesser use of video games. First, for both boys and girls, early experiences with video products greatly affect later choices, so negative experiences will lead to less video play. Second, video gaming on all platforms correlates with general computer familiarity and skill. Given that computer skills are listed among the top ten qualities/skills that employers look for in new hires and that computer skills are critical to many future professions (Job Outlook, 2004), parents, teachers, and employers should be interested in these trends.

Peers And Play

Judith Rich Harris created a stir a few years back when she wrote a book entitled *The Nurture Assumption* (1998) that questioned whether "parents matter" in the socialization and upbringing of children. Although she severely undercredits the role of parents by focusing on genes (see good rebuttal by Borkowski & Ramey, 2001), she did focus conversation on the often under-discussed topic of the role of peers in the formation of children's lives. In this segment we will look at the role of peers and group play as they pertain to gender. Four major findings stand out in the literature on group play.

1. Both boys and girls sex-segregate in their play.
2. Boys tend to play in larger groups, girls in smaller groups.

3. Girls play in more structured settings, boys in less structured settings.
4. Peers reinforce gender-typed behavior and punish gender-atypical behavior in their friends.

Although there are many interesting studies in this area, in this case I do not want us to focus on the "who, what, where, and it depends" of variation. Instead, think about the potential outcomes of these findings. Researchers have firmly established that children self-segregate into single-sex play (Maccoby, 1988; Winsler, Caverly, Willson-Quayle, Carlton, Howell, & Long, 2002). Researchers are less clear on why children choose **sex segregation** so strongly. For this book, the question we will consider is "why does it matter?"

Sex segregation leads to both boys and girls feeling more comfortable with single-sex arrangements and learning the ways of that "culture." Martin & Fabes (2001) found that the more both girls and boys played with same-sex partners, the more their behavior became gender-typed and differentiated. The segregation leads to the development of different sets of social skills, styles, expectations, and preferences. Martin and Fabes introduce the notion of "social dosage," where play in sex-segregated groups also increases children's level of adhesion to societal gender expectations. It is like "check" in poker where a player who wants to stay in the game doesn't have to up the bid but he/she must match the bid to keep playing. So, even a child who is only mildly interested in gender-typed play has to "check" by matching their behavior to the others' in order to keep playing with the group. If someone raises the bid, a check will require a higher investment.

Combined with sex segregation is the set of findings indicating that boys tend to play with groups of 7 to 8 friends, whereas girls tend to play in 2s (dyads) or 3s (triads). One of my favorite authors, Carol Shields, provides the following description in one of her novels that really captures these results. In this passage a mother describes her teenaged son and daughter.

> Richard's friends are random and seasonal. There are the friends he swims with in the summer and the casual sweatered football friends. There is a nice boy named Gavin Lord whom we often take skiing with us but forget about between seasons. There is a gaggle of deep-voiced brothers who live next door. For Richard, they are interchangeable; they come and go; he functions within their offhand comradeship. In their absence he is indifferent.

> Meredith's best friend is a girl named Gwendolyn Ackerman, an intelligent girl with a curiously dark face and a disposition sour as rhubarb. She is sensitive: hurts cling to her like tiny burrs, and she and Meredith rock back and forth between the rhythm of their misunderstandings; apology and forgiveness are their coinage. It is possible, I think, that they won't always be friends. (Shields, 1976, pp. 41-42)

Related to group size, as well as expectations, boys are more likely to be involved in "low structure" play, whereas girls are involved in "high structure" play (Carpenter, Huston, & Holt, 1986). Low structure play involves few rules, low monitoring by adults, and lots of freedom (think about "king of the mountain"). High structure play involves set rules, high monitoring, and conformity (think about a board game such as "Sorry"). These three elements taken together (sex segregation, group size, and play structure), yields boys' play patterns that differ from girls' play patterns. you see that play as a boy is different from play as a girl. Most importantly, what skills do children learn from this play? In large groups, boys (or children in those types of situations), learn leadership, negotiation, assertiveness, and aggressiveness. In small groups, girls (or children in those types of situations) feel the loss of a group member more acutely. Consequently, the conflict is more emotional and intense, and they learn how to be cooperative, conciliatory, and to pay attention to feelings and communication. Indeed, the small size alone facilitates those types of connections among the group. Children who cross groups learn how to work with different sets of expectations and experiences.

Finally, peers enforce gender rules with each other. Peers chide friends who cross gender lines (e.g., Witt, 2000). Both boys and girls are socially sanctioned for being inappropriate to their gender, although there is variation in what is "allowed."

Schools

My mother likes to tell the story that in 4th grade, I came home and told her that I was confused by the fact that some girls pretended to be dumber than they really were. I was not imaging it; at ten years of age, some girls really do learn to hide some of their talents (Garrod, Smulyan, Powers, & Kilkenny, 2004). To be fair, being "too" smart is also something for which boys pay a price. Much of middle and high school experience is one of "fitting in," so any attribute that makes you stand out in a non-conforming way is one that may be problematic Steinberg, 2004).

There is strong evidence that educators' expectations of boys and girls differ and that the behavior of educators toward them also differs (as reviewed by Gayle, Preiss, & Burrell, 2006). Girls are expected to be nice, compliant, noncompetitive, and avoid conflict. Boys are expected to be assertive and cutting-edge. Look at Table 6.5 that lists the kindergarten awards from a school in the Midwest. What is being rewarded? This school is rewarding thinking and learning in boys, cooperation and caring in girls. In elementary school, teachers reward girls for tidiness and congeniality. Teachers give boys more latitude; after all, "boys will be boys" (Sadker & Sadker, 1994). One year, I had a student in my class who was the mother of four daughters. She came into class angry one day because she had recently returned from parent-teacher conferences. She reported that after the end of each meeting she had to ask the teacher how each daughter was doing academically, because the teacher had spent the entire meeting reflecting on the girl's social skills.

Table 6.5 Kindergarten Awards*

Boys' Awards	Girls' Awards
Very Best Thinker	All Around Sweetheart
Most Eager Learner	Sweetest Personality
Most Imaginative	Cutest Personality
Most Enthusiastic	Best Sharer
Most Scientific	Best Artist
Best Friend	Biggest Heart
Mr. Personality	Best Manners
Hardest Worker	Best Helper
Best Sense of Humor	Most Creative

* Deveny (1994)

Although there is much quality research on gender and education, we will focus on two major projects that summarize findings from decades of research. More importantly, both projects received mainstream media attention and K-12 educators took the findings seriously. Although Basile (1995) reports that the results from these projects have resulted in some concrete positive changes in schools, evidence exists which suggests that many of the gender "issues" in the classroom remain today (Gayle, Preiss, & Burrell, 2006).

Sadker and Sadker's (1994) book *Failing at Fairness: How America's Schools Cheat Girls* found that boys dominate classroom communication. For instance, teachers gave boys more "floor time", called on boys more often, and allowed boys to speak without asking permission. On the other hand, teachers frequently admonished girls to raise their hands when answering. Teachers were mostly unaware of these behaviors such as calling on the boys more frequently, and it did not matter what the sex of the teacher was. If you recall Chapter 5 on stereotypes, these situations most likely reflect a default to gender stereotypes on the teachers' parts, not a systematic effort to treat boys and girls differently. Sadker and Sadker conclude that boys are rewarded for competitiveness, aggressiveness, and gaining the teachers attention even by acting up, whereas girls are rewarded for waiting their turn and being polite. In addition, teachers often perceive girls' higher grades as due to conscientiousness rather than talent or ability.

"School Gender Gap"

In 1992, a study commissioned by the American Association of University Women focused on gender differences in educational opportunities (AAUW, 1992). They, too, found that teachers "shortchanged" girls unwittingly. Teachers forced boys to work out problems they did not understand, but would tell girls what to do. This pattern of "helping" girls was strongest in "masculine" subjects such as math and science where the perception is that girls are less capable. Interestingly, researchers find a similar pattern with parents when they helped their children with cognitive tasks. Parents tend to be more task-oriented and problem-solving with sons, while they "aid" and cooperate with their daughters. In fact, girls tend to get better grades in math and science than boys; however, they also take fewer science and math classes (Caplan, Crawford, Hyde, & Richardson, 1997). A by-product of these differences in treatment is that boys become better at receiving, coping with, and learning from specific criticism of their work. These differences in treatment and expectation also vary by social class, ethnicity, and race. For instance, in a laboratory study, Murray (1996) found that ethnicity associated with minority groups outranked gender in its negative effects on teacher ratings of students' habits, skills, and maturity.

Finally, education has a large impact on career preparation. Educational practices continue to perpetuate stereotypes and patterns of "women's work" and "men's work." Although these findings are most striking in math and the sciences, they appear across the board and start early. Not only do girls see math as "male," they also come to believe they are less able at math and science, are less encouraged to complete higher-level courses, and, in fact, don't complete as many high-level science and math courses (e.g., Barnett & Corzazza, 1998; Caplan, Crawford, Hyde, & Richardson, 1997).

Krupnick (1984) found similar patterns of gender inequity in teachers' treatment of students in college classrooms. Higher education bears a less egalitarian history than do U.S. grade schools (Nasaw, 1981). Educating an entire society as a democratic goal is a relatively recent idea – public schooling was not prevalent in the U.S. until the 1850s (Nasaw). When we look at higher education, although Harvard was founded in 1636, in was not until 1833 that Oberlin College became the first to admit women. In the past, even learned individuals argued especially against higher education for women (review by Kimmel & Mosmiller, 1992). Some argued that "too much" education would physically deform women, by destroying their figures and complexions, make them mentally or emotionally unstable (some said it would "make their brains swell"), and make the blood run from their uterus to their brain and disrupt reproduction. Even when education became available to women, "making better mothers" was still the main reason provided as motive (Grave, 1998).

Scholars and social critics hotly debate the findings regarding gender and education. Some critics argue that recent attention to girls' education has made the classroom hostile to boys (Sommers, 2000). A more reasonable argument may be that grading practices favor those with tidy and orderly work, a bias that ends up favoring girls. As far as I know, there is no empirical data supporting the idea that classrooms are hostile to boys; however, it is true that boys generally have lesser academic achievement than girls. A major recent review indicates that men are less likely than women to get bachelor's degrees. Furthermore, women complete their college degrees in a shorter amount of time and get better grades than do men (King, 2006). When behavioral problems combine with learning disabilities, lower grades, higher dropout rates, and racial inequities, there is no doubt that we should all be concerned with boys' educational attainment opportunities – a trend some researchers call boys' "underachievement" (West, 1999). It may also be true that psychologists, parents, and teachers, may develop their behavioral standards more strongly normed on girls' behavior. Consequently, a larger number of boys than girls are seen as problems and/or diagnosed with behavioral problems (McIntyre & Tong, 1998). However, the lack of women in various careers and the lower scores on standardized tests (especially in math) suggest that there are still inequities in the educational system that systematically disadvantage girls.

On the good news front, several scholars point out that much of what "works" in education works for both men and women (e.g., Galliano, 2003). Consequently, policies that reduce harassment in schools (sexual and otherwise) and create engaging hands-on curricula benefit us all. Overall, the study of gender and education deserves more research attention and all of us should acknowledge its important policy implications.

Although this book focuses on the U.S., gender and education is a worldwide issue. Women have higher rates of illiteracy in every geographic region. In particular areas, the differences are dramatic. For instance, 50% of the women in sub-Saharan Africa are illiterate compared to 30% of men (United Nations Educational, Scientific, and Cultural Organization, 2000). Why do we care? Literacy is an indicator of well-being and economic viability. The poorest individuals are also those with the least access to knowledge - a situation that perpetuates poverty and further disadvantages individuals with very few resources abroad and in the U.S. At the end of the chapter, I've included some website addresses were you can further explore global literacy conditions.

Societal-Level Sources Of Socialization

Sources of socialization must be understood alongside the context of set larger economic, social, political, and religious structures. Even if individual teachers, friends, or parents never said "Nice girls don't..." or "Real men do..." many aspects of society do send clear messages about gender roles. One way to think about these societal level influences is to borrow a distinction often used by early gender analysts. Men's roles were referred to as "public" and women's roles as "private" – references are made to a "public/private split" or public and private "'spheres" (e.g., Elshtain, 1981; Welter, 1966). Generally speaking, men's influence in public spheres supersedes women's.

In reference to public spheres, men wield most of the corporate, political, religious, and fiscal clout in the U.S. and internationally. The snapshot of the major power structures in the U.S. reveals a systematic control of resources and power by men ("patriarchy"). In the corporate world, although women make up almost half of America's labor force, only eight Fortune 500 companies have women CEOs or presidents, and 67 of those 500 companies have no women corporate officers at all – the upper-management positions are held entirely by men (Gettings, Johnson, Brunner, & Frantz, 2007). However, these percentages improved since 1995.

If we look at U.S. government, currently 74 women serve in the U.S. House of Representatives and 16 in the U.S. Senate (Amer, 2008). A policy group analyzed the percent of women and men appointed by governors to top-ranking policy positions and found that 30% of the positions went to women and 70% to men (Center for Women in Government, 1999). When it comes to religion, every major world religion is dominated by male clerics and the religions stemming from Abraham (Judaism, Christianity, and Islam) provide primarily male images of divinity (Bynum, 1986). Below we will take a closer look at religion and political activities as sources of gender socialization. Chapter 14 explores gender in the workforce, so the implications of the economic imbalances will be explored later in this book.

Religion

The role of religion in the exploration of gender studies is relatively recent and comparatively understudied in relation to gender and economics or politics (King & Beattie, 2004). Currently, over 80% of Americans identify with a religious group and roughly 75% describe their religious outlook as "religious" or "somewhat religious" (Boorstein, 2006; Mayer, Kosmin, & Keysar, 2001) In the American Religious Identification Survey (ARIS) in 2001, 77% of the respondents identify as Christian, (24% of the total sample identified as Catholic; and Baptist representing the largest Protestant group at 16% of the total sample), Jewish, Islamic and Buddhist denominations accounted for less than 4% of the total affiliations. Fourteen percent indicated no religion and 5% refused to designate. ARIS was based on a random telephone survey of 50,000 American residential households in the continental U.S.A. (Mayer, Kosmin, & Keysar, 2001). In the survey, the question was phrased ""What is your religion, if any?". Gender differences in religiosity were apparent in this survey (see Figure 6.2) and support previous research which has reliably shown that women describe themselves as more religious than do men.

Figure 6.2
Note – Figure represents population estimates rather than actual number of respondents the numbers are extrapolated from their sample.
Note: Secular is a term meaning not associated with religion. For instance, Thanksgiving is a secular holiday, Christmas, Ramadon, and Passover are religious holidays.

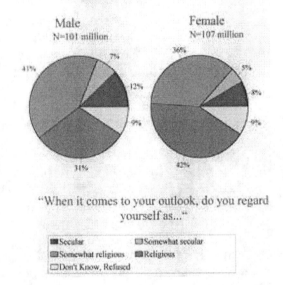

EXHIBIT 4
Outlook of U.S. Adult Men & Women:
Religious or Secular

Source: http://www.gc.cuny.edu/faculty/research_briefs/aris.pdf (Mayer, Kosmin, & Keysar, 2001; p. 20.).

Despite the apparently large role that religion plays in both men and women's lives, comparatively little academic work in psychology has focused on gender and religion. King (2004) suggests that one reason for the paucity of research on gender and religion is the existence of a "double-blindness." King argues that gender studies in the social sciences, humanities and natural sciences have been "religion blind" (p. 1); whereas, religious studies have been "gender blind" (p. 2). King notes that there is progress in our understanding of the links among gender, religion, and cross-cultural diversity.

Empirical psychological research regarding religion, like most psychological research, tends to focus on the impact of religion on the individual. In addition, the published work can be categorized into two major arenas. First, researchers have explored the role of religiosity as a predictor of several important health-related outcomes. For instance, meta-analyses indicate that spirituality has moderate effect sizes for stress reduction (Ano & Vasconcelles, (2005), higher quality of life (Sawatzky, Ratner, & Chiu, 2005), better psychological well-being (Hackney & Sanders, 2003; Maselko & Kubzansky, 2006), and mortality reduction (McCullough, Hoyt, Larson, Koenig, & Thoresen, 2000). Well-designed studies, such as those cited, statistically control for other variables that also contribute to well-being such as social support and physical exercise. Spirituality appears to play a unique role in positive well-being. The second major arena of research in psychology on religion has also focused on the relationship between religious attitudes and other important social attitudes such as prejudice (e.g., Hunsberger & Jackson, 2005) and political attitudes (Calavita, 2005). Generally speaking, fundamentalist Christianity is associate with more prejudiced and more conservative political views, except for African American conservative Protestants who tend to be more liberal (Woodberry, 1998). The percentage of Americans who identify as "conservative" Protestants (defined by denomination, beliefs, and/or self identification) is approximately 10-20% and regional, ethnic, racial and social class variations affect identification with various subgroups such as Evangelicals, Fundamentalists, Charismatics and Pentecostals (Woodberry, 1998).

Several issues arise when religion is analyzed as a source of gender ideology. First, religious beliefs are marked by large variations across individuals even within the same denomination. Woodberry and Smith (1998) reviewed several surveys and found that conservative Protestants in the U.S. disagree more about gender role attitudes than does the general population. In other words, the standard deviation is larger for conservative Protestants than other religious groups. Second, there is often a disconnect between official writings of the religious group and the private beliefs of individuals who practice a particular religion. The Catholic Church specifically forbids any birth control devices except "natural family planning" which relies on planning intercourse around a woman's most fertile time (Pope Paul VI, 1968). However, surveys of American Catholics indicate that only 36 percent of Catholics believe that birth control is wrong ("Poll," 2001). Finally, religion as discussed and practiced in the U.S. today is difficult to study as separate from politics and other major societal changes. Bayes and Tohidi (2001) argue that the increase in the exchange of information associated with globalization has led to more prominent public discussions of religion and gender. For instance, during the 1995 United Nations World Conference on Women in Beijing, China, religion was one of the key issues. Bayes and Tohidi (2001) illustrate that the conference generated alliances between cross-cultural and cross-religious groups that may have previously been viewed as disparate. In particular, they note coalitions between some conservative Catholic and Muslim delegations who argued that women's roles are divinely ordained and biologically determined to be complementary to masculine roles. Related to the view of women's roles is the primacy of motherhood, the constriction of sexuality to heterosexual marriage, opposition to abortion, and an emphasis on religious values (Bayes & Tohidi). Feminist scholars emphasize the relationship between the view of women in decidedly biological terms and religious attitudes aimed at controlling women's sexuality (Gross, 1996).

Given the variation in religious experiences, what is the message from religion regarding gender? Nason-Clark (1995) argues that religious teachings regarding women can largely be summarized as "know your place," while acknowledging that the "place" may change according to a particular doctrine. Hawley (1994) also asserts that most religions have a view on "appropriate behavior" for women (Hawley, 1994). Many religious also indicate a "place" for men but the place is less constricted than for women. In particular, most conservative religious views on women suggest a need for deference to husbands; whereas men only give deference to a deity. Peterson and Runyan (1999) suggest that most fundamentalist religious doctrines promote traditional family structures that privilege the power of males as heads of family, community leaders and religious authorities, and reserve the greatest "power/sacredness/

authority to a definitively male deity or prophet" (p. 103). Women's roles tend to be restricted to family-oriented activities and piety is seen as a major pillar of womanhood (Welter, 1966). They have less visibility and power in public spheres.

Religion also appears to have a strong influence on individual gender roles. Donelson (1999) found that religion was the strongest predictor of gender-role attitudes for adolescents. Fundamentalist Protestants have been found to have more traditional attitudes on gender roles than less fundamentalist Protestants even after controlling for other individual variables such as political ideology (e.g., Gay, Ellison, & Powers, 1996; Hoffmann & Miller, 1997). Traditional gender roles support the role of the husband as the head of the household and the primacy of motherhood as a woman's role. In an older study, Hertel and Hughes (1987) found that Euro-American fundamentalists had more traditional gender attitudes than Baptists, Catholics, Methodists, Lutherans, Presbyterians, Episcopalians, Jews, and those reporting no religious affiliation. In a study with a fully macro lens, the proportion of fundamentalists in a state positively correlated with conservative gender attitudes above and beyond individuals' own religious affiliations and beliefs (Moore & Vanneman, 2003).

The notable blending of religion and politics in the current "era of the religious right" in the U.S. (Martin, 1996) has also increased the tension between fundamentalists and non-fundamentalists on the relationship between religion and gender roles. For example, a Christian group named the "Promise Keepers" received a copious amount of press when they started to have large scale revival-type meetings for men (www.promisekeepers.org). The organization is based on seven principles, one of which reads "A Promise Keeper is committed to building strong marriages and families through love, protection and biblical values." This principle is based on their belief that a man should be the head of the family consistently with the biblical verse Ephesians 5:23: *"For the husband is the head of the wife as Christ is the head of the church..."* and its "matching verse" 22 which states: *"Wives submit to your husbands, as to the Lord"*. Evans (1994) a pastor in the Promise Keeper movement, writes the following advice to men.

> "Sit down with your wife and say something like this: 'Honey, I've made a terrible mistake. I've given you my role. I gave up leading this family, and I forced you to take my place. Now, I must reclaim that role'...I'm not suggesting you ask for your role back, I'm urging you to take it back...there can be no compromise here. If you're going to lead, you must lead."

Movement statements such as the one above ignited much criticism from both liberal religious and secular writers including a *New York Times* article entitled "Women and the Promise Keepers; Good for the Gander, but the Goose Isn't So Sure" (Goodstein, 1997). In an interesting deepening of the surface debate, qualitative research suggests that conservative Protestant women may be entering into a type of "agreement" whereby traditional gender roles for them are associated with higher expectations for standards of commitment and support from their husbands (Gay, Ellison, & Powers, 1996). The discussion of Promise Keepers is an interesting glimpse into a very modern debate about an old subject.

Finally, the *practice* of religion shows interesting gender variation. Church attendance is correlated with better health and well-being outcomes for men and women but the relationship is stronger for men (Maselko & Kubzansky, 2006). Donelson (1999) illuminates the "paradox" of religion and gender, noting that women are generally in secondary positions in the church and society yet more religious by most measures (e.g., frequency of prayer, attendance at religious services, and reported feeling of closeness with God). Gender differences in religiosity also appear to hold true across ethnic minorities in America (Ghorpade, Lackritz, & Singh, 2006). In addition, high levels of religiosity are particularly marked for African Americans; although there is evidence that in younger African Americans fewer gender differences exist; Lesniak, Rudman, & Rector, 2006). Fundamentalist Christianity has a strong following in Asian Americans, in part due to international proselytizing (England, 2004; Ghorpade, Lackritz, & Singh, 2006). Hispanic Americans account for more than 45% of all Catholics under the age of 30 in the United States and 73% of Hispanics are Catholic (Johnson-Mondragón, 2005).

Evidence confirms that women's stronger religiosity is also found in Judaic and Islamic settings (Stark, 2002). Islamic men and women appear to experience strength from their religion and potential conflict. Ali, Liu, and Humedian (2004) suggest that Muslim women may face conflict with American society over the wearing of the hijab (clothing covering the head, face, or body), attitudes toward polygamy, and general xenophobia toward Islamic individuals. Islam is also marked by a deep commitment to marriage which can intensify the outcome for women of domestic violence if it occurs because divorce is not seen as an option (Hassouneh-Phillips, 2003). Research on Judaism tends to focus on Israeli Jews. Judaism, like Christianity and Islam, shows tremendous variation from strongly orthodox to more liberal religious attitudes. U.S. Jews tend toward more liberal beliefs (Hyman, 1995). Rabbi Ellenson (2004) suggests that the Jewish tradition of allowing rabbis to interpret religious doctrine in light of changing "context and sensibilities," explains why American Jews hold more egalitarian views on gender roles. Boyarin (1997) argues that traditional European Judaism allowed for strong women and more passive, receptive and scholarly males than non-Jewish European males. He notes that the Zionist male ideal is the more aggressive and self-reliant like non-Jewish European male ideals. Generally speaking, in contrast to *conservative* U.S. Protestants, Jewish individuals show more liberal gender attitudes (Albert & Porter, 1986).

Overall, when we look at gender and religion it is sometimes easy to get absorbed in practices that may chafe at our understanding and our views of human rights. Interestingly, some of the most horrific practices such as honor killings and genital mutilation are actually cultural practices that span several religions and are not often sanctioned by the local religions (Parrot & Cummings, 2006; Souad, 2004; World Health Organization, 1999). Honor killing is the killing of a female (and/or her family members or friends) for supposed sexual or marital offenses. These killings are referred to as "honor" killings because the woman is typically murdered by her own relatives or relatives to restore honor to the family. Female genital mutilation normally consists of the removal of some of or the entire clitoris and cultures that practice it believe that a girl cannot be considered to be an adult until she has undergone this procedure. Although these practices are indicative of serious gender inequality, a focus on the most severe outcomes of cultural practices against women may draw attention away from the much more pervasive attitudes and images associated within mainstream American religious traditions.

Politics

Traditional political activity is another public sphere seemingly dominated by men. As mentioned above, men are far more likely to serve in public office than are women and this finding is supported internationally (Peterson & Runyan, 1999). Although individual women have yielded significant power, women as a group, are underrepresented at each level of government – local, regional, state, and national. This inequity in access to power is often referred to as a "structural inequity" (p. 7; Peterson & Runyan, 1999). In the 110th U.S. Congress (starting January 2007), there were a record number women serving: 74 women in the House (20 Republicans, 54 Democrats) and 16 women in the in Senate (5 Republicans, 11 Democrats). In percentages, women comprised 14% of the house and 16% of the Senate (Amer, 2008). A report asked "Why don't women run for office?" and found that well-qualified women are less likely than their male counterparts to consider running for public office (Lawless & Fox, 2004).

Two key factors are associated with this gender disparity (Lawless & Fox, 2004). First, women do not perceive themselves as qualified. Second, women do not receive as much encouragement as men do in the candidate emergence process. When women do run for office, they are as successful in securing posts as men. In addition, women and men are equally positive toward the activities associated with campaigning such as attending fundraisers. In a finding that also fits with the concept of the public and private spheres, women were more interested in local-level politics than national and were more interested than men in serving on local school boards. Men and women are also equally likely to vote and some elections show a "gender gap" where men and women differ statistically in their endorsement of a candidate (Conway, Steuernagel, & Ahern, 2005). A gender gap in presidential elections has been apparent since 1980 (Center for American Women and Politics, 2005). For instance, in 2000, 43% of women voted for George W. Bush compared to 53% of men.

Several factors point to a trajectory of increased women's participation in politics including larger numbers of women in law schools, comparatively larger numbers of women candidates than in the past, and changing attitudes toward more positive responses toward women candidates (Conway, Steuernagel, & Ahern, 2005). Conway, Ahern, and Steuernagel (2005) also argue that a focus on public policy rather than traditional political participation yields a picture of a widening and deepening role of women. Women's role in public policy is particularly apparent in the areas of education, reproductive policy, childcare, and marriage and divorce law. Women's role in health care, employment policy, economic equity (housing, credit, retirement) and the criminal justice system is less apparent.

The relative lack of women in traditional political positions belies the fact that women have been – and continue to be – politically active in other realms. African American women, in particular, have a rich history of activism (Cole & Stewart, 1999; Dixson, 2003). Women have also played important roles in specific types of activism and appear to lend credence to movements associated with traditionally feminine arenas such as caring for the environment and children's rights (Culley & Angelique, 2003; Edelman, 2000). The recent vaulting of Cindy Sheehan to celebrity status as an anti-war activist rests, in part, on the fact that she is the *mother* of a dead soldier (Houppert, 2006). Activist women tend to view their gender as both an aid and a hindrance (Culley & Angelique, 2003). Finally, some scholars have argued political involvement can be broadened beyond activities such as voting and running for office to include other forms of civic engagement. If civic engagement includes situations such as providing care to others, women are fully represented (Herd, Meyer, & Harrington, 2002).

"Women in Politics"

When we consider traditional politics as a source of socialization, we see that the politics have often been cast in stereotypically male terms (Conway, Steuernagel, & Ahern, 2005). As the research above indicates, several key variables affecting women's participation appear to be changing. However, stereotypic female roles also continue to work against traditional political activities. Analyzing data from the past 50 years, Atkeson and Rapoport (2003) found that men have stayed consistent is being more willing to indicate likes and dislikes about political candidates and parties and less likely to answer "I don't know" as compared to women. Figure 6.3 shows the pattern of "I don't know" responses in response to specific questions about candidates or policies from Atkeson and Rapoport's study. The authors argue that political socialization needs to change as well as women's already changing access to resources and political structures.

Figure 6.3: Average percent of men and women answer "don't know" to specific questions regarding candidates or policies 1952-2000

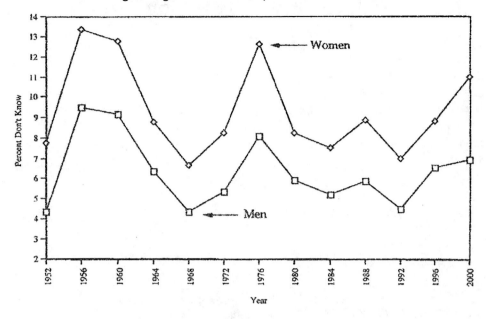

Source: (Atkeson & Rapoport, 2003)

Conclusion

As men and women we are in contact with many sources providing us with gender-related messages. What I hope that you take from this chapter is that boys and girls receive fairly consistent messages about what it means to be a boy or a girl from multiple sources in their lives. Interactions with individuals, groups and major institutions of society serve to reinforce stereotypic gender roles. It is not a matter of a stray comment or image. It is a progression of feedback and images from day one that add up to strong shapers of gender roles.

Additional ways to think about the material in this chapter

- Who and what were the strongest sources of socialization regarding gender in your life?
- What were the central messages you received about appropriate gender roles for your sex?

Global Connection Opportunities

❖ http://www.religionfacts.com/homosexuality/comparison_chart.htm
  o This site provides a "comparison chart" on a variety of world religions and their general views on homosexuality. Although very broad, it provides an interesting context to think about religion and sexuality.

Chapter 7
Gender and Cognition

Try To Solve These Two Logic Problems

1. Part of your new clerical job at the local high school is to make sure that student documents have been processed correctly. Your job is to make sure the documents conform to the following alphanumeric rule:

    "If a person had a D rating, then his or her documents must be marked code 3."

    You suspect the secretary you replaced did not categorize the student's documents correctly. The cards below have information about the documents of four people who are enrolled at this high school. One side of the card tells a person's letter rating and the other side of the card tells that person's number code. Indicate only the card(s) you definitely need to turn over to see if the documents of any of these people violate this rule.

D	F	7	3

2. In its crackdown against drunk drivers, Massachusetts law enforcement officials are revoking liquor licenses left and right. You are a bouncer in a Boston bar, and you'll lose your job unless you enforce the following law:

    "If a person is drinking beer, then he or she must be over 21 years old."

    The cards below have information about four people sitting at a table in your bar. Each card represents one person. One side of a card tells what a person is drinking and the other side of the card tells that person's age. Indicate only the card(s) you definitely need to turn over to see if any of these people are breaking this law.

Drinking Beer		Drinking Coke			25 years old		16 years old

How did you do on the logic problems? Was one easier than the other? The answer to #1 is D and 7; the answer to #2 is "drinking beer and "16 years old." It is essentially the same question, but only 25% of people get #1 right, whereas 75% of people get #2 right. The example should help you think about the kinds of contextual influences that can influence how we answer cognitive questions. The field of exploring cognition is complicated even without adding in the gender piece. In this chapter, we explore gender differences in cognition. To spoil the conclusion, there are very few differences. However, in these few areas, the etiology, or theories regarding the reasons for the differences, is fascinating. Furthermore, results vary substantially by what kind of cognition is measured and how it is measured.

For centuries, scholars would have scoffed at a chapter on gender differences in thinking. After all, everyone knew that men were smarter than women. Why even ask the question? All of the individuals in positions that required cognitive power such as government and clergy were men. Most people were illiterate and the vast majority of literate individuals were men. The presumption of difference also allowed for the status quo to stay in place. After all, if men were in positions of power because women were unable to perform in these roles, then there would be no reason to change the system.

Early science focused on "flawed" measurements such as the weighing of brains. In general, it appeared that the smarter the animal, the weightier the brain. Men's brains were and are heavier than women's. The average brain weight of an adult male is 49.5 ounces – just over 3 pounds – while women typically have a 44-ounce brain, a one-third-pound difference; however,

women have 55.4 percent gray matter vs. 50.8 in men (Gur, Turetsky, Matsui, Yan, Bilker, Hughett, & Gur, 1999). Researchers evolved to a more sophisticated notion of cranial capacity (volume rather than weight – often indexed to the size of the body). Cranial capacity varies according to factors such as age, environment, and body size. However, as Purves et al (2001) point out, the ability to judge intelligence from brain capacity is akin to trying to judge athletic ability from body type – it is too imprecise. In addition, when comparing across species, what measures can be used to compare intelligence across species? Of course, we still measure brains. But now research is more sophisticated and focuses on the role of gray matter and specific functionalities and use 3-D magnetic resonance imaging to look at the differences. Most importantly, the important debate over the measurement and the meaning of these differences continues (Sala, 2007).

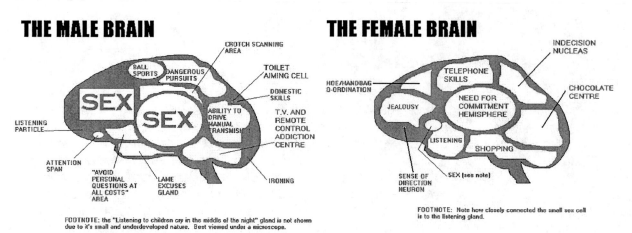

THE MALE BRAIN

THE FEMALE BRAIN

FOOTNOTE: the "Listening to children cry in the middle of the night" gland is not shown due to it's small and underdeveloped nature. Best viewed under a microscope.

FOOTNOTE: Note how closely connected the small sex cell is to the listening gland.

Whenever I think about the differences between men's and women's brains, I often think of those silly "cartoons" where men's and women's brains are mapped by area. The largest area in the men's brain is "sex" and includes smaller areas for "remote control addiction center" and "lame excuse gland" whereas the largest area in women's brains is "need for commitment" with smaller areas for "irrational thoughts" and "chocolate." Several versions circulate on the e-mail circuit, but they are all similar. In this chapter, we will seriously evaluate research-based findings on cognition.

Psychology uses "cognition" to refer to thinking, learning, and remembering. Psychological research on cognition has focused on mathematical, verbal and spatial skills. We will review the findings on those key areas. In addition, I will profile two additional areas of "thinking" differences that are intriguing in terms of research design and popular response – moral development and attribution.

Cognitive Differences

What matters when a researcher wants to measure **cognition**? The past few years has seen a large increase in multiple and complex perspectives on intelligence (e.g., Gardner, 1983; Goleman, 1997). We now know humans vary on their aptitudes and talents across a wide range of "intelligences" such as spatial, linguistic, musical, kinesthetic, mathematical, intrapersonal (self) and interpersonal (others). When we turn to gender differences, the research focuses namely on cognitive attributes that are related to standard cognitive function – namely, academic success. Interestingly, gender differences are not apparent in very "standard" ways of assessing intelligence such as IQ (intelligence quotient). The developers of IQ tests such as the Stanford Binet choose not to use any question that men and women answer significantly differently on during initial piloting phases of items (Maddox, 2002). Although the average score for men and women on IQ tests do not differ, the variances (standard deviations) differ. Men are overrepresented in both the high and low ends of the IQ range – they are overrepresented in the "genius" categories and it the mental retardation range (Halpern, 2000). Scientists continue to debate why this may be, but it does appear to be more biologically based than socially based.

Researchers have established some consistent but small gender differences in verbal, math, and spatial skills. See Box 7.1 for a discussion of the analyzing gender differences. We will first review the findings and then turn to theories about the causes of these differences. When we examine gender differences in these areas we will also look at data across the lifespan. It is both interesting and useful to assess when tests can begin to detect these differences if they exist.

Box 7.1: Analyzing Gender Differences and Similarities

Researchers examine patterns of similarities and differences between men and women because it helps us
- understand the role of research methodology in understanding both similarities and differences
- debunk "accepted" beliefs from the past such as "men are smarter than women"
- learn about the role of culture, perceptions, expectations, and situational influences in eliciting gendered behavior
- focus on is the contexts and conditions under which similarities and differences emerge

What do we need to think about when we read about differences?
- Research publishing practices privilege topics for which significant differences have been found. Rejecting the null hypothesis of "no difference" is the standard in psychological research.
- Effect sizes from meta analyses of gender research are small.

Spatial Skills

The area of cognition that shows the largest gender difference is **spatial skills**. However, visual-spatial skills are best thought of in five different categories and only some of them yield gender differences (Halpern, 2000). Figure 7.1 shows a sample task for each of the five areas.

1. *Spatial perception.* **Spatial perception** refers to being able to understand the spatial positions of objects by ignoring distracting information. For instance, in Figure 7.1., the rod-and-frame task requires a participant to line up the stick "the rod" parallel to the outside edges of a rectangle while a frame rotates within the rectangle.

2. *Mental rotation.* **Mental rotation** refers to the ability to imagine how three-dimensional objects will look when they are rotated in space. For instance, as shown in Figure 7.1, a respondent must decide which of the images is not the same figure as the original figure. Or, an object is shown in a series of panels each with a different rotation and the respondent must pick out what the next rotation would look like. Items regarding mental rotation are a traditional component in much of the K-12 standardized testing.

3. *Spatial Visualization.* **Spatial visualization** refers to complex processing of spatial information. For instance, in the embedded figures task shown in Figure 7.1, the participant decides whether the image on the left "a" is in the more complex image on the right "b."

4. *Spatiotemporal ability.* **Spatiotemporal ability** refers to understanding visual information that is moving. In Figure 7.1, the participant must estimate the speed of a ball that "disappears" into a background.

5. ***Generation and maintenance of a spatial image.*** In this category, the tasks rely on individuals being able to keep an image in mind for future tasks. In Figure 7.1, the respondent has to hold the shape of a letter in mind in order to answer the question correctly.

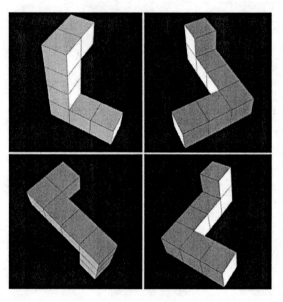

Certainly, there are other visual-spatial skills that underlie and overlap with these types of tasks. In addition, researchers are often interested in measuring completion time as well as accuracy. Gender differences appear in each of the five categories *except* spatial visualization (Halpern, 2000). The largest effect sizes for gender differences are found in the mental rotation tasks (the effect sizes fall in the "medium" range). The differences in the other areas are small. Recall from Chapter 2 that Cohen gives us a guide for social science effect sizes generated from meta-analyses (statistical reviews of several studies on the same topic) where ~.20 is small, ~.50 is medium and ~.80 is large. Spatial gender differences appear early in life, can be reliably measured by approximately age 10 (Halpern, 2000), and appear to stay consistent throughout the lifespan (Meinz & Salthouse, 1998).

Figure 7.1:

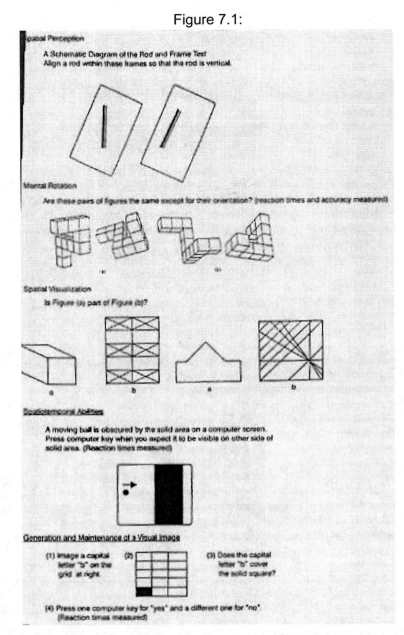

Why do we care about spatial skills? A variety of careers such as engineering, architecture, chemistry, and construction require strong spatial skills. In addition, spatial skills may drive some of the higher-level math understanding. Additionally, there is evidence that spatial skills seen in the laboratory are also replicated in real life situations (Halpern & LaMay, 2000). For instance, in a study that will probably lead some of you to say "I told you so," researchers found that when giving directions, men are more likely to give North, South, East, West directions. Women use more "left" and "right" directions and landmarks (e.g., "take a left after the big yellow house") (Dabbs, Chan, Strong, and Milun, 1998). Before you start gloating, both strategies appear to be equally effective no matter who's asking for help.

"How the Body Works: the Colorful Right Hemisphere"

Mathematical Skills

Mathematical skills show some gender variation. It appears that in elementary school, girls outpace boys in computational skills. However, boys show higher mathematical problem-solving skills than girls. In addition, as we've mentioned before, boys disproportionately outscore girls in the highest end of mathematical abilities (e.g., Halpern; 2000; Richardson, 1997). Finally, research exists that supports the idea that it may be the spatial skills advantage of men that drives the mathematical difference. Casey, Pezaris and Nuttall (1992) found that statistically controlling for the component of math scores due to mental rotation erased the gender difference usually seen.

Verbal Skills

Meta-analyses indicate that **verbal skill** tests yield small gender differences. Some sub-measures yield bigger differences. For instance, a large gender difference exists for speech errors, where more men are likely to use pauses, errs, and ums. Oftentimes, scientists refer to this as "verbal production." Men show an advantage in verbal analogies (e.g., ORCHESTRA : MUSICIAN :: (A) story : comedian (B) band : singer (C) garden : leaf (D) troupe : actor (E) government : lawyer. The answer is "D."). Women show an advantage in anagrams, writing, verbal ability tests,  reading comprehension, generating synonyms, and memory for words. However, verbal differences are generally small (effect sizes around .2 or lower). Developmentally, we know that girls speak and use more complex sentences earlier than boys (e.g., Gazzaniga, Ivry, & Mangun, 1998; Horgan, 1975), and girls maintain this edge throughout elementary school.

Recall that men show higher variability than women in IQ, spatial, and math ability (Hedges & Nowell, 1995). In verbal skills, the most striking differences are in the lower ends of ability. For instance, boys are twice as likely than girls to be classified as learning disabled, four times more likely to stutter, five times more likely to show mild dyslexia, and ten times more likely to show severe dyslexia (Sutaria, 1985).

One of the more interesting current debates is over whether the differences between men and women are lessening. Some studies supported a decrease in both the spatial and verbal differences. Debate erupted over whether the gap *really* was decreasing or whether it merely *appeared* to be decreasing. The controversy focuses on the types of measures used in studies with standardized tests versus more specific measures and tasks in empirical studies used for meta-analyses. In addition, the composition of the types of students taking tests like the SAT and ACT are changing. So, for instance, fewer men are going to college and therefore the men taking the exam may now be a different group than before. Overall, at this moment, a consistent "closing of the gap" cannot yet be supported (Halpern, 2000). Another curious "blip" in the data pertains to the verbal components of the SAT. Although, on most verbal tests, women show an advantage, for the SAT men have an advantage and have since the 1970s. Why the SAT produces data that is out of the ordinary with other verbal skills data is not yet fully understood.

Before we turn to theories about the causes of these differences, let's remember to ask the question "Why should we care?" As psychologists, we care about these differences because the question of why they exist is fascinating, and the related theories seeking to explain them use a blend the nature and nurture reasoning to explain the influences that shape us. Policy makers may use the differences psychologists identify to assess academic progress and award scholarships. Finally, you may care, because the general findings indicate strong similarity and overlap between men and women.

Theories Regarding Verbal and Spatial Gender Differences

Biological Theories

Scientists have proposed several biological theories that may help explain the verbal and spatial differences between men and women. Indeed, spatial and verbal skill gender gaps are probably the most biologically influenced differences that we will review in this book, and they are best explained by biopsychosocial perspectives. Biopsychological perspectives focus on the physiological factors associated with determining behaviors and mental processes. In the introduction to her book on sex differences in cognition, Halpern writes of her own surprise in assessing the newest research.

The literature on cognitive abilities is filled with inconsistent findings, contradictory theories and emotional claims that are unsupported by the research. Yet, despite all the noise in the data, clear and consistent messages could be heard. There are real, and in some cases sizable, sex differences with respect to some cognitive abilities. Socialization practices are undoubtedly important, but there is also good evidence that biological sex differences play a role in establishing and maintaining cognitive sex differences, a conclusion that I wasn't prepared to make when I began reviewing the relevant literature. (p. xvii, 2000)

We will look at four major biological theories: brain lateralization, gonadal hormones, genetic variation, and evolutionary theory.

Brain Lateralization and Structure. Many studies have now confirmed differences in the functional organization of men's and women's brains. One of these differences involves how we use the brain's two hemispheres (e.g., Wagner, Phan, Liberzon, & Taylor, 2003). Each brain has two hemispheres that communicate through the corpus callosum. You may recall that the perception pattern of hemispheres is "crossed" (see Figure 7.2).

Figure 7.2

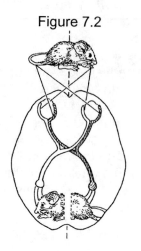

That is, information obtained on your right side (through your right eye or right hand) crosses to your left hemisphere and vice-versa. The corpus callosum readily communicates information between the hemispheres. However, humans apparently vary in the extent to which they are "lateralized." Lateralization refers to the functional specialization of the hemispheres. The more lateralized an individual is, the less communication between the hemispheres. In the majority of people, language skills are more likely to be located on the left side of the brain (you can remember this with language (L) = left (L)). Spatial skills are more likely to be located on the right side of the brain. How do researchers know about lateralization? Most early brain findings came from studies of individuals who experience trauma to the head. These early studies found that women recovered language skills from a stroke on the left side of the brain better than men did (McClone, 1978).

Men tend to be more lateralized than women (Wagner, Phan, Liberzon, & Taylor, 2003). That is, women appear to have more communication between the hemispheres – often referred to as bilateral organization. Handedness also appears to be related to lateralization. Left-handers have better *spatial skills* on average than do right-handers but the language findings are less clear (Hines & Collaer, 1993). In addition, men are more likely to be left-handed. Scientists have linked prenatal hormones to brain organization – including lateralization (Geschwind & Galaburda, 1987). In related findings, women's corpus callosa appear to be larger than men's. Prenatal hormones appear to increase the size of the corpus callosum and a larger callosum indicates that the two hemispheres can communicate more readily. Overall, the findings suggest that men's brains are more lateralized with language development more concentrated on the left and spatial ability on the right. Women are more bilateral and show more language development on both hemispheres. Newcombe (in press) describes the amount of support for the lateralization process' role in spatial skills as "dubious."

Another theory focuses on the relationship of where specific skills (e.g., which hemisphere) are processed. The left hemisphere is better at processing information in a "piecemeal, analytic and sequential manner" whereas the right hemisphere is better at processing information that is "integrative and holistic" (Banich & Heller, 1998, p. 1). These differences in types of processing then line up well with specific types of skills: holistic for spatial and sequential for language.

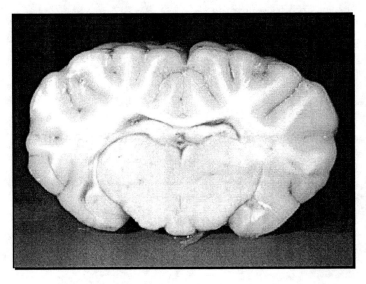

Another brain-structure biological theory focuses on the role of white matter (Gur et al., 1999). White matter is the portions of the brain and spinal cord that are white and composed of axons and dendrites. It helps transfer information between distant regions of the brain and is therefore linked to spatial abilities. The white matter carries the nerve impulses originating in the gray matter. Individuals with more white matter appear to be better at spatial skills. Although it is not clear why, men have a larger amount of white matter than women. This interesting finding should inspire more research in this area.

Finally, brain research has focused on "where" information is processed. Even in infants, boys' brains appear to process information in different parts of the brain than girls,' for instance, in response to hearing words (Molfese, 1990). In research with functional magnetic resonance imaging (fMRIs), scientists can gather images of where the activity is taking place. One set of research that received much media coverage was a study where they had men and women view images ranging from neutral (non-threatening animals) to disturbing (mutilated human bodies). Women showed activity in more areas of the brain, whereas men showed activity in fewer areas. In addition, in a surprise memory task a few weeks later, the women recalled the images more fully and used nine areas of the brain to do so, compared to men's two areas of the brain (Canli, Desmond, Zhao, & Gabrieli, 2002). Our "A closer look at an interesting study" for this chapter details a study on language processing (Baxter, Saykin, Flashman, Johnson, Guerin, Babcock, & Wishart, 2003).

Box 7.1: A closer look at an interesting study...

Who did the study?

Baxter, Saykin, Flashman, Johnson, Guerin, Babcock, & Wishart (2003)

What did they study?

They assessed brain activation patterns of men and women involved in a language task.

Who did they study?

Ten women and nine men who were right-handed, healthy and for whom English was a first language. The men and women did not differ on age, education, or a vocabulary test.

How did they do the study?

Respondents were scanned with a fMRI which provides an image of a slice of the brain approximately every 1.5 mm. As they were scanned, the respondents completed a semantic (language) task. Researchers presented them with auditory pairs of words through earphones where one word represented a larger category (e.g. beverage) and the other sample from the category (e.g. milk). Respondents squeezed the bulb if the category and the example matched.

What did they find?

Men and women were equally accurate on the task; however, men showed primarily left hemisphere activation whereas women showed activation on both the left and right. See Figure 7.3.

What is so interesting about it?

Cool technology. Functional MRIs are expensive and time consuming to analyze, hence the small sample size. *[Scientists estimate that a typical scanning session requires 60-90 minutes plus 4-8 hours to interpret each scan because there are so many images (Cosgrove, Buchbinder, & Hong, 2000)]* However, this study provides a current model of the types of brain comparison gender studies we are likely to see for many years to come. The findings support and enhance the brain lateralization theories regarding gender differences. The sophistication of the scan allows us to really see the processes that had only been hypothesized earlier or "guessed" at through more crude measures.

Figure 7.3:

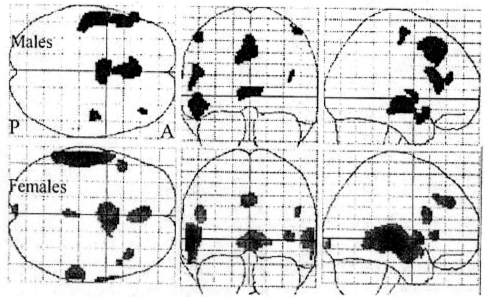

Brain scan from the "A closer look at an interesting study." The images on the top are for males; whereas the bottom images are for females. The "P" stands for posterior – meaning the front of the brain (toward your nose); whereas the "A" stands for anterior – meaning the back of the brain. The difference is most notable in the middle pictures from the scans. Note how there is activity on both sides for the women and more concentrated on one side for the men.
(Figure 1 from Baxter, Saykin, Flashman, Johnson, Guerin, Babcock, & Wishart; 2003, p. 268)

In brain structure research, we quickly run into the "chicken-egg" problem of causation. It makes sense that a difference in brain structure could lead to a difference in behavior. However, behavior may also affect the brain structure. Our old experiences may prime us to respond to our new experiences. We already have evidence that learning experiences can alter brain structures (e.g., Ungerleider, 1995).

Gonadal Hormone Theories. In Chapter 4, we learned that the brain is organized prenatally so that it can be activated by puberty-related hormones. Many of the cognitive functioning theories focus on this prenatal brain organization. One piece of evidence that speaks to the theories is the fact that spatial gender differences are seen before puberty, indicating that the organization may be a larger player than the activation. Other evidence for gonadal hormone influence come from the researchers I profiled in Chapter 2 when discussing how the media treats "hot topics." Kimura and Hampson (e.g., 1994) have linked natural menstrual hormonal fluctuations to cognitive functioning. Women who are ovulating (high progesterone and estrogen) have the highest verbal skills and when they are pre-menstrual (lowest progesterone and estrogen) they have the lowest verbal skills. Spatial skills show the opposite pattern. In addition, men appear to show fluctuations in skills as related to their seasonal hormonal fluctuations (men also show daily cycling of testosterone levels) (Svartberg, Jorde, Sundsfjord, Bønaa, & Barrett-Connor, 2003). When men's testosterone is high (Fall) their spatial skills are better (Kimura & Hampson, 1994). Interestingly, men's spatial skills are best when their testosterone is higher than women's but not as good when men's testosterone is at its peak. Newcombe (in press) who described the support for lateralization as "dubious" argues that the role of sex hormones as a reason for gender differences in spatial skills is *likely* despite the "murky" data on their role due to the complexity of the relationship.

Genetic Theories. As we saw in Chapter 4, some genetic anomalies appear to affect cognitive functioning. For instance, we know that three or more sex chromosomes appear to lead to reduced cognitive functioning. In addition, you'll recall that individuals with Turner's syndrome (XO) have very poor spatial skills. It appears that the Y chromosome and its accompanying masculinization of the fetus enhance spatial skills. Most likely, the genetic theories will dovetail with the gonadal theories, and future research will focus on the hormonal organization of the brain.

Evolutionary Theories. As suggested earlier in this book, evolutionary theory focuses on the hunter/gatherer structure as the primary influence on spatial skills (e.g., Jones, Braithwaite, & Healy, 2003). The theory argues that hunters (primarily men) needed to be able to pick out a 3-D figure against a background and as it moved. In addition, men may need good spatial skills to navigate territories for best access to fertile women. Gatherers (women) needed to be good at finding stationary objects in context and remembering where they were. While brain structures are likely to be affected by evolution, these very precise theories regarding specific behaviors are tenuous. For instance, spatial skills are required for other activities including basket weaving and gathering food at great distances from villages. Furthermore, not all past societies are so simply organized into hunter/gathers. Newcombe (in press) argues that evolutionary theories regarding spatial skills are beset with untested assumptions.

"The Theory of Evolution in 2 Minutes"

Socialization Theories

Socialization arguments regarding the gender difference in mathematics span the types of gender development theories we have reviewed. Math is a gender-typed subject where boys are expected to do well and are rewarded. As we have seen in Chapter 6 on sources of socialization, there is sufficient evidence to suggest that boys are encouraged to do better at math than are girls. In addition, math teachers are likely to be male, and both men and women model stereotypic roles when it comes to math. For instance, a child may get the following type of response from his/her mother "I'm not very good at math, ask your father"). Benbow (1998) and Halpern (2000) provide a summary of the research in the area of psychosocial influences on math differences. First, girls have more negative attitudes towards math than boys; however, the overall findings regarding attitudes toward math are very small with men being slightly more positive than women (d = .14; Hyde, Fennema, & Ryan, 1990). Second, girls see math as less important to their future careers than do boys. Third, girls have less confidence in their ability to do math than do boys. Interestingly, it appears that women have less confidence especially when thinking about "masculine" tasks such as visual spatial ability (Beyer, 1990). Fourth, both boys and girls tend to see math as gender-linked to men. Fifth, teachers, peers, and parents give girls less encouragement to study advanced math. Finally, women take fewer math courses (especially advanced math courses) than men. This differential in the number of math courses is probably the major factor driving the gender differences found on mathematical reasoning tests with older students. Recall that girls get better grades than boys, so these findings are set against no great "actual" deficit. Overall, all of these factors together help create and maintain a culture where it is easier for boys to exceed in math in comparison to girls.

Socialization theories more specific to the verbal and spatial gender differences focus on the types of activities in which boys and girls are involved. In general, our society encourages boys to be more active ("go outside and play") and girls to be more passive ("do a puzzle, read a book") and adults provide different toys to boys and girls. Interestingly, "boy toys" are often the type of toys that help develop spatial skills (e.g., building blocks and Erector Sets) (Boehm, 1986).

Another interesting set of activities to analyze are team sports. Think about basketball. If you play basketball, it is all about moving through space yourself while other 3-D objects are also in motion. For many years, boys were much more likely to be involved in team sports. Perhaps, we will see some changes now that a larger number of girls are involved in team sports. Over time, the experiences of boys and girls have deviated substantially from each other, with boys

spending more time than girls doing activities that enhance spatial skills. Even the differences in the time that boys and girls spend playing video games could be a factor. Boys play three times the number of minutes per week as compared to girls (Wright et al., 2001). And, computer and video game usage has been linked to improved spatial skills (Terlecki & Newcombe, 2005). Also, we are very likely seeing situations where children seek out activities that match their talents and proclivities. A child who is even slightly predisposed toward good spatial skills may enhance them by a spending a large amount time playing video games.

Some of the most interesting studies hinge on the idea that spatial skills can be taught and enhanced. Law, Pellegrino & Hunt (1993) found the traditional sex difference in spatiotemporal reasoning, and then provided both the boys and girls in their study with practice and feedback. Although the practice did not eliminate the gender gap, both the boys and the girls improved. The ability to improve at spatial skills appears to cross ages and types of tasks (Halpern, 2000).

Socialization and access to opportunity are also the major explanatory factors in understanding race, ethnic, and class variations in cognitive functioning. Simply put, no evidence backs biological theories in regards to these socio-cultural groups. However, measures such as standardized tests show large differences between these groups. These differences are almost entirely accounted for by variables such as access to opportunities, the quality of education, home environments, and nutrition. Gender merely compounds the "problem" for individuals who come from disadvantaged backgrounds. Recall the conceptual models from Chapter 1 regarding how to think about the gender link to race, ethnicity and class. When it comes to cognitive skills, the model shown in Figure 7.4 best fits the data by suggesting that gender differences would precede cultural differences, and that cultural differences could greatly impact the overall findings.

Figure 7.4

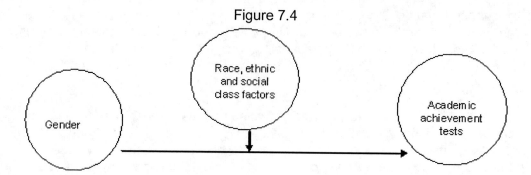

Combining the evidence for biological and socialization theories indicates that gender differences in cognition are very likely to be biopsychosocially driven. If male and female children are born with a predisposition toward various cognitive abilities, these abilities are then enhanced by cultural expectations and psychological reinforcements. BUT, before we leave this topic, let me remind you that when differences are found, they are small (Hyde, 2005). The research and the theories are fascinating, but you don't want to develop theories that are bigger than the actual findings or policies that end up disadvantaging either sex.

A good example of how the discussion of gender differences in cognition can get quickly out of control, I direct you to a recent commotion over some remarks by the President of Harvard, Lawrence Summers. Summers touched off a national debate by suggesting that innate abilities (or lack thereof) may be the reason that women are underrepresented in the sciences and engineering (Summers, 2005).

> It does appear that on many, many different human attributes-height, weight, propensity for criminality, overall IQ, mathematical ability, scientific ability-there is relatively clear evidence that whatever the difference in means-which can be debated-there is a difference in the standard deviation, and variability of a male and a female population. And that is true with respect to attributes that are and are not plausibly, culturally determined. (Summers, 2005, ¶4)

He made this comment as part of prepared remarks for elite conference on the topic of the under-representation of women and minorities in the sciences and engineering. Keep in mind, his academic training is as an economist. Several women researchers walked out of the conference, Summers apologized multiple times, and pledged funds for gender research (Fish, 2005; Fogg, 2005; Monastersky, 2005). As an observer, I was most interested in the level of coverage it engendered and the intensity of those arguing that there either is or is not research support for his assertions (e.g., Brown, 2005; Muller, Ride, & Rouke, 2005; Singer, Barkley, & Taylor, 2005). The American Psychological Association quickly published a collection of articles on the topic entitled *"Why aren't more women in science: Top researchers debate the evidence"* (Ceci & Williams, 2007).

Another side of me was disappointed that an administrator in higher education felt free to make that kind of comment without a nod to the complexity of the research on this topic. However, for this book, the situation nicely illustrates that this is not a dead conversation. It is alive and well in academia and in the press. A set of remarks coming from the President of the most famous university in the U.S. carries with them far-reaching ramifications. His words potentially connote power and affect others' views of the topic. As the resulting press furor suggested, his words quickly became part of mainstream American media.

We now turn to cognitive gender differences with fewer biological linkages but interesting implications for gender and thinking. We will look at moral development and attribution processes.

Moral Development

Cognitive development theory, as suggested in Chapter 3, argues that children's maturity affects their cognitive understanding of gender. Developmental maturity for children affects their cognitive understanding of all topics. Most children gain an ability to think in more complex ways. **Moral development** is related to stages in cognitive development. We will examine an intriguing discussion regarding gender and moral development that occurred several years ago. The discussion over the relative "stages" of men's and women's moral development illuminates some key research and the social implications of interpretation. In reality, meta-analyses suggest a small effect size regarding differences in men's and women's moral reasoning (e.g., Jaffee & Hyde, 2000). The continued debate regarding these finding in both popular press and academic journals over "women's moral reasoning" 'and "men's moral reasoning" propels a more in-depth analysis of the elements in the discussion.

How would you respond to the following scenario?
In Europe, a woman was near death from cancer. One drug might save her, a form of radium that a druggist in the same town had recently discovered. The druggist was charging $2000, ten times what the drug had cost him to make. The sick woman's husband, Heinz, went to everyone he knew to borrow the money, but he could get together only about half of what it would cost. He told the druggist that his wife was dying and asked him to sell it cheaper or to let him pay later. But the druggist said no. The husband got desperate and broke into the man's store to steal the drug for his wife. Should the husband have done that? Why?

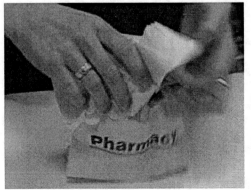

The scenario above is a variation of the famous "Heinz Dilemma" long used in moral reasoning research. Kohlberg (1973) created this dilemma that places several important values up against one another to judge individuals' moral reasoning. Whether or not an individual supports Heinz' action is inconsequential to the research. What interests researchers is the *reasoning* behind the answer. Kohlberg's theory posited three major levels of moral development, each with two stages. Those of you familiar with Piagetian theory will recognize the language.

Table 7.1

Kohlberg's Theory of Moral Development
Level I. **Pre-conventional** Stage (individual oriented) Stage 1: Obedience and Punishment Orientation Stage 2. Individualism and Exchange Overall, the focus of Level 1 reasoning is on consequences for self (ego-centric). Focus is also on rules and obedience with the aim to avoid punishment and gain rewards.
Level 2. **Conventional** Stage Stage 3: Good Interpersonal Relationships. Concerned about Others. Conform to rules to gain approval from others. Stage 4: Maintaining the Social Order Emphasis on justice and society's need to have laws in order to function. Overall, Level 2 reasoning shifts from obedience to a more relativistic outlook. In addition, there is a concern for good motives, such as others' or society's needs for order.
Level 3. **Post-conventional** Stage Stage 5: Social Contract and Individual Rights Stage 6: Universal Principles Overall, Level 3 reasoning sees laws as based on a social contract that can be changed through mutual agreement. Decisions should be based on universal moral principles.

One of the key criticisms of Kohlberg's work is that he developed this theory after collecting data only with male respondents. His original 1950s sample was comprised of 72 boys, from middle- and lower-class families in Chicago. At the time, it was unfortunately not unusual for psychologists to assume that whatever was true for men would also be true for women. In general, psychologists assumed a human condition for which men were the exemplars. After developing the theory, researchers assessed both men and women and found that men scored higher on moral reasoning than women. Keep in mind that if the research proved explanatory of universal stages of moral reasoning, it suggested that men's moral reasoning was "better" than women's. Take a closer look at Table 7.1. We need to focus on Level 2 and its two stages. Men score an average that lands them in Stage 4, whereas women on average score in Stage 3.

Gilligan (1982), who worked with Kohlberg and admired his ideas and work, challenged the gender findings of his research. She did not argue with the method of his research nor its fundamental views. Coding respondent's answers to moral dilemmas is an extremely complex venture and coders are highly trained in how to conduct the interview and the types of prompts that may go with them. Her key problem was with the interpretation of Stages 3 and 4. She argued that there is no reason to think that an emphasis on others is less cognitively developed than an emphasis on the need for social order. Gilligan argued that Kohlberg relegated "female-type" thinking (caring and responsibility to others) to lower stages and "male-type" thinking (individuality, rationality) to higher stages. Gilligan posited that Stages 3 and 4 should actually be equivalent, not hierarchical. Gilligan developed a theory of the "ethics of care" to represent the type of moral reasoning behind Stage 3 and the "ethics of rights" to represent the reasoning behind Stage 4.

A notable comparison that Gilligan reports is 11-year-old Jake's answer to a complex question as compared to 11-year-old Amy's. The question reflects one of the probes used after children respond to Heinz' dilemma.

> Question: When responsibility to oneself and responsibility to others conflict, how should one chose?
>
> Jake: "You go about one-fourth to the others and three-fourths to yourself."
>
> Amy's answer is 112 words long and starts with "Well, it really depends on the situation. If you have a responsibility with somebody else, then you should keep it to a certain extent, but to the extent that it is really going to hurt you or stop you from doing something that you really, really want, then I think maybe you should put yourself first. But... (pp. 35-36).

The quote nicely captures Gilligan's argument the boys are responding with judicial responses whereas girls are drawing from a more relational basis. Gilligan suggested that women's socialization to be caretakers leads them to "**ethics of care**" thinking and to defining themselves through connection. In contrast, men's socialization to become independent contributes to "**ethics of rights**" reasoning and to defining themselves as separate from others. However, the major data source for Gilligan's theory was interviews with women who were pregnant, considering abortion, and ambivalent. Most of the women argued either *for* or *against* their own abortions based on the views of others such as their partners or parents. Gilligan interpreted this reasoning to be evidence for an ethic of care.

Before examining the empirical evidence regarding Gilligan's theory, I want to introduce another book that garnered tremendous response and also argued for the theory that women and men "think" in different ways. In *Women's Ways of Knowing: The Development of Self, Voice, and Mind (*Belenky, Clinchy, Goldgerger, & Tarule, 1986) Belenky and her colleagues reacted to another theory developed from research conducted solely with men. Perry (1970) developed a stage theory regarding the intellectual development of college students. In Perry's theory, students proceed from dualistic thinking to a more constructed way of understanding and assessing. Belenky et al's theory is less of a stage theory although it did suggest a sequence. Table 7.2 lays out Perry's and Belenky et al.'s major points. Belenky et al. argued that women's socialization leads to different learning strategies than those recognized and rewarded in typical universities. However, like most of the gender material we have looked at, this must be understood in terms of the social context. Would we not argue that different experiences of many types (gender, maturity, culture) could affect learning styles? Is gender the fundamental organizing principle here? Or, is learning style the issue at hand, and instructors and students alike can come to recognize variation in the pattern.

Table 7.2

"Women's Ways of Knowing" (Belenky, Clinchy, Goldgerger, & Tarule, 1986)	Perry's (1980) Intellectual Development Stages (Eight stages group into four)
Level One: Silence or absence of voice. - Women students feel mindless and voiceless, subject to whims of external authority	**Dualism/Received Knowledge:** 1. Basic Duality 2. Full Dualism -Knowledge is absolute -All problems are solvable -Authorities provide the right answers
Level Two: Received Knowing: Listening to the voices of others. -Women students feel they can receive knowledge, but not create it	**Multiplicity** 3. Early Multiplicity 4. Late Multiplicity -Multiple perspectives acknowledged -All points of view equally valuable
Level Three: Subjective Knowing -Truth and knowledge are private and subjectively known or intuited	**Relativism** 5. Contextual Relativism: 6. "Pre-Commitment": -Knowledge is contextual and relative
Level Four: Procedural Knowing: Separate & Connected -Women students are invested in learning and applying objective procedures for obtaining and communicating knowledge	**Commitment in Relativism** 7. Challenges to Commitment 8. "Post-Commitment" -Personal commitments made out of relativistic frame of reference -Capable of original thought
Level 5: Constructed Knowing -Women students view knowledge as contextual and can create knowledge found objectively or subjectively	

Gilligan and Belenky et al's work highlight important discussions in the field of gender. Both books represent concepts of "thinking" that are very different from those with which we started the chapter. The theorists strongly believe in a consistent form of female socialization. Both argue that previously undervalued forms of thinking and reasoning should be more highly valued. Some argue that these "women's ways" theories rely on fundamental stereotypes of women (caring and connected) and then flip the judgment of these characteristics from negative to positive (e.g., Jody, 1998).

Gilligan's book, *In a Different Voice: Psychological Theory and Women's Development,* was tremendously popular. It spoke to many women in a powerful way. By suggesting that women's moral reasoning was equally valid compared to men's, and that it was uniquely informed by society's expectation for women, she touched an important nerve. Her work, and the work of others who support the notion that a "woman's voice" comes from women's experience, resonates with many women who feel that women's unique experiences are not recognized or valued by society or academia. Furthermore, many women who feel left out of "male models" of human existence are much drawn to theories that speak to alternative experiences. Despite the fact that the empirical support for these theories is weak, I think it is crucial to continue to discuss why these theories appear to appeal to so many people. They may also have served to tap dimensions or emotions about experience that other materials appeared to miss. However, these works ultimately do not serve to "prove" that men and women think differently.

Gilligan's work received a number of important criticisms. First, her research with women facing abortion decisions made for awkward comparisons. Abortion decisions are real; responses to the Heinz Dilemma are hypothetical. Are they really comparable? More importantly, what in men's lives can really compare to an abortion decision? In Chapter 2, I argued that it is methodologically unsound to compare men and women without measuring both groups with a comparable measure. Gilligan's study is a prime example of this problem. In fact, Belenky et al.'s involves the same problem. They compared their own sample to Perry's without sampling a new group of men to directly compare men and women with their own theory. This criticism does not negate claims about "women's ways" that might be made from the data – we just don't know if these constructs may not also be true of "men's ways" or if men's and women's ways are different. Belenky et al. suggested that men with similar life experiences might show a similar pattern to women. However, support of their theory (such as the linking of life experience to knowing) needs to be empirical in nature.

The empirical support for Gilligan's work is mixed. In general, both men and women use reasoning consistent with an "ethics of care" and an "ethics of rights" (Boyes & Walker, 1988; Walker, 1984). Women appear to be more likely to use an "ethics of care" than men, and men more likely to use an "ethics of rights" than women (small effect sizes found in a meta-analysis by Jaffee & Hyde, 2000), but both men and women use both. Finally, the type of moral dilemma elicits the type of reasoning. Dilemmas that deal with relationship concerns elicit more care-based reasoning for both men and women (see Table 7.3) than do dilemmas that are more rights-based.

"What are Ethics?"

Table 7.3: A moral reasoning problem based on a friendship dilemma (based on Selman's (1980) social moral development research)

Charlene and Joanne have been good friends since they were five. Now they are in high school and Joanne tried out for the school play. As usual she was nervous about how she did, but Charlene was there to tell her she was very good and give her moral support. Still Joanne was worried that a newcomer in the school would get the part. The new girl, Tina, came over to congratulate Joanne on her performance and then asked if she could join the girls for a snack. Right away, Charlene and Tina seemed to hit it off very well. They talked about where Tina was from and the kinds of things she could do in her new school. Joanne, on the other hand, didn't seem to like Tina very well. She thought Tina was a little pushy, and maybe she was a bit jealous over all the attention Charlene was giving Tina.

When Tina left the other two alone, Joanne and Charlene arranged to get together on Saturday, because Joanne had a problem that she would like to talk over with Charlene. But later that day, Tina called Charlene and asked her to go see a play on Saturday.

Charlene had a dilemma. She would have jumped at the chance to go with Tina, but she had already promised to see Joanne. Joanne might have understood and been happy that Charlene had the chance to go, or she might feel like she was losing her best friend when she really needed her.

How does this dilemma compare to the Heinz dilemma? Can you imagine a response with moral reasoning based on an ethics of justice? An ethics of care?

As is consistent with cognitive developmental theory, no strong evidence exists for race, ethnic, or class differences in moral reasoning (e.g., Wilson, 1995). However, additional research with individuals from other types of cultures (such as collectivist societies such as China that focus less on the individual) may yield interesting patterns of differences in moral reasoning. Evidence of cultural variation would more closely align with Gilligan's argument about socialized differences. Evidence has amassed that strongly suggests that individuals' moral reasoning will reflect that which is morally relevant to the culture at hand (e.g., Boyes & Walker, 1988; Wood, 1996). Finally, in an interesting twist, despite Gilligan's claim that the Kohlberg's framework and measure were gender biased, in fact, no consistent gender differences have been established even when using his original framework (e.g., Walker, 1984; 1986; Wood, 1996). Consequently, the whole discussion has led to more important theoretical and methodological discussions than actual gender-difference discoveries. Hyde (2005) writes "Gilligan's ideas have permeated American culture. One consequence of this over inflated claim of gender difference is that reifies the stereotype of women as caring and nurturant and men as lacking in nurturance (p.590)." Wood (1996) ends her review of the research with a thoughtful comment about the culture-bound theories.

> My own perspective is that while I believe both Gilligan and Kohlberg have developed sound theories about how it is that morality may develop, both are polarized views which restricted their positions in a nearly sexist manner. To say that all men or all women reason in only one way is to assume that gender roles are fixated and negates other conditions which may display differences. Both models, it seems are disproportionately culture bound (p. 381).

Patterns of Attribution

Attribution is the process of suggesting a cause for an outcome. One of the easiest ways to think about attribution is to think about an exam. It turns out that people are more likely to start the process of attribution if an outcome or occurrence is negative and unexpected. It leaves us asking "Why?" But, for instance, if you find $20 on the street, are you racked with anxiety about why? Doubtful. You probably put it in your pocket and happily move on. Assume that you expected to get a "B" on an exam and the grades are posted and you actually received a "C." This unexpected and negative event will likely lead you to ask "Why?" What are some reasons? You didn't study enough? The test was too hard? You're dumb? Wiener (1974) provides a classic way to categorize attributions along two main dimensions. First, attributions are either internal (about the individual) or external (about the situation). Second, attributions suggest that the cause is either stable (always true) or unstable (comes and goes). Table 7.4 shows sample responses for each of the four possibilities.

Table 7.4

	Stable	**Unstable**
Internal	*I'm dumb.*	*I didn't study hard enough.*
External	*That teacher is always too hard.*	*That exam was too hard.*

Predictable patterns in attributions occur. For instance, people are likely to make external unstable attributions about negative events. That makes sense, right? You would want to think it was a fluke. When positive events occur, people lean toward stable, internal attributions. If you had gotten an "A" on the exam, is it because you're smart or because the exam was too easy? We are likely to give the former reason. "*We are likely*" is a misleading when it comes to attribution patterns though. Individuals who are clinically depressed are more likely to attribute occurrences opposite to the way non-depressed individuals usually do (Abramson, Metalsky, & Alloy, 1989). Table 7.5 shows this pattern. As you might expect, it is not clear which direction the relationship goes. Is it depression that leads to the depressive attribution style? Or, it is a depressive attribution style that leads to depression? Or, do they both inform each other? Think about it, how would it make you feel to think that every time something went wrong, it was due to something permanently "wrong" about you? However, the evidence appears to point to individuals with a pessimistic or helpless attribution style being more prone to depression after the occurrence of negative events (Abramson, Metalsky, & Alloy, 1989).

Table 7.5: Attributions for success or failures

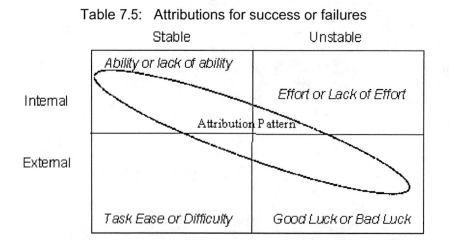

	Stable	Unstable
Internal	Ability or lack of ability	Effort or Lack of Effort
	Attribution Pattern	
External	Task Ease or Difficulty	Good Luck or Bad Luck

*Attribution Pattern: Depressed and non-depressed individuals show a flip pattern. Non-depressed individuals make stable-internal attributions for **positive** events and unstable-external for **negative** events, depressed individuals make stable-internal attributions for **negative** events and unstable-external for **positive** events. Adapted from Weiner, 1986.*

Gender complicates the picture. Women are twice as likely as men to be diagnosed as clinically depressed (Mazure, Keita, & Blehar, 2002) and more likely to use the "depressive attribution style" than are men (Gladstone, Kaslow, Seeley, & Lewinsohn, 1997). But, again, the chicken-egg problem is at hand. More recently, the question of whether non-depressed women show different attribution patterns than men has been re-examined. In early research, two major theories were posited. First, people looking at men's and women behavior (attributions about others) tended to attribute men's successes to ability and women's successes to luck (Deaux & Emswiller, 1974). Second, men and women appeared to use the same attribution pattern that the "others" did when assessing their own attributions! One of the best-known studies found that 75% of men chose to play a game of skill over luck, compared to 35% of women (Deaux, White, & Farris, 1975).

The current findings are less clear-cut. Some evidence exists that observers are still more likely to attribute women's successes to luck. However, a meta-analysis has detected an underlying research design explanation. Gender differences in attributions are most strongly seen in studies where the task was "masculine" (all effect sizes were small) (Swim, & Sanna, 1996). The gender pattern for attributions about one's own successes and failures also shows interesting variations. For instance, the wording of the attribution question appears to have an effect on the gender outcomes. When asked to give information about the outcome ("how much ability did you have?") meta-analyses reveal that men are more likely to use ability attributions and less likely to use luck attributions than are women (regardless of positive or negative outcomes) (Frieze, Whitley, Hanusa, & McHugh, 1982). When we add the depression piece back in, we have evidence that non-depressed women use more "depressive attribution" than do non-depressed men; however, depressed men and women both use more depressive attributions. This pattern appears to be stronger for negative events than positive events (Gladstone, Kaslow, Seeley, & Lewinsohn, 1997).

When you think about attributions, you need to know that they are very strongly affected by culture and experience. We see significant international variation in the types of attributions that people make about each other and themselves (Mezulis, Abramson, Hyde, & Hankin, 2004). In the studies conducted with U.S. populations, there is less evidence of cultural variation. However, one recent study of adolescents suggests that teens from higher socioeconomic status backgrounds (SES) were *more* likely to suggest pessimistic attributions for negative events than were teens from lower SES backgrounds. The researchers did not find the same pattern for positive events. The authors postulate that lower SES teens are more likely to experience negative events and may therefore adopt more psychologically healthy attributions in response to negative events. Their race data supports their hypothesis as they found that African American teens also use a lower number of pessimistic attributions than do European American teens (Waschbusch, Sellers, LeBlanc, & Kelley, 2003). Fascinating findings are likely to come from this kind of cultural variation research. Such research helps us better understand specific ethnic groups as well as the larger implications of attribution patterns.

"Psychology Lessons: What is the Fundamental Attributions Error?"

Despite the mixed research on attributions, I chose to spend some time on them in this book because whether you are a man or a woman, you may find it useful to analyze your own attribution patterns. If someone leans toward depression, there is ample evidence that some cognitive restructuring (thinking differently) can lessen depressive symptoms. A good layperson's guide that has been shown to help people is Burns' 1981 *Feeling Good: The New Mood Therapy* (Burns, 1999).

This chapter focused on thinking and surveyed differences in cognition, moral development, and attribution. My hope is that this chapter has given you a chance to think more fully about the biopsychosocial approach to gender differences as well as the personal, social and political significance of finding and discussing gender differences and similarities.

Additional ways to think about the material in this chapter

- What do you think accounts for the "popularity" of studies and theories that espouse a difference between men and women?
- What role do you think the construction of achievement tests plays in the results researchers find using them?

Global Connection Opportunities

❖ http://nces.ed.gov/surveys/international/G8report.asp
  - o This site has the report "Comparative Indicators of Education in the United States and Other G8 Countries: 2004" it is a report that compares the U.S. to the other G8 countries (Canada, France, Germany, Italy, Japan, Russian Federation, United Kingdom) in four areas: (1) the context of education; (2) preprimary and primary education; (3) secondary education; and (4) higher education.
❖ http://www.unicef.org/publications/index_29995.html
  - o "The GAP Project is a yearlong multimedia assessment of global progress towards gender parity in education. Using various media - photo, video, web and print - the project examines why the Millennium Development Goal of gender parity in education by 2005 was not met, and highlights innovations that can help ensure that all children are in school by 2015. The report is the first step in the ongoing evaluation of progress and is being published as part of UNICEF's contribution as the lead agency of the UN Girls' Education Initiative."

Chapter 8
Gender and Feeling

A. *Emotionality*
B. *Moods*
C. *Stress*
D. *Mental Health Disorders*

From *"Harry Potter and the Order of the Phoenix"*

Hermione looked at the pair of them with an almost pitying expression on her face. "Don't you understand how Cho's feeling at the women?" she asked. "No," said Harry and Ron together. Hermione sighed and laid down her quill. "Well, obviously, she's feeling very sad, because of Cedric dying. Then I expect she's feeling confused because she liked Cedric and now she likes Harry, and she can't work out who she likes best. Then she'll be feeling guilty, thinking it's an insult to Cedric's memory to be kissing Harry at all, and she'll be worrying about what everyone else might say about her if she starts going out with Harry. And she probably can't work out what her feelings toward Harry are anyway, because he was the one who was with Cedric when Cedric died, so that's all very mixed up and painful. Oh, and she's afraid she's going to be thrown off the Ravenclaw Quidditch team because she's been flying so badly."

A slightly stunned silence greeted the end of this speech, then Ron said, "One person can't feel all that at once, they'd explode." (Rowling, 2003, p. 99).

Poor Ron. Doesn't it seem like too many feelings might make someone explode? And, certainly, Ron's comments reflect a societal view that women are more emotional than men and that men are confused by the whole thing. But, what's the real story? In this chapter we will explore stereotypes of men's and women's emotions and gender differences in reported emotional states and moods. We will then explore how men and women respond to stress and mental states that potentially reflect both stress and emotional reactivity.

Emotionality

In her book summarizing the research on gender and emotion, *Speaking from the Heart,* Stephanie Shield's (2002) titles a chapter "Emotional = female? Angry = male?" Indeed, her chapter's title reflects some of the more enduring findings from the study of gender and emotion. First, people believe that women are more emotional than men. Second, people hold gender-specific stereotypes about individual emotions. Namely, people see women as more likely to feel and show happiness, sadness, and fear, and men more likely to feel and show anger. Finally, both the appraisal of emotion and the experiencing of emotion are very context-dependent. We judge our own and others' emotion by the situation which prompted it. So, for example, women are expected to be more emotional about relationships than are men. Let's take a look at each of these of these sets of findings.

Stereotypes and Facts about Emotion

In general, most of the stereotypes are about the expression of emotion or the "outward display" (showing emotion) rather than the internal subjective experience of emotion (feeling emotion). Indeed, women self-report more emotional expressiveness than do men (Fischer, 2000). People also believe that men and women differ more in the display rather than the experience of emotion (Johnson & Shulman, 1988). There is support of a similar experience of emotion - both men and women report similar internal experiences in response to emotional stimuli (e.g., happy when something good happens) (Fischer, 1993). Both sexes are also aware of the different standards regarding the expression of emotion by men and women (Stoppard & Gruchy, 1993). Additionally, regardless of "feeling," men certainly talk about emotions less so than women do (Shields). As we saw in Chapter 6 on sources of socialization, parents monitor children and peers monitor each other when it comes to gendered behavior regarding emotion. Who is up for being a cry-baby? In line with these socialization theories, most scholars argue that men's comparatively lower emotional responsiveness is due to "lack of practice" (e.g., Jansz, 2000).

Although considerable research supports the socialization-based theory that we shape and reinforce the expression of emotion, interesting neurological research exists that may eventually lead to more insight on women's emotional expressiveness and men's restricted expressiveness. Canli, Desmond, Zuo & Gabrieli, 2002) using MRI technology found that emotional visual images triggered more areas in women's brains than in men's at the time the images were shown (e.g., mutilated bodies). Nine areas known to be associated with emotion were triggered in women's brains, compared to two in men's. In addition, in a surprise "test" three weeks later, women recalled more of the images than did men. The study could be detecting the way that men and women process and remember emotion. However, this study could also be reflecting chicken-or-the-egg logic. Women's socialized and rewarded interest in emotions may cause brain responses and/or the brain's structure may be enhancing the interest in emotions.

Specific Emotions

When it comes to specific emotions, anger appears to be the emotion that is most distinctive from the others (Shields, 2002). Hess, Senécal, Kirouac, Herrera, Philippot, and Kleck (2000) report the findings from two different studies that explored specific emotions. First, respondents estimated how men and women would react to emotional situations. Second, respondents

 estimate their own emotional reactions (in terms of behavior) to a variety of situations. Consequently, the first study assessed stereotypic views on gender and emotions and the second study assessed how self-perception fit the stereotype. An example of an anger situation scenario provided to the responses is "Someone learns that somebody close to him has been spreading negative rumors." The researchers assessed nine different emotions: happiness, serenity, sadness, fear, disgust, contempt, anger, shame, and guilt. The anger we expect from men is apparent in this study. Participants expected men to be significantly more likely to express anger in the situations designed to provoke sadness, shame, fear, and anger.

Figure 8.1 shows the data from one of their scenarios. The figure shows the respondents estimates of the percentage of men and women who would respond to the "fear" situation with each of the seven emotions. The graph shows that the respondents believed that the men would show more anger in response to fear than would women. If you are someone who ignores graphs – don't! It is important to learn how to read them. Take another look. There were other significant gender differences (look for the asterisks). In addition to the anger expectation, women were expected to show more sadness, fear, disgust, shame, and guilt than men. The article shows a similar graph for each of the seven emotions. Overall, participants expected women to respond more with disgust and shame in each of the emotional situations except for the one dealing with sadness.

Figure 8.1: Respondents views of how men and women would react to fear scenarios from Hess, Senécal, Kirouac, Herrera, Philippot, and Kleck (2000).

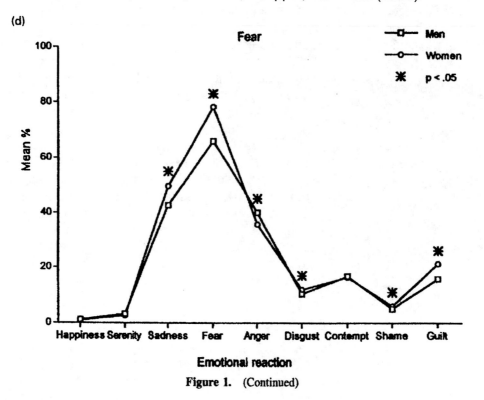

Figure 1. (Continued)

The authors suggest that the findings support the idea that the prevalent stereotype for women is withdrawal (fear/sadness) and self-direct (shame/guilt), whereas men's emotional reactions are more active (anger).

How well did the respondents' own self-perceptions fit these stereotypes? First, when comparing men to women, the researchers found an expected pattern. Women reported a higher probability of showing behaviors congruent with sadness and fear, whereas men reported a higher likelihood of responding with anger. When compared to the "stereotypical" estimates, the most consistent finding was about sadness. Women were more likely to (and expected to) respond with sadness to negative situations. The parallel finding is that men are more likely to react with happiness to negative situations (keep in mind it is a relative number). Overall, there was a general consistency between the self-perceptions and the stereotypic beliefs. As we saw in our chapter on stereotypes, many scholars argue that emotional responses by men and women are very likely both reflecting and supporting (through self-fulfilling prophecy) the stereotypes.

Before we leave this topic, spend some time thinking about anger as an emotion. Why do people respond to it differently from other emotions? From a more overtly political view, you may ask who is entitled to anger? What language do we use to describe it? "Out of control" vs. "just angry"? We will revisit this when we look at context-dependent emotions below.

Context-dependent emotions. Shields (2002) argues that the general standard for emotional display for both men and women is "manly emotion." Manly emotion is felt but not displayed. If it is displayed it is supposed to represent "passion in the service of reason." In addition, the definition of "excessive" is set low. One may shed a single tear – not a crying jag or

sobbing. Ample examples exist (particularly from politics) where emotion can prove to be the icing on the cake – where a single tear indicates deep feeling from a man. In comparison, a woman crying can indicate that she is not fit to run a government during trying times. Shield's argues that both men and women face a double bind. Women face the expectation that they will be "appropriately nurturant (as shown in part through extravagant expressiveness), yet conform to the overarching standard of manly emotion (p. 174)." For men, the bind is how to "approximate the elusive ideal of manly emotion (p. 174)" where they have to balance between being "inexpressive" as men should be and being "sensitive" the way that good fathers and partners should be. Earlier in the book, Shields poses and answers the question "Are there gender differences in emotion?" She responds with the following:

> Of course there are. What is interesting about these differences, however, is that they are far more context-dependent than the prevailing emotion stereotype leads us to expect" (Shields, 2002; p. 40).

Huston-Comeaux & Kelly (2002; Kelly & Huston-Comeaux, 1999) found that emotion reactions are seen as "overreactions" when the situation involves men's anger in achievement contexts and women's happiness and sadness in interpersonal contexts. They had participants rate the appropriateness of the responses shown in several scenarios which were written to show an overreaction. For instance, the "angry achievement" scenario read like this "Cindy was hired with the understanding that she would become the next Head Manager. When that position recently became available, the company did not promoter her. Cindy reacts by hanging fliers all around the town that discredit the company. A happy interpersonal scenario read "Jack has been dating his college sweetheart for 6 years. This past weekend he got engaged. Jack starts loudly singing "The Wedding March" out his apartment window so everyone can hear the good news." (Huston-Comeaux & Kelly, 2002, p. 4) Recall that due to the random assignment of this experimental design, the "only" variables that should account for differences in ratings would be the gender of the respondent and/or the gender of the actor in the emotion scenario. In this study, the gender of the actor played the largest role. The findings suggest that participants saw men's overreactions as inappropriate in achievement situations and saw women's overreactions as inappropriate in interpersonal situations. The authors suggest that this study provides empirical support for the idea of the "double bind" put forth by Shields. Participants saw both men and women as inappropriate when acting excessive in their "own" domain fields. These ratings appear to be based on stereotypes. So, the double bind comes in where we are viewed negatively if we are not emotional about the right things (in this case, men=achievement; women=interpersonal), but if we are "too" emotional we are also seen negatively. Interestingly, the researchers also asked about "sincerity" and participants saw women as sincere when angry and men when happy. Overall, the importance of this research hinges on the fact that, as observers, we bring our context-specific stereotypes to our views of others' emotions. If I was a physician, how might I respond if a male patient was really angry about his work situation?

"The Power of Human Emotion 'Conversations with Robyn'"

Overall, the findings on emotionality suggest that the empirical differences emerge in studies of the *display* of emotion. Although called a variety of terms, the general idea is that men have a "restrictive emotionality" and respond to situations with less emotion than do women. We have to be careful here with the terminology because the implication is that "lesser" means "worse than." There is no evidence that it is bad for men to respond the way that they do, or good for women. Rather, scientists can link both types of emotional expression (restricted and internal) to negative health outcomes. We will return to the health outcomes later in this chapter when we look at stress and mental disorders.

Recent research has illuminated an interesting confluence between gender stereotypes, display of emotion, socialization, and, potentially, evolutionary theory. Becker, Kenrick, Neuberg, Blackwell, & Smith (2007) established that people are faster and more accurate at detecting angry expressions on male faces and happy expressions on female faces. The researchers indicated that there may be a more "hard-wired" or evolutionary reason for the difference such as the adaptive purposes of identifying and angry man (potential harm) or a happy woman (potential comfort). In addition, the difference may be driven by prominent media images displaying angry men and happy women.

Finally, we must acknowledge that most emotion studies utilize self-reports methodology. Self-report means that a respondent indicates how he/she felt after the fact (**retrospectively**). Self-report gives us a very good picture of what people believe to be true about themselves. Emotions and moods are internal states and except for moods involving high arousal which could be measured physiologically, **self-report** makes sense. However, the timing of self-reporting matters. The longer a person is away from the actual event, the larger the discrepancy between the actual and the perception of the actual. In the next section on moods, I'll give you a better feel for the difference between retrospective and prospective measures. But, to reiterate the central finding of this segment with the self-report piece more fully taken into account, mostly white male college students believe that they feel more emotion than they show, and profess no great interesting in talking about emotion.

Moods

In line with the belief that women are more emotional than men is the idea that they are moodier than men are. The central idea behind moodiness is the speed of the "up and down" or mercurial nature of changing emotions. In particular, people believe that women are likely to be "moody" during the premenstrual phase. Good research exists in this area that might surprise you a bit. First, a couple of reminders. Men show fluctuations in their hormone levels both in a 24 hour daily cycle and by the seasons. Women's hormonal fluctuations are more directly tied to their menstrual periods. As shown in 8.2, estrogen and progesterone are high during ovulation and low prior to menstruation.

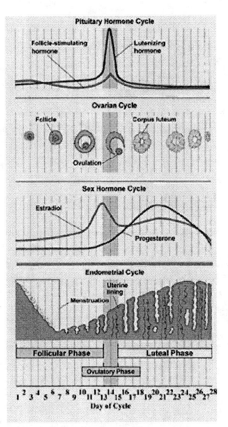

Try to think of some of the hypotheses. How about women having more fluctuation than men? Women's fluctuations being tied to their periods? How about the moon? By the way, it is the fluctuation in hormones that appears to be tied to mood changes – not the fact that it "low" or "high" but rather influx. In fact, some researchers believe that a subsection of women are just particularly sensitive to hormonal fluctuations (less than 1/3 of women). In addition to biologically based theories of mood fluctuation, there are some other theories such as the belief that moods are tied to the lunar cycles. However, we know that other systematic factors affect our moods. Students often think of non-systematic variables that, in fact, do affect our moods such as the weather. But, what is a normal cycling event? The days of the week are a "normal" cycle – Monday blues, TGIF, weekend highs, etc. Rossi and Rossi (1977) provide useful terms to capture these ideas by labeling the biologically-based cycles "body time" and the socially-based cycles "social time."

How would a researcher study the relative impact of social and body time on moods? Obviously, a researcher would need some men and women in similar circumstances – same age, occupation, etc. However, mood researchers also added in women who were on birth control pills (BCP) (McFarlane, Martin, & Williams, 1988). Birth control pills keep the levels of hormones relatively stable and at a level that "fools" the body into thinking it's pregnant. When women have a "period" with BCPs it is due to a drop in hormones; however, the absolute level is still higher

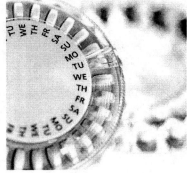

than normal-cycling women and the overall drop is very small. This chapter's "closer look at an interesting study" profiles one of these mood studies.

Box 8.1: "A closer look at an interesting study..."

Who did the study?

McFarlane, Martin, & Williams (1988)

What did they study?

They assessed the mood fluctuations as potentially linked to the menstrual cycle, lunar cycle and/or days of the week.

Who did they study?

15 women using oral contraceptives, 12 normal cycling women and 15 men. Ages ranged from 19-26, all were college students.

How did they do the study?

They had the respondents fill out daily check sheets regarding moods (prospective) for approximately 60 days. At the completion of the study they were asked to recall their average mood for each day (retrospective). In addition, women were asked to recall where they were in their menstrual cycles.

What did they find?

Women recalled having the classical menstrual mood pattern retrospectively, but prospectively did not experience it. Men and women did not differ significantly in fluctuation. Day of the week effects were strong.

What is so interesting about it?

Although this study has a small sample, it was designed in such a way to control for many previous methodological problems. The prospective and retrospective materials allow for interesting comparisons. Finally, the researchers were able to rule out some other common theories about cycling moods (e.g., the Transylvania Effect!).

Let's review the findings from this study and their other study (McFarlane & Williams, 1994).

1. In retrospect, women believed that they had the classic menstrual mood pattern (pleasant moods at ovulation and more negative moods premenstrually); however, there was almost no evidence for this pattern in the prospective tables.

2. Women were NOT moodier than men; they were as stable day-to-day or across days.

3. Cycling is the norm for both men and women. Two-thirds of the men and women showed marked positivity on days corresponding to some standard cycle (lunar, menstrual, days of the week). Researchers measured these fluctuations against each person's own normal standard deviation.

4. Both men and women showed days of the week (social time) effects. However, when comparing retrospective data to prospective data both men and women recalled the week stereotypically. Keep in mind that these participants were students so a traditional workweek model (Monday blues, weekend highs) tends to work. However, Tuesdays tend to be more blue than Mondays.

5. No support for the idea that our moods follow the moon.

6. My advice to you? Activate these stereotypes in a way that works for you. Remind the important men in your life when it is a weekend morning (testosterone is highest in the morning) and remind women when it is a weekend day when they are ovulating. Perhaps you'll get a self-fulfilling prophecy effect.

Overall, the facts support the idea that stereotypes about menstrual moods and days of the week strongly influence the memory of those moods.

Stress

Feelings contain a component of **subjective** experience. How do I feel? Subjective or individual responses to events are part of the human experience. As psychologists, we are interested in predictable patterns to these subjective experiences. Are women more likely to respond in a particular way? Men? Two areas where the subjective experience of feelings my men and women directly affect health outcomes are stress and mental disorders such as depression. We will explore both of these areas in the next sections.

Stress refers to negative emotional experiences related to a person's relationship with his/her environment (Taylor, 2003). Predictable physiological, cognitive, and behavioral changes accompany stress. Individuals vary in their reaction to stress. Normally, we think of stress in

terms of "stressors" – events in the environment that cause negative emotional experiences. Classic stressors include crowding, illness, bad relationships, deadlines, etc. Over time, we've come to understand that even "positive" events can be stressors (such as weddings or graduations). How an individual subjectively perceives the stressor affects whether it is experienced as a stressor. Personalities, perceptions, and biological constitutions all affect how individuals perceive and experience stress. In addition, we distinguish between acute stressors and chronic stressors. Acute stressors are short-term, often intense, stressors (e.g., an upcoming exam); chronic stressors are long-term, usually lower level, stressors (e.g., financial concerns, illnesses like diabetes).

"What is Stress?"

As already indicated, stress is a physiological experience. Early research focused on **"fight or flight"** responses. Organisms experience arousal in response to a perceived threat and get ready to flee (flight) or attack (fight). Although adaptive to be able to respond this way, it is physically unhealthy to be in prolonged aroused states. Selye (e.g., 1956) proposed a specific model of stress based on the fact that all stressors appeared to produce similar physiological responses and that this response leads to exhaustion (the General Adaptation Syndrome). Overall, flight-or-fight and Selye's theories are sound and have been complemented and expanded by a greater understanding of the psychological processes involved in human perception and experiencing of stress.

Two areas of stress research have indicated potential for gender differences. First, predictable gender differences could arise in the types of stressors: namely, negative events, uncontrollable events, ambiguous events, task overload, and stressful life events. Consequently, we are likely to see some gender specific patterns. For instance, men are more likely to be soldiers and therefore more likely to experience war-related post-traumatic stress disorder (PTSD). Women are more likely to be survivors of sexual trauma and more likely to have PTSD related to those experiences (Koss, Bailey, Yuan, Herrera, & Lichter, 2003). Women are also more likely to experience role overload for balancing parenting and employment because employed mothers experience more intense home obligations than do employed fathers (Jacobs & Gerson, (2004).

The second major gender differences stress theory is a new theory which examines mechanisms that men and women use to deal with stress. Taylor, Klein, Lewis, Gruenewald, Gurung, & Updegraff (2000) have advanced a theory of **"tend and befriend"** to complement "fight or flight." In this theory, individuals or organisms affiliate with one another in response to stress. They argue that this social and nurturing response is more likely to be seen in women than in men. In addition, it is preserving of self and offspring. Interestingly, there is also research suggesting that men and women respond to stress with different physiological patterns. Women are more likely to release the stress hormone oxytocin in respond to stress. Oxytocin is modulated by estrogen and therefore more likely to be modulated in women. It appears that high levels of oxytocin for men and women are related to calmer, more social behavior. The "tend and befriend" theory will need additional research; however, women are more likely than men to turn toward others in times of stress (a small effect size of .20, Tamres, Janicki, & Helgeson, 2002). Regardless of gender, unchecked stress has been linked to poor physical and mental health outcomes. Stress directly affects psychology (e.g., increased blood pressure and decreased immunity), but it also increases poor health habits (e.g., increased smoking, decreased sleeping) and it affects health behaviors (such as seeking health care).

Mental Disorders

Part of the human condition is the existence of mental disorders and mental illnesses. For this segment, we are interested in the mental disorders that show significant gender differences. Table 8.1 shows the mental disorders that show large gender discrepancies: alcohol abuse, phobias, mood disorder, generalized anxiety, and anti-social personality disorders.

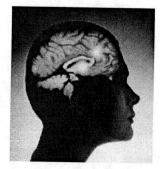

Table 8.1

Percentage of Americans who have ever experienced psychological disorders that show gender significant gender variation. Listed in order of overall population prevalence[1]

Disorder	TOTAL	Gender	
		Men	Women
Major Depressive Episode	17%	13%	21%
Alcohol Abuse with Dependence	14%	20%	8%
Phobias	11%	7%	16%
Generalized Anxiety	5%	4%	7%
Anti-Social Personality	4%	6%	1%

[1]   Kessler et al. (1994) Percentages rounded up to whole numbers for ease of comparison.

Please keep in mind that most mental disorders do *not* show gender differences in prevalence rates, including the most serious disorders of schizophrenia and bi-polar depression. We will examine each of the major areas of gender differences in mental disorders after discussing overall gender issues in the diagnosis and treatment of mental illness. For each of the areas, the primary theories regarding the difference center on gender roles, not biological sex differences.

Diagnosis and Treatment

As we look at rates and try to understand differences, we need to consider two key findings. First, mental health professionals are likely to bring gendered stereotypes to their diagnoses. Consequently, due to the view that some are more vulnerable than men, the prevalence rates of mental disorders in women may be inflated overall, or inflated for specific seemingly gender-related disorders (e.g., bulimia). Clinicians appear to be especially likely to consider gender in depression and personality disorders (Potts, Burnam, & Wells, 1991; Sprock, Crosby, & Nielsen, 2001). Race and ethnicity have been shown to influence diagnosis and treatment although the gender difference appears to stay stable in most ethnic and racial groups (Fernando, 2002; Loring & Powell, 1988). In part, these problems are exacerbated by limited information about mental health in society's subgroups and a relatively homogenous group of therapists. Fortunately, mental health professionals are taking these challenges seriously and progress is being made (McLaughlin, 2002). However, women are still proportionally more likely than men to be prescribed drugs for psychological problems (Cafferata & Meyers, 1990). Finally, individuals and their therapists might each have beliefs and notions about what constitutes good mental health based on gender.

Second, women are much more likely to talk about their symptoms and seek treatment than are men (Lin, Goering, & Offord, 1996; Moeller-Leimkuehler, 2002; Rickwood & Braithwaite, 1994). Again, this difference appears to be consistent across ethnic and racial groups and is true for physical health problems. Ciarrochi and Deane (2001) found the traditional gender difference in seeking help, but also found that, regardless of gender, individuals who were less skilled at managing emotions were less likely to ask for help and benefit from help. However, gender roles clearly influence this type of behavior for men and women. Feminine gender roles allow for acknowledging weakness and asking for help. Masculine gender roles prize independence and "walking it off." In their extremes, both roles can be detrimental. Women can be overly dependent on others (and/or medications provided by others) to help with problems and therefore less likely to believe they can do things themselves. Men can be overly anxious to mask problems with behaviors such as drinking or drugs.

Although every mental disorder is more complicated and more highly connected to multiple causes than any one theory can predict, there is a simple way of talking about these gender roles and mental disorders that I find helpful. Please accept this as a large brush stroke, not a precise idea. Several times in this book, we have seen patterns where women are more likely than men to go inwards with emotions rather than outwards (e.g. shame versus anger). The broad stroke theory suggests that while women go inwards, men go "outwards" with their feelings with behaviors such as anger and alcohol abuse. We know that men are less likely to talk about their emotions. Outward expressions allow men a way to "deal with" their emotions that fits the masculine role. We will see this general pattern of inward/outward several times as we look at some of the disorders.

Mood Disorders – Depression

Depression fits in the category of mood disorders. Classic clinical depression shows the largest gender discrepancy; women have higher rates of depression than do men. The topic of gender differences in depression has received abundant research attention. Mental health professionals consider depression as the "common cold" of mental disorders. One in five women will have a depressive episode in their lifetime and one in ten men (Kessler et al., 1994). In addition to being a prevalent disorder, depression's direct link to suicide makes it a disorder deserving of serious attention. Research on suicide itself indicates that women attempt suicide more often than men but men "succeed" four times more often than women because they use more lethal methods (e.g., a shotgun compared to pills) (National Institute of Health, 2000). Figure 8.3 shows data on suicide for European American and African American men and women. Both African American and European American men are more likely to commit suicide than women and that African American women have the lowest rates. Also, note the spike in the elderly ages for European American males.

Figure 8.3

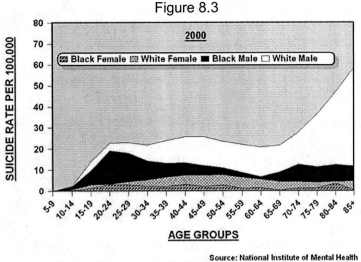

Source: National Institute of Mental Health
Data: Centers for Disease Control And Prevention, National Center For Health Statistics

Many of us have had a day or several days where we pull ourselves under our comforters, are sad, and eat cookies. Consequently, it is important to distinguish run-of-the-mill sadness from "clinical depression." Traditionally, mental health professionals indicate that an individual may wish to seek help for depression if their symptoms have lasted for over two weeks. Table 8.2 lists traditional depressive symptoms

---

Symptoms of Depression
- persistent sadness or unhappiness
- lethargy loss of interest in previously enjoyable activities
- irritability
- sudden change in appetite
- disruption of normal sleep pattern (sleeping more or less)
- physical discomfort
- difficulty thinking or concentrating
- thoughts of suicide or death

National Institute of Health (2000)

Many individuals suffering from depression have indicated that they would kill themselves if they "had had enough energy." Indeed, suicide risk is greatest for individuals coming out of a deep depression who have enough energy to enact the suicide. Famous individuals who have suffered from severe depression and/or committed suicide include rock musician Kurt Cobain, artist Georgia O'Keefe, writer Sylvia Plath, first lady Barbara Bush, and playwright Tennessee Williams (Yapko, 1998).

Why the gender differences? The causes of depression are varied and include personality, biological, genetic, and/or environmental factors. A biochemical change in the brain accompanies depression. However, as with many disorders, it is unclear whether external factors such as stress or grief cause the imbalance or if the imbalance makes a depressed person more susceptible to responding to external factors with depressive symptoms. Despite the large gender difference in incidence rates, depression for men is equally serious. The finding that men are less likely to seek treatment has spurred the National Institute of Mental Health to launch a campaign entitled "Real Men. Real Depression" (www.menanddepression.nimh.nih.gov.) that, in part, has placed posters in high traffic areas such as airports with a diverse group of photos of men with the text *"It takes courage to ask for help. These men did."* (Kersting, 2005)

Gender differences in depression emerge around the age of 15 (Nolen-Hoeksema & Girgus, 1994). It appears that girls are more likely than boys to have risk factors for depression prior to adolescence. However, these risk factors lead to depression in the face of the challenges associated with adolescence (Nolen-Hoeksema & Girgus, 1994). Research points to gender similarities and differences in the symptoms and experiencing of recurrent major. Women tend to have an earlier age-at-onset, more frequent depressive episodes, and a greater number of depressive symptoms than do men (Smith, Kyle, Forty, Cooper, Walters, Russell, et al. (2008). The American Psychological Association published a report on a summit regarding women and depression that profiled the major causes of gender differences in depression (Mazure, Keita, & Blehar, 2002). Let's first take a look at the biological factors and then the psychosocial factors.

"What is Depression?"

Biological Factors: Research implicates two major biological factors in depression – genetics and sex hormones (National Institute of Mental Health, 1995). Genetic research indicates that genes may provide a risk factor for depression. However, at this time, no specific genes have been identified and there is no known sex-related link. Sex hormone research currently provides more biological insight than does genetic research. Researchers believe that fluctuations in sex hormones during the menstrual cycle trigger biochemical changes that make women more vulnerable to mood disorders such as depression. Research supports the role of neurotransmitters in triggering depression, especially serotonin (Yapko, 1998). With all of the advertising, you may be familiar with the names of depression treatment drugs such as Prozac, Paxil, and Zoloft. All of these drugs are SSRI's which stands for selective serotonin reuptake inhibitors – they work by regulating serotonin. Current research delves more fully into the role of estrogen, progesterone and testosterone on the mood variations potentially associated with fluctuating hormones (NIMH, 1995). Animal models suggest that how stress affects estrogen may provide a useful line of research.

Psychological and Social Factors. Even in disorders with strong biological factors such as schizophrenia, biological/genetic factors at best explain approximately 50% of the occurrences (Grigorenko, 2005). Psychological and social factors play a role in all mental disorders. For depression, research has focused on life stress and trauma, interpersonal relationships, and cognitive style.

Life stress and trauma. Approximately 80% of all major depressive episodes for women are preceded by a severe negative life event (Mazure, Keita, & Blehar, 2002). Stressful life events affect both the onset of depression and the individual's experiencing of the depression (Kessler, 1997). The experience of sexual abuse as a stressor has been shown to have a direct biological link to the function of the hypothalamic-pituitary-adrenal axis (HPA). The HPA axis is a major part of the neuroendocrine system, which helps regulate various body processes such as digestion, the immune system, and energy usage. An overactivation of the HPA axis is linked to depression (and Alzheimer's and obesity) (Raber, 1998; Weiss, Longhurst, & Mazure, 1999). In addition, women are more likely than men to experience depression in response to stressful events. Social stressors more likely to be experienced by women than men include poverty, economic inequity (even if above the poverty line) and discrimination. Psychological stressors that are more likely to be experienced by women than men include childhood sexual abuse, adult sexual assault, and domestic partner violence. A review of the literature in this area suggests that at least 60% of women diagnosed with depressive illnesses had been victims of some sort of abuse (Blumenthal, 1995). Nearly all women who had experienced *severe* childhood sexual abuse developed depression later in life (Blumenthal, 1995). Recent research has honed in on some psychological mediators that affect the mental health outcomes. For instance, shame and self blame and avoidant coping strategies appear to be linked to poorer outcomes (Whiffen & Macintosh, 2005). Identifying more positive coping strategies can help mental health professionals more fully aid abuse victims.

Sexual assault has also been linked to suicide – traditionally through depression, post-traumatic stress disorder, and or increased risky behavior (Ullman, 2004). Depression and post-traumatic stress disorder are also outcomes seen in the victims of partner abuse (Campbell, 2002). Given the high probability of mental distress related to abuse and assault, researchers have called for improvement of the availability and accessibility of mental health services for those survivors who are less likely to consult the formal system (Koss, Bailey, Yuan, Herrera, & Lichter, 2003). More importantly, as a public health issue, some researchers have argued that gender differences in depression rates could be lowered by effectively decreasing violence against women.

Cognitive Style. In Chapter 7 on cognition, we saw that women were more likely than men to respond to life events in helpless and hopeless ways. Current models look at the ways in which cognitive styles mediate the repulsion between stress and depression. One of the more interesting spurs of research in this area focus on the process of "**rumination.**" Rumination involves repetitive and passive focus on the symptoms of distress. Excessive rumination results in decreased problem solving, fewer beneficial behaviors and increased depressive symptoms (Nolen-Nocksema, 1995). Women are more likely to ruminate than are men (Nolen-Nocksema, 2000).

Relationships. Another interesting strand of research analyzes the role of relationships in women's lives. Arguing that relationships are more central to women's self-concept than to men's, researchers suggest that there is a depression risk called "unmitigated communion." Women who overly respond to others stressful events tend to neglect themselves and take on the problems of others (Helgeson & Fritz, 2000).

Finally, recent research combines the focus on rumination and relationships and analyzes a process known as "co-rumination" (Byrd-Craven, Geary, Rose, & Ponzi, 2008; Calmes, & Roberts, 2008; Hyde, Mezulis, & Abramson, 2008; Jose & Brown, 2008; Nolen-Hoeksema, 2008). Co-rumination is a passive, repetitive discussion of symptoms or problems with a close other. Evidence suggests that adolescent girls engage in higher levels of co-rumination which contributes to more positive relationships but more depressive symptoms. For adolescent males, it appears to improve relationships but not affect depressive symptoms

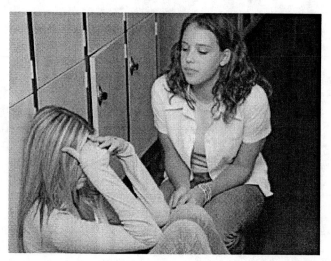

Overall, despite fascinating new insights into factors involved in depression, the reasons behind the large gender differences in depression rates needs additional research and the facts will remain complex and interrelated.

Alcoholism. Before alcoholism was added to the official list of mental disorders (the Diagnostic and Statistical Manual of Mental Disorders (current version is the DSM IV – TR, American Psychiatric Association, 2000 – new version due in 2012), the prevalence of overall mental disorders in women looked much higher. However, recognizing the psychological disorder that prompts alcoholism has helped psychologists understand both disorders and alcoholism more fully. Men are more likely to drink alcohol and more likely to abuse alcohol although women's rates for both have risen in the past several decades. Why do men abuse alcohol more than women? First, women receive more social sanctions for drinking heavily than do men and therefore may be less likely to choose alcohol as a way to "escape." When women do abuse alcohol they tend to do so at home and they are more likely to be sexual abuse survivors. Secondly, men appear to mask symptoms more with alcohol than do women. So, for instance, a male phobic may be more likely to drink to calm himself, whereas a female phobic may be more likely to present to a physician for a prescription.

"Alcoholism"

Racial and ethnic variations exist in alcoholism rates. In terms of gender, the Native American population appears to be the only subgroup where women have the same rates of alcoholism as men. A recent study also suggests that although Native American alcohol abuse rates are higher than European American rates, they appear to less so than originally thought and anecdotally reported (Spicer, Beals, Croy, Mitchell, Novins, Moore, & Spero, 2003). In large scale comparisons, European American men have higher alcohol abuse and substance abuse rates than Hispanic, Asian, African American and other minority cultural groups (Adrian, 2002; Cherpital & Borgers, 2002). Indeed, despite stereotypes regarding substance abuse in minority groups, there appears to be no basis for this belief (Adrian, 2002). Additionally, men of color who are more aligned with mainstream values appear to have higher rates of alcohol and substance abuse (Cherpital & Borgers, 2002). Mexican American individuals drink more than Mexicans but less than European Americans (Adrian, Dini, MacGregor, & Stoduto, 1995). Native American, African American, and Hispanic men are all more likely to die from alcohol related diseases than are European American men mostly due to access to health facilities.

Both gay and lesbian individuals are at higher risk for substance abuse; however, the causes of this risk appears to be entirely psychosocial and due to reactions to real and perceived rejection by society and its accompanying depression and possible self-hatred (e.g., Hughes, 2003).

Figure 8.4

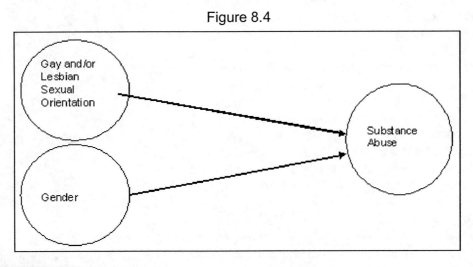

Figure 8.4 shows a situation where there is no direct relationship between gender and sexual orientation for the outcome variable of substance abuse. Men are more likely to abuse than women, and lesbian and/or gay individuals are more likely to abuse than heterosexuals. However, this is also a case where further research may yield information more like an interaction – where, for instance, gay males are more at risk than lesbian women. The research at this point does not support an interaction but does support the idea that both gender and sexual orientation are risk factors.

Anxiety and phobias. Diagnostically, clinical and counseling psychologists categorize generalized anxiety disorders and phobias in the same larger category of anxiety disorders. Generalized anxiety disorders refer chronic anxiety and exaggerated worry; whereas, phobias refer to fears of specific events or items (e.g., text anxiety, fear of flying). Both disorders show strong gender differences in prevalence. Despite the large gender differences, it is yet undetermined why they exist. Current theories focus on female reproductive hormones and their related cycles. In addition, reproductive hormones appear to influence how and when women experience their anxiety (Pigott, 1999). Certainly, there are some phobias such as agoraphobia that have a clearer connection to gender roles. Agoraphobia is the fear of being in public places from which someone feels they cannot escape. Many agoraphobics become completely homebound. Women are more likely to be agoraphobics. Women's likelihood to be stay-at-home mothers, their increased likeliness to see themselves as powerless and to be more willing to admit fears have been indicated as possible factors in the higher prevalence for women (Watkins & Lee, 1997). International data on agoraphobia provides more support for underlying biological causes that are exacerbated in certain psychosocial environments (Gater, Tansella, Korten, Tiemens, Mavreas, & Olatawura, 1998).

Eating disorders. Eating disorders involve extreme disturbances in eating behavior. Traditionally, psychologists categorize these disorders into three sets: anorexia, bulimia, and binge-eating (NIH, 2000). People who suffer from eating disorders can experience a wide range of physical health complications including minor complications like teeth, stomach and esophagus problems from vomiting as well as serious conditions, such as heart or kidney failure. Anorexia nervosa is the most serious eating disorder and one of the diagnostic guidelines involves a body weight less than 85% of the expected weight. Anorexia involves severely distorted body image and eating obsession. Anorexics tend to not eat, eat only certain foods and use the whole range of unhealthy weight control behaviors such as vomiting, pills, etc. Somewhere between .5 and 3.5% of women are expected to suffer from anorexia in their lifetimes. Bulimia involves binge eating accompanied by compensatory behavior such as vomiting, laxatives, diet pills, compulsive

exercise, etc, and approximately 1-4% of women are expected to suffer from bulimia in their lifetimes. Binge eating involves binging with no compensatory behavior (2-5% prevalence rate). Eating disorders tend to present during adolescences or early adulthood. Women are more likely to develop eating disorders than are men. Researchers estimate that for anorexia and bulimia, approximately 5-15% of the individuals are male, whereas as many as 35% of binge eaters are male (NIH, 2000). In a recent study of over 1,000 college students, 7% of total sample reported eating behaviors that would be diagnosed as an eating disorder this represented 9% of the women and 2% of the men (Donley & Vachon, 2001). As with all surveys of this type, students struggling with these issues might have been more or less likely to return the survey so the numbers have to be used with caution. However, this was a well-designed study with a large enough sample to provide less concern about sampling bias.

The causes of eating disorders are complicated and tend to be interwoven with other disorders such as depression. In addition, the onset of eating disorders at puberty suggests the potential role of gonadal hormones (McCabe & Vincent, 2003). Physiological changes may precede or stem from the psychological aspects of eating disorders. As with all psychological disorders, family variables play are role (such as criticism) as do individual issues (such as low self-esteem and need for control) (McCabe & Vincent, 2003). No *one* cause can predict eating disorders (Polivy & Herman, 2002). However, the large gender discrepancy in eating disorders causes researchers to also look more closely at social predictors (Griffiths & McCabe, 2000). Eating disorders are distinguished from some of these other disorders due to the rise in their number (which may, in part, be due to an increase in diagnosis) and its co-incidence with increased societal pressure for women to be thin (Presnell, Bearman, & Stice, 2004). Consequently, although not the only cause, media images and pressure to be thin does play "a" role in eating disorders for both men and women. In addition, when the western ideals of beauty is introduced into developing nations, there appears to be a corresponding increase in eating disorders (e.g., Wassenaar, le Grange, Winship, & Lachenicht, 2000).

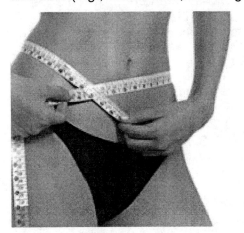

The pressure to be thin is much greater for women than men, and girls appear to have a stronger relationship between their responses to media and their body esteem (Murnen, Smolak, & Mills, 2003). In addition, cultural variations within the United States shed some light on the role of the media. Although all girls can be at risk for eating disorders, European American girls appear to have the greatest risk. Research suggests that African American girls have a wider view of ideal body shapes and value other physical attributes of beauty outside of thinness (Barry & Grilo, 2002; Perez & Joiner, 2003; Sorbara & Geliebter, 2002). Hispanic, Native, and Asian American women tend to have lower rates of eating disorders than European Americans, although not as low as African American women. Unfortunately, these rates may be increasing to become more in line with European American rates (Walcott, Pratt, & Patel, 2003). Overall, the danger appears to be in the internalization of the ideal and vastly unattainable image of beautiful women as thin (Hermes & Keel, 2003).

Personality Disorders

Personality disorders affect individuals' self-image, their ability to have successful interpersonal relationships, and range of emotion – often displaying inappropriate impulse control (Millon, 2004). Individuals with personality disorders often experience conflicts with others and others experience conflict with them. Seven major "types" of personality disorders exist. The personality disorder that yields the largest gender difference is anti-social personality disorder (Grant, et al., 2004). Table 8.3 shows the prevalence of the seven types of personality disorders by gender.

Table 8.3 Prevalence of DSM-IV Personality Disorders

	Avoidant	Dependent	Paranoid	Antisocial	Obsessive-Compulsive	Schizoid	Histrionic
Male	1.9%	.40%	3.8%	5.5%	7.9%	3.2%	1.9%
Female	2.8%	.60%	5.0%	1.9%	7.9%	3.1%	1.8%

Grant et al. (2004)

Antisocial personality disorders involve a lack of moral or ethnical sensitivity and the absence of guilt or anxiety about hurting others. Serial killers often carry this diagnosis which in common usage is called a "sociopath or psychopath." Individuals with this disorder are thoughtless and rarely have good interpersonal relationships (Millon, 2004). Thankfully, it is a rare disorder, but the gender difference of almost 3 males to 1 female gives pause regarding its cause and display. Again, gender roles appear to exacerbate this disorder. A traditional male role with its emphasis on power, domination, uncommunicativeness, competitiveness and emotional restriction nicely supports the behaviors of an individual with this disorder.

Conclusion

In this chapter, we reviewed the research on gender differences in feelings. Men and women tend to have similar emotions and moods. However, there is strong public belief in the existence of gender differences in moods. So, Ron, in our opening passage from *Harry Potter,* better represents public beliefs than empirically established differences. Women and men do appear to display their emotions differently and respond to stress differently. Finally, gender role internalization appears to be directly linked to some well-established differences in mental disorders such as alcoholism and depression.

Additional ways to think about the material in this chapter

- Think about the extent to which you (and your friends and family) display emotion. In what ways does the culture in which you were raised affect this display (or lack thereof)? What role does gender play?
- Think about the difference between men and women in terms of depression rates. How does the socialization of both men and women affect the diagnosis and experiencing of depression?

Global Connection Opportunities

- ❖ http://www.bbc.co.uk/science/humanbody/mind/articles/emotions/faceperception1.shtml
- ❖ This site describes research associated with a BBC (British Broadcasting Corporation) series regarding the human face. On the right you will see a link to "psychology tests" where you can test your own ability to read faces.

Chapter 9
Health and Sexual Behaviors

A. *Health and Lifestyle*
    1. Health Risks and Life Expectancy Rates for Men and Women
    2. Theories regarding the sex gap in health rates
B. *Sexual Attitudes and Behavior*
    1. Sexual Behavior
    2. Sexual Attitudes

U.S. Life Expectancy Data What do you notice right away?		
	Male All races	*Female All races*
At birth in 1900	*46.3*	*48.3*
At birth in 2000	*74.3*	*79.7*

This chapter is the first of three on gender-related behaviors. In this chapter, we explore health behaviors and sex and sexuality. I teamed these two topics because both involve physically related outcomes and behaviors and their links to psychological processes.

One of the more intriguing paradoxes in the field of health is that women have longer life expectancies than men but they also have more functional impairment and medical disorders throughout adulthood. At every age, men have higher mortality rates than women. The health differences between men and women are also striking given the common belief that women are the weaker and more vulnerable sex. We will first look at differences in men's and women's health risks, then we will look at life expectancy rates and theories about why women live longer. Finally, we will quickly discuss the implications of women living longer.

Health Risks and Life Expectancy for Men and Women

Obviously men and women are at risk for diseases that are related to their sex (e.g., prostate cancer for men, ovarian cancer for women). However, the differences go beyond the predictable. Men are more likely to suffer from **acute** short-term diseases whereas women are more likely to suffer from **chronic** long-term diseases. Men are more likely to die earlier from heart disease, and they die more often from the flu. Almost every autoimmune disease (diseases where the body is at some level attacking itself) has higher rates of occurrence in women. For instance, women are nine times more likely to get systemic lupus erythematosus, three to four times more likely to get rheumatoid arthritis, four times more likely to get scleroderma, and two to three times more likely to get multiple sclerosis (Foreman, 1998). In addition, due to their long life expectancy, women are more likely to develop age-related disease such as osteoporosis and osteoarthritis.

Women have higher **life expectancy** rates in all western industrialized nations. Table 9.1 shows U.S. life expectancy rates for 1900 and 2000 by gender and race. As you look at the data, consider a few key points. First, infant mortality rates affect "at birth" life expectancies – the higher the infant mortality rate, the lower the life expectancy. Second, for as long as data have been collected on this topic, women show the life expectancy advantage. In the U.S., the gap has been approximately 6 years since 1900. Third, life expectancy varies tremendously from one nation to another; Japan is in the top three (men = 78.7, women = 85.6); sub-Saharan African countries show the lowest rates, e.g., in Zambia of 42.5 for women and 42.1 for men. The World Health Organization (WHO) reports that the AIDS epidemic in Africa has drastically affected life expectancies where the averages would be expected to be in the low 60s rather

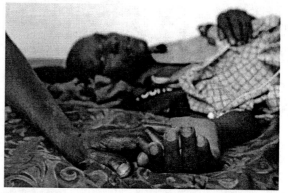

than the low 40s without AIDS. Given the longevity edge of women, national life expectancy rates that are closer together for men and women is not a good sign for women. In general, they indicate preference for male children, higher maternal deaths, and generally poorer treatment of women. Many Middle Eastern countries have similar life expectancies for men and women. For instance, in Kuwait, it is 76.4 for males and 78.73 for females (CIA, 2008). Russia shows one of the world's highest sex gaps of 73.1 for females but just 59.2 years for males.

Table 9.1
Life Expectancy Rates in 2000 by Race and Gender United States

	All races[1] both sexes	*All races male*	*All races female*	*White males*	*White females*	*Black males*	*Black females*
At birth in 1900	47.3	46.3	*48.3*	46.6	*48.7*	32.5	*33.5*
At birth in 2000	77.0	74.3	*79.7*	74.9	*80.1*	68.3	*75.2*

[1] Includes white, black and all other census races (Arias & Smith, 2003)

Before we turn to theories on the reasons for this gap, let's review the leading causes of death for men and women. Table 9.2 shows the top ten causes of death for men and women in the U.S. for 2005. Take some time with this chart. The causes rank differently for men and women. Is there something that strikes you about the causes of death for men as compared to women?

Table 9.2
Leading causes of death for all ages by sex (2005 data)

All	% of deaths	MEN (Ranking)	WOMEN (Ranking)
1. Heart Disease	34%	#1	#1
2. Cancer	30%	#2	#2
3. Cerebrovascular (Stroke)	8%	#5	#3
4. Chronic Lower Respiratory Disease (e.g., emphysema)	7%	#4	#4
5. Unintentional Injury	6%	#3	#6
6. Diabetes Mellitus	4%	#6	#7
7. Alzheimer's	4%	#10	#5
8. Influenza & Pneumonia	3%	#7	#8
9. Nephritis (Kidney Infection)	2%	#9	#9
10. Septicemia (bacterial infection of the blood)	2%	NA	#10
Suicide		#8	NA

National Center for Injury Prevention and Control (2005).
Note: Shading indicates a different ranking for men or women.

When you take a careful look at the some of the causes of death for men (but not for women) such as injury and suicide, note that men appear to participate in more risky behavior. In fact, these "lifestyle" choices are some of the major reasons behind men's lower life expectancies. Let's take a look at some of the primary theories for this gap.

Theories Regarding the Sex Gap in Life Expectancies

Researchers assert several theories to explain gender differences in longevity. Keep in mind that most of the theories involve psychologically-based arguments that involve lifestyle or behavioral choices that differ by gender.

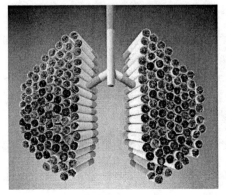

Smoking Rates. For decades men smoked at a much higher rate than women. Unfortunately, women began to catch up with men in this area. Currently 25% of adult men and 23% of adult women smoke (Centers for Disease Control, 2001). Although smoking rates are dropping overall in the United States, women's rates are dropping more slowly than men's (between 1965-1993 men's dropped 24%, women's 11%). Women are also beginning to smoke at younger ages. Smoking rates among female high school seniors increased from 18% in 1991 to 24% in 1997 whereas for teenaged men the percentage stayed fairly stable. If the trend continues, women smokers will soon outnumber men smokers even if the overall percentages for both are down.

Among racial and ethnic groups, smoking prevalence was highest among American Indians/Alaska Natives (32.7 percent: 33.5 for men and 31.7 for women) and lowest among Hispanics (16.7 percent: 21.6 for men and 11.9 for women) and Asians (12.4 percent: 18.5 for men and 6.3 for women). African Americans show rates similar to European Americans, around 23%; however, the gender gap is larger with 27.7 percent of men smoking and 17.9 for women. Note that Native Americans and European Americans are the only ethnic groups who do not show the gender gap. In addition, although Asian rates are lower overall, some Asian American groups show very high rates; female Laotians have a 42% prevalence rate (American Lung Association, 2003). For both men and women, smoking has been directly indicated in heart disease and lung cancer. Women are twice as likely as men to develop lung cancer from smoking (Senay, 2004). For women, smoking has also been linked to osteoporosis, cervical cancer, spontaneous abortions, stillbirths, premature menopause, infertility, and low birth weight babies.

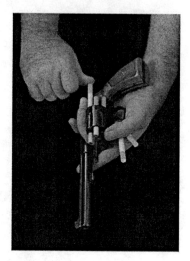

"Healthbeat – Smoking Rates"

Risky Physical Behavior. Men are more likely than women to engage in a wide variety of risky behaviors. Men abuse alcohol and illegal narcotics more than women do. Men are more likely to be homicide victims than are women. Greater access to firearms, social expectations for aggression, and peer group support for violence are the top reasons suggested for male homicide rates.

Men are also more likely to be suicide victims than are women. Men are more likely to choose more dangerous (and effective) methods for suicide such as firearms as compared to methods such as drug overdoses. In addition, men are more likely to die in car accidents than women because men are more likely to drive under the influence of alcohol and more likely to speed. In 2001, men had over twice the fatality rate in traffic accidents compared to women (28,545 compared to 13,396; US Department of Transportation, 2002). If one narrows the age range to 25-44, the top cause of mortality for men is accidents and other injuries, whereas for women it is cancer. Keep in mind that the overall death rate for this age group is still low. Finally, before we imagine that all physical risk involves large crushing metal, men are more likely to risk their health risks by not wearing seat belts, not applying sun screen, not wearing helmets, carrying weapons, eating high-fat diets, and many more.

The Later Onset of Hypertension and Coronary Artery Disease in Women. Heart disease is the number one killer of both men and women. However, men are more likely to die earlier from heart disease; women peak 10 to 20 years after menopause. Research on heart disease has employed "interesting" methodology reflecting the type of bias we discussed early in this book. Most of the major studies of heart disease, including one called "Normal Human

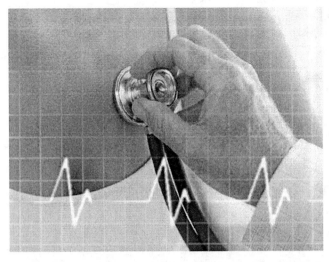

Aging" and one using 45,000+ participants, have been conducted solely with men (reviewed by Mastroianni, Faden, & Federman, 1994). Please note those dates – they are not in 1890. Keitt (2003) provides a categorization of the two camps of researchers prior to the pressure to include women "one group saw females as smaller versions of males and thus viewed the study of women as unnecessary; the other group believed that women were too complicated to study because their hormonal cycles made them difficult subjects and led to complicated data" (p. 254). After considerable lobbying, the Women's Health Equity Act passed in 1991, and more complete studies (on several health topics) have been launched (see Office of Research on Women's Health, 2003). Does it matter? In this case, the idea that "male experience=human experience" did matter. Box 9.1 indicates new findings on how heart disease shows up in women. Women exhibit a wider array of first symptoms, so health prevention materials can overlap but also need to differ for men and women. In addition, despite all the important attention and money given to breast cancer, heart disease is still the number one killer of men and women. Current clinical trials on heart disease show solid improvement regarding the inclusion of women in the studies (Keitt, 2003). Finally, in another example of the importance of including both men and women in clinical trials, a recent study found that a low dose of aspirin wards off the risk of heart attacks for men but not for women (Ridker, et. al., 2005).

Box 9.1: How and When Heart disease presents in women

Women's Experience of Heart Disease

Women...
- tend to develop heart disease ten to 15 years later than men.
- are more likely to have angina (chest pain caused by lack of oxygen to the heart) as the first symptom of cardiovascular disease (CVD). In men, the first symptom is more often a myocardial infarction, or MI (a heart attack).
- are more likely to have Prinzmetal's angina, a form of chest pain due to a spasm of a coronary artery (a major artery of the heart) rather than to blockage of the artery.
- may be more likely to delay seeking treatment when they have possible heart attack symptoms — and less likely to receive appropriate treatment when they do seek help. Women need to be aware that their heart attack symptoms may not be "typical," such as severe chest pain. Instead, symptoms may be more subtle and include fatigue, nausea, abdominal pain, "indigestion," shortness of breath or difficulty breathing, weakness, or even jaw pain.

Heart disease risk factors where women are at higher risk than men...
- who are menopausal and/or older than 55 experience rising "bad" low-density lipoprotein (LDL) cholesterol and triglyceride levels, to the point that they tend to be higher than they are in men.

- experience decreased "good" high-density lipoprotein (HDL) cholesterol levels as they get older. Fortunately, women seem to benefit as much as or even more than men from LDL cholesterol and triglyceride lowering.
- tend to have higher blood pressure than men do, especially after age 65. Like raised LDL and triglyceride levels and lowered HDL levels, high blood pressure is a risk for heart disease.
- of any age who have diabetes are more likely than men to develop heart disease. Diabetic women who have heart attacks also tend not to recover as well as men.
- may experience changing levels of cardiovascular risk with the use of hormone replacement therapy (HRT).

Women's Health Interactive (2001)

The Effects of Stress. Researchers debate the role of stress in longevity. You can imagine how easy it is to start a fight by someone arguing that either men or women have more stressful lives. Let's make it less argumentative by saying that the difference lies in the perceived stress and the body's response. As we discussed in greater depth in the prior chapter, women and men do differ in their physiological responses to stress. However, in addition, men are more likely to respond to stress with physically risky behaviors such as alcohol abuse. Finally, it is important to recognize that being an ethic minority and/or being working class or low income in the United States are technically "health risks" due to increased stress, more risky jobs, and poorer access to health care.

Social Support. Psychologists refer to the physical and psychological comfort provided by other people as "**social support**." Social support appears to buffer stress (Frazier, Tix, Klein, & Arikian, 2000), and women have larger social networks and qualitatively better social support (Porter, Marko, Schwartz, Neale, Shiffman, & Stone, 2000). Ethnic and racial variations exist in social support. For instance, Mexican Americans tend to have larger social support networks than European Americans (Gamble & Dalla, 1997), and African Americans actively involved in religious activity (which tends to enhance social support) live approximately 14 years longer than those who are not religiously active (Boldt, 1998). Why does social support reduce stress? Several factors are at play: simply being with others, increased problem-solving ("two heads better than one"), and talking out problems. All have been shown to have a positive effect on cardiovascular, hormonal, and immune systems.

Occupational Hazards. Men are much more likely to die or be maimed at work. Look back to Table 9.2, these work-related deaths are included in the "unintentional injury" category. Men numerically dominate risky fields such as fire fighting and police work. In addition, they are more likely to be employed in physically dangerous work with machinery such as construction sites and manufacturing plants. Women's work is less risky in terms of acute mortality but there are some hidden dangers. For instance, exposure to tobacco smoke can be up to five

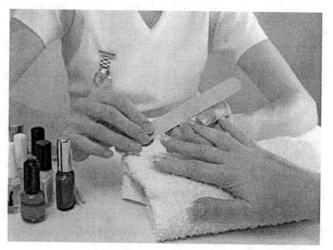

times higher in restaurants than other work places and approximately 80% of waitstaff and 53% of bartenders are female (Flagler, 2003). You may have some trouble guessing one of the more health-risky female-dominated professions. Manicurists. Recent reports suggest most manicurists are still not adequately protected from the chemicals (particularly those associated with acrylic nails) (Hukill, 1999). The chemicals used for nails have been linked to eye, skin, and lung irritations. Finally, both men and women are at risk from work situations where psychological demands are high but control or decision-making is low – these types of work situations are associated with higher stress and higher rates of heart disease (Ganster, Fox, & Dwyer, 2001).

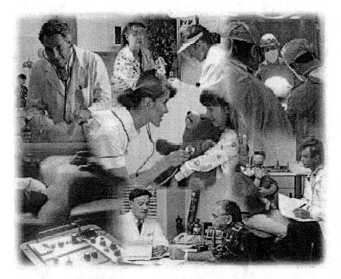

Access and Use of Health Care. As we saw in the chapter that discussed mental disorders, women are more likely to describe symptoms and seek out medical help. Masculine gender roles are associated with invulnerability and, therefore, it is not surprising that men might be less likely to acknowledge illness. Consequently, women's serious conditions are more likely to be caught earlier and treated more effectively. Gender differences in health care interactions appear to result largely because women are more likely to admit the need to seek medical advice and thus to initiate it themselves (called "self-referral"). A more serious concern appears in ethnic and racial variations in health care access. Low income Americans and people of color regardless of social class standing have less access to health care. Health care facilities are farther away and more hassle (e.g. taking a bus) to access. Furthermore, individuals without health insurance often do not get regular check-ups and/or delay presenting symptoms to a physician due to the cost of visits. Consequently, they are less likely to receive an early diagnosis and early diagnosis is associated with better prognosis. Finally, there are also cultural variations in beliefs about how often and if health care professionals should be consulted. Differences in health care access result in some horrendous statistics. For instance, African American women's breast cancer rates are similar to European American women's rates, but African American women are much more likely to die from breast cancer. African American men's prostate cancer rates are similar to European American men's rates, but African American men's death rates are much higher. Figure 9.1 shows how race may affect death rates from cancer. African Americans, in general, have lower access to health care. Then, the gender effects may come into play, such as men accessing health care less frequently than women.

Figure 9.1

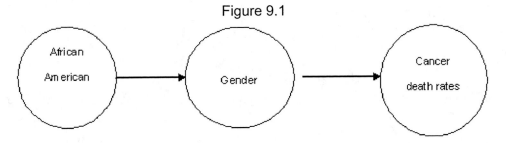

It is also important to note that despite many good strides in the past few years, the medical profession is still overwhelmingly male and European American. The fact that the medical profession is largely homogenous affects health care provider-client interactions at many levels. Again, as with mental health professionals, the medical profession is making good strides in terms of training providers and addressing treatment inequities in the system. Larger issues such as access to health care have to be debated and solved at government levels.

Overall, the key idea to take from these findings is the large number of detrimental health behaviors that are controllable and due to lifestyle factors. The masculine gender role with its emphasis on risky "macho" behavior encourages men to act in ways that are dangerous to their health. Earlier we saw that Russia had one of the widest sex gaps in the world. As a tie to the arguments made above, the most common explanation for Russia's gap is the high incidence of male alcohol abuse, which led to high rates of accidents, violence, and cardiovascular disease. Fortunately, since 1994, life expectancy has been improving for men in Russia, in part due to decreasing alcoholism rates (WHO, 2000).

Implications of Women Living Longer. Women's longer life expectancies produce several social and policy implications. First, Women are more likely to be widowed and/or live alone than are men. Second, women are more likely to live a portion of their lives needing assistance. Over 75% of the residents in nursing homes are women. Finally, women in the older cohorts are more likely to live in poverty than are men. The highest rates of poverty are found among older women of color who live alone. All of these considerations pose policy questions in regard to the role of state and federal government in funding social, economic and health care related interventions.

Sexual Attitudes and Behavior

As we saw in earlier in this book, men's and women's physical sexual structures are largely similar. For men, penile stimulation triggers the most intense arousal and for women it is the stimulation of the clitoris and the Gräfenberg spot (the "G-spot," a sensitive area on the top front segment of the vagina). Sexual arousal and sexual feelings are extraordinarily mediated by psychological and cultural influences. Although the urge to have sex and to procreate is animalistic, how we feel this urge and respond to it is very human. Consequently, sexuality shows tremendous variability. In this section, we will first examine heterosexual behavior, then childhood sexual abuse, and we will look at sexual attitudes and explore variations in sexual orientation. Finally, we will review media influences on sexual attitudes and behaviors. We will cover rape in Chapter 10 with aggression.

Sexual Behavior

Most of the research on sexual behavior is self-report. As we have seen before, self-report has its costs and benefits as a measurement tool. With sexual behavior, feminine and masculine gender roles lead to men's likeliness to exaggerate their sexual behavior and women's likeliness to diminish theirs. Although many double-standards exist in our lives, the double standard for sexuality is one of the most researched gender-based ones, and one of the strongest double-standards. For women, their behavior often gets classified into one of two very disparate categories – Virgin or Whore. We don't have much language for the vast majority of sexual behaviors that fall "in-between" these two categories. At what point does a woman become a whore? A skank? A slut? Who determines where the line is? In addition, women who choose virginity or just choose not to sleep with a particular person run the risk of being called "frigid," "cocktease," or worse. Finally, premarital sex is less acceptable for women than men. It is a no-win situation. For men, the traditional masculine role is to be a full time stud. Men are supposed to be ready and willing at any time and to pursue all potentially leads. All in all, it is clear that women are the "gatekeepers." They are the ones who set the limits and say no. Men

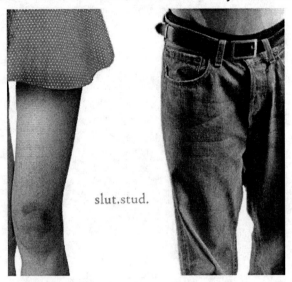

slut.stud.

try to initiate sexual activities more and devise more strategies for doing so. The double standard for sex means that the same sexual behavior performed by a man as compared to a woman will be judged very differently. Before we look at specific sexually-related behaviors, acknowledge that there appears to be very little variation across ethnic, racial, and social class groups in heterosexual behavior. Below we look at several topics that have consistently yielded reliable gender differences: sex drive, masturbation, intercourse, age at which individuals become sexually active, number of partners, fantasies, and infidelity. Then, we look at three more serious examples of gender imbalance associated with sex: sexual coercion, sexual abuse of children and prostitution.

Sex Drive. Across a wide variety of measures, men appear to have a stronger sex drive than women do (review by Baumeister, Catanese, & Vohs, 2001). Men report having more frequent thoughts about sex, more frequent sexual fantasies, more varied sexual fantasies, a higher level of desired frequency of intercourse, a higher number of desired partners, more masturbation, more preference for variation in sexual practice, less willingness to forego sex, less refusal of sex, and more initiation of sex. In addition, unlike many other gender differences, little evidence can be found that supports findings in the other direction. The authors of this review point out that these findings cannot be generalized to other important variables such as enjoyment of sex, but they bluntly conclude that "men desire sex more than women" (p. 269).

Researchers have advanced several biological theories for this higher sex drive, including the confirmed role of testosterone in both men's and women's sex drive, the newly explored role of neurological correlates, and evolutionary theory proposing that women need to be more selective and less promiscuous than men. However, psychosocial theories are involved too. Certainly, part of the masculine ideal is a high sex drive, and some men may be exaggerating its role in their life and or just enjoying and enhancing its meaning. However, researchers suggest that culture plays a stronger role in dampening women's sex drives than in enhancing men's sex drives. For instance, religiosity is linked to fewer partners and a higher age at first sexual experience for women (e.g., Seidman, Moser, & Aral, 1992).

Masturbation. A higher percentage of men masturbate than women. In addition, men masturbate more often than women. In a meta-analysis of sexual behaviors and attitudes, the gender difference in the frequency of masturbation was the largest behavioral difference established (*d* = .96; Hyde & Oliver, 2000). In college samples of single individuals, men masturbate three times more often than women (Leitenberg, Detzer, & Srebnik, 1993). In a national sample, 81% of men report having masturbated in the past year, and 72% of women (Janus & Janus, 1993). The more educated people are the more likely they are to masturbate, but we don't really know why (Laumann, Gagnon, Michael, & Michaels, 1994). In addition, African American men and women are less likely to masturbate than are European American men and women (Laumann, Gagnon, Michael, & Michaels, 1994).

Men's higher masturbation rates are more likely linked to men's higher sex drive; however, cultural and education variation suggests that gender and cultural roles also play a role. Interestingly, although women talk about most sexual matters with each other more than men do, men do talk about masturbation with each other more than women do (Park, 2002).

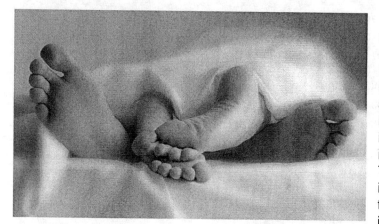

Intercourse. Research on sex is not only constrained by self-report, it also is constrained by how individuals define a variety of sexual behaviors. In general, when asking about heterosexual contact, individuals are asked about sexual intercourse (vaginal-penile), anal intercourse, and oral sex. Tremendous variability across individuals and studies exists. For this segment, we will look at when individuals become sexually active and the number of partners in heterosexual intercourse. There do not appear to be any large gender differences in the frequency of intercourse; however, there is tremendous individual variation both men and women. On average, American couples have intercourse one to three times a week in their 20s and less than that as they age (Smith, 1991). For married couples, the length of the marriage is negatively associated with intercourse frequency (meaning the honeymoon really is over!), but more happily the higher the level of marital satisfaction the higher the frequency of intercourse (Christopher & Sprecher, 2000).

Becoming Heterosexually Active. Current data suggest that by age 17 the majority of men (72%) and women (66%) have become sexually active (Mott, Fondell, Hu, Kowaleski-Jones, & Menagahn, 1996). Boys become sexually active sooner than do girls. At age 13, 15% of boys have been sexually active and 3% of girls. Despite concern about large age gaps between young female partners with older male partners, most teenagers appear to have intercourse with someone very similar in age. In the past, men's first partners tended to be a casual sex partner or a prostitute whereas women's were in committed relationships. However, both men and women now describe their first sexual partner as someone toward whom they feel emotional attachment or love (Miller, Christopherson, & King, 1993).

Number of Partners. Surveys suggest that men report a median of 8 partners across their lifetimes, whereas women report having a median of 3 (Langer, 2004). As a good reminder of how medians and means can differ (covered in Chapter 2), in this same survey, the average (mean) results were 20 for men and 6 for women. The means were higher than the medians due to a small number of individuals with a very high number of partners. When you think about it, the numbers do not add up. With whom are these heterosexual men having sex? Although some argue that it is possible that some women have an extraordinary number of partners to make up for the gap from those women having fewer, but the data do not appear to bear this out. Instead, it appears that men are over-reporting and women are underreporting. No major differences are apparent by ethnicity, race, or social class.

Infidelity. Although infidelity can occur in any relationship, most of the research focuses on marriage. In national samples, 25% of men and 16% of women report having an extramarital affair (Laumann, Gagnon, Michael, & Michaels, 1994). A strong relationship exists between permissive sexual attitudes and willingness to have an affair, a relationship that in conjunction with the double standard may help explain the gender gap in infidelity. Finally, in survey research on attitudes, gay men indicate the most accepting attitudes toward non-monogamy compared with both lesbian and heterosexual couples. Researchers also explore the role of gender in reactions to infidelity. In general, the

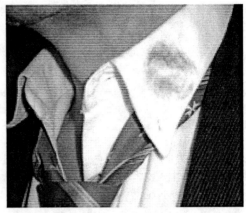

findings suggest that men are more upset by the *sexual* aspect of infidelity whereas women are more upset by the *emotional* component (Buss, Larsen, Westen, & Semmelroth, 1992; Cann, Mangum, & Wells, 2001). One study has found that heterosexual men are the most likely to be distressed by imagined sexual jealousy as compared to heterosexual women, lesbian women, and gay men (Sheets & Wolfe, 2001).

"Infidelity Basics – Dr. Sheri Meyers"

Sexual Coercion. We will discuss rape in the next chapter on aggression. Rape is primarily a crime of power and control with sex as the weapon. However, it would be incomplete to discuss sexuality without acknowledging sexual coercion or unwanted sexual actions. In research with married couples, 2-10% of women report being forced to do something sexual they did not want to (Laumann, Gagnon, Michael, & Michaels, 1994). Marital sexual coercion is highly related to other physical violence within the marriage. In one disturbing study, the monthly frequency of sex among couples where the husband was violent was 2.5 times higher than in couples with non-violent husbands (DeMaris, 1997).

Childhood Sexual Abuse. Finally, we must address childhood sexual abuse due to the gender differences in rates and in its long-lasting impact on the survivors. Fairly large variations in the prevalence numbers exist for childhood sexual abuse. Knowing the prevalence of childhood sexual abuse is important for researchers in understanding the problem and designing interventions. Differences in prevalence rates do not change the horrific facts of any one child's abuse. Several methodological factors are associated with the differences (as reviewed by Goldman & Padayachi, 2000). First, researchers obtain their data from differing sources. They may collect data from children referred to social services, from police and hospitals, or through retrospective surveys with adults who self-report childhood sexual abuse. Second, researchers vary how "childhood" is defined and how they frame the questions about abuse. Third, evidence supports both overreporting and underreporting of childhood sexual abuse. Finally, the evidence conflicts over whether there has been an increase or decrease historically in sexual abuse because social mores and reporting have both changed. With all of these caveats in mind, let's take a look at the common findings regarding childhood sexual abuse.

The most recent large scale review indicates that approximately 17% of adult women and 8% of adult men were sexually abused as children (Putnam, 2003). Girls, younger children, children with disabilities, and children with dysfunctional parents are all at higher risk for sexual abuse. *Sexual* **abuse** accounts for approximately 10% of all childhood abuse. The median age at first abuse for both men and women is approximately 10 years old (Finkelhor, Hotaling, Lewis, & Smith, 1990). For women, most of the abuse included genital contact or more severe abuse, for men it is mostly genital contact (Anderson, Martin, Mullen, Romans, & Herbison, 1993). Approximately 40% of the abuse was by a family member, 46% by an acquaintance, and the rest by strangers. Men were more likely to be abused by strangers than are women (Finkelhor, Hotaling, Lewis, & Smith, 1990). Overall, it appears that there are few racial and ethnic variations in childhood sexual abuse (Lau, McCabe, Yeh, Garland, Hough, & Landsverk, 2003; Sines, 2003). African American youth are more likely than other racial groups to be placed in foster care, but it does not appear to be from greater rates of sexual abuse at home.

The vast majority of perpetrators of sexual abuse are men. Women account for less than 20% of the abuse. Theories regarding the preponderance of male perpetrators focus on gender role socialization, in particular men's socialization to be aggressive and to link sex and aggressiveness. Furthermore, another factor may be men's reduced likelihood of confiding emotions which may leave them more likely to act on their frustrations. Finally, it is important to note that many male perpetrators are themselves young (teenagers) at the time of the abuse.

Finally, the outcomes of childhood sexual abuse are strongly documented and can be severe. Childhood sexual abuse for women has been linked to risky adult sexual behavior, alcohol abuse, depression, revictimization as adults, anxiety, and sexual dysfunction, particularly for women who received no treatment as children (Beitchman, Zucker, & Hood, 1992; Wilsnack, Wilsnack, & Kristjanson, 2004). For men, adult sexual dysfunction is the most common correlate. And, the type of sexual abuse influences the adult impact of the abuse. For instance, girls who are abused by fathers or stepfathers exhibit more symptoms. And, children who experience physical abuse in conjunction with sexual abuse and/or fear in conjunction with the abuse have poorer health outcomes (Beitchman, Zucker, & Hood, 1992). Children who report the abuse to understanding parents and/or others appear to have the best health outcomes (McCarthy, 1998).

One of psychology's concerns with childhood sexual abuse is that children have not developed the cognitive framework to understand or process the events beyond knowing they are unwanted. Overall, outside of a few cases where an older child has a consensual relationship with an older person, childhood sexual abuse is a serious social concern with a significant negative impact on individuals and our society overall. It is a problem that perpetuates additional abuse and poor physical and mental health outcomes.

Prostitution. Women are more likely to work as prostitutes than are men, and men are much more likely to hire a prostitute than are women. Factors associated with becoming a male or female prostitute include poverty, poor life prospects, school failure, tedious job, turbulent relations with family-of-origin, and physical and sexual abuse (Bullough & Bullough, 1996; Markos, Wade, & Walzman, 1994). Of course, as several researchers have noted, these conditions are merely necessary but not sufficient. If they were sufficient, we would have many more prostitutes. Most prostitutes start the profession due to contact with someone in the business. In addition, most prostitutes start the profession when they are teenagers.

Prostitution includes its own social class distinctions with practitioners who range from streetwalkers to call girls – reflecting the social distinctions in our larger society. Men who access female prostitutes do so mainly for one or more of the following reasons: sex without emotional involvement, a type of sex unavailable with their partner, frequent absences from home, a view of sex as only appropriate with '"bad girls," and problems that preclude them from finding partners (Freund, Lee, & Leonard, 1991). Most male prostitutes' clients are men – many of whom do not consider themselves gay. Male prostitutes are less likely than female prostitutes to have "pimps" or business managers. In one study of 224 male prostitutes, 47% self-identified as heterosexual, another 18% as homosexual, and 36% as bisexual (Boles & Elifson, 1994).

Prostitution is a dangerous job in terms of both violence and disease. Health professionals are now calling upon their own profession to seriously address the risks of sex workers nationally and internationally. Calling upon their colleagues to put aside their moralistic responses and focus on the "conditions of sex work" instead of the nature of the work, Wolffers and van Beelen (2003), suggest that focus must be placed on "vulnerable work situations with violent, non-paying clients in unprotected places; and lack of protection by police and legal systems" (p. 1981). Overall, the causes and correlates of prostitution are a microcosm of society's view of the relationship between gender and sex. Box 8.2 highlights this issue with our "Closer look at an interesting study…" on suicide risk among teen streetwalkers.

Box 8.2 A closer look at an interesting study...

Who did the study?

> Kidd & Kral (2002).

What did they study?

> Suicide experiences in street youth – most of whom were involved in sex trade.

Who did they study?

> Twenty-nine street youths from downtown Toronto - 10 males, 19 females. In order to be interviewed, respondents must have been 1) under the age of 24, 2) out of their parents' home for at least one week and on the street.

How did they do the study?

> They conducted semi-structured interviews with the respondents who were found through outreach programs and through referral to others from those being interviewed. A semi-structured interview means there are set questions such as "If it is all right, we will talk about suicide now. You can tell me about a person you know who has committed suicide, and if you want you can tell me about your own experiences with suicide," but also plenty of freedom to follow up on the threads of the conversation.

What did they find?

> Approximately 76% had attempted suicide. Suicide thoughts and attempts appear to be connected primarily to feelings of low self-worth, isolation, lack of control, and rejection. Most of the youth reported childhood abuse at home (52% physical abuse, 44% sexual abuse – a respondent could re represented in both categories).

Most of the studies we've looked at in this book have been quantitative. This study reflects the benefits of qualitative research. My own view is that these two types of research, quantitative and qualitative, are best considered next to each other. Both complete a side of the story that the other cannot. As you read the quote below, note the type of richness a researcher can get from a qualitative interview. Keep in mind that the quantitative data can help contextualize this type of quote to help us understand if this type of experience is normative or unique. Unfortunately, we know that this woman's experience is normative for kids on the street.

"Home was my dad molesting me and my mom on coke. And my dad leaving and my mom's boyfriends molesting me and my mom on coke. Same trip. I used to get beat a lot when I was a kid. I had a lot of suicidal tendencies, if that's what you're looking for. Home was rough. Home was poor. My mom was bringing tricks home and stuff and shit and fucking up big time. I don't know... it was pretty rough so I went to the streets and then I started prostituting. I was eleven and a half when I started selling myself. That was rough. I got raped a couple of times. I got stitches in my pussy, 37 of them to be exact, from a knife. I hung myself when I was thirteen. I hung myself three times in a year. I don't know... the rest was just junk [heroin]. I used to do heroin and cocaine a lot, but I quit because I overdosed too many times p. 419."

Before we examine gender differences in sexual attitudes, Table 9.3 provides a summary of the material on sexual behavior covered in the previous sections.

Table 9.3: Summary of gender differences in sexual behavior

Sexual Behavior	Women	Men
Sex drive		Higher sex drive
Masturbation		Higher frequency of masturbation
Age at which individuals become sexually active	Become sexually active later than do boys	
Number of partners	Average ~ 3	Average ~ 12
Infidelity	16% of married women	25% of married men
Sexual coercion	More likely to be forced to do something sexual against their will	
Sexual abuse as children	~17% of girls	~8% of boys More likely to be perpetrators
Prostitution	More likely to work as prostitutes	More likely to hire prostitutes (of either sex)

Sexual Attitudes

Attitudes toward Sexual Behavior. Over the last few decades, both men and women have become more liberal in their sexual attitudes. However, gender differences exist on some attitudinal dimensions. Men separate love and sex more than do women (Hendrick & Hendrick,

1995). Men are more likely than women to view love as a "game" and as a game to be played with many partners. However, this latter view is fairly rare for both sexes. Women appear to do more "love planning" and are more likely to view each partner as a potential long-term partner.

One of the more common measurements of sexual attitudes is the extent to which people view sex outside of marriage as wrong. In general, men hold more liberal attitudes than women toward premarital sex and older individuals hold more conservative views than younger individuals. In a meta-analysis of sexual attitudes, the gender difference in the view of premarital sex in a casual relationship was the largest attitudinal difference established (d = .81; Hyde & Oliver, 2000). The researchers found a medium-sized effect when the premarital sex was

between committed or engaged individuals, with men still being more liberal than females (d = .49 and .43 respectively). For instance, Werner-Wilson (2001) measured over 1000 high schoolers' attitudes by asking "What is your attitude about teenagers having full sexual relations (sexual intercourse) before marriage?" Responses ranged from 1 (always wrong) to 5 (always right). Male students averaged a score of 2.51; whereas female students averaged 1.15. As would be expected, the men were also more likely to have experienced intercourse.

One set of findings indicates that young men perceive more pressure to have intercourse than do women. These findings fit with other research that supports the idea the men and women follow a type of "sexual script" when they are in sexual situations. A sexual script is an unwritten set of rules and guidelines about how to act which include the idea that men are supposed to push for sex, whereas women are supposed to resist – in part to protect the reputations of both parties.

Table 9.4 shows data from a national representative survey of 15-24 year-olds (Kaiser Family Foundation, 2003). European Americans are more likely than all the other ethnic and racial groups to report that they feel pressure to have sex again once a relationship has become sexual. In addition, African American and Latino youth report that abstinence is less realistic than do other groups. However, in general, the data suggest gender, racial, and ethnic similarity.

Table 9.4: Percent of young adults who strongly or somewhat agree with the sexual attitude statements (Kaiser Family Foundation, 2003).

| | Gender | | Racial and Ethnic Group | | | |
	Men	Women	European American	African American	Latino American	Asian American
If you have been seeing someone for a while, it is expected that you will have sex	55%	38%	47%	49%	40%	42%
There is pressure to have sex by a certain age	61%	54%	57%	61%	57%	54%
Once you have had sex it is harder to say no the next time	62%	48%	61%	45%	46%	47%
Waiting to have sex is a nice idea but nobody really does it	64%	60%	59%	71%	66%	54%

Overall, the research on sexual attitudes suggests similarity between men and women and a general liberalization of attitudes over time. When gender differences are found, men tend to be more "liberal." For instance, the most consistent gender difference in sexual attitudes is the extent to which individuals endorse premarital sex. Men are much more likely to view premarital sex as acceptable. Indeed, as we saw with in the section on sexual behavior, their actions parallel these attitudes.

Variation in Sexual Orientation. As with many of the topics we've discussed, there is large variation in the sexual behaviors of individuals. Despite human interest in having tidy categories, sexual orientation also shows variability. Terms such as heterosexual, homosexual, and bisexual cannot adequately convey the variation. In fact, many have argued that the best way to think about sexual orientation is as a continuum with one end anchored with "exclusively homosexual" and the other end "exclusively heterosexual." Figure 8.2 shows an example of this logic using a six point scale.

Figure 9.2: The Kinsey Continuum

0	1	2	3	4	5	6
Exclusively heterosexual behavior	Primarily heterosexual, but incident of homosexual behavior	Primarily heterosexual but more than incidental homosexual behavior	Equal amounts of heterosexual and homosexual behavior	Primarily homosexual but more than incidental heterosexual behavior	Primarily homosexual, but incidents of heterosexual behavior	Exclusively homosexual behavior

The Kinsey Institute for Research in Sex, Gender and Reproduction *(2003)*

This is a continuum of *behavior*. Think about how much more varied it would be if thoughts and fantasies were measured. In general, comparing several types of surveys, it appears that 4-6% of men and 2-4% of women are predominantly homosexual for a major part of their lives (e.g., Le Vay, 1996). A much larger portion of the population falls into one or another of the Kinsey categories 1 through 5. For instance, up to 20% of men and 17% of women in the U.S. have reported homosexual behavior (Sell, Wells, & Wypij, 1995). In addition, it is simplistic to portray relationships as the result of our biological urges. Who we fall in love with at any given time is more complicated than any original biological tendency (Diamond, 2003).

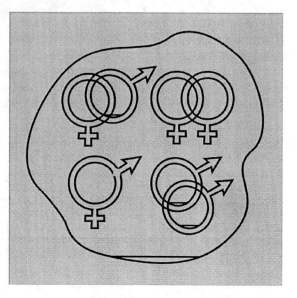

How does gender enter into our discussion of sexual orientation? Recall our early distinction between gender identity and biological sex? These same shades of gray enter into the discussion of gender and sexual orientation – as do gender roles. Research on men and women and sexual orientation yield few consistent themes because the findings rely on individuals' self-definitions. Self-reporting in sexual behavior is always inaccurate to some degree, but self reports regarding sexual variation are even more likely to be influenced by cultural and social expectations. However, gender role differences appear in some arenas, and they reflect the different socializations with which we are now familiar. Women, regardless of sexual orientation, rank emotional expressiveness and equality in their love relationships as more important than do either gay or straight men. In addition, other gender role differences play out in the type of sexual behavior and number of partners. In general, lesbian women have longer lasting relationships and fewer partners, whereas gay men have more partners and shorter-term relationships. Gay men are also more likely to find partners in bars and cruising than are lesbians (for reviews Elze, 2002; Fisher & Akman, 2002). Although this is not a text on human sexuality, I must assert that research clearly suggests that, as a group, homosexual individuals are psychologically "normal" and any maladjustment to homosexuality most often stems from the discrimination and social views against lesbians and gays. In terms of relationships and sexual satisfaction, gay and lesbian couples report levels similar to those of heterosexual couples (Kurdek, 1991).

Media and Sexual Behavior. As a review from Chapter 5 on gender expectations, recall that media is very sexualized. Both men and women are encouraged to be sexual. Specific images are associated with specific media. For instance, rock videos are aimed at adolescent men and show women as ready and willing at any time.

Pornography shows distinct gender differences. For the purposes of this book, we will look at consumption patterns and the effects of pornography, but before we do that we need to define the terms. Oftentimes, people use the term pornography to refer to sexual material that is *not* acceptable to them as the viewers, whereas they use the term "erotica" to refer to sexual material that is acceptable to them (e.g., Allgeier & Allgeier, 2000). Of course, what happens when these two views collide? What if one person finds images of children in sexual positions

arousing and acceptable and another does not? Table 9.4 shows a definition of pornography put forward by two of the foremost feminist writers on the topic of pornography. Read it carefully. If and how individuals, communities, and societies chose to define pornography reflects a myriad of complicated social and legal issues.

Table 9.4

Catharine Mackinnon's and Andrea Dworkin's statutory definition of pornography (from the Indianapolis ordinance at issue in American Booksellers, Inc. v. Hudnut)

"Pornography" under the ordinance is "the graphic sexually explicit subordination of women, whether in pictures or in words, that also includes one or more of the following:

(1) Women are presented as sexual objects who enjoy pain or humiliation; or

(2) Women are presented as sexual objects who experience sexual pleasure in being raped; or

(3) Women are presented as sexual objects tied up or cut up or mutilated or bruised or physically hurt, or as dismembered or truncated or fragmented or severed into body parts; or

(4) Women are presented as being penetrated by objects or animals; or

(5) Women are presented in scenarios of degradation, injury abasement, torture, shown as filthy or inferior, bleeding, bruised, or hurt in a context that makes these conditions sexual; or

(6) Women are presented as sexual objects for domination, conquest, violation, exploitation, possession, or use, or through postures or positions of servility or submission or display."

Indianapolis Code § 16-3(q).

The statute provides that the "use of men, children, or transsexuals in the place of women in paragraphs (1) through (6) above shall also constitute pornography under this section."

In contrast to the erotica/pornography definition offered above, I prefer the distinctions made by Fisher and Barak (2001) where "erotica" indicates non-violent consensual sex, "degrading pornography" indicates images that degrade women, and "violent pornography" where violence and sex are intricately linked. However, each of these categories requires a judgment call, so for this section, we will *in*accurately use pornography as a generic term for sexually explicit material.

Although the numbers of women customers is growing, most pornography consumers are heterosexual men (Adult Video News, 1998). In a representative sample, 23% of men and 11% of women reported having watched X-rated movies (Laumann, Gagnon, Michael, & Michaels, 1994). In addition, one percent of men and no women reported using "dial-a-porn" telephone sex. In a college sample, men indicated an average of 6 hours of X-rated material per month, whereas women reported 2½ hours per month (Padgett, Brislin-Slutz, & Neal, 1989) – these are averages across all the students so they include individuals who answered zero. The amount of pornography on the internet has grown quickly and allows the consumer both privacy and easier access to those who share atypical interests (e.g. bestiality). Not surprisingly, viewers of internet pornography think that it has a greater negative influence on others than on themselves. Interestingly, women view internet pornography as having a stronger influence on men than other forms of pornography, and women are more likely to support restrictions on pornography (Lo & Wei, 2002).

"A Drug Called Pornography"

Analyses of the images on the internet reveal consistent themes. An analysis of the images on 31 free internet porn sites found that much of the imagery involved the theme of women as victims where the perpetrator was not shown (Gossett & Byrne, 2002). In another analysis of images, the common themes were close-ups, erect penises, fetishes, and masturbation (Mehta & Plaza, 1997). In a larger study of 9,800 images (Mehta, 2001), approximately 20% of the images involved children or adolescents (a similar percentage was found in a study with by Rimm, 1995, with a more questionable methodology). In general, it is the degradation of women and children that raises the largest level of concern. Although some scholars have overstated the direct link between the consumption of pornography and actual sexual actions, there are still many reasons to be concerned about the images contained within pornography and the consumption rates. Below I've summarized the major ideas and concerns as supported by empirical research (drawn from the review by Fisher & Barak, 2001). First, despite the prevalence of pornography, the majority of men do not choose to access it and choose the less

violent and degrading options when given a choice (see Bogaert, 2001). There exists a subset of men with violent sexual histories who seek out sexual stimuli of the violent nature. Second, men are more likely to access pornography than women. However, there are very few individual predictors of "which" men are more likely to do so. In general, previous use of pornographic materials best predicts current use of materials.

Finally, there is no evidence to suggest that pornography "causes" rape. However, sometimes in their zeal to respond to this erroneous charge, researchers such as Fisher and Barak (2001) gloss other findings associated with continued exposure to pornography. Most notably, pornography endorses and promotes the "rape myth" that suggests that women actually "want" to be forced to have sex. It corresponds to the idea that women say "no" but mean "yes," and the images in pornography often show women responding favorably to a rape. Empirical studies of pornography consumption support the idea that viewers of pornography become more willing to endorse the rape myth and more callous toward the objectification of women. These findings are particularly strong when violent pornography is studied and is evident in both short- and long-term effects. In addition, people who view pornography are also more likely to be discontented with the appearance of their intimate partner and marital values. Some of the more famous studies of the effects of pornography include Malamuth & Donnerstein (1984), and Zillmann and Bryant (1988). Violent pornography portrays women as willing victims and men as enjoying the infliction of pain – images that are flattering to neither gender. If you'd allow me an editorial note, the fact that research does not support a direct link between rape and pornography is NOT a reason to be less concerned about violent pornography. Rather, the research allows us to focus on what we should be worried about, exposure to material that dehumanizes.

Overall, this chapter has focused on health and sex related behaviors that are heavily mediated by psychosocial influences. The gender differences apparent in these fields can be directly linked to common views of stereotypical masculine and feminine behavior. In the next chapter, we will look at aggression and helping behavior, other human behaviors highly affected by gender stereotypes.

Additional ways to think about the material in this chapter

- Think about the last woman and man you knew who died. What was the cause of death? How well does this individual's life fit with the research on this topic?

Global Connection Opportunities
- *https://www.cia.gov/library/publications/the-world-factbook/fields/2102.html*
- *This site leads to the World Fact book and this particular URL is to life expectancy rates. Spend some time thinking about*

Chapter 10
Hurting and Helping Behaviors

A. *Aggression*
   1. *What are the gender differences in aggression?*
   2. *What is aggression?*
   3. *Gender differences in aggression across the lifespan*
   4. *Causes of aggression*
B. *Violence*
   1. *Rape*
   2. *Domestic Abuse*
C. *Pro-social behavior*
   1. *Empathy*
   2. *Helping*
   3. *Nurturing*

Dear Annie: I am 22 years old and engaged to "Jared," a wonderful man. The problem is that I have been taking my anger out on him physically. I realize that it is not right to hit a person, especially someone you love, but I cannot seem to stop doing it. I know if it were the other way around, if Jared were being physically abusive to me, I would leave him in a heartbeat.

You've done a few columns about women who abuse the men in their lives, so I hope you can help me. Jared has said, "If you hit me again, it's over," but he stays. I keep promising to do better, but I always wind up hurting him anyway.

I admit we both have a drinking problem. Although the abuse usually happens when one or both of us are drinking, the truth is, I sometimes hit him when I am perfectly sober. I once hit him so hard that I broke my hand in the process.

Lately, I have been trying hard to cut back on my alcohol consumption, and I've been doing very well. I am proud of myself for that. However, being sober means I'm more aware of how much Jared drinks. He has no intention of doing anything about it, which of course makes me really angry.

I feel such guilt and pain about hurting him. I do sincerely love Jared, and I want to stop the abuse because I would hate to lose him. Can you help me figure this out? -- Abusive and Engaged

Dear Abusive: Hitting so hard that you break your hand means you are way out of control. It's good that you recognize the problem and truly want to stop. Now, you need to take responsibility for your actions and develop new strategies for dealing with your anger and hostility. Please do not finalize your marriage plans. You and Jared need time to work on the abuse and alcohol problems before you make your destructive relationship legally binding. Couples counseling may help get you started.

There are support groups for abusers, and although they are mostly for men, you could also benefit. To find out if there is one in your area, contact the National Domestic Violence Hotline at 1-800-799-SAFE (1-800-799-7233) (ndvh.org) for assistance and information.

Annie's Mailbox is written by Kathy Mitchell and Marcy Sugar – item ran SUNDAY, OCTOBER 5, 2003.

In this chapter we will explore behaviors that attempt to harm (aggression) and behaviors that attempt to help (prosocial behaviors).

Aggression

Did it surprise you that the person writing the letter at the beginning of this chapter was female? Why? One of the reasons may be that the masculine gender role intricately links with aggressive behavior. Another reason is that men are much more likely to cause physical harm to others than are women. In this section we will explore gender differences in aggression. We will conclude with the gender differences in the forms of aggression that impact the lives of men and women most fully – domestic violence and sexual abuse.

What Are The Gender Differences In Aggression?

Generally stated, men are more aggressive than women. For instance, if we look at crime statistics, men are overwhelmingly more violent than women. Men committed over 85% of the murders from 1960-1990, and men are much more likely to be involved in assaults, armed robberies, and rape (Daly & Wilson, 1988). Both men and women are more likely to be killed or assaulted by men. Although more women commit more violent crimes than ever before, men are still the primary perpetrators of crime (Bureau of Justice Statistics, 2003). Although the evidence that men are more aggressive than women is compelling when analyzing violent crime, looking at aggression across a variety of contexts gives us a better sense of the gender dimension.

What Is Aggression?

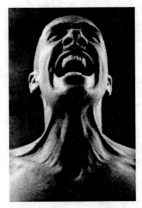

Aggression refers to behavior intended to harm. Psychologists distinguish between "hostile" aggression and "instrumental" aggression. Hostile aggression is an end in itself. A person aggresses against another in order to cause them harm. Instrumental aggression is a means to an end. In this case, the person aggresses in order to get something (Strube, Turner, Cerro, Stevens & Hinchey, 1984). A classic example of the latter is a child who bonks another child over the head to gain a toy. Researchers studying aggression pay attention to a combination of factors including environmental (frustration, heat, crowding, alcohol) and personality (Type A, hostile, narcissistic) variables. Evidence supports the idea that humans contain some innate (inborn) motives towards aggression. Humans can respond to threats with aggression as well as compete for resources with aggression. Of course, as with many human characteristics, aggressive behavior varies tremendously across individuals and cultures.

Measuring aggression is not easy and as you will see as we look at the research, much of the variation in the studies comes from differing measures of aggression. To further compound the problem, few studies exist which assess the several measures found to be related to aggression in one population. Consequently, we rarely know the relationship between forms and manifestations of aggression. Think about a time that someone has hurt you. How did they do so? I suspect that many of you can come up with examples that show why aggression is complicated to study. Namely, aggression need not be physical. You can hurt someone in a variety of ways. Let's take a look at some variation in measures of aggression that yield different patterns of gender differences.

Provocation. One of the key factors behind aggression is provocation. Both men and women respond to perceived threats and or acts of aggression with aggression. Aggression that produces pain or physical injury receives a more physically aggressive response from men than women (Eagly & Steffen, 1986). In a meta-analysis, Bettencourt and Miller (1996) found additional evidence that the types of factors that provoked men and women varied by gender. For instance, men are much more likely to respond with various forms of aggression than women to suggestions that they are intellectually incompetent. In fact, the authors suggest that these differences in reactions to provocations may help explain the overall difference in aggression. Related to this idea is the fact that men more readily feel provoked or offended than do women. Campbell (1993) found that men are more likely to see a

variety of events as a threat to their personal identity – a theme that was almost absent in the women's reports. Campbell also suggests that men and women describe their own aggression differently. Women describe their anger as an *expression of emotion* whereas for men describe their aggression as *feeling more in control* (even if they are acting out of control).

Physical and verbal aggression. As we have seen, men are more physically aggressive than women; however, the number of physically aggressive acts gives a very lopsided image of aggression among and between men and women. Researchers found that when they measured both physical and verbal aggression the image of aggression changed. First, when both types of aggression are measured in children, the gender difference in the number of incidences disappears or is dramatically reduced. Second, it originally appeared that girls used verbal aggression more than boys, and boys used physical aggression more than girls (Archer, Pearson, & Westeman, 1988; McCabe & Lipscomb, 1988). While it is true that the overall number of incidences is much closer if all types of aggression are measured, newer research that distinguishes between verbal and indirect aggression finds a more carefully delineated gender difference.

Direct vs. indirect aggression. Researchers now distinguish between direct and indirect aggression. Direct aggressions are actions aimed at the target and clearly coming from the aggressor, and indirect aggressions are actions that allow the aggressor to conceal his/her identity. Bjorkqvist, Lagerspetz, and Kaukiainen (1992) provide a more complete list used in research with children, shown below. As you read these categories, keep in mind the "intent to hurt" component of aggression. I need not tell you that these behaviors can/do hurt.

Direct Physical Aggression:
* hits, kicks, trips, shoves, takes things, pushes, and pulls.

Direct verbal aggression:
* yells, insults, says he/she is going to hurt the other, calls the other names, and teases.

Indirect aggression:
- shuts the other person out of the group, becomes friends with another as a revenge, ignores, gossips, tells bad or false stories, plans secretly to bother the other, says bad things behind the other's back, says to others "Let's not be with him/her," tells the person's secrets to a third person, writes notes in which the other person is criticized, criticizes the other person's hair or clothing, and tries to get others to dislike the person.

As you might suspect, men are more likely to engage in direct aggression as compared to women. In addition, women are more likely to engage in indirect aggression. Men use indirect aggression the least. Men's aggression patterns indicate the most use of verbal aggression, followed by physical aggression, with indirect aggression as a distant third. These gender patterns hold up across cultures and ages (Oesterman, Bjoerkqvist, Lagerspetz, Kaukiainen, Landau, Fraczek, & Caprara, 1998). To help you get a feeling for the magnitude of these differences in one study of youth, boys were seven times more likely than girls to use physical aggression and twice as likely to use verbal aggression (as measured by peer ratings). On the other hand, girls were twice as likely as boys to use indirect aggression (Salmivalli, Kaukiainen, & Lagerspetz, 2000). As you think about these differences, remember that women are more acutely aware of the potential repercussions of their aggressive behavior. Doesn't it make sense that women might lean toward aggressive behaviors that allow their identities to be masked?

In a study of adolescents, Salmivalli, Kaukiainen, and Lagerspetz (2000) found that social rejection was highly correlated with aggressive responses for both boys and girls. In other words, peers choose to reject someone who is aggressive and/or rejection from the group may lead to more aggression. In addition, they found that individuals who were aggressive tended to be aggressive in both direct and indirect ways. However, they also found that indirect aggression was positively related to acceptance for boys but not for girls, and they found that social status affected both the use and perception of aggression. For instance, a popular person may be able to use indirect aggression to his/her benefit whereas a person with less status could not. Green, Richardson, and Lago (1996) found that males with strong social networks reported more indirect aggression than direct aggression – interestingly, this social network difference was not related to type of aggression in women. These studies give examples of the subtle and complex measures that are needed in aggression research; although they will yield complicated results!

Gender Differences in Aggression across the Lifespan

As with any gender difference in adulthood, researchers look toward childhood to see when the difference shows up. Again, the definition of aggression plays an important role. Keep in mind that the "intent to hurt" is a different motive than rambunctiousness. One classic study in this area distinguished between physically aggressive behavior, level of physical activity, and

level of "rough-and-tumble" play (DiPietro, 1981). Rough-and-tumble (R & T) play is non-aggressive but high contact play. The researchers traveled around in a mobile laboratory containing a trampoline and a beach ball and watched either boys or girls play in same-sex trios. They only found a difference in R & T play, not in activity level. Simply put, although girls were as likely to jump vigorously on the trampoline, boys are more likely to jump on top of someone as part of playing on the trampoline! In their study, boys showed more physical aggression but the difference was not statistically significant perhaps because there were so few incidences.

When looking at the role of parents in R & T play, fathers are more likely to engage in R & T with their children than mothers (Paquette, Carbonneau, Dubeau, Bigras, & Tremblay, 2003). Interestingly, the age and sex of the child are larger determinants of parent-child R &T than other factors such as the socio-economic status of the family. The amount of time children spend in R & T play declines over time. Researchers suggest that R &T allows for the development of a variety of social skills, including dominance. Of course, the need to dominate can get out of hand. Finally, Paquette, Carbonneau, Dubeau, Bigras, and Tremblay (2003) found a small relationship between rough and tumble play and physical aggression for boys but not for girls, a finding that should encourage some additional research on this topic.

Like rough and tumble play, incidences of physical aggression decline with age. In fact, unless you've worked with toddlers, it may surprise you to know that the incidence of physical aggression is highest at age 2 and decreases throughout the school years. The gender difference in physical aggression is also the largest at younger ages (Hyde, 1984; Paquette, Carbonneau, Dubeau, Bigras, & Tremblay, 2003). Cross-cultural evidence suggests that the use of verbal aggression surpasses the use of physical aggression by the age of 15 (Bjoerkqvist, Lagerspetz, Kaukiainen, Landau, Fraczek, Caprara, 1998; Oesterman, et al., 1998). Both cross-cultural and international data support boys' more aggressive tendencies. Some evidence exists that gender differences in aggression can be due to a small number of boys who exhibit a greater amount of extreme behavior (Hyde, 1984). Finally, in a sample of older Americans (ages 55-89), indirect forms of aggression were more common than direct (Walker, Richardson, & Green, (2000). Overall, male-on-male aggression is the most common aggression, followed by male-on-female, and ending with female-on-female. In addition, male-to-male aggression is more likely to involve two strangers, where male-to-female aggression is more likely to be between intimates (Hilton, Harris, & Rice, 2000).

Causes of Aggression

Biological Factors. Biological factors are clearly involved in aggression. We know that for both men and women, the amygdala is involved in physically aggressive behavior, and we also know that testosterone is correlated with physical aggression. We know from animal studies that electrically stimulating the amygdala results in aggressive behavior and that animals responding to aggressive stimuli show higher activity levels in the amygdala. Furthermore, lesions on the amygdala can yield excessively tame animals, and epileptic seizures affecting the amygdala can result in aggressive

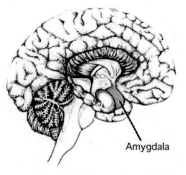

Amygdala

behavior. However, although the amygdala plays a role, the causal connection is not directly clear for humans, and there is no reason to suspect a gender difference. Testosterone, on the other hand, provides us with some correlational evidence. For instance, as we've seen, men are more physically violent and have higher testosterone levels. In addition, athletes using steroids have higher levels of aggression than athletes not using steroids (steroids convert to testosterone). However, these studies are correlational; the more aggressive athletes may lean toward steroid use.

Other fascinating studies include studies that measure athletes before and after games. Usually, testosterone rises immediately prior to a match, is higher after a match, and is higher after a win than a loss (e.g., Booth, Shelley, Mazur, Tharp, & Kittok, 1989). In animal studies, castrated male rats injected with testosterone become more aggressive, as do female rats injected with testosterone. However, to make it all more complicated, researchers have also linked testosterone to positive outcomes (such as helping) and they have found high estrogen (not just high testosterone) to be related to elevated aggression. Overall, reviews suggest that testosterone has a small but consistent correlation with aggression, but is far from being the definitive factor in explaining the gender differences in human aggression (e.g., Book, Starzyk, & Quinsey, 2001; Harris, 1999). Finally, there is growing evidence that if a hormone-aggression link is found, it is probably due to hormonal differences set prenatally at the time of brain hormonal organization rather than at hormone activation time such as puberty (Ramirez, 2003).

Evolutionary Theory. Evolutionary theorists argue that male aggression arises from their need to attract female mates (Laland & Brown, 2002). Evolutionary theorists tend to see aggression as instrumental in mating or attaining food. However, critics of the theory particularly challenge the idea that men are aggressive for women. Fischer and Mosquera (2001) argue that empirical and ethnographic evidence from humans indicate that men's aggression is more likely to aim at gaining respect from their fellow man more than at gaining attention from a female mate. Evolutionary theorists also tend to ignore data on mothers' aggression. If someone has warned you not to come between a mother bear and her cubs (or any mother and her young), take it seriously! Some of the most physically aggressive behavior in the animal kingdom comes from mothers protecting their young. Human research on this topic would be interesting, although difficult and ethically questionable to create a realistic scenario in which to test humans.

Socio-Cultural Factors. As with almost all of the behaviors we've looked at, situational and context variables greatly affect aggressive behavior. Both men and women are aware of the expectations for them within a wide range of situations. As we saw with sexual behavior, gendered expectations can act to enhance or diminish behaviors. Research on the socio-cultural factors involved in aggression focus on aggression and dominance as part of the masculine role and the lack of aggression and subordination as part of the feminine role. Consequently, we find support for socio-cultural views in the research explored below that finds evidence of social support for men's aggression and social sanctions against women's aggression.

Social Support for Men's Aggression. As indicated earlier in this book, the masculine gender role involves many dimensions, including strength, holding one's ground, and independence. Aggression is one potential avenue for demonstrating those traits. Boys are often taught how to fight, along with when to turn the other cheek. Peers will tease both boys and fathers who walk away from a fight. Society often reacts poorly to men who reject military service, such as conscientious objectors – they are looked upon with suspicion and portrayed as wimps (D'Emilio, 2003). Even if we don't directly say "Be aggressive" to men, we believe that aggressiveness is part of manhood. Most of us expect boys and men to be aggressive. As we have seen with other stereotypes, this leads us to shrug off stereotypical behavior. In response to a boy's seemingly run-of-the-mill aggression, you can see people smile and say "Boys will be boys." Finally, there is evidence that men are sanctioned if they are too nurturant. For instance, Rane and Draper (1995) found that respondents watching videos of men's nurturant behavior towards children ranked the more nurturing men as less masculine.

At a larger societal level, we know that boys and men are surrounded by violent images and provided with few prosocial models. Although girls and women are surrounded by the same images, the perpetrators of violence in the media in fictional and real settings are overwhelmingly male. One fascinating study tried to capture the level of socio-cultural support for aggression and was able to correlate this level of support to sexual aggression (Baron, Strauss, & Jaffee, 1988). This study found that communities with higher levels of support for aggression had a higher reported number of rapes even after controlling for important variables such as socioeconomic factors and population size (a finding replicated by Hogben, Byrne, Hamburger & Osland, 2001).

Although the results are fascinating, I think the more interesting facet of this research is how they operationalized (decided how to measure) socio-cultural support for aggression. In this research, they measured three categories. First, they measured the popularity of violent magazines, such as *Soldier of Fortune*. Second, they measured governmental-related violence such as corporal punishment in schools, death sentences handed down, and the actual number of executions per 100 homicide arrests. Third, they measured something they referred to as socially-approved violent or aggressive activities. In this category, they 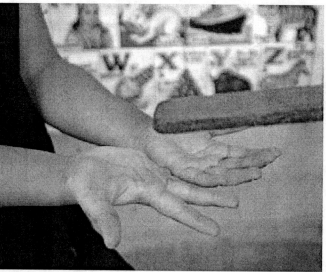 assessed rates such as National Guard enrollment and expenditures, hunting licenses issued, and number of high school football players who continued the sport in college. Any one of the factors may appear trite to you – but that is why this study is so interesting! No social event or behavior is ever about one factor; these researchers pulled together a mosaic of indicators that served to create a fairly accurate measure of the socio-cultural acceptance of violence.

Social Sanctions for Aggression. For women, society suggests that physical aggression is inappropriate. Eagly and Steffan's (1986) meta-analysis found evidence that women's behaviors were tempered by "expected negative consequences" of their own aggressive behaviors. Negative consequences included violence in response, relationship disruption, and the potential  harm to the other. In a related set of findings, Cox, Stabb, and Hulgus (2000), also found that women were more likely than men to suppress anger feelings. Overall, it is clear that socialization plays a major role in men's and women's suppression and expression of aggression.

Verbal Skills. Another argument for gender differences in aggression combines biology and culture and involves the use of verbal skills. As we've seen, girls develop verbal skills more quickly than do boys. Consequently, the argument advances that girls learn to use words to resolve conflict sooner than do boys who rely on physical methods more fully. Indeed, boys and girls both use physical aggression less as they age, but boys continue to use more physical aggression than girls. Piel (1990) suggests that differences in verbal skills may also account for the fact that poor and working-class children appear to have higher levels of physical aggression. Piel found that children with low language maturity were more likely to select physically aggressive behaviors. Although more research is needed, the verbal edge that girls have may play a role in promoting early gender differences in aggression – differences that are then exacerbated by continued socialization and enhanced by biological dimensions.

"Correlation Between Violence and Lack of Verbal Skills"

How to Decrease Aggression

Several interventions appear to be successful in reducing aggression (review by Baron & Byrne, 2003). First, the presence of non-aggressive others helps reduce aggression. Providing "models" of nonaggression and/or individuals who urge restraint reduces aggression. Secondly, individuals can be trained in social skills and perspective-taking that can reduce aggression. Some of this training can be short term and still very effective. Some researchers indicate that individuals can more effectively be trained in the cognitive aspects of empathy rather than the affective (Richardson, Green, & Lago, 1998). In other words, I can be trained to think about how someone else may feel even if I can't feel how they would feel. Finally, researchers have developed a technique referred to as the "incompatible response technique" (e.g., Baron, 1993) where an angry individual is confronted with an emotion incompatible with anger (such as humor). Despite the fact that this technique can backfire, most of us cannot hold two disparate emotions at the same time.

We are going to look at two specific types of violence that reflects gendered aggression – rape and partner violence. You'll find it interesting to note prior to reading this segment that the prevention and intervention strategies for batterers and rapists include work on perspective-taking and increasing empathy.

Violence

How do we think about violence in a way that is useful for a practical understanding of the issues? Is it appropriate to speak about "violence against women" when women are not the only victims? What do we know about efforts to decrease violence? These are difficult questions. We will not be answering them in this book. However, I hope to provide you several angles through which to judge these kinds of questions by looking at two major types of gendered violence: sexual coercion (rape), and partner violence. First, we need to discuss the range in the statistics available on this topic. As you are aware, statistics vary by how and why they are collected and who collects them. When we are looking at statistics such as the number of rape victims a year, the numbers may vary significantly. Perhaps one researcher asked individuals to report retrospectively while another relied on actual rape complaints filed with police officers. You may ask whether it matters. I would argue two points with you. First, it doesn't matter to the individual person who has been violated – it is a horrific crime no matter what. Second, it does matter to policy makers. Having a sense of the actual scope of the problem better allows us to design appropriate interventions. It helps us understand the problem better. Consequently, I understand why the researchers continue to "fight" over the results. Before we start, please acknowledge that everyone involved in this work at a legal, counseling, or policy level indicate that rape and other forms of violence are underreported -- even if they argue about the level of magnitude of the underreporting.

Rape

The fear of sexual violence and/or the experience of sexual violence touches all women's lives. Sexual violence touches men's lives too. Men are the perpetrators, the friends and relatives of victims, and victims themselves. Over the past several decades, scientists and practitioners have developed a much clearer sense of the role and meaning of rape in our society. The feminist movement has fueled much of the impetus to better understand rape and its impact.

Researchers consistently find that approximately 15% of women report being raped at some point during their lifetime, and 2.1% of men (Tjaden & Thoennes, 2000). In study representing nearly 25% of 18-24 year-olds in the United States at the time it was conducted, 27% of women reported being raped or the victim of attempted rape (Koss, Gidycz, & Wisniewski, 1987). This study produced the widely-cited statistic of "1 in 4" women having been raped." Of course, that number also includes attempted rates so it is not accurate to use the statistic as it is stated in the quotations above. In their study, forty-five

percent of women reported having been pressured to have intercourse when they didn't want to. In a different study, college men are more likely to report experiencing unwanted kissing or fondling than intercourse (Waldner-Haugrud & Magruder, 1995).

683,000 forcible rapes occur every year, which equals 56,916 per month, 1,871 per day, 78 per hour, and 1.3 per minute.

Additional statistical insights come from the National Crime Victimization Survey (Rennison & Rand, 2003). Ninety-nine percent of the individuals arrested for rape are men. Most male victims have male perpetrators. Most women survivors of rape knew their attackers. Approximately 70% of rapes are committed by a man the woman knows – the vast majority of these rapes are committed by friends or acquaintances rather than family members. For male victims, the stranger rate is approximately 50%. Although anyone is at risk for rape and accounts of the age of victims range from 2 ½ weeks old to 94 years old, over 75% of rape victims are between the ages of 12-28. The survey only provides rape statistics for individuals who are age 12 or more so the numbers on boys and girls younger than 12 are educated guesses. Most rapes occur between victims and attackers of the same race. The only racial comparison available in this report is between African Americans and European Americans. African Americans report a higher rape rate than European Americans. For the past several years there have been approximately 250,000 rapes a year.

"Sexual Assault Awareness"

Two popular feminist slogans many years ago read "Rape is power, not sex" and "Rape is sex as a weapon." The slogans served to raise the consciousness of the impetus behind rape. Prior to our current understanding, professionals and laypeople alike saw rape as the inevitable result of men's sexual urges. Women were often accused of "asking for it" by their clothing, their behavior, or their very existence. We still occasionally see remnants of this misguided and dangerous belief system in rape trials and other public venues, but activists, including many rape survivors, have reduced them.

How do we know that rape is about power and not about sexual desire? That rape is violence where sex is the weapon? One of the reasons we know that rape is about violence and power is that rapists report domination as the major reason behind their attacks. Interviews with rapists reveal that the main "benefits" of rape include 1) a method of revenge and/or punishment, 2) a means of gaining access to unwilling or unavailable women, 3) a bonus added to burglary or robbery, and 4) a recreational activity described as an adventure and an exciting form of impersonal sex that gained the offender power over his victim (Scully & Marolla, 1985). Clinical work with rapists supports these conclusions. Groth (2001) writes that rape is a "pseudosexual act, a pattern of sexual behavior that is concerned much more with status, hostility, control, and dominance than with sensual pleasure or sexual satisfaction (p. 13)." Even date rapes, which may start with a certain level of sexual arousal, end as rape when the male partner becomes angry and progresses regardless of the woman's wishes.

Another reason we know that rape is about power is that rape is used as a military tactic and a colonization device. Historians provide ample evidence that soldiers were taught to rape as a means to dominate and terrify another group. In addition, rape is almost always a component of "ethnic cleansing" (Websdale & Chesney-Lind, 1998). Historians have documented mass levels of rape in Nazi Germany, Bosnia, Croatia, and Rwanda. In the former Yugoslavia, militias from both Christian and Muslim sides of the conflict trained their soldiers to rape. In addition, colonization often involves rape to create pregnancies that result in children who can be used to the colonizers' advantage. Sometimes colonizers raped to start the genetic "purification" of indigenousness peoples. Other times, children helped build a workforce. For instance, during the United States' long slavery period, children born to slaves were "assigned" the condition of the mother (slave or free), not the father. Regardless of the "difficulty" of establishing paternity, it licensed rape by slave owners and their sons to create more slaves.

Another mistaken belief about rape is that rapists represent a small and mentally ill portion of the male population. Unfortunately, only 3% of rapists are considered "insane" by the courts (most with antisocial personality disorder commonly referred to as "sociopaths" Black, 1999). The research suggests that relatively few qualities distinguish rapists from men who don't rape.

Rapists appear to be "normal" to most people. In studies of college populations, alcohol use, athletic affiliation, and fraternity membership have all emerged as predictors (Ullman, Karabatsos, & Koss, 1999). Researchers have implicated alcohol use by either the attacker or victim in over 2/3rds of rapes. It is crucial to note that alcohol makes it more difficult to hear "No" and to say "No." Athletic organizations and fraternities are notorious for promoting a whole array of behaviors that "hyperfit" the masculine gender role (e.g., alcohol, physical and sexual aggression).

In addition, researchers have found several factors to be associated with committing sexual assault and therefore represent some of the ways that rapists differ from non-rapists: a history of family violence, multiple sexual partners, low self-worth, impulsiveness, and delinquency (Schiefelbein, 2002). Belief factors correlated with sexual assault include belief in the rape myth, hostility towards women, and low religiosity. Men with a predisposition to sexual violence appear to be more likely to rape with exposure to pornography; otherwise, as noted earlier in this book, pornography links to belief in the rape myth, and reduced compassion for rape victims (Seto, Maric, & Barbaree, 2001).

Rape survivors report a variety of effects including psychological and physiological effects as well as social and economic consequences (Koss & Kilpatrick, 2001). The primary psychological effects include post-traumatic-stress syndrome, anxiety, and depression. Rape survivors often show more risky behaviors after the rape including alcohol, drug abuse, and smoking. Physiological effects can include HIV and other sexually transmitted diseases and chronic health problems most likely related to the psychological effects. Women who have been raped are at greater risk for additional sexual victimization (Cloitre, 1998). As compared to victims of other physical assaults, rape survivors are more likely to blame or question themselves. In addition, survivors of acquaintance rape (which includes rape by a partner) are more likely to feel betrayal than are survivors of stranger rape (Wiehe & Richards, 1995). Rape recovery is slow but possible. For individuals' reading this book, psychological help is available free or at low cost. Contacts can be made through your campus, a rape prevention group, a victim's advocate program, or through national hotlines.

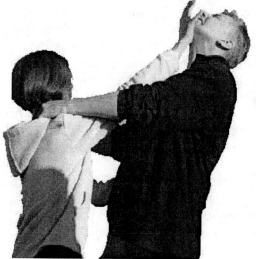

Efforts to prevent and decrease rape focus on women's self-protection, program's designed for men to better understand sexual violence (such as through a college program), treatment groups for men who have committed rape, and reforms to the criminal justice system which treat the victims more justly. With the large number of women's rapes being perpetrated by acquaintances, the focus on women's self-protection MUST be accompanied by other forms of awareness. Table 10.1 shows a college campus' website content on reducing acquaintance rape. The focus is on behavioral changes such as directly communicating ones real feelings. Researchers are now exploring another form of response to rape. Koss and her colleagues (2003) are exploring the potential for "restorative justice programs" that hold an offender accountable for his/her actions. Interestingly, it is the victim and community members who decide on the form of reparations (Koss, Bachar, & Hopkins, 2003). Cambell's (2008) review of the literature indicates that the existence of rape crisis centers, restorative justice programs, and sexual assault nurse examiner programs are all improved responses to rape victims; but, also concludes that for too many victims postassault help seeking becomes a "second rape" in terms of response from authorities.

Table 10.1

Reducing the Risk: Acquaintance Rape

Acquaintance rape is forced sexual contact or intercourse between people who know each other. The rapist may be the victim's girlfriend, boyfriend, lover, partner, date, family member, neighbor, teacher, employer, doctor, classmate, etc. Force can include emotional and economic coercion, physical restraint, beating, and the threat of harm, with or without a weapon. Though frequently as premeditated and as violent as stranger rapes, acquaintance rapes are rarely reported. They are often trivialized by society as "not so bad" or not "real rapes."

Suggestions for the Possible Assailant
- Treat your partner the way you would want to be treated.
- Assume that "no" always means "no". Ask if you are uncertain about what your partner wants you to do.
- Acting aggressive and dominant can be dangerous. It can create a climate in which forced sex may occur.
- Be aware that committing rape has severe consequences for both you and the victim (e.g. emotional distress, disease, prison).
- You don't always have to make the first move sexually.
- Understand which behaviors constitute rape and do not engage in them.

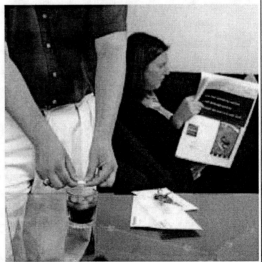

Suggestions for the Possible Victim/Survivor
- Trust your instincts. Listen to your inner voice and act on it.
- Ask yourself, "Am I able to say 'no'?" And "Am I comfortable with what is happening?"
- You can't tell if someone has the potential to rape based on how they look or because they have been nonviolent in the past.
- If you don't like what someone is doing, you can reject the activity without rejecting the person.
- Acting passive and submissive can be dangerous. It can create a climate in which forced sex may occur.
- Take care of yourself on a date: Be prepared to pay your own way, have access to a phone, arrange for transportation, and consider dressing in a way that allows you to move freely and quickly.
- Get out of the situation as soon as you sense danger or feel afraid.
- Learn about your ability to protect and defend yourself. Take assertiveness training and self-defense courses.

Suggestions for Either Partner

- Think about what you really want and communicate this to your partner. Make sure they understand you.
- Listen to what your partner is saying. Pay attention to nonverbal messages as well.
- Set limits for yourself and for your partner (e.g. "I will be home by 12," or "Keep your hands above my waist.")
- Believe and act as if your needs are important. Respect yourself and your partner.
- Feel good about yourself. If you don't feel good about yourself, get involved in activities and with people who will help you feel better.
- Drink responsibly. Most acquaintance rapes happen when one or both partners is drunk or high.
- Know which behaviors constitute rape.
- Be aware that you always have the right to say no to sexual activity regardless of whether or not you have had sex before.
- Use peer pressure to help stop abusive behaviors which may lead to acquaintance rape. For example, when over-hearing someone talk about taking advantage of a partner sexually, let them know you think this is wrong. Silence can be mistaken as approval. If you know about a situation which has the potential to result in a date rape, do something to stop it or tell someone who will do something.

The Aurora Center for Advocacy & Education (2003)

In an article titled "Rape: A Century of Resistance," Rozee and Koss (2001) conclude with a summary that describes the accomplishments of a collaboration to address sexual violence and lays out a path to accomplish what yet needs to be done.

At the dawning of the 21st century, we are proposing new ways of looking at both rape prevention and education efforts in the Decade of Behavior. Feminist researchers, practitioners, and activists can contribute a unique perspective to the dialogue about solutions to the problem of violence against women. In particular, we contribute the oppositional view of an oppressed majority, the understanding that violence is a gendered phenomenon (O'Toole & Schiffman, 1997), and the belief that power is at the root of gender relations. We have provided a foundation for prevention and avoidance that is based in social and cognitive theory, relies on women's strengths, and does not require women to change their social behavior to achieve effective self-protection. Most research on rape resistance is still focused on stranger rape although known perpetrators commit most rapes. Research is still needed on resistance to rape by intimates, especially dates and acquaintances. Very little is known about women's resistance to marital rape. We need further program development, especially prevention programs that are theoretically grounded and are assessed in relation to the program goals. We need to encourage curricula on relationship violence, not just isolated programs, and we need to lobby for the adoption of these programs into public schools... Partnering with community rape prevention initiatives may be an effective method for larger rape education efforts. Rape researchers can do much to communicate our findings about rape resistance and men's prevention programs by creating more structured connections between researchers and community practitioners. It is crucial that academics bring new ideas to the table that are grounded in theory and empirical data. It is equally crucial to listen to the wisdom about program design and implementation contributed by rape activists in the community. We must simultaneously continue to work on improving laws, and changing institutions and cultural mores that exacerbate both the problem of rape and the damage to its victim-survivors. We need a research demonstration project on community-based justice as applied to violence against women, particularly rape. Everyone agrees that the criminal justice system is broken when it comes to processing acquaintance rape cases and other sexual offenses against women, but much of the anti-violence movement has focused on incremental change in existing processing, not on thinking outside the box. Investigating the efficacy of community-based methods of legal resolution may be a fruitful new path (pp. 306-307).

Partner Violence

Table 10.2 lists the findings from the executive summary of the results of the National Violence against Women Survey, "Extent, nature and consequences of intimate partner violence" (Tjaden & Thoennes, 2000). Read it carefully to get a sense of the scope and magnitude of the problem. Despite its prevalence, I have found that students who have not experienced partner violence personally or close by have trouble understanding the role of both partners.

Terminology is important scientifically and politically because the terms affect how people view the "issue." I will use the term "partner violence" to match the current research. You may see the terms domestic violence, family violence, marital violence, couple violence, battered women, and/or violence against women. Although the term partner violence partially obscures the fact that women are overwhelmingly the victims of severe physical violence within a relationship, it also conveys two important points. First, it conveys the fact that men are also victims of partner violence and includes violence in same-sex couples. Second, it conveys the idea that you don't need to be married or cohabitating to be at risk. Although after the age of 25 most Americans are married, it is clear that violence is occurring in dating relationships and among teens as well as adults.

"Domestic Violence – Why Doesn't She Just Leave?"

One of the reasons besides its prevalence that researchers have focused on "wife beating" is the legal history of marriage. For centuries, wives literally became the property of men when they married (Kelly, 1994). Legally, people are allowed to treat their property as they see fit. Despite the fact that many of us use the term "rule-of-thumb" carelessly, it actually comes from an old English law suggesting that men could not hit their wives with any stick thicker than their thumb (Kelly, 1994). The U.S. has come a long way in a short time from a country where wife beating wasn't illegal in all the states until the 1920s. Improved responsiveness to partner violence is directly a product of the feminist movement that emerged in the 1970s. From that point to now, the problem has been named, battered women's shelters developed, law enforcement workers and lawyers trained, and research on the topic has mushroomed. However, as many critics argue, the problem is still often seen as "Why does she stay?" rather than "Why does he continue to batter her?"

Table 10. 2
Summary of findings from the executive summary of the results of the National Violence Against Women Survey "Extent, nature and consequences of intimate partner violence" (Tjaden & Thoennes, 2000).

1. **Partner violence is pervasive**.
   - Percent of women reporting that they were raped and .or physically assaulted by a current or former spouse, cohabiting partner or date: 25%. Percent of men: 8%
   - It is a criminal justice and public health issue.

2. **Women experience more partner violence than men do**.

3. **Racial and ethnic variation is apparent in partner violence**.
   - Rates are highest in African American and Native American populations, followed by European American and Hispanics. Asian Americans have the lowest domestic violence rates.

4. **Violence against women is part of a systematic pattern of dominance and control**.
   - Violence is often accompanied by emotionally abusive and controlling behavior – often escalating.

5. **The violence that women sustain has larger and more long-term physical results than the violence sustained by men**.

6. **Violence exists in both gay and lesbian couples**.
   - Men living with men experience a higher level of violence than women living with men. Women living with women experience the lowest rates.

7. **Stalking is a larger problem than previously recognized**.
   - Approximately 5% of women and 0.6% of men report being stalked by a former partner.

8. **Most intimate partner victimizations are not reported to the police**.
   - It is estimated that 1/5 of all rapes, 1/4 of all physical assaults and 1/2 of all stalkings were reported to the police.

Batterers. What do we know about batterers? They are overwhelmingly male. They are violent and dangerous. Their threats are not "just threats." Of all of the battered women murdered by their former partners, 75% were killed while attempting to leave an abusive relationship (Tjaden & Thoennes, 2000). Batterers are individuals interested in control and dominance but also very impulsive themselves.

Many battered partners speak of trying to do "everything" right so as to not enrage their partners. But, sadly, nothing can be done right, because the batterer uses anything to trigger an attack. Even more disturbing is the fact that battering is likely to increase when a woman is pregnant. Many researchers argue that the pregnancy makes the male feel less in control and increases anger at the woman and jealousy of the baby (Campbell, Oliver, & Bullock, 1998). Research on marital violence suggests that batterers minimize their actions, tend to see their wives as their property, and speak of "gaining control" and "showing who is boss" (Dell & Korotana, 2000). Male batterers of women are also strongly committed to a masculine gender role (Copenhaver, Lash, & Eisler, 2000). A meta-analysis supports a consistent relationship between hypermasculinity and hostile beliefs about women and attitudes supportive of partner violence (Murnen, Wright, & Kaluzny, 2002).

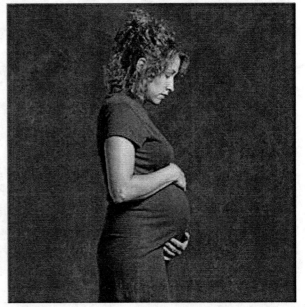

In terms of social policy, some of the most important findings suggest that batterers are much more likely to come from abusive homes themselves and that battering is often linked to alcohol abuse (Rosenbaum & Leisring, 2003). The latter was true for men who battered women and men who battered men. These are important findings because disrupting the cycle implies positive results for the next generation. In the literature, this repeating of violence across generations is often referred to as "the intergenerational transmission of domestic violence" or "the family as a training ground for domestic violence." Figure 10.1 shows a recent attempt to raise awareness of the issue.

Figure 10.1 Ad run in the *New York Times* to raise awareness of family violence

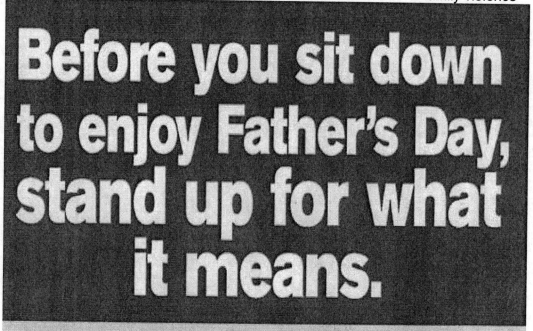

We know the realities of violence against women and children - as witnesses and victims, as friends and companions of those who have suffered. That's why 350 of us, men from all walks of life, have committed to turn our private concern into public action.

We call ourselves "founding fathers" because we intend for this crucial beginning to give way to a new kind of society - where decency and respect require no special day on the calendar, where boys are taught that violence does not equal strength and where men stand with courage, lead with conviction and speak with one voice to say, "No more."

On this Father's Day, we ask you to give rather than receive.

End Abuse (2003) – Family Violence Prevention Fund

Research aimed at statistically predicting further violence in a relationship found that the most significant predictors of continued abusive behavior were the batterer's history of alcohol abuse, the severity of abuse in the relationship, the batterer's general violence, and the level of psychological abuse in the relationship (Cattaneo & Goodman, 2003). Interestingly, the victim's own assessment of the dangerousness of her partner was also predictive, suggesting that the women themselves have an accurate sense of the risk. This latter finding has important policy implications as it may suggest, for example, that police officers could have the victim help assess the risk.

The Victims of Partner Violence. Contrary to most people's typical reaction to battering, most battered women do leave the relationship or try to leave. It is also true that many go back. McGee (1999) reviews the literature and her own work with battered women to provide an extensive list of reasons why women "stay" in violent relationships. I have summarized the major reasons to include:

- they fear him and an escalation of violence.
- they love him and want the relationship but not the violence.
- they do not have the financial means to escape.
- they do not trust the police and legal system to protect them.

- they believe or are subject to religious and cultural beliefs that you stay in a marriage no matter what.
- batterers often physically and emotionally isolate their victims; the victims may not feel they have anyone else.
- they stay "for the sake of the children."
- the psychological destruction that comes with the battering may lead them to believe that they "deserve" the violence.
- they come from homes that were violent and see it as "natural."
- they stay to "help" the batterer and believe he can change.
- they stay due to the shame and social stigma of being a battered partner.
- they believe the batterer's promises that it won't happen again (see below).

Walker (1984) was one of the first researchers to catalog the progressions and cycles of partner violence. She identified the "cycle of violence," the pattern that is often played out in violent relationships. Phase I of the cycle is a gradual escalation of violence that may be over hours, days, or months. Phase II is the acute battering incident. The assailant attacks his partner, and the battering may last for hours, days, or even longer. In Phase III the batterer promises to change and never batter again. He is contrite and may even enter therapy. Although not all battering follows this cycle, Walker found that 65% of all women report a tension-building phase, and 58% report a "loving, contrition" phase.

Women Initiating Partner Violence

What do we do with the knowledge that women initiate physical violence? In fact, in some research, they initiate violence at a level equal to men's (Archer, 2000). First, it is important to acknowledge that women initiate violence and that some women batter their male and/or female partners. Second, it is important to acknowledge that gender differences in partner violence still exist (White, Smith, Koss, & Figueredo, 2000). Men initiate violence that leads to more severe injuries than women do. Third, it is important to note that women who continually initiate violence in relationships are likely to come from similar backgrounds as male batterers (namely violent, dysfunctional families), although there is still evidence of additional differing variables that  predict violence for men and women (Riggs, O'Leary, & Breslin, 1990). Finally, it is important to note that violence initiated by women often begets a more severe retribution of violence from men (e.g., Riggs & O'Leary, 1996). In a thoughtful summary of research on partner violence in dating teen couples, Capaldi and Gorman-Smith (2003) tie together many of the threads that we've covered.

> Even assuming mutual conflict, the findings regarding physical aggression for these young couples are a challenge to interpret. Viewing of the couples' problem-solving interactions for the OYS [Oregon Youth Study] sample suggested that physical aggression may be a complex form of intimate communication that is related to proximal factors such as irritability, impulsivity, attention seeking, sexual ownership display, and sexual signaling and arousal. It also shows parallels to rough-and-tumble play between family members (Maccoby, 1980). It appeared that physical aggression was often a

privileged liberty allowed to the romantic partner, especially in the case of the young men's tolerance of female physical aggression. Perhaps physical aggression plays some role in breaking down distance and awkwardness for some young couples and helps establish physical intimacy. However, the potential for escalation in severity of physical aggression during heated altercations for couples with a very physical interaction style would appear to be a strong risk (p. 266).

To summarize, we know that men who batter and women who are battered are more likely to come from abusive homes. We know that battering cuts across social class and racial lines and those families under stress are more likely to experience violence. Racial and ethnic variation in partner violence exists, although it is under-researched. In general, physical violence rates are highest in African American populations and lowest in Asian American populations (Capaldi & Gorman-Smith, 2003). Ethnicity and racial variation is difficult to pull apart from other social environment factors. Good research would have to have access to ethnic and racial populations that reflected social class and other environment variability. Despite clear evidence of partner violence with gay and lesbian populations, we know that victims in these populations have less access to intervention resources than do heterosexual victims. This lack of access is, in part, due to the fact that gays and lesbians, as a stigmatized population, felt it necessary to hide partner violence even from the community for so many decades (Girshick, 2002; West, 1998), despite the involvement of many lesbians in the domestic violence movement. See Box 10.1 for a moving poem regarding gay male partner violence.

Box 10.1 Rigoberto Gonzalez' poem "Crooked Tongue."

Crooked Man

He owns a crooked tongue
that jams his grief inside his crooked mouth
and no one hears the news that
I have died.

Neighbors say I'm still inside
his crooked house, which, when I entered
months ago was not a dark cocoon of wood
and bone. I should have known

better, people will declare when
I'm finally extracted like a nail.
But until then I'm not mistaken in
the kinder things I've learned

about this man who wants to change his crooked, crooked
ways. He apologizes when he strikes, he
craves forgiveness. When I drop it
on his tongue he savors it—

coaxes out the peppermint
to soothe my wounds. No touch
can heal the way his does, starving pain away
with promises. No promises can hold more hollow bowls.

Only Bluebeard's wives have grown
so wise, seeking out forbidden rooms
because they want to wear the secret of their lover's
lust—passion so dangerous it's fatal.

This man I love will never tell
his side of it. He mourns in silence.
If only he could sing my ecstasy—imprisonment
within his crooked, crooked heart.

I will conclude this section on partner violence with a quote from a website where individuals have posted their stories. I chose this one because it has so many of the characteristics we've come to see in partner violence situations.

> My ex-husband began hitting me before we were married. Instead of seeing it as a 'red flag,' I embraced the belief that it had happened only because of who I was and something I must have done. I embraced this philosophy during 26 years of marriage. It was always 'my fault' and if I could 'change,' the emotional and physical abuse would end. Of course, it didn't. In the meantime, I became increasingly fearful, anxious, and depressed. I became an alcoholic, which only increased the beatings. I became an 'expert' at lying about why I couldn't come to work, why I couldn't make social engagements, and at applying make-up to cover the bruises. After one particular beating, I told my ex-husband I thought I had a broken rib. He said, "You know where the hospital is, go there." On the day my youngest son went away to school, there was an altercation, and my ex-husband and son pulled out of the driveway, while I lay unconscious on the garage floor. When I regained consciousness, my glasses were broken, I had two black eyes, a chipped tooth, and a split lip. I left that night.
>
> (Anonymous, n.d.)

Prosocial Behaviors

Psychologists use the term prosocial to refer to behaviors that are meant to help others. We will look at three prosocial behaviors – empathy, nurturing, and helping. One of the key aspects of prosocial behaviors is that they need to be voluntary and intentional actions (with or without a cost to the person doing the action) (Grusec, Davidov, & Lundell, 2002).

Empathy

Empathy refers to a sensitivity and responsiveness to others' feelings. Any "Star Trek: The Next Generation" fan will remember that Counselor Troi was half human and half "Betazoid." People from the fictitious planet Beta were telepathic and could sense others people's feelings, so the writers of the program called her an "empath." Stereotypical views hold that women are more empathetic. Interestingly, if you ask women, they will tell you they are very empathetic and more empathetic than men. Self-report studies on empathy yield large gender differences (Trobst, Collins, & Embree, 1994). Observers think that women are more empathetic than men.

How would you measure empathy? Although self-report is one of the most common methods, other researchers use physiological measures to assess arousal in response to someone else's pain. For instance, researchers will measure physiological distress such as the change in heart rate or the change in the electrical properties of the skin (galvanized skin response) in response to a child's pain or a graphic car accident. In their review of the literature, Eisenberg, and Lennon (1983) found large gender differences in self-report and in common signs of distress, but no gender difference when physiological responses are measured. Finally, before we leave this topic, recall that empathy skills reduce acts of aggression.

Nurturing

Nurturing tends to refer more specifically to the care of young children although researchers have often used animals in their studies. Originally, many researchers assumed that women would "naturally" be more nurturing. Tied to the concept of "maternal instinct," many argued that women come "wired" to be more nurturing. Indeed, there is very little current psychological research on this subject because the argument was essentially "put to bed" a couple of decades ago. The overall finding was no gender difference in nurturance and strong evidence that nurturing is a relationship between a child and an adult that takes skill, practice, and time to master. Berman (1981) summarizes the research into two major categories on which I have elaborated:

1. Measures of nurturance can be self-report, behavioral, and/or physiological. In self-report measures, women report being more nurturing than do men. In behavioral and physiological measures, the difference is essentially non-existent. However, behavior is strongly influenced by past behavior, and women are more likely to have child care experience. So, for instance, gender differences in nurturing are more apparent for parents than for non-parents – because both male and female non-parents have little experience with babies.

2. Hormones appear to play little role. Hormones may enact a stronger role in nurturing one's own biological children as linked to breast feeding and its subsequent hormonal changes (Weisenfeld, 1985). However, as many fathers, adoptive, and foster parents can attest, nurturing is largely an issue of caregiver attitude.

Furthermore, in an exhaustive review of anthropological and other social science research, Hrdy (1999) concludes that motherhood is neither instinctive nor automatic.

As you might suspect, research on nurturing was laden with policy and social implications. The notion that women were "naturally" more suited to childcare clearly supported the status quo of men's and women's roles. Humans have a proclivity to default to biological arguments. We tend to see others' talents as more in-born than they really are. A pianist may have a natural sense of music – but he or she must still practice to be good. I often see this in students' discussion of writing – they act as if good writers have been struck by a muse. However, even if ideas and motivation might come to others more readily, good writing is only attainable through practice, practice, practice! Childcare is no different. Spending time getting to know any individual child's needs and wants can potentially lead to positive nurturance (or negative!) for anyone. I wonder if any of you have a relative like one of mine? When her children were young, she thoroughly dominated their care. No one else fed, changed, or played with the children. Occasionally, she would acquiesce and let her husband "Harold" hold the baby. Inevitably,

Harold would do something not to her liking or even clumsy – to which she'd respond that Harold was hopeless with the baby! Now, I ask you – when would Harold ever have a chance to get better?

Finally, as the flip side to aggression, we expect men to be less nurturing than women. One of my favorite studies is an older one that measured men's and women's responses to pictures of baby animals. In this study, women and men rated the overall attractiveness (emotional appeal) of the babies in the pictures either alone or with same-sex friends. What do you think happened? While there were some gender differences overall, the interesting results were those from within the context. Women in groups rated the babies as more attractive than when alone, and men rated the opposite (solo  men rated the babies as more attractive than men in groups) (Berman, 1976). This study nicely represents the situational context of our gendered behaviors – women exaggerated when with a group to "show" their femininity, whereas men understated their ratings to "show" their masculinity. Stand by a cage at a pet store sometime and watch the behavior. Let's say there is a baby rabbit in the cage. Women will come up and be perfectly at ease saying gooshy things like "Look at the cute little baby bunney-wunney," whereas a man around men will say things like "Look, a rabbit" – but we know that he is actually thinking "Look at the cute little baby bunney-wunney"!

Helping

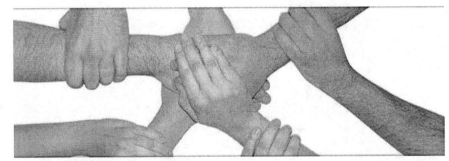 What do you think of when you think of helping behavior? Do you imagine a burly guy ripping open a burning car door to save a child? How about a person staying up late on the phone talking to a friend who is down? Much of the early research on helping behavior focused rather exclusively on physical helping. If you watch your local news for their reporting on local "heroes," they are inevitably people who physically helped someone else. Interestingly, this view of helping aided a gender bias in helping research. When defined as physical help, men are more likely to help than women. Do you know why? Helping research clearly indicates that possessing the ability to help is one of the strongest predictors of helping. So, for instance, individuals trained in first aid are more likely to help in health emergencies. Consequently, both the expectation that men should be physically able to help and their own beliefs in their physical ability both aid the fact that men are more likely to help in physical situations. If you add to the picture the fact that women are more likely to ask for help, the picture looks rather lopsided.

However, newer research has helped to paint the picture in more subtle tones. Men are more likely than women to help strangers in short-term public encounters (Eagly, 1998). Women are more likely to help in long-term emotional support of family and friends. Men are more likely to risk themselves physically in order to help. In fact, when Becker and Eagly (2004) looked at less three prosocial behaviors that are moderately dangerous (living kidney donations, *Peace Corps* volunteering, and *Doctors of the World* volunteering), they found equal representations of men and women. Consequently, the overall finding is that the type of help needed is, in itself, a situational demand responded to differently by men and women. In a recent study, men offered more help than did women to a female target but the amount of empathy respondents felt for the target affected how often help was offered. Furthermore, gender differences appeared in the "type" of person men and women responded to with empathy (Oswald, 2000). Both men and women are more likely to help when they have role-models who help (Stukas, Switzer, Dew, Goycoolea, & Simmons, 1999), and the typical social psychology findings fit the helping literature in that people are less likely to help if the person in need is seen as undeserving, poorly dressed, apparently lesbian or gay, and/or too "different" from the person who could help. Women also judge helping to be more important than men, but men and women found helping equally personally satisfying (Killen & Turiel, 1998).

"Pay It Forward"

The Bureau of Labor Statistics provide data that indicate European Americans are more likely to volunteer compared to African, Hispanic and Asian Americans (2009, http://www.bls.gov/news.release/volun.t01.htm). However, in each of these racial groups, women are more likely to volunteer than men (e.g., overall 29% compared to 23%). As depicted in Figure 10.2 the data would suggest that gender has a direct effect on volunteerism and is likely influenced by race.

Figure 10.2

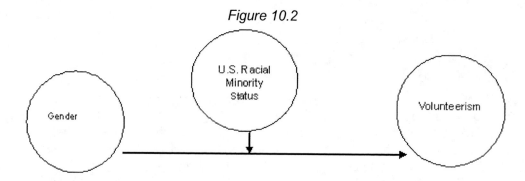

Here is a sampling of a few more interesting findings about gender and helping that enhance the primary findings. In a study that found that women were more likely to help than men, they also found that women were more likely to help in a nurturant way than in a problem-solving way, whereas men were equally likely to use either of the two helping modes (Belansky & Boggiano, 1994). Another study of media sources analyzed the modeling of helping behavior in children's books and found that men's helping behavior was mostly physical, whereas women's helping behaviors were equally emotional and physical (McDonald, 1989). Finally, in a finding that speaks well for prosocial behavior across gender, the researchers found that as people age, they begin to see helping as more as a matter of personal choice than an obligation (Killen & Turiel, 1998).

Our "A closer look at an interesting study" shown in Box 10.2, focuses on some gender-related findings regarding helping.

Box 10.2 A closer look at an interesting study...

Who did the study?
George, Carroll, Kersnick, & Calderon (1998).

What did they study?
Gender-related patterns of helping. They asked participants to describe a friend's problem and then measured several key factors including closeness of the relationship, severity of the problem, controllability of the cause of the problem, empathy of the helper, sympathy toward the person with the problem, anger toward the person with the problem, quality of the help offered, amount of time spent helping, and self-efficacy (beliefs about ones general ability to help or make a difference).

Who did they study?
Over 1,000 participants (aged 17-89 yrs) from a large community sample. The researchers gained participants from a method known as "snowball" sampling. In other words, you start small and ask a few people and then have them refer you to others. So, just as the snowball rolling down the hill picks up snow and becomes larger, this sample also become larger the more referrals are made. It is a convenient way to get a sample; however it is not a good way to get a sample that best "represents" the larger population.

How did they do the study?
Respondents described situations where a friend had a problem and then completed questionnaires describing factors that influenced their actions toward their friend.

What did they find?
Overall, women spent more time helping, gave higher quality help, and felt more empathy and sympathy in response to their friends' problems. For both men and women, self-efficacy (beliefs about ones own ability to help) and perception of problem severity are the greatest direct predictors of helping.

What is so interesting about it?
The large sample helps give the study generalizability. Measuring so many factors that may influence helping allows the researchers to best understand which factors make the most difference. The authors note that the study contrasts with earlier work that suggests that men are the more helpful gender. More importantly, their work suggests the type of clustered ideas we've seen before: namely, that women's help is associated with sympathy, empathy, and the closeness of the relationship; whereas men's help is more closely associated with controllability, responsibility, and who is at fault.

Overall, this chapter has looked at gendered behaviors associated with hurting and helping others. Gender roles have a large influence over men's and women's behavior in these arenas.

Additional ways to think about the material in this chapter

- http://www.psychologymatters.org/bandura2.html
  - APA article regarding how non-violence can be learned.
- http://www.volunteeringinamerica.gov/
  - A site dedicated to volunteering — it includes several interesting data sources regarding gender comparisons.

Global Connection Opportunities

- http://www.unifem.org/campaigns/vaw/issue.php
  - A site devoted to a United Nations campaign to reduce violence against women at an international level.
  http://www.womensenews.org/article.cfm/dyn/aid/2022/

Chapter 11
Gender and Communication

A. Verbal Communication
B. Non-verbal Communication

Let's say a guy named Roger is attracted to a woman named Elaine. He asks her out to a movie; she accepts; they have a pretty good time. A few nights later he asks her out to dinner, and again they enjoy themselves. They continue to see each other regularly, and after a while neither one of them is seeing anybody else.

And then, one evening when they're driving home, a thought occurs to Elaine, and, without really thinking, she says it aloud: "Do you realize that, as of tonight, we've been seeing each other for exactly six months?" And then there is a silence in the car. To Elaine it seems like a very loud silence. She thinks to herself: Geez, I wonder if it bothers him that I said that. May he's been feeling confined by our relationship; maybe he thinks I'm trying to push him into some kind of obligation that he doesn't want, or isn't sure of.

And, Roger is thinking: Gosh. Six months.

And Elaine is thinking: But, hey, I'm not so sure I want this kind of relationship, either. Sometimes I wish I had a little more space, so I'd have time to think about whether I really want us to keep going the way we are, moving steadily toward... I mean, where are we going? Are we just going to keep seeing each other at this level of intimacy? Are we heading toward marriage? Toward children? Toward a lifetime together? Am I ready for that level of commitment? Do I really even know this person?

And Roger is thinking... so that means it was... let's see... February when we started going out, which was right after I had the car at the dealer's, which means... lemme check the odometer... Whoa! I am way overdue for an oil change here.

Dave Barry (1995; pp. 59-61)

This chapter explores gender differences in verbal and nonverbal communication. Research has established fewer differences in verbal communication and a greater number of nonverbal communication than you might expect. Overall, as with every domain we have explored, the similarities strongly outweigh the differences and the context of the behavior is the strongest factor associated with the outcome (Dindia & Canary, 2006).

For communication to happen, an individual must first have a thought to communicate ("I'm hungry"), then decide on a way to communicate that thought (point to McDonald's or say "I'm hungry."), then the other person must receive the message and decode its meaning ("Does she want *me* to make dinner?"). This decoding of the message will include variables such as the tone, the body language, and the content. In addition, any history between these two individuals will affect both the transmission of the message and the reception of it. Just one exchange contains many potential miss-hits. The Dave Barry "skit" that started the chapter is a great example of how and why miscommunications can happen between any two people. Think about what's involved in this interaction. It is no wonder we have many miscommunications in our lives.

Research indicates that most people spend 50-75% of their day communicating (Klemmer & Snyder, 1972; Rice & Shook, 1990). College students spend 69% of their communication time speaking and listening and 31% percent reading and writing (Barker, Edwards, Gaines, Gladney, & Holley, 1980). The form of communication has changed with email, social networking, Web 2.0 sites, texting, and cell phones; however, college students still spend a high proportion of their day in communication behaviors (Jones & Madden, 2002).

In 1973, Robin Lakoff, a linguist, was one of the first scholars whose work flamed a lively discussion about gender differences in verbal communication. In her article "Language and Woman's Place", she argues that women speak differently than men. Women's speech reflects their lower position in society by sounding more tentative and less powerful. In particular, she argues that women use verbal modifiers that made their speech appear to be more tentative. For instance, women are more likely to use "sort of" or "I think;" Whereas, men are more like to state something directly "I like this.") Lakoff argues that women's speech both reflects their lesser power and contributes to lessening their power by perpetuating meeker stances.

Eckert and McConnell-Ginet (2003) explore the extensive amount of empirical research and debate prompted by Lakoff's article. They group the debates into two helpful questions: 1) Do women and men speak differently? and 2) Are gender differences in speech due to socio-political experiences? We will address both questions in this chapter for verbal and nonverbal communication. As you might expect, the empirical research on communication yields a much more complex and changing picture of gender and communication than Lakoff originally suggested.

Gender Differences in Verbal Communication

You'll recall from the chapter on cognition, women maintain a slight advantage in language skills when compared to the average skills of men. Verbal communication in this chapter refers to the way that individuals talk, rather than the cognitive processes involved in language. Think about it. If you were male, what would you do to sound feminine? If you were female, what would you do to sound masculine? Both of you would take your voice to a different pitch... but what else?

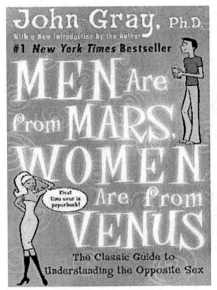

Stereotypes of men and women and popular accounts of gender differences suggest there are huge differences in the manner in which we speak and our motivation for communicating. Research on beliefs regarding gender differences in communication suggests consistent beliefs that there are differences (Hall, 2006). Much less empirical evidence exists than these accounts would suggest. John Gray (1993) sold over 8 million copies of *Men are from Mars, Women are from Venus*. He argues that after a long day of work, men want to retreat to their caves, whereas women want to talk. He argues that women speak in metaphors and generalizations, whereas men speak sparsely and literally and interpret others liberally. Are we that different? Not really. Communication scholar Dindia (2006) summarizes the data best when she notes the difference is more like "men are from North Dakota, women are from South Dakota" (p.3).

"John Gray: Communication Keeps Passion Alive"

Deborah Tannen is another high profile writer in this area. Unlike John Gray, she is an academic and a linguistic researcher. Her book *You Just Don't Understand: Women and Men in Conversation* (1991) was on the *New York Times Bestseller* list for nearly four years. Although she bases her book more fully on empirical research, she, to o, overemphasizes the differences between men and women. As one of her main devices, she distinguishes between men's "report-talk," used to state facts and give advice, and women's "rapport-talk," used to make connections with others and empathize. She joins other writers in using the term "genderlect" to describe this gender difference. In addition, like Gray, she argues that knowing about the differences and acknowledging them (not evaluating one as better than the other) can improve communication between the sexes. As consumers of this research, we need to be able to appraise these

types of popular books that fail to say "on average" or "slightly more likely" when reviewing these assertions. Verbal communication is an area of gender research with tremendous overlap between the two curves. On a very practical note, it is fair to say that any two individuals who enter into a conversation with different motivations are likely to end in a miscommunication. I have learned to tell my friends "I just want to complain and have you agree with me," but I have also learned to ask students "Do you want advice from me?" All of us, whether male or female, allow the situation and the context to influence how we talk and what we expect.

In the following sections, the research regarding several key domains within communication is reviewed: voice pitch, amount of speech, interruptions, topic introduction, and tentative "vs." dominant speech.

Voice Pitch. Biologically speaking, men have a lower voice pitch than do women because men have longer vocal tracts (Tatham & Morton, 2006). However, nature would predict less exaggeration at both ends of the spectrum than the actual pitches used by men and women. By as early as ages 4 to 5, before puberty has had its chance to alter their voices biologically, boys will lower their voices and girls will raise theirs (Tatham & Morton). These children are likely mimicking the tones and pitches that they hear. Much of it is probably unconscious, but the findings suggest that boys and girls associate voice pitch with gendered behavior.

Amount of Speech. Women are often stereotyped as "clucking hens" when they are together – talking incessantly and about trivial things. Interestingly, men actually do more talking than women overall, and both sexes vary considerably by situation. James and Drakich (1993) reviewed the literature on "quantity" of speech using the tally method discussed in Chapter 2. They found that in more than half of the studies evaluated, men spoke more than women, and in less than 10% of the studies, women spoke more than men. The rest of the studies found no difference. Men tended to speak more than women in formal situations such as meetings or classes, whereas women tended to speak more in informal situations. In addition, other research has suggested that men take longer turns when speaking, whereas women tend to speak in "bursts" (Smith-Lovin & Robinson, 1992). Finally, Smith-Lovin, Skvoretz, and Hudson (1986) found that men and women speak an equal amount of time in same-sex situations (an average of 25 contributions per interaction with 5 others on a task), but in the mixed-sex situations, men tend to make a larger number of contributions (31 compared to 45).

Losey (2002) analyzes how often Mexican American and European American students spoke in a bilingual Spanish/English class for adults. In this setting, ethnicity and gender interacted. Overall, European American students spoke more than the Mexican American students did. Compared to a hypothetical situation where each student would be contributing equally, Mexican American men spoke four times more than expected and Mexican American women spoke half as much as expected. The author hypothesizes that the Mexican American women in this case were quieter than the other students because they were experiencing the "double whammy" of being both female and Mexican American and the expectation to be quiet. Figure 11.2 depicts these findings in an ethnic/gender diagram showing that although being Mexican American altered (in this case exaggerated) finding in regard to gender and speaking aloud.

Figure 11.2

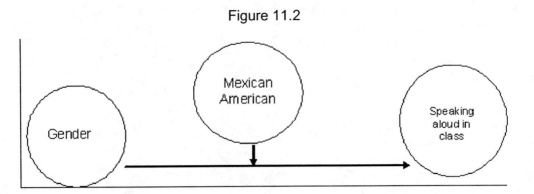

Interruptions and Overlaps. Observers, and those being interrupted, often see interruption as dominant. Sociologists Zimmerman and West (1975) distinguish between interruptions and "overlaps," where the second speaker starts to speak before the first speaker has finished. Overlaps occur at "transition relevant" places. In other words, it would not sound out of place. Interruptions, on the other hand, involve the second speaker breaking into the first speaker's at "inappropriate times." Observers and speakers are more tolerant of overlaps than interruptions. Cultures vary in how much simultaneous talk is normal. Tannen (e.g., 1984) indicates that individuals from some cultures may feel shut out or bored if others do not overlap and interrupt. For instance, African American culture tends to be "high involvement," where speakers see overlaps as supportive of the conversation (Kochman, 1981). Interestingly, African American heterosexual couples also tend to show more equal contribution (less asymmetry) than European American couples (Houston Stanback, 1985). Think about a situation where a European American raised not to "interrupt" may perceive an overlap as inconsiderate. Fascinating geographic and cultural differences also exist. For instance, Tannen suggests that observers might view Jewish New Yorkers as more aggressive and hostile than Christian Californians. However, domination was not the motive of the speakers and they may not have even dominated the conversation, they were just more likely to overlap and interrupt (Tannen, 1994).

The gender findings regarding interruptions are not consistent. When researchers find differences, they tend to be in formal situations, and men interrupt more often than do women. In informal situations, overlap and interruptions are more equal. James and Clarke's (1993) review of the research suggests that even in public behavior, men do not interrupt more. However, in more private interactions, men appear to use silence and interruptions more than women to control the conversation. However, the research on this topic is dated, and scholars need to explore the arena more fully. For instance, we need to know more about differences among demographic groups such as age cohorts and social class and more fully understand when individuals feel silenced. Indeed, Eckert and McConnell-Ginet (2003) exhort readers to look for dominance patterns in silence and speech. Silence tends to equal powerlessness, and the vast majority of public "speakers" in our culture are men because more leaders are male.

Topic Introduction. The successful introduction of conversational topics comprises another fascinating area of gender research in communication. Fishman (1978) found that in conversations between wives and husbands, husbands' conversation topics were much more likely to "succeed." Succeeding meant that the partner took up the conversation topic and discussed. The finding was striking, with 96% of the topics introduced by men succeeding as compared to 36% of the wives' topics. Women appear to facilitate the conversations of their partners more fully than do men. One of the reasons for this difference may be the gendered use of "back-channeling." Back-channeling refers to responses that facilitate a conversation such as "hmmm, "yes" "right'. Women appear to use these phrases more often than men (Edelsky & Adams, 1990).

Hannah and Murachver (1999) randomly assigned men and women to be trained to converse in either a facilitative style or a non-facilitative style resulting in four types of conversants. Then, they brought in untrained people and studied conversations between their trained speakers and an untrained participant of the opposite sex. Participants paired with a facilitative speaker spent more time speaking than those paired with a non-facilitative speaker. Interestingly, the effect was stronger for men. Women tended to be responsive regardless of their partners' speaking style. This study exemplifies how researchers separate a behavior typically viewed as gender-based (i.e., facilitative communication skills) from sex in order to distinguish the role of the behavior from the actor. Studies such as this one can also help us understand that individuals can learn new behaviors and that new behaviors can elicit a different set of responses.

Tentative "vs." Dominant Speech. In Lakoff's original work on gender and language, she argued that men use more dominant speech patterns and that women use more tentative, less powerful patterns. This distinction is also referred to as "direct vs. indirect" speech. Evidence for these patterns included women using more meaningless phrases ("oh, "you know", and the slang use of "like"), empty adjectives instead of intellectual evaluation ("It was lovely."), and more hedges and qualifiers. Overall, although Lakoff's original article prompted good research and excellent discussion, scholars now believe that most of her arguments were exaggerated or more complicated than a simple gender analysis could address. The next few paragraphs address verbal hedging and should give you a good example of why the research topic is so difficult to study.

The category of hedges and qualifies includes the verbal expressions such as "tag questions," where a statement is made and then qualified such as "it is cold in here, isn't it?" A person can also hedge their comments by making them sound more like a question than a statement (referred to as "uptalk"). Try lilting the last part of this comment instead of stating it more flatly: "It is time to end the meeting." I think it's fun to listen to the various ways students ask questions or make statements in class. One of the more interesting dominant forms from some students starts out with "Don't you agree that..." It *can* be taken as quite a challenge (i.e., "I dare you to disagree with me.").

The research on tag questions is very complex because speakers use tags for very different reasons. The type of tag associated with the less powerful communication is one where the speaker is asking for confirmation: "The ball was out, wasn't it?" Linguistic researchers refer to this as "epistemic modal" function; but I just want you to understand how tags can function in various ways. You can understand how repeated use of this kind of tag might make the speaker appear to be uncertain or unwilling to make a stand. Tags can also be facilitative, where a speaker adds the tag to encourage or facilitate a conversation (Holmes, 1982). Eckert and McConnell-Ginet (2003) use the example of "Great performance, wasn't it?" In this case, it is not that you are unsure of your own opinion about the performance, you are opening a dialog. In softening," tags tone down a criticism such as "you were a bit noisy, weren't you?" "Challenging" tags are meant to silence the other person: "You thought you could pull the wool over my eyes, didn't you?" Overall, there is no clear strong finding about tag use and gender, but it's important that you understand where some of the ideas have come from, and why the research is so challenging to conduct.

Dominant speech includes more behaviors such as directive comments ("Close that window." versus "It's cold in here, isn't it?") and commands and threats. Interestingly, however, when the speakers are in interpersonal conflict, women tend to be more direct and confrontational while men tend to avoid conflict (Gottman, 1994; Wood, 1994). Dominant speech can also include the use of cuss words. Profanity is often considered inappropriate for both women and children. However, as you might pick up from listening around campus, younger women do not appear to be as swayed by this expectation as older women are! Listeners must consider profanity in the context of the interaction. For instance, if I'm angry with someone and fling an epithet, observers may perceive my behavior very differently than if I'm trash-talking on a basketball court or hanging with my friends. Nicotera and Rancer (1994) indicate that men tend to pursue more argumentative patterns of speech. Women, as compared to men, see argumentative patterns as hostile and combative and interpret the strategy as dominating. Of course, both men and women use argumentativeness when provoked, and the research on the use and perception of argumentativeness is another area of communication where ethnic racial, class, and geographic variations are likely to be seen. Finally, when women are speakers, their politeness of speech can often lead to increased liking by the audience (Carli, LaFleur, & Loeber, 1995).

Research supports gender differences in communication more strongly in formal interactions and where gendered behavior is expected. So, for instance, I'm a heterosexual woman I may speak in a more "feminine" manner if I'm flirting with a male, or if I've been led to believe I'll be interacting with someone who is very traditional, or if I think there will be retaliation for not conforming to the expectation. Think about it. If you were female and interviewing for a job at Hooters-type restaurant, how would you want to act if you really needed that job? Indeed, Hall (1995) found that phone sex workers draw on many stereotypic views of women in order to create their phone personalities. For instance, in one taped 2-minute message, the woman "loves to shop, she wears feminine clothes (in a breathy voice she says "I went to my favorite store, Victoria's Secret, and bought satin bikinis, …"), she likes to look at herself in the mirror, and she lies in bed half the day fulfilling male fantasies" (p. 192). Listened to a trailer for a movie lately? It is usually a male voice speaking in short declarative statements, like "In a time before peace, in a land at war, there lived a warrior…."

Speech patterns vary by social class too. Middle-class white women's speech sets the standard for stereotypically feminine patterns. Historically, society has expected white middle-class women to epitomize "feminine" speech – refined, submissive, and responsive to others. Look at Figure 11.3 showing findings from Labov's research (2001). The graph depicts an analysis of the full pronunciation of "ing" verb endings by gender and social class in casual conversation across five Philadelphia neighborhoods. Contrast the completed ending "Are you heading for the library?" with "Are you headin' for the library?" in working-class situations both men and women are "allowed" to use the shortened ending. However, in upper-middle-class contexts, you get a gender split, where women use the full ending more than men do. The author suggests that this class split rises from a greater emphasis on middle-class women appearing to be gentile and well raised.

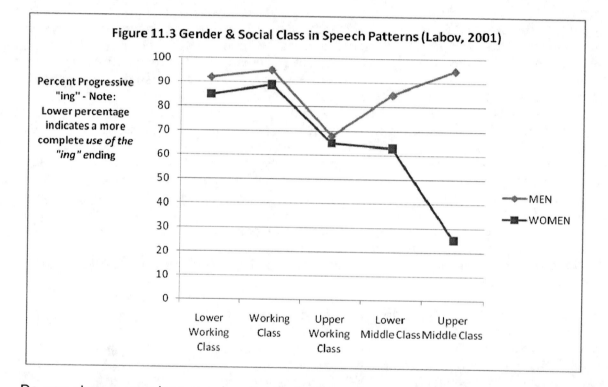

Do you change your language by situation? Many of us do. I find that I use more casual phrases such as "ain't" when I'm around folks who aren't university-educated. It makes me feel like I fit in and am not holding myself above them. Language signals who we are. Many individuals who live across cultures report using at least two language sets. For instance, in the non-fiction book *Hope in the Unseen* (Suskind, 1999), a reporter follows an African American high school student from a poor inner-city school to the Ivy League Brown University. The student, Cedric Jennings, learns to use more formal speech at college and more slang back at home. He is also shunned for using the "wrong" language in either situation and often feels alienated, especially from his white upper-class college peers. Or, read this quote from a gay man who talks about the fact that his sexual identity is always part of his consciousness like "a part-time job."

> It's like a part time job.... I don't close anything down. I mean I'm always gay... I'm always thinking with a gay sensibility but I do check my language at work and say "My friends and I went out" hoping that the people I'm talking to who know I'm gay will go "Oh okay ... let's assume they were gay, right. Okay, get on with the story." (Miller, 2002, p. 3)

The importance of these examples is that they give credence to the idea that individuals can and do change their language to "fit in" with their perception of the appropriate behavior for any particular group. If you extend that argument, you can better understand the women's language may be due more to expectation than to any predisposition to speak a certain way.

One other important note about verbal communication is that the same behavior performed by a woman and a man may be perceived differently and/or labeled differently. Take the idea of gossip. Many people think of women as gossips. But, what does it mean to be a gossip? Gossip usually refers to negative talk about others who are not in the room. However, if you were to hear a group of men talking negatively about someone else, would you label it gossip? Cameron (1997) analyzed the talk of a group of college men and found that they often used derisive terms such as "faggot" and "wimp" to describe some of the men who were absent and somehow different from the group. Think about how you might perceive a group of women referring to an absent woman as a "dyke" or a "bitch." Interestingly, observers could perceive both the homophobia and the implications of the speech (e.g., women being catty, men being what?) very differently. In fact, women may not technically gossip more than men, but their speech behaviors are labeled as gossip just as their? Disagreements may be labeled as bickering rather than arguing (as reviewed by Eckert & McConnell-Ginet, 2003).

Self-Disclosure

Many of us have had the experience of sitting next to a stranger on a bus or plane and suddenly knowing "way too much" about this individual's personal life. When we share information about our personal lives, researchers call this "self-disclosure." Look at Figure 11.2 and note that the theorists depict the self much like an onion. The idea is that our most private thoughts are like the middle of the onion – smelly and harder to reach. The circumference of the onion indicates topics of conversation, each of which has layers to it. Self-disclosure theory suggests two important dimensions. First, as people get to know one another, they cut into the "onion" both deeper and wider (referred to as "social penetration theory"; Altman & Taylor, 1973). Secondly, most individuals match each other in their self-disclosure rates. As our conversation partner shares more private experiences, we tend to match the rate. "Reciprocity" refers to this matching phenomenon, and our desire for balance in our relationships drives the process. Most of us feel more vulnerable when someone knows something personal about us and we don't know something about him or her. Think about it, have you ever surprised yourself by sharing something more personal than you expected to? I suspect your partner's self-disclosure preceded yours. So why does our seatmate tell us their life story? The explanation for the bus situation is that your seatmate knows they will not be seeing you again and is therefore free to self-disclose.

"Interpersonal Communication: Self-Disclosure"

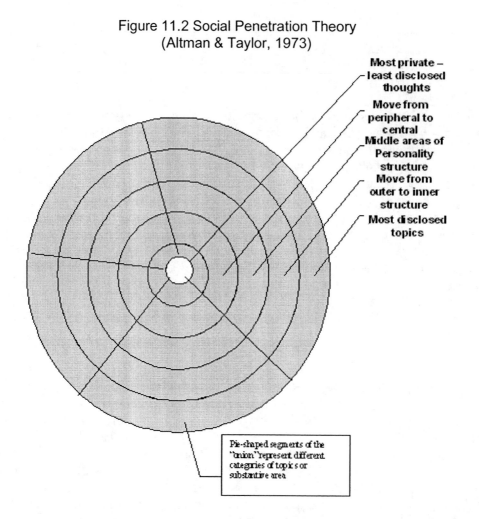

Figure 11.2 Social Penetration Theory
(Altman & Taylor, 1973)

Most private – least disclosed thoughts

Move from peripheral to central

Middle areas of Personality structure

Move from outer to inner structure

Most disclosed topics

Pie-shaped segments of the "onion" represent different categories of topics or substantive area

The gender differences found in self-disclosure are consistent and robust. Women cut the onion faster and deeper than do men. So, which combinations of men and women show the highest rates of self-disclosure? As you might expect, from the highest rates of self-disclosure to the least follows this order: women with women; women with men; men with men. In interactions between men and women, it is the woman who sets the rate of disclosure and, due to reciprocity, the man follows suit.

However, one of the key findings in research on same-sex interactions is that most men and women had similar objectives for the conversation, including offering helpful advice, talking about topics of interest to the other person, and showing interest (Clark, 1998). The type of topics may vary. So, while men may talk about sports more than women do, most people talk about other people, their own surroundings, and their common leisure activities. In an analysis of e-mails written by men and women about a recent holiday, Colley and Todd (2002) found that women wrote more about social and domestic topics (nightlife, shopping), whereas men wrote more about the location and journeys associated with their holidays. The women also showed a higher incidence of rapport and intimacy maintenance in their emails – especially when writing to male friends. In this study both men and women showed higher levels of self-disclosure with opposite-sex friends. An example of a self-disclosure from an email was "There were some great beaches and I went paragliding, I've never been so scared in my life! (p.384)" The authors suggest that the high level of self-disclosure with opposite-sex friends indicates an interest in establishing and increasing intimacy. Although the sample was small in this study, e-mail analysis will be an interesting new arena for communication research.

What To Make Of All This?

You'll recall the complex question asked earlier in this chapter: "Are gender differences in speech due to socio-political experiences?" Clearly our society still produces strong stereotypes regarding gender and communication. Are individual men and women merely reflecting these stereotypes and responding to expectations? And, if so, what are the implications, and why would it matter? Let's return to the question of domination and submission and review the finding of topic introduction. You can see that it would be easy to interpret the findings to suggest that men are exerting their dominance by controlling the conversation, pushing their own agenda, and quieting someone else's. However, you can also see how women's facilitative behavior helps elicit this behavior. In addition, it matters what the motivation of both individuals is, how  observers would interpret the interaction, and how personal and societal expectations can influence that interpretation. Overall, the evidence on gender differences in verbal communication strongly suggests that it is socially constructed and that individuals and societies could choose to change a variety of verbal communication patterns once they have been recognized as useful or not useful.

Gender Differences in Non-Verbal Communication

"If you have to choose between verbal and nonverbal messages – trust the nonverbal."

-Advice to a college student from a mother

Is this good advice? If you can interpret the non-verbal correctly, it is excellent advice. As communicators, we convey a majority of the meaning of our messages non-verbally. Consequently, forming non-verbal messages (encoding) and translating nonverbal behaviors into meaning (decoding) are important skills. Interestingly, as you may recall from Chapter 2 on understanding differences, some of the strongest, most robust gender differences established by research reside in the arena of non-verbal behavior (e.g., Dindia & Canary, 2006; Guerrero & Floyd, 2006; Hall, 2006). When the term "partner" is used it indicates another person in a dyad – it does not necessary indicate friendship or romance. The material below explores nonverbal sensitivity, smiling, gazing, space, and touch.

Nonverbal Sensitivity

From childhood, women appear to be more accurate decoders of non-verbal expressions than men are – on average, they have a higher level of nonverbal sensitivity (Feldman & Tyler, 2006). In an early tally review of studies of people's ability to judge emotions by vocal and facial cues, women were better decoders in 84% of the studies (Hall, 1978). For instance, women appear to be better at judging the emotion of the individual in a picture. Women also appear to enc ode their emotions such that others can decode them more easily (e.g., disgust, fear, pleasantness, and anger) (Wagner, Buck, & Winterbotham, 1993). Currently research continues to support this female advantage in nonverbal sensitivity (Hall, 2006). A socialization argument regarding these findings on encoding would suggest that society teaches men to mask their emotions. This expectation is similar to the expectation that "big boys don't cry." The arguments about why women are more accurate non-verbal decoders are more complicated.

One of the more challenging hypotheses argues that subordinate (or oppressed) individuals (those lower in power, dominance, and/or status), regardless of gender, will be better at non-verbal decoding than those who are dominant because they have to be (Henley, 1977). Think about it. Does it not behoove you to be able to ascertain quickly whether your boss is in a good or bad mood? Have you had the experience of being able to keep a low profile on a day that you've decoded a grumpy boss? Can you think of a situation when a boss would need to discern the moods of his subordinate coworkers?

Research provides inconsistent support for the "oppression hypothesis" (Hall, 2006). Gender differences parallel power-related differences in some of the nonverbal behaviors (such as interruptions and bodily openness) but some behaviors are more likely to be seen in women regardless of power (e.g., greater decoding skill). Hall argues that power may be the root cause but the other social factors associated with the display or coding of a behavior modify the expression. Gender differences most likely result from traditional gender role expectations. I think you will find that exploring the social, political and interpersonal ramifications of communication is of practical importance to you personally and professionally.

Interestingly, individuals who are motivated to be good non-verbal decoders can develop the skill. Box 11.1, "A closer look at an interesting study…" profiles a study where researchers look at a variety of factors that may increase or decrease an individual's ability to decode nonverbal behaviors. Note that individuals who travel are better at non-verbal decoding than are individuals who stay close to home.

Box 11.1: A closer look at an interesting study...

Who did the study?

> Swenson & Casmir (1998)

What did they study?

> People's ability to interpret accurately the facial expressions of emotions in others. They assessed characteristics about those judging the emotions, such as their gender, whether or not they had traveled, and their area of study.

Who did they study?

> 1560 college students from the United States, Germany, South Africa (Black), and Japan.

How did they do the study?

> They showed the students black-and-white slides depicting each of five emotions (happiness, sadness, anger, fear and surprise) on the faces of male/female, young/old actors who were European-American; African-American, and Asian.

What did they find?

> Gender was the variable that most influenced the accuracy of judging emotions. Women were more accurate than men in their judging. Cultural background did not appear to make much difference, nor did the judging of emotions on the faces of individuals from similar cultural backgrounds. However, travel also influenced accuracy in that individuals who traveled outside their own countries were better at judging emotion.

What is so interesting about it?

> The sample size is large for studies of this kind, and there were even numbers of individuals from each of the four cultures. Despite the fact that other variables were measured, gender was still the predominant variable that influenced the accuracy of judgment. Authors suggest that these findings also indicate that individuals can "learn" to be better judges of emotions through experiences such as travel and/or interactions with individuals in a variety of experiences.

Smiling. Have you ever been told to "smile?" If you've been told it rather often, you are probably female! Women are expected to smile more than men, and they actually do smile more than men and return smiles more often (Hall, 2006; Henley, 1977). Examinations of gender differences in smiling are contingent on gender role expectations. Women are generally more expressive of emotions and women are "supposed" to facilitate interaction. In a more overtly socio-political argument, the underlying theory is that it makes dominant individuals "feel better" to think of a submissive person as happy. In a meta-analysis of 400 comparisons of gender and smiling, LaFrance, Hecht, and Paluck (2003) found that women smile more in social interactions However, the moderators they identified clearly illustrate the role of gender role expectations –

for instance, the gender differences were larger when the individual were aware of being observed and are not apparent until the adolescence. Women also receive more smiles than do men (Hall, 2006).

"People Smiling"

Gazing

Researchers have also explored eye-contact as a consistent gender difference. Even as children, girls gaze longer at others than do boys (Kleinke, Desautels, and Knapp, 1977). Even more interestingly, boys tend not to like others who gaze at them for a long time, while girls do. By adulthood, women in same-sex non-romantic dyads tend to spend more time in direct mutual gazing, whereas men in same-sex non-romantic dyads tend to converse with one man talking and the other averting his gaze (Mulac, Studley, Wiemann, & Bradac, 1987). Overall, women gaze more and are gazed at more so than are men (Hall, 2006).

One of the non-verbal results that often surprises my students is the finding that men prefer to sit across from someone whereas women tend to sit adjacent to partners (Hall, 2006). The key feature to physical orientation studies is whether the person is a stranger or a friend. Women prefer to sit across from men who are strangers (to keep an eye on them?), whereas men prefer to sit adjacent to strangers (to avoid long gazes?). One theory asserts that gazing is often coded as aggressive both for humans and other animals. Think about the questions "Are you eye-balling me?" or "Whadda YOU lookin at?" These questions are really a challenge to someone asking, "Is that gaze friendly or hostile?" Whenever I discuss these finding in class, the students who have the most examples to offer have usually worked at restaurants seating same-sex and opposite-sex couples and enjoy watching them jockey for seat positions.

Space

When I was a child, my family went on a car trip one year in our Volvo station wagon. My parents were in the front seat, my 13-year-old brother and my maternal grandparents were in the middle seat, and I (at 11) was in the far back where there wasn't a seat! If you had looked into the middle seat, you would have found my teen-aged brother flopped in his spot, my grandmother fully condensed such that her arms and legs did not move away from her body, and my grandfather approaching one-half of the actual space available across the whole middle row with his legs parted and his arms crossed and everything expanded. Down the road we went, not realizing we were epitomizing the research on gender and physical space.

218

"Personal Space Etiquette"

In general, men take up more physical space than women, beyond the person's actual physical size. Have fun in class one day and watch the body language associated with how men and women students sit in the classroom desks. In one study of children, boys used between 1.2 and 1.6 times more space than girls (Harper & Sanders, 1976).

Moreover, as mentioned in the chapter on socialization, boys use more physical territory in their play than girls. Men also have a larger "personal space" and feel more uncomfortable if it is invaded. Men will sit farther away from others than will women (Hall, 2006).

Touch. Touch comprises a very complex area of research in gender and nonverbal differences. As humans, we touch for many different reasons, and who initiates touch is not always clear. Let's start with the data considering touch among equal-status individuals. As children, both girls and boys engage in more same-sex touch than opposite-sex touch (Major, Schmidlin, & Williams, 1990). As adults, women appear to initiate touch more often, although men initiate touch to intimate areas more than women (Willis & Dodds, 1998). In informal situations, researchers find very few gender differences (Major, Carnevale & Deaux, 1981). In a study where men and women were asked to comfort a same-sex friend, women offered more hugs than did the men (Dolin & Booth-Butterfield, 1993).

When measuring same-sex touching, homophobia may be a factor. One of my favorite things to do at movie theatres is to watch for the "homophobia seat" – my name for the unclaimed seat that usually ends up between two teenaged boys. Indeed, research suggests that more homophobic individuals provide less same-sex touch, and that men are more likely to be homophobic than women.

Studies on touch between non-equal-status individuals indicate that higher-status individuals usually initiate touch more often than lesser-status individuals. Think about it. Would you touch your boss? Would you touch your professor? Certainly, it is much more likely that a teacher would touch a student on the shoulder than vice-versa. As with other communication studies, scholars hypothesize that gender differences in touch may be linked to status as related to gender. However, although status probably plays a role, the initiation-of-touch research does not continue to support a gender difference in this area. It may be that the differences suggested and/or found were artifacts of the way the research was done (that is, no differences were actually there because the "right" other factors were not being measured) or the differences existed and society has changed such that they are no longer as strong or present. As we have seen, both the type of relationship and the level of commitment make a difference. Stewart, Cooper, and Stewart (2003) sum up the research by commenting "Although there may no longer be a clear-cut distinction of who initiates touch more often, men and women continue to attach different meaning to touch." Future research on touch will probably not clear up the findings. The context of touching varies so dramatically across situations and individuals that consistent findings are unlikely to be established unless they are findings particular to a specific culture or subculture.

What To Make Of It All?

This chapter should help to hone several arguments that are crucial to the study of gender similarities and differences. First, good research on complex behavior is difficult to conduct. Second, the context of the behavior is crucial to understanding the implications of the behavior. Finally, gender is intricately linked to other social factors such as power and therefore it is extremely difficult to disentangle the antecedents and consequences of gender when measuring behavior.

Additional ways to think about the material in this chapter

- ❖ http://nonverbal.ucsc.edu/ Dane Archer is a renowned nonverbal researcher. There are several interesting links off this central site – most aimed at selling the related videos. But each link has sample photos with questions/answers where view photos and interpret behaviors. In particularly, I recommend the "Interpersonal Perception Task."
- ❖ http://www.yourofficecoach.com/Topics/direct_or_indirect_communicator.htm This site for professionals never mentions gender or sex but does a good job of laying out the types of phrases associated with direct and indirect communication and the situations under which each might be the most helpful. When are you more or less likely to use each type of communication?

Global Connection Opportunities

- ❖ http://nonverbal.ucsc.edu/gest.html – "World of Gestures" link at the site described above.
- ❖ http://bb.mhc.ab.ca/bbcswebdav/users/cpayne/website/portfolio/cultcomm/dnt_undrstnd.htm
  Good overview of cross cultural variation in communication styles and behaviors.

Chapter 12
Gender Experience across the Lifespan:
Relationships, Parenthood & Aging

Chris and Pat face each other. They believe they are making a life-long commitment to one another. What are they promising each other? To love? To honor? To obey? To initiate the conversations about "us"? To take out the trash every Thursday? To write the holiday cards? Does it matter what gender Chris and Pat are? And, what will their gender effect? Will it affect their expectations of each other? Of themselves?

Throughout this book, we have painted a picture of the gender role expectations on men and women. We have analyzed the biological and socio-cultural factors associated with gender differences in behavior. This chapter takes a more "lifespan" approach. We will look at gender over the lifetime with special attention to relationships and parenting.

Relationships

Childhood & Teen Socialization

Let's assume a heterosexual romantic relationship between two people in their mid-20s who are European American and raised middle-class. Rick and Maria have recently gotten engaged.

Assuming upbringings that reflect the research on gender that we have covered, what do we know about Rick and Maria? Let's take Maria first. We know that Maria probably has an XX chromosome pattern and developed physically and cognitively more quickly than Rick. Maria has undoubtedly been rewarded for producing neat and tidy school work and caring for others. She has probably stayed close to home and teachers when in her playing and has small friendship groups with other girls. Rick, on the other hand, with his XY chromosomes, has larger friendship groups, is more likely to be intellectually challenged by his teachers, and has more physical latitude. Rick and Maria's parents and peers have acted to both overtly and subtly teach the meaning of "boy" to Rick and the meaning of "girl" to Maria. Both Rick and Maria will have paid a social cost for crossing gender lines; however, Rick's choices of appropriate gender behavior are narrower than Maria's. Social, cultural, religious and political messages surrounded both of them in all forms of media. Both are likely to know the stereotypes about men and women and conform to them to some degree. Rick "should be" strong, independent, and able to aggress if needed. Maria "should be" concerned about others, nurturing, and dependent.

Rick and Maria hit their teenage years. What happens? Adolescence brings a tightening of the gender expectations for both of them. Psychologists refer to this process as "gender intensification" (Hill & Lynch, 1983). During early adolescence and related to the onset of puberty, boys and girls experience increased pressure to adopt gender rigid attitudes and behaviors. Given that teens are actively working to know who they are as individuals, how they identify in terms of gender roles is one of the dimensions they must "figure out." Consequently, both boys and girls tend to take on more stereotypical behaviors and attitudes. For both men and women, puberty brings a change of body experience and in expectations for their behavior.

"The Age of Puberty"

For girls, puberty corresponds with an increase in body image concerns, dropping self-esteem, and increased risk for depression. There is an increase in sexual exploration and, for a substantial minority of girls, sexual abuse. Puberty is a risky time for girls. The average age of menarche (the start of menstruation) in the U.S. is 12.4 (Chumlea, Schubert, Roche, Kulin, Lee, Himes, & Sun, 2003). Although since the early 1970s, the age of menarche has leveled off it has dropped substantially across time mostly due to improved nutrition. For instance, the average age of menarche in the early 1900s in the U.S. was probably closer to 14 (Museum of Menstruation and Women's Health, n.d.). Both Hispanic and African American girls have slightly earlier ages of menarche than European American girls (12.25, 12.06, and 12.55 respectively), although it is not clear why this is true (Chumlea, et al., 2003).

In addition, menarche is considered the last event of puberty for girls, hormonal and bodily changes precede menarche by approximately two years. Fascinating research exists on "early vs. late" onset of puberty for girls. In general, early maturing girls are self conscious about their changing bodies and uncomfortable about the attention they may receive regarding their physical maturation (Archibald, Graber, & Brooks-Gunn, 1999; Weichold, Silbereisen, & Schmitt-Rodermund, 2003). In addition, early maturing girls are at higher risk for psychological problems and substance use (e.g., Wiesner & Ittel, 2002). Late maturing does not appear to be a risk factor for girls; in fact, it may offer some psychological and social protection against risk factors.

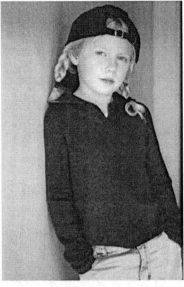

In terms of behavior, some research I did a few years ago gives an interesting glimpse into expectations for girls. In many publications, tomboyism is portrayed as unusual – behavior displayed by a narrow percentage of girls. However, when researchers ask girls/women to "self-identify" – the vast majority of women indicate that they were tomboys. In my study, I surveyed college students, their same-aged friends who did not attend college, the students' mothers and grandmothers (Morgan, 1998). In this three generational study, 77% of the younger women (no difference by education), 69% of the mothers and 46% of the grandmothers claimed they had been tomboys. Tomboy behavior was largely a matter of "doing boys' stuff" such as playing football, climbing trees, and pretending to be Hans Solo instead of Princess Leia when role playing movie characters. Most interesting, when asked to report when they stopped tomboy behavior, the average age for the younger women was 12.6 (nearly the same as the age of menarche) – although some reported they never stopped! In response to a question regarding "who/what" influenced the change in behavior, most reported that they were encouraged by peers to by more "ladylike." However, my favorite answer will always be the three-word response "Sister Mary Catherine." Overall, this research suggests that girls who are tomboys merely have a larger repertoire of behaviors and are then pressured into more stereotypical behaviors. My mother finds this research funny because I was a "girly-girl" and not a tomboy, so I was one of the 23% doing research on the other 77%!

For boys, puberty is also a time of rapid change. Like girls, they are often surprised by their bodies. Girls' menarche is paralleled by boys' "semenarche" or first ejaculation. We don't know much about how boys interpret these events, as like many male experiences, men are supposed to be quiet and stoic. In the reverse of girls' experience, early puberty for boys is usually positive and associated with higher social status and greater body satisfaction. Late maturing boys have

lower self esteem and higher body dissatisfaction than early or normative pubertal boys (Alsaker, 1996). However, as with girls, early maturation does appear to be correlated with greater substance use (Wieser & Ittel, 2002). For boys, the first physical sign of puberty is usually testicular enlargement which begins on average at age 11.6 years. However, it is the body mass and height that comes late in males' puberty. Overall, both men and women have better puberty experiences if they are informed about the changes that will occur. In addition, in those cultures where puberty is "celebrated" through rites of passages, adolescents often have more positive experiences with puberty than in those cultures that don't have a rite of passage of some kind.

Puberty Experience Stories

17 year old man reflecting on his first wet dream…
When I had my first wet dream, I had no idea what was going on. I thought I had wet my bed. It was a really strange feeling for me. I remember liking the dream, but I felt very embarrassed. I thought that maybe I had some sort of psychological problem. And who was I going to ask about it – my mother?" "Chad" as quoted in Pollack (2000)

48 year-old woman reflecting on learning about menstruation…
My brother took his role as older brother very seriously. You had to teach a little sister not to be dumb, since they are dumb already by definition. In his considered opinion, the necessary information included stuff about the mysteries of the female body. So when he was 6 or 7 – I would have been 4 or 5 – he came home from school one day and announced to me that "girls' butts bleed, and yours will too!" Well, of course I had to beat him up … To his credit, he always came back and corrected things later, when he got new information. As he got older, he'd be a bit more circumspect: "So, remember what I told you before about girls' butts bleeding? I think it's actually more like this …" (Personal Communication, 2004).

Romantic Partnership and Marriage

Rick and Maria are engaged to be married. How might their gender affect their relationship? Wood (2000) suggests several areas of romantic relationships that are gendered. She argues that men and women may vary on the topics of talk introduced, how they show support, the inequity of their household jobs, and, as we've seen in previous chapters, the initiation and extent of violence. In addition, evidence exists that men and women deal with relationship conflict in different ways. Gay and heterosexual men tend to withdraw and lesbians and heterosexual women tend to want to "talk it out" to restore the intimacy (Gottman, 1994; Rusbult, Zembrodt, & Iwaniszek, 1986). In addition, research from several decades supports the idea

that women take more responsibility for maintaining conversations and relationships. Interestingly, women are more likely than men to initiate break-ups – a finding that is most likely linked to their willingness to initiate conversations about the relationship. Indeed, the phrase "let's talk about us" signals a problem to men, whereas it may only be a woman's attempt to increase intimacy (Wood, 2000). Indeed, gay male couples discuss their relationships less than lesbians do (Wood, 1999).

The other major way that gender comes into heterosexual relationships is the societal expectation for the "wife" and "husband." Before I discuss marriage in my gender courses, I often have students compare and contrast the differences between "Velma" born in 1880 and "Tiffany" born in 1980. Women's roles have changed more rapidly than men's, so we will focus more exclusively on women. Scholars note that for men, the largest change is in the role as "father," so we explore fatherhood more fully when we discuss parenthood later in this chapter. Table 12.1 highlights the differences the students usually generate in regard to Velma and Tiffany.

Table 12.1

Velma (born 1880)	Tiffany (born 1980)
* more likely to be born into a rural situation	* more likely to be born into a suburban or urban situation
* more likely to marry earlier	* more likely to marry later
* will have more children	* will have fewer children
* fewer educational opportunities	* more educational opportunities
* fewer occupational opportunities and expectations for homemaking	* more occupational opportunities and higher expectations
* more likely to marry for financial security	* able to marry for love
* more social restrictions	* fewer social restrictions

In my class notes on marriage, I keep a clipping from a catalog showing a framed print for sale. The print's title is "The Greatest Moments of a Girl's Life" and the sales pitch reads "it is a print that your grandmother might have had. It chronicles the proposal, the wedding sand the joys of parenthood." Indeed, there are six panels to the print showing a young European American upper-class couple who appear to be in the 1920's. The panels read "the proposal," "the trousseau", "the wedding," "The first night in their new home" and "the new love" (a picture of both parents leaning over a bassinette). Currently, when I ask my female students to imagine other "great moments" of their lives they provide additions such as "my high school graduation," "my college graduation," and "my first job." The additions by my students reflect historical change and current opportunity structure for female college students. But, the print represents the most idealized version of women's "romantic lives." Overall, the list comparing Velma (1880) and Tiffany (1980) is fairly accurate – except for age at marriage. Students often hold a "Romeo & Juliet" notion of marriage in the past. In fact, in the 20th century, marriage was usually contingent on a man's ability to support his family which often meant waiting to inherit land or get established in a business. Consequently, that average age at marriage (first marriage) for women in 1890 was 22 whereas for men it was 26.1 (U.S. Bureau of the Census, 2003). In 2002, the average age for women was 25.3 and for men 26.9. While the age at marriage is higher currently, please note there is not a huge difference and the difference is larger for women. In fact, in the last hundred years in the U.S., the 1950s showed the youngest age at marriage (men= 22.8; women = 20.3 – something that contributed to the baby boom!). Note that the age gap between men and women is approximately two years. The gap is a common finding related to men's need to be financially secure when marrying. So, when Velma was thinking about marriage what would be on her mind? She would be interested in someone with financially security who could support the raising of children and her in her old age. Of course, if he were of similar age, race, and religion the match would be best received. In what would Velma's suitors be interested? Given that one of the crucial reasons for marriage was procreation, suitors would be looking for women who appeared to be able to have lots of children. If you had to pick proxies for procreation, what would you pick? You'd probably pick young and health (and good looking wouldn't hurt). I have a friend whose grandfather took his intended home to meet his father. After being introduced the grandfather asked her to turn around and then declared "You can marry her, she's got good breeders' hips."

"Marriage Basics"

Many students balk at the portrayal of marriage as a practical arrangement; however, for many centuries, marriage has been both political and practical (Cott, 2002; Hartog, 2002). Interestingly, some researchers argue that you can still see the vestiges of the old system. For instance, analyses of single ads suggest that men are more likely to mention their financial status and women are more likely to mention their looks (Willis & Carlson, 1993). In a more recent study with a related finding, Smith and Stillman (2002) found that personal ads placed by lesbian women carried fewer physical descriptors than those placed by heterosexual women. In everyday language people will discuss men "marrying" down and women "marrying up" a process described by scholars as the "marriage gradient." What do we say when we see an attractive young woman with a less attractive much older man? "He must be rich!" In addition, some pundits "worry" about the potential marriage partners for a high status woman. This exchange of status for beauty is not uniformly consistent across cultures; however, the idea that marriages involve an exchange of attributes and resources is fairly universal.

Of course, people "married for love" in the past and still do. However, love is a much stronger motive and expectation for marriage now than in the past. Research on current couples indicates that for both men and women "love" was their main impetus for marriage. One fascinating older study found social class differences in expectations for marriage (Rubin, 1976). Working class women were more likely to expect to be satisfied if their husbands' had steady work, did not drink excessively, or beat them; whereas middle class women had "higher standards" expecting "everything"

out of marriage including love, companionship, and support. In a recent study, Sprecher & Toro-Morn (2002) compared ethnic groups of U.S. undergraduates and also revealed social class variation across ethnicity. They found that middle/upper class students were more likely to espouse the importance of "passionate love" in entering marriage than were lower/working class students. However, in general, the sample greatly endorsed the idea that love should be part of marriage. Social class has consistently been shown to be related to young ages at first marriage in the U.S. and in other countries (e.g., Andres & Adamuti-Trache, 2008; van Poppel, Monden, & Mandemakers, 2008). Ethnicity and social class, as we have seen often, are intertwined especially when it comes to marriage (Sarkisian, Gerena & Gerstel, 2007).

It is clear that marriage partners play a different role in men's and women's lives than they use to. In particular, the reality is that men and women who marry nowadays are much more likely to live together without children with each other than couples in the past. Longer life expectancies combined with lower birth rates mean longer lives together without children – a demographic fact that is likely to affect the kinds of attributes men and women look for in their partners. Specifically, emotional intimacy with ones partner is a relatively new cultural expectation (Cott, 2002; Hartog, 2002).

Before Rick and Maria got engaged, they will have largely been attracted to the same types of qualities in each other. Both men and women believe that potential mates should be similar to themselves, loving, supportive, and secure in their relationships (Klohnen & Luo, 2003). They will enter into this marriage expecting that they are marrying for love and that their partner will be their best friend. Furthermore, despite the high divorce rates, they expect that their marriage will last. Most of us tend to believe that "divorce is for other people." They will each bring with them their perceptions of the meaning of "a good marriage" "a good husband," and "a good wife." Box 12.1 discusses an interesting view of a popular urban myth regarding being a good wife. A variety of cultural backgrounds will predispose them to more traditional view of marriage including: highly religious cultures, working class cultures, and traditional ethnic minority cultures.

Two themes emerge when researchers analyze ethnic variation in marriage expectation. First, the more acculturated ethnic individuals are to dominant culture ideas, the more they may experience conflict with their parents and grandparents over marriage expectations. Women appear to express this conflict more so than men do (e.g. Chung, 2001). Second, in general, African American populations produce demographic patterns that are striking different from other races and ethnicities. African Americans are less likely to marry and to be married than are European Americans and are more likely to have non-marital children (Besharov & West, 2002; Tucker & Mitchell-Kernan, 1995). The usual factors that affect marriage rates such as greater acceptance of nonmarital sex and unwed parenthood also affect African Americans. However, special circumstances create increased pressures on African American marriage rates including the lasting effects of slavery and early laws prohibiting marriages for blacks, and high poverty rates which correlate with fewer economic reasons to marry. Finally, many scholars have indicated that African Americans create and sustain larger family and friend networks that nurture adults and children with or without the traditional marital rites (Taylor, Tucker, & Chatters, 1997). Overall, the implications of the demographic variations in African American families also lead to marital expectations for young African Americans that systematically differ in a predictable way from young European Americans. Namely, marriage is less of a "necessity" for African Americans than it is espoused by European Americans.

Box 12.1

Why This Urban Myth?

You may have seen the following advice in some form. On the Internet and in other sources it is references as an excerpt from a "1950s home economics textbook" and is often referred to as "How to be a good wife."

1. Have dinner ready: Plan ahead even the night before, to have a delicious meal on time. This is a way of letting him know that you have been thinking about him, and are concerned about his needs. Most men are hungry when they come home and the prospects of a good meal are part of the warm welcome needed.

2. Prepare yourself: Take 15 minutes to rest so you will be refreshed when he arrives. Touch up your make-up, put a ribbon in your hair and be fresh looking. He has just been with a lot or work-weary people. Be a little gay and a little more interesting. His boring day may need a lift.

3. Clear away the clutter: make one last trip through the main part of the house just before your husband arrives, gathering up school books, toys, paper, etc. Then run a dust cloth over the tables. Your husband will feel he has reached a haven of rest and order, and it will give you a lift too.

4. Prepare the children: Take a few minutes to wash the children's' hands and faces if they are small, comb their hair, and if necessary, change their clothes. They are little treasures and he would like to see them playing the part.

5. Minimize the noise: At the time of his arrival, eliminate all noise of washer, dryer, dishwasher, or vacuum. Try to encourage the children to be quiet. Be happy to see him. Greet him with a warm smile and be glad to see him.

6. Some DON'TS: Don't greet him with problems or complaints. Don't complain if he is late for dinner. Count this as minor compared with what he might have gone through that day.

7. Make him comfortable: Have him lean back in a comfortable chair or suggest he lie down in the bedroom. Have a cool or warm drink ready for him. Arrange his pillow and offer to take off his shoes. Speak in a low, soft, soothing and pleasant voice. Allow him to relax and unwind.

8. Listen to him: You may have a dozen things to tell him, but the moment of his arrival is not the time. Let him talk first.

9. Make the evening his: Never complain if he does not take you out to dinner or to other places of entertainment; instead try to understand his world of strain and pressure and his need to be home and relax.

10. The Goal: Try to make you home a place of peace and order where your husband can relax.

Interestingly, one of the several websites that looks into "urban myths" (stories commonly believed to be true which do not have any evidence of having occurred) has been unable to locate the textbook that is often cited as the source (www.snopes.com). The authors of the website muse on the reasoning behind these points as an urban myth and suggest that's distribution helps us say "look how far we've come" (Williams & Williams, 2003). It gives us something to laugh at and about which we can feel smug. Of course, many texts from the 1950s have material in them that is directly akin to this advice, so it is not untruthful, but perhaps exaggerated. Another modern website supports the idea that there is humor in looking back by providing a modern day version of the list – one still replete with stereotypes!

Now, the Updated Version for the 90's Silicon Valley Woman

1. Have dinner ready: Make reservations ahead of time. If your day becomes too hectic, just leave him a voice mail message regarding where you'd like to eat and at what time. This lets him know that your day has been rotten, and gives him an opportunity to change your mood.

2. Prepare yourself: A quick stop at the "LANCOMB" counter on your way home will do wonders for your outlook and will keep you from becoming irritated every time he opens his mouth. (Don't forget to use his credit card!)

3. Clear away the clutter: Call the housekeeper and tell he r that any miscellaneous items left on the floor by the children can be placed in the Goodwill box in the garage.

4. Prepare the children: Send the children to their rooms to watch television or play Nintendo.

5. Minimize the noise: If you happen to be home when he arrives, be in the bathroom with the door locked.

6. Some DON'TS: Don't greet him with problems and complaints. Let him speak first, and then your complaints will get more attention and remain fresh in his mind throughout dinner. Don't complain if he's late for dinner; simply remind him the leftovers are in the refrigerator and you left the dishes for him to do.

7. Make him comfortable: Tell him where he can find a blanket if he's cold. This will show you care.

8. Listen to him: But don't ever let him get the last word.

9. Make the evening his: Never complain if he does not take you out to dinner or to other places of entertainment, go with a friend or go shopping (use his credit card).

10. The Goal: Try to keep things amicable without reminding him that he only thinks the world revolves around him.

("Now", n.d.).

So, each of us brings the lessons of our experience and culture to the "wedding table." Strangely enough, even if Maria & Rick were to bring liberal egalitarian ideals to their marriage, research suggests they will play out more traditional roles. Evidence suggests that college men and women cite egalitarian ideals but experience less equality (Steil, 2000). Both men and women tend to be unrealistic about marriage; however, women tend to be unrealistic about equality, whereas men tend to be more unrealistic about romance (Larson, 1988). Research indicates that unrealistic marital beliefs diminish interpersonal satisfaction in hetero, gay, and lesbian intimate relationships (e.g., Kurdek, 1993; Larson, 1988). Unrealistic expectations can be personal (expecting your partner to read your mind) or m ore practical such as the egalitarian expectation that we will "share" kitchen duties. Women, in particular, have shown significant change toward more egalitarian views. For instance, Botkin, Weeks, O'Neal, and Morris (2000) found statistically significant changes in college women's expectations and attitudes between 1961 and 1996. Who is most idealistic about marriage? In might not surprise you, but college

students *engaged* to be married were more idealistic (e.g. unrealistic) than were students in serious relationships and/or married students (Bonds-Raacke, Bearden, Carriere, Anderson, & Nicks, 2001)! If you are looking for good news, some research has supported the idea that students who discuss the research or marriage can become less idealistic (Sharp & Ganong, 2000). Personally, I also am comforted by the research that supports the positive correlation between equality in a marriage and satisfaction (e.g., Steil, 2001).

When discussing the difference between 1880 and 1980, students often do not mention one other important difference. Tiffany is less likely to get married than Velma would have been. The vast majority of men and women will marry at some time in their lives. In 1970 the percent of men between the ages of 40-44 who had never married was 4.9 and for women 6.3; by 2002 the number had doubled or more (US Bureau of the Census, 2003b). For men 16.7 had never married and for women 11.5%. However, even with the change toward "less" marriage, marriage remains incredibly "popular."

Divorce
The divorce rate has risen rapidly in the past century. It currently stands at approximately 50%, whereas in the early 1900's it was less than 10% (US Bureau of the Census, 2003c). How is divorce gendered? As discussed above, t he expectations that men and women bring to the marriage are gendered. Furthermore, women's labor force participation has almost certainly been causally related as well as correlated with divorce. Indeed, women's economic independence has been linked to divorce across many countries (Barber, 2003). However, we

need to be careful about arguments that appear to indicate that women working "wrecks' families. Most research indicates that economic opportunities merely "allow" women to leave marriages that are already troubled. In addition, Sen (2002) argues that economic independence may not be linked to divorce for younger cohorts of women because women's labor force participation will be the norm for these groups. Finally, new research indicates that financial stability is linked to a lower risk of divorce perhaps by a woman's personal satisfaction linking to higher marital satisfaction (Rogers & DeBoer, 2001; White & Rogers, 2000).

However, gender experiences are also reflected in the outcomes of divorce. Namely, the economic impact of divorce plays out differentially based on gender. On average, women's post-divorce standard of living is 27% *below* their rate at marriage; whereas, men's post-divorce standard of living 10% *above* their rate at marriage (Peterson, 1996). In fact, the numbers may be larger in both directions *(*Braver & O'Connell, 1999).

Friendships

Rick and Maria may expect each other to fill their intimacy needs, but like their ancestors, they will also initiate and maintain friendships throughout their lives. The research on gender and friendships overwhelmingly supports two findings (Wood, 2000). First, both men and women value friendship. Second, the similarities in the ways that men and women engage in friendships outweigh the differences. Oftentimes the research on friendships poses a deficit model for men – namely, they aren't as good at interpersonal interaction as women. In particular, men are less skilled at providing verbal comfort to others (e.g. Kunkel & Burleson, 1998). However, as we have seen in other domains, both men and women provide emotional (expressive such as "talking it out") and material (instrumental such as physically helping out) comfort in their friendships. Wood and Inman (1993) provide evidence that women may prioritize emotional care over instrumental and vice versa for men. More research is needed in this field. Finally, as we saw in the chapter on communication, both men and women tap *women* for their emotional needs.

As we look at friendships, researchers often point back to the types of skills boys and girls learn in their childhood friendship circles. Girls, in their smaller groups, focus on building relationships, often include others and tend to be cooperative and supportive. Boys, with their larger groups, tend to jostle for status and authority, and focus on goals. When we look at friendships, the research can be discussed in three categories: friendships between women, friendships between men, and cross-sex friendships.

Friendships between Women. Women's friendships with each other tend to be emotional, disclosive and personal and talk is the action (Wood, 2000). Bonding through talking appears to be consistent across working class, middle class and upper middle class women (Gouldner & Strong, 1987; Walker, 1994). Women feel that they know each other in layered and complex ways (e.g. (Rubin, 1985). However, ethnicity does appear to play a role in how women view their friendships. Samter, Whaley, Mortenson, & Burleson (1997) studied Asian American, African American, and European American friendships and found the largest differences between African American and European American women. European American women were much more likely than African American women to view their same sex friends as providing emotional support. One of the arguments that the authors' provide is that the emphasis on network and enmeshment in the African American community creates less of a need for the support of individual to need specific support. However, the authors provide several other interesting theories and, therefore, Samter, Whaley, Mortenson, & Burleson's study is our "closer look at an interesting study "discussed below. Armstrong (2000) also found that the friendship/support networks of older African American and European American women differed on several dimensions despite the fact they were equally useful to the women.

Box 12.2 A closer look at an interesting study...

Who did the study?
Sampter, Whaley, Mortenson, & Burleson (1997)

What did they study?
The role of gender and ethnicity in perceptions of same-sex friendships.

Who did they study?
199 college students – 40% Asian American, 30% African American, & 30% European American.

How did they do the study?
Respondents completed measures assessing 1) the important of comforting skill in same-sex friendships, 2) the relative significance of emotion-focused versus problem-focused goals, and 3) the effectiveness of a variety of comforting strategies.

What did they find?
They indicate that the most consistent and strong finding was a difference between African American and European American *women*. European American women were more likely to rate their same-sex friend as having the capacity to provide emotional support than were African American women.

What is so interesting about it?
I chose this study because the authors do a fine job of laying out the central finding and then providing several key and potentially conflicting arguments regarding "why" they found what they found. First, African American women might truly see the goal of emotional support from their same-sex friends as less central. The focus on enmeshment in African American communities may lessen the view of single friends as providing support. Second, the authors indicate that their measure may be "culturally bound." Their measure of emotional support relies heavily on items that prioritize or reflect *talking* as the primary means of support. Talking may be more prized among European American women. Finally, the authors argue that emotional support really does play less of a role in the same sex friendships of African American women as compared to European American women. Consequently, the discussion component of this article is a fine example of thoughtful and multiple ways to think about one set of data.

Friendships between Men. When men discuss their friendships, they often mention doing things together, findings that Swain (1989) called the "closeness of doing." During these times when men are doing things other than talking, they feel that they are have meaningful time with their friends and developing camaraderie and closeness. Floyd (1995) suggests that men communicate in more "covert" ways but are not less caring or affection. As with women, social class, racial, and ethnic variations do not appear to show differences, but less research exists on the topic (Franklin, 1992).

Cross-Sex Friendships. Despite the occasional "problem" of the boundary of sexual interest that sometimes arises in cross-sex friendships, both men and women value their friendships with each other. As might be gleaned from the previous sections, men feel more able to discuss emotions with women, and women mention the fun they can have with male friends (Wood, 2000). In an exhaustive review of the research on male-female friendships across the lifespan, Monsour (2002) outlines several key points. First, the benefits of cross-sex friendships share the same benefits of same-sex friendships such as social support, fun, companionship and loneliness protection. Second, cross-sex friendships offer the unique aspect of an "insider's

perspective" on the other gender. Third, cross-sex friendships appear to have significant impact on each person' view of themselves. Finally, cross-sex friends play varying roles across the lifespan. For instance, in early childhood they provide fun, in adolescence they provide help with self-exploration, and in later years, social support becomes the key factor. Monsour (2002) notes barriers to cross-sex friendship which include the potential for gossip about the relationship, jealousy of partners, and the extent to which men and women work in sex segregated workplaces.

Lesbian and Gay Friendships. Research on lesbian and gay friendship networks indicates that lesbian women and gay men are disproportionately likely to have other lesbians and gays as friends but also tend to have these friends be of similar ethnicity and social class (Weinstock, 1999). In addition, if lesbian women and gay men are parents, they are likely to be friends with individuals with similar parenting styles. Finally, although lesbian women and gay men often have close ties with their families of origin, they are more likely than heterosexuals to build a family-type network out of friends. Weinstock (1998) and others argues that these networks are largely in response to rejection from family members and the need to know of safe connections. Figure 12.1 indicates how sexual orientation may affect friendship networks. Gender affects types of friendships directly but sexual orientation may change the needs and demands for friendship networks.

"Friendship"

Figure 12.1

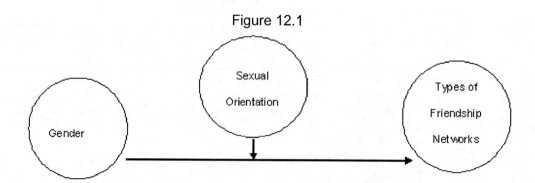

When we discuss friendship, we must remember that across gender, social class, ethnicity, race, and education, people are overwhelmingly likely to become friends with individuals like themselves. Research clearly supports the "birds of a feather flock together" hypothesis (McPherson & Smith-Lovin, 2001). Finally, friendship networks are not static. Vanzetti and Duck describe this lifelong fluctuation nicely "Friendships continue to be maintained, lost, gained, and placed "on hold" for possible reactivation at a later time." (1996, p. 411)

Parenthood

As you will recall, my students argued that Velma born in 1880 would have more children than Tiffany born in 1980. Indeed, the fertility rate in the U.S. in 1900 was approximately 4.0 births per woman whereas for the past several years it has fluctuated around 2.0 births per woman (Downs, 2003). In another interesting way to look at the data in 1976, 20% of women with children had 5 or more children; by 2002, only 3.6% had 5 or more children. Currently, Hispanic women have the highest fertility rate at approximately 2.4 births per woman. In addition to having fewer children, today's women tend to become mothers later in their lives than women in the past. In only thirty years, the average age at which women experience their first birth has risen almost three years (from 21.4 in 1970 to 25.0 in 2000 (Mathews & Hamilton, 2002). One reason behind this rising number is the larger percentage of women attaining college degrees and "delaying" childrearing. Finally, just as fewer women today marry, fewer women have children. In 1976, 10% of women had no children; whereas 17.4% are childless today (Mathews & Hamilton, 2002). Although some of the rise is due to infertility problems associated with waiting longer, the choice to not have children contributes the largest amount to the number. I will address the psychological impact of childlessness a bit later.

So, if Maria is in the 82% of women who will have children, what should she expect for herself and for Rick? As we just learned, she is likely to have her first child around the age of 25 and will probably have just two children. If both children are out of the house when the youngest is 20, she'll be 47 and facing at least 33 years living without children, most with Rick, if she lives to her life expectancy of 80. Again, we see the power of demographic changes on individual lives and why the expectations for marriage are rising! However, as psychologists we wonder about the changing meanings of motherhood and fatherhood.

Motherhood

Ample evidence exists which points to the idea that motherhood is intricately linked to womanhood. Women who become mothers are often idealized and the expectation that women should be mothers and should *want* to be mothers is evident historically and in most classic psychological theories (Hare-Mustin & Broderick, 1979; Zucker, 1999). However, more recently the view has been challenged and the rise of reliable birth control has given women much more choice about the spacing of children and the choice to become a mother. Regardless of the social backdrop to motherhood, the experience of becoming a mother is life changing for most women. Crawford and Unger (2004) illuminate five major themes from women's experiencing of motherhood.

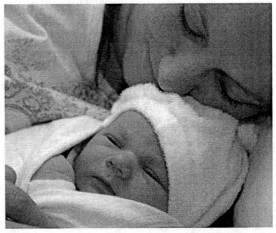

1. Becoming a mother results in large, significant, and permanent changes in identity and life circumstance.
2. Motherhood can involve feelings of intense love, competence, and achievement.
3. Motherhood is a constantly changing relationship, as both child and mother grow and develop. Mothers and children move from a relationship of profound inequality to one of equality. Throughout the process, the mother moves from meeting physical needs to meeting intellectual ones; emotional demands remain constant.
4. Both child and mother must confront the limitations of love and care.
5. Mothers and children must adapt to a society that is structured as though children did not exist and does not provide necessary support for those who care for the young (pp. 352-353).

As with most "universal" experiences, there is considerable individual variation in how motherhood is experienced. Paris & Helson (2002) followed 48 college educated, full-time mothers from their early 20's when all were unmarried and childless to age 27 during a time when gender roles were much more traditional (late 1950s – early 1960s). Their study provides a glimpse into the experiencing of motherhood at time when women had very few choices regarding work/family relationships. The authors focused on two dimensions: positiveness toward motherhood and satisfaction with motherhood. Table 12.1 provides examples for high, medium and low positiveness about parenting. The quotes give a good sense for the type of struggles associated with fulltime mothering.

Overall, a woman's experience of motherhood will be largely determined by her own personality, her partner, the quality of her relationship with her partner, and the pressures and expectations of her cohort of peers and society. If a woman has a positive experience mothering, it builds and reinforces her view of herself as a good and capable mother. Mothering enhances her self image. However, a poor experience mothering can lead to a loss of confidence and a diminished identity and sense of self.

"Dispelling Motherhood Myths"

Table 12.1

Examples From 27 Year Old Fulltime Mothers Regarding The Positiveness Of The Experience Of Motherhood (Paris & Helson, 2002).

High

"I was extremely happy (after first child was born).... I enjoyed the occupation of being a full-time housewife and mother more and more as time passed by.... Responsibilities were new to me in this field; however, they were challenging and exciting... (Regarding gratification in motherhood) A feeling of being needed.... also a felling of great accomplishment and a feeling of joy in observing my child grow and develop.... I feel I am a 'good mother.' I enjoy devoting a substantial amount of my time to the care and welfare of my children. I enjoy the responsibilities involved in child care."

Medium

"I've never known what real love was like until our first child was born. I did find out though how self-centered or selfish a person is until they have had to sacrifice for their child. Not that the sacrifice is an unhappy event.... (Regarding surprises after having a child) Boy were there surprises! I never realized the responsibilities or sacrifices necessary. Before having children I always thought if you were a good disciplinarian your children would be perfect. Now I find that's only about a small fraction of the guidance you must provide.... My children aren't perfect, nor is their mother. I'm trying my best to raise them to be good adults. If I know inside I have tried my best, then I don't feel I should ever have to be ashamed of the end result."

Low

"Naturally more responsibility, tied to the house almost 100% (after first child was born) ... (Regarding breast-feeding) No – O.K. for other but not for me. Why bother when modern science has made it so easy and better for the child... (Regarding being a 'good mother') Yes, at least I try as hard as possible to make her feel I have a real interest in her, her life, her toys, her games, etc.

Mothering is experienced differently for a variety of subsets of women – most notably teen mothers, single mothers, African American mothers, and lesbian mothers. In a brief summary, these are conditions that change both the experiencing of motherhood and the potential meaning of motherhood for women. Lesbian mothers experience more social rejection and have to combine a very mainstream activity (mothering) with the marginalized identity of lesbian, a finding that is also true for gay fathers (Hequembourg & Farrell, 1999). African American mothers are more likely than European American mothers to form extended family networks with other women and African American women are less likely to equate motherhood with dependence on a man (Collins, 1997; Dickerson, 1995). Single mothers often struggle with financial difficulties and good child care is a worry as they do not have a "backup" parent (Paterson, 2001). Another notable social change is the rise in the number of women who have chosen to become single mothers (Hertz, 2007). Teen mothers produce some of the poorest well-being outcomes for both mothers and their children. Most teen mothers struggle with financial difficulties, poor motherhood training, and blunted personal and career aspirations. However, even under those conditions, many teen mothers are still able to overcome many of the barriers (Brooks-Gunn, Schley, & Hardy; 2000; Coley & Chase-Lansdale, 1998). Across the many varieties of mothering, children with mothers who have adequate financial and social support have an excellent prognosis for positive well-being.

Fatherhood

Over the past few decades the role of fathers in their children's lives has changed dramatically. Shapiro, Diamond, and Greenberg (1995) suggest several key components to this change. First, historical changes leading to births at hospitals and men's workplaces being away from the family led to increased separation from children as compared to agrarian times. In fact, several generations of children grew up with little fatherly involvement and influence. More recently, the feminist movement and a men's movement have refocused the discussion on the importance of men's financial and psychological roles in children's lives. One contributor to bringing men "back" into children's lives is the increase in women's labor force participation creating a need for men to do more parenting and housework. In addition, men are more present at the birthplace and we have a better understanding of the impact of father absence. Father absence has been linked to later psychological problems for both boys and girls, just as father's presence often improves both children's and mothers' well being. Men's experiencing of fatherhood is often accompanied by subjective and objective pressure to be a good provider to his family.

Fathers are often emotionally shut out of the pregnancy, expected to provide support to the mother but be silent about their own emotions and experiences. Expecting fathers tend to feel protective toward their partners and most appear to be surprised by the feelings of mortality and vulnerability that come with children – as well as the

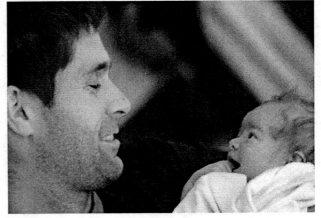

overwhelming sense of love that often accompanies parenthood (Shapiro, Diamond, & Greenberg, 1995). In addition, the fathering behavior of new fathers is directly linked to the experiences with their own fathers (Kost, 2001). However in contrast to fathers in the past, current fathers appear to be more active participants in the details of day-to-day childcare, more expressive and intimate with their children, and play a larger part in the socialization process of their children (Rotundo 1985). In short, their parenting behavior more closely parallels mothering. They also appear to be less gender-role bound, but more research is needed. Personally, I look forward to the research in the next several years that will reflect on men's increased role in parenting and its effects on men and their children.

Finally, in recent years, policy makers have paid considerable attention to the notion of "deadbeat dads" – fathers who do not pay their court ordered child-support. Recent data suggest that approximately 85% of custodial parents are mothers, of which 88% receive a part or all of the support awarded by the court (~45% receive all, another 37% receive some) (Grall, 2003). Unfortunately, approximately 12% do not receive any child support and many more have no support arrangement. Many parents do not seek support because they are financially unable to do so, and many parents do not pay support because they are financially unable to do so. Legislators passed laws that allow for custodial parents to "attach" the wages of the person owing support. The last significant change was in 1993 (Office of Child Support Enforcement, 1998). These laws allow the government to remove the support payments from a paycheck prior to the worker receiving it and have, therefore, improved compliance rates.

"How Guys Think About Fatherhood"

Childlessness or Childfree

The idea that motherhood intricately links to womanhood drives much of our beliefs about childless women. Newer research distinguishes between voluntary childlessness (often referred to as "childfree") and involuntary childlessness (childless). Past perceptions of childfree women painted them as selfish and maladjusted (as reviewed by Somers, 1993). Currently, even in the best circumstance, people tend to project that childless or childfree women will be lonely and racked with regret. However, the research indicates that childless/childfree women *actually* appear to be more likely to be associated with a variety of positive outcomes including better well-being and higher marital and career satisfaction (Somers, 1993). In addition, consistent

findings exist regarding the voluntary childfree women. They tend to be better educated, urban, less religious, less traditional, more career oriented, and better paid than are mothers. As you might expect, childfree women tend to show higher levels of overall well-being than childless women and report lower levels of child-related regret (Jeffries & Konnert, 2002).

However, both childfree and childless women appear to gain the "benefits" of not having children. Studies with childless individuals past the age of 50 indicate that the perceived advantages are fewer worries or problems, financial benefits, greater freedom, and career flexibility; whereas, the perceived disadvantages were lack companionship/being alone/loneliness, lack of support and care when older, and missing the experience of parenthood (Connidis & McMullin, 1999).

Unfortunately, both childfree men and women believe that they are viewed negatively by others – especially their family members. Women report feeling this negatively more acutely than do men (Somers, 1993). In Box 11.2 I've included a poem written by a former student. I've included it because I think it is well written and because she was a student who told me that my lecture on childlessness was the first time she had ever been presented with an "alternative" to the feeling that others have labeled "mandatory motherhood" (Russo, 1976).

Childless

Coerce me not into thy folding arms of virtue.
Cast me not into a barren mandate of time.
Place me high onto the pedestal of freedom
Please for me to find
Existence
Inside my unmothering womb.
Pressure not my breast for weaning
Nor your personal ideals of womanhood
Punish not my sins of solo ties
Nor my limits as a curse

Lori Garofalo (Unpublished)
Used with permission

Abortion

Abortion has been legal in the U.S. since the 1973 Supreme Court decision *Roe vs. Wade.* Reproductive choice via birth control options and abortion is now a major component of women's lives. Being able to control when and if they have children has radically transformed women's family and career choices. In this section, I will profile abortion in the U.S. today and the research on the psychological implications of abortion.

Approximately half of all pregnancies in the U.S. are unintended and approximately half of the unintended pregnancies are terminated by abortion (Alan Guttmacher Institute, 2003). More than half of the abortions obtained are from women under the age of 25. In addition, African American women and Hispanic women have abortion rates higher than European American women. Several scholars argue that higher pregnancy and abortion rates in ethnic minorities may be linked to less access to contraceptives. Even without good access to birth control, most women obtaining abortions report using a contraceptive the month they became pregnant. Abortion rates have dropped in the last 20 years and currently rest at approximately 1.3 million a year (Alan Guttmacher Institute, 2003). If you were to profile women who obtain abortions, you would find them to be young, poor, unmarried, poorly educated and more likely to be from an ethnic minority group. However, it may surprise you to know that over 60% of abortions are among women who have already had one or more children. Overall, the three major reasons that women give for obtaining abortions are that a baby would interfere with work or school, that they cannot afford another child, and that they do not wish to be single mother or are having problems with their partners. Abortions occurring in the first 12 weeks of gestation account for 88% of all abortions and are not associated with any future child-bearing problems (Alan Guttmacher Institute, 2003).

"Abortion, the Procedure"

As you might suspect, researchers explore the psychological effects of abortion (Katharine Dexter McCormick Library, 2001). In order to understand these findings, you must recognize that pregnancies are stressful events, and unwanted pregnancies are particularly stressful. In general, one of the major responses to abortion by most women is relief (Major, Cozzarelli, Cooper, Zubek, Richards, Wilhite, & Gramzow, 2000). In contrast to some theories suggesting that there is a "post-abortion syndrome" with severe psychological symptoms, most research indicates that fewer than 20% of women have negative psychological outcomes associated with abortion (Bradshaw & Slade, 2003). Several factors help predict negative outcomes including poor mental health prior to the abortion, poor support from family and friends, feeling pressured into the abortion decision, strong religious beliefs against abortion, and a belief prior to the abortion that she will have trouble coping. Major et al. (2001), followed 442 women who received 1st trimester abortions and assessed them one month after the abortion and two years later. Seventy percent of the women indicated that they would make the same decision over again if they had to and that the overall benefits outweighed the costs. Interestingly, as you might expect, the experience of relief and other positive emotions decreased over time and negative emotions increased. Overall, women's pro-abortion mental health is the best predictor of post-abortion mental health and their subsequent feelings about an abortion. Researchers have conducted very few studies regarding men and abortion. However, the research suggests that men take the abortion decision seriously and that some men view the decision as a turning point in their lives (Coleman & Nelson, 1998; Marsiglio, & Diekow, 1998).

Lifespan & Aging

Remember our couple Rick and Maria? What can they expect as they age? When we last left them, they were about to get married. Let's say they married, decided to have their 2.2. children, did not divorce, and spent their 20's, 30's and most of their 40's balancing their work/family needs. We know that the both Maria and Rick were likely to behave more gender-role traditionally during their childrearing years. As they face midlife, both Rick and Maria will evaluate their success in meeting their early adulthood goals. Sometimes this reevaluation will lead to substantial changes in life including changes in marital status and occupational choices. However, despite common beliefs only a minority of people dramatically alter their life structure in an event referred to as a "midlife crisis" (Lachman & James, 1997). Maria and Rick will begin

to feel the physical effects of aging and may adjust their lifestyles to express other qualities in "age-appropriate" ways. For instance, my husband gave up rugby for soccer! The aging of their own parents intensifies this experience of turning inward, reevaluating and feeling mortal.

Women often find accepting midlife more difficult than men because of the double standard of aging that judges the physical signs of aging more harshly in women than men. Unfortunately, men judge aging women even more harshly than women do (Kogan & Mills, 1992). Newer research does suggest that the double standard is declining and that individual are more upbeat about middle age and find the time more satisfying (Menon, 2002). Men and women both experience a widening gap between the age that the feel (their subjective age) and their actual age (objective age) but women show a large gap than men (Montepare & Lachman, 1989). Finally, men and women have more positive view of aging experience longer longevity (Levy, Slade, Kunkel, & Kasl 2002).

Research on gender and aging reveals two major purposes of gender and aging studies. Sinnott and Shifren (2001) suggest that one purpose is to look at traditional gender difference comparisons, an event they label "gender-by-performance" comparisons. Meta-analyses and individual studies exist to flesh out the existence of gender differences in older men and women. As you might expect by now, the results are largely mixed when it comes to the big research areas of cognitive functioning and personality changes. However, as we've covered, gender differences exist in aging and health. In addition, even though both aging men and women are likely to experience caregiving, women are more likely to be caregivers and women appear to experience more negative symptomology in response to caregiving, possibility as related to response to stress (Yee & Schulz, 2000).

The second major purpose of gender and aging studies focuses on gender role development and change. Overwhelming evidence exists to suggest that both men and women become less gender role rigid as they age. Men tend to focus more on family and friends and less on work; women tend to feel more efficacious and powerful (Sinnott & Shifren, 2001). Guttman (1994) argues that older men rework their aggressive personalities to become peacemakers whereas women shift from passive to more assertive roles. Regardless of the direction of the change, men and women both gain satisfaction and a sense of freedom from this widening of roles. One argument suggests that men and women can abandon gender role categories as they change from "Mom and Dad" into individuals focusing on wholeness and the meaning of life. As with all lifespan research, scholars must attend to differences that may reflect the cohort in which individuals were raised as well as measures that may not be able to equally valid across age or cohort groups.

Women and Aging

One aspect of gender and aging that deserves special attention is the role of widowhood for women. Because women are very likely to outlive their spouses and partners, they are likely to live through and grieve the loss of loved ones. In a recent study of 55,000 older women, Wilcox, Evenson, Aragaki, Wassertheil-Smoller, Mouton, and Loevinger, (2003) found that the loss of a husband negatively affected mental and physical health. Most of the women showed resilience and began to recover or regain their previous state of health. Interestingly, although the strategies for recovery were diverse, there were some strategies appear to be ... use of social support in the community, learning new ways to cope, the decrease in stress now that the person is no longer a caregiver.

"Inspiration on Aging"

Conclusion

Rick and Maria face an interesting relationship and a life filled with costs and benefits caused by gender and/or informed by gender. They also face a life filled with all the ebbs and tides caused by being human. The next chapter focuses on the role of work in men's and women's lives.

Additional ways to think about the material in this chapter

- What messages did you receive about partnerships and children when you were a child?
- What are the implications of a rapidly changing society for romantic relationships in the future?

Global Connection Opportunities

❖ http://www.nationmaster.com/graph/peo_mar_rat-people-marriage-rate
  - This site lists marriage rates by country. Make sure to click on the tab that shows the map. A marriage rate is the number of marriages per 1,000 people per year.

Chapter 13
Gender Experience: Work and Work/Life Balance

A Day in the Life of…

A day in the life of me! Single parent extraordinaire, I am the busy working mom of two boys, ages 7 and 22 months. Oh yes, and expecting baby boy number three soon as well. What is life like as a single mother of two sons? Let me tell you about a typical day in my life.

My day begins at 6:20 am when my alarm goes off. I have gotten really good at ignoring the alarm, so thank goodness for toddlers with internal alarms or I would be late to work on a regular basis. So I drag myself out of bed in hopes of snagging a shower before the little one wakes up. Oops…too late…I hear Ethan in his room attempting to escape from the crib. Lucky for me he hasn't actually figured out how to escape yet, but each day he is getting closer. As I approach, I see he has thrown one foot up over the top rail of the crib, and is now yelling "I stuck!" at the top of his lungs. So much for letting his big brother sleep a few more minutes.

Having successfully unstuck Ethan, I go to try to convince Noah, my older son, to get out of bed. Noah is very good at going back to sleep when I leave the room, so I have to actually get him out of the bed and stripped down to his underwear before I can safely leave to take my shower. That is no guarantee that he will actually be dressed when I get out, but I can hope for the best. I check once more on Ethan to make sure he isn't terrorizing the cat or his big brother, and dart into the bathroom. Ahhhhhh! A shower at last! Of course, I don't dare stay in long, or who knows what chaos I will find when I emerge.

Upon emerging from the shower, I once again check to make sure everyone is still alive, and proceed to get dressed. This usually means grabbing the first pair of pants I can find that still fit (don't get me started on maternity clothes) and then attempting to find a shirt to match that isn't too wrinkled. Everything I own is somewhat wrinkled since

I am lucky to iron once a year, if that. Today is a good day if I can find both socks and shoes that match – then I'm off and running! A quick check to make sure Noah is dressed, I grab some clothes for Ethan and hustle the boys downstairs. I stuff all of Ethan's medications, clothes, and other necessary toddler paraphernalia into his bag and chase him throughout the house to get his coat on. All the while I'm calling to Noah "have you fed the cat?" and "did you put your homework in your backpack" and "get your shoes and coat on right now or I'm leaving without you and it's going to be a long cold walk to school!" I don't really mean this last one (honestly!)

Getting out the door is the hard part...from here on out things get easier. Wrestle Ethan into his car seat, make sure Noah remembered his backpack. Run back in the house because I forgot my purse. Finally, we are off! What day of the week it is determines where the boys need to go – and since it is Tuesday that means taking Ethan to his Grandma's (my mom's) house, and then drop Noah off at the sitter. Thank goodness for Grandma and a wonderful sitter who feed my boys breakfast and get Ethan dressed in the mornings.

Now I can go to work. This takes all of 3 minutes from the sitter's house. There are definite advantages to living in a small city – it doesn't take very long to get anywhere. Work is actually my downtime, crazy as it seems. I can go in and forget about misplaced homework papers, mismatched clothes, and whether or not the boys remembered to brush their teeth. I joke with my midwife that if I need to go on bed-rest she will have to order me to work 24/7, since work is the only place where I actually get off of my feet and can sit and do nothing. Not that I sit and do nothing all day. I work as an accountant though, and it's a pretty sedentary and fairly stress free job. Which is nice. Every busy parent needs some time each day where you can talk to and interact with other adults. But I must admit, if I ever win the lottery my resignation letter is already written!

4:15 pm rolls around and it is time to round up the boys. First I'm off to the sitter to pick up Noah, then on to my parent's house. Tuesdays are especially nice, because I know my mom always fixes dinner for us on Tuesdays. Yes, I am spoiled! I actually get to kick back at her house and play with my children for a whole half hour or so. This is probably the highlight of my day. After dinner, I sit and help Noah with his homework, then send him off to change into his basketball clothes. While I'm helping Noah, Ethan is usually monopolizing my dad – either wrestling with him on the floor, or demanding he read him a book. I am fortunate to have such great parents, and that my children have formed a close bond to both of them!

As usual on Tuesdays, I have to drag the boys kicking and screaming (well, almost) from my parent's house to get Noah to basketball practice on time. Again, I don't have far to go, only a few miles. I love to watch Noah practice, though usually I am too busy chasing Ethan, trying to keep him off the courts or from stealing the balls. They are both pretty tired by the time practice is over at 7:30 pm. At last, we are headed home for the day.

Most nights Ethan goes to bed at 7 pm, but on basketball night it is closer to 8 pm. Chances are he has fallen asleep in the minivan on the way home. Being tired myself, I am often lazy and just pull his coat and shoes off and lay him down fully clothed. Heck, he doesn't care, why should I? Noah still has to shower and have a snack, then around 9 pm I can get him tucked in as well. Both boys are pretty good about going to bed when I tell them it is time, which is good because I am usually out of energy for arguing by this point. Now I get some me time.

Okay, so me time isn't much fun. This is when I throw a load of laundry in, wash the dishes that have been sitting in the sink since yesterday, clean out the litterbox. All of the fun stuff that goes along with maintaining a household. I'm lucky to make it until 10 pm, and it's time for me to give up and go to bed myself. Once upon a time I used to read and watch TV in the evenings, but I can't seem to keep my eyes open to do that anymore. (Except on Thursday nights – no one is allowed to disturb me during Survivor!) A quick brush of the teeth, change of clothes, and I can fall into bed now (I don't even have to turn the bed down, since I never bother to make it up in the first place.) Another day down, with no trips to the emergency room or other crises - it has been a good day. Now if only I could convince the baby inside me to settle down so I could actually get some sleep I'd be all set! And that is a day in the life of me, single mom extraordinaire!
Carolyn George ©2003 Used with Permission
http://www.theladiesconnection.com/dayinlife.html

When I was a girl, my grandfather would lean back in his chair and assert "Boy, have times changed." He would mainly use this phrase when reflecting upon the social roles of men and women. Although there were times when I thought he was just being stubborn and resisting any type of change (as was his nature), the older I got, the more I realized that as a man born in 1909, he had, in fact, witnessed a particularly rapid period of change in men's and women's lives. Perhaps the most noticeable and notable change is in the area of employment. In the year he was born, 10% of all married women were employed, in the year he died, 1997, approximately 55% of all married women were employed. This chapter looks at the change in women's employment rates, the pattern of men's and women's work lives, the status of the labor force market, and the research pertaining to work/life balance for men and women.

The Engender Workplace

When analyzing labor force participation, it is helpful to think about the agricultural paradigm from which both men and women have shifted. Briefly, the U.S., and much of the developed world, have seen a rapid shift from rural agrarian economies to more urban **industrialized economies** (normally dated from the 1850's on) (Baxandall, Gordon, & Reverby, 1995; Evans, 1990; Hymowitz, & Weissman, 1984; Lerner, 2005). Generally speaking, in agricultural based economies, each member of the family contributed to the family's economic wealth and it was advantageous to have many children to help work the farm. In industrialized economies, the norm was for men to leave the home to work a job (e.g., a factory job), the woman to care for the home front. Children, instead of being an economic asset, are more of an economic liability in industrialized societies. Interestingly, the rise of "women's magazines" focusing on how women can make the home a haven away from work correspond to industrialization. *Ladies' Home Journal* started publishing in 1883. College educations were rare (in 1940, 4.6%

of the population over the age of 25 had completed a college degree) (U.S. Census Bureau, 1942) and women's education was promoted primarily for the role of being a good mother, not for career or self-improvement reasons. Currently, approximately 30% of men and women have college degrees (actually 28% for men and 30% for women) (Stoops, 2004). At the turn of the century, single women who married were expected to stop working. This pattern stayed fairly level until World War II. The deployment of so many workforce able men to the forces, left many jobs unfilled. Women were actively lobbied to fill these positions (Honey, 1985). For many women it was the first time they had experience employment, and/or the first time they had experienced work that was challenging and well-paid. After World War II, there was a concerted government campaign to push women back into the home with the emphasis on their civic duty to return these jobs to men (Honey). However, the percentage of women employed for wages did not drop back to the level of pre-war percentages. In the 1970s, in correspondence to the 2nd wave of the women's movement (the 1st wave being the period leading up to the right to vote in 1920), **women's labor force participation** radically shifted upwards. Table 13.1 shows the rate of employment for single, married, and widowed/divorced women from 1900 to 2002.

"Women's Roles Shift in the 1950's"

Table 13.1
Labor Force Participation Rates by Year and Marital Status

Year	All Females	Single	Widowed, Divorced	Married
1900	20.60	45.90	32.50	5.60
1910	25.50	54.00	34.10	10.70
1920	24.00	na	na	9.00
1930	25.30	55.20	34.40	11.70
1940	26.70	53.10	33.70	13.80
1950	29.70	53.60	35.50	21.60
1960	37.70	58.60	41.60	31.90
1970	43.30	56.80	40.30	40.50
1980	51.50	64.40	43.60	49.80
1990	57.60	65.00	46.40	59.00
2002	59.60	67.40	49.20	61.00

Sources: Long (1958) and U.S. Department of Labor (2004).

Overall, women's labor force participation has changed rapidly. However, women have always played an important role in the economic viability of families and a smaller percentage have worked for wages less than men (Baxandall, Gordon, & Reverby, 1995). The largest changes, and the changes most likely to catch the eye of the public and policy makers, are the increase in the number of middle-class women who are employed, and the increase in the number of *mothers* who are employed. Currently, approximately 65% of women with children under the age of 6 (important because they are not yet of school age) are in the labor force. In addition, 56% of mothers of children under the age of one are employed (Bureau of Labor Statistics, 2004). However, these numbers can belie the fact that poor women have always worked for wages, often in under-recognized jobs. If you look at work associated with wages, at the turn of the century the vast majority of jobs available to women were domestic jobs. Women both went out to do domestic work (e.g., maids and nannies) and brought in domestic work (laundry and seamstresses) – especially, women of color who would be less likely to be able to secure other forms of work (Dill, 1994; Dudden, 1983; Palmer, 1989). Even in the more rural areas, the taking in of male borders was extremely common. Women were likely to cook and clean for their own families plus borders. For instance, in 1900, a full 10% of married women and 4% of single women reported having boarders (Sobek, 1997). For married women, when boarders were considered along with other occupations, the occupation rate was closer to 15% than the 5.7% normally reported.

In addition, women of color have had patterns that have varied from European American women. For instance, African American women and Asian American women tend to have employment rates higher than European American women (Fullerton, 1999). Scholars suggest that the high employment rate of African American women can be contributed to higher rates of single parenthood, higher rates or African American men's unemployment, and fewer social sanctions against being employed (Fullerton).

Figure 13.1

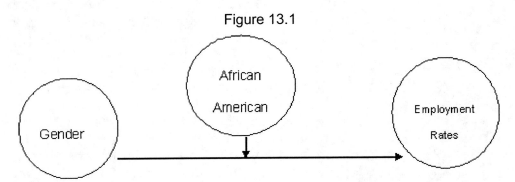

Figure 13.1 depicts the predicted relationship between race and gender and employment rates. In this situation, gender has a direct relationship to employment, particularly if one is African American. As suggested, there is more emphasis on employment for African American women as compared to European American women (Chavous, Harris, Rivas, Helaire, & Green, 2004) and there are more employment opportunities for African American women than African American men (Fullerton).

Asian American women's higher employment rate is often linked to higher education and cultural emphasis on academic and business success (Fullerton); however, ethnic differences within the Asian American racial group are likely to show high variation. The heavy emphasis on women as family caretakers and mothers and its corollary of an emphasis on men as breadwinners contributes to the lower employment rates in Hispanic women. Table 13.2 shows the percent of racial groups labor force participation by gender for the age group most likely to have the highest rates of employment (35-44 year olds). When you examine these numbers, you see the racial variations in women's employment, as well as the noted trend of higher unemployment rates for African American males.

Table 13.2 show employment rates as broken down by race.
Labor Force Participation Rates by Gender and Race for 35-44 year olds

Demographic Group	Asian	African American	European American	Hispanic
Men 35-44	91.80%	85.00%	94.00%	91.40%
Women 35-44	72.90%	79.9%	78.10%	67.90%

Source: Fullerton (1999)

The Types of Work Done By Men and Women

Two major differences appear when you compare men's and women's work. First, men tend to work in different types of women than do women. Second, the work patterns of men and women tend to differ. When we compare men's and women's employment, Figure 13.2 is a helpful way to conceptualize the difference. The largest triangle represents all of the jobs available. The higher up in the triangle, the fewer the number of jobs and the higher the prestige. CEOs of corporations would exemplify a job high in the triangle. The lower in the triangle, there are more numerous, but less prestigious jobs. For instance, plentiful employment exists for food servers. The bottom of the triangle represents job functions or types. There is a large arrow pointing to a line on the triangle. It represents the "**glass ceiling.**" The glass ceiling is aptly named as it refers to the existence of an invisible barrier that prevents women from being promoted beyond middle management. The term glass ceiling conjures up the visual image of a person who cannot get through the ceiling but can see other people walking around up there. In addition, perhaps it is glass because it can be shattered? The term has been linked to a 1986 article for the *Wall Street Journal* written by Hymowitz and Schellhardt. Researchers have established that there is a glass ceiling for women and for individuals of color in the U.S. workforce (U.S. Department of Labor, 2000). Recently, labor force observers have coined the term **"glass walls"** to refer to the experience of women who are not given full lateral access to information and experiences that would allow for further upward movement in a pyramid type corporation (e.g., Trollvik, 2005). Overall, the benefit of Figure 13.2 is that it represents two important comparison of men's and women's employment. Women work in fewer types of jobs and in less prestigious work.

Figure 13.2

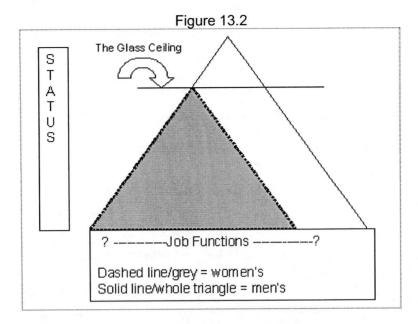

Let's take a closer look at the types of men's and women's employment categories. The type of work that men and women do is one of several contributors to the wage gap. The **wage gap** is the existence of a persistent difference between the average pay for men and the average pay for women. Currently, the wage gap stands at .74 cents to the dollar (women make 74% of what men make). We will return to more contributors to the wage gap later in this chapter. When you think about men's work and women's work, do any stereotypes come to mind? In general, women's work is often thought of in "cleaner" indoor environments; whereas, men's work is often thought of in more outdoor, physical environments. As the labor force shifts from manufacturing to more service jobs, that perception may also shift. Many college students are also likely to think of "white collar" jobs when they think of work. Table 13.3 shows the top 10 occupation categories for men. Look at the men's work. Note how many of the jobs are in a physical environment. Now, look at the women's work. Note how many of the jobs are in offices – a substantial minority of women work in clerically related work. Table 13.3 illustrates another very important point. It shows the extent to which men tend to work in fields with other men and women in fields with other women. Economists have defined a field as "**male dominated** or **female dominated**" if 75% or more of the workers are of a particular gender.

Table 13.3
Top 10 Occupations for Men and Women

MEN (over 16 working full-time) (72,903)*			WOMEN (over 16 working full-time) (63,737)		
Occupation	# of men	Percent of occupation – male	Occupation	# of women	Percent of occupation - female
Other executive, administrative, & managerial	8,543	.59	Administrative support (includes clerical)	8,361	.76
Construction trades	6,151	.98	Other executive, administrative, & managerial	6,028	.41
Transportation and material moving	5,211	.90	Retail Sales	4,270	.63
Mechanics and Repairers	4,545	.95	Teachers (elem. & secondary)	4,242	.75
Equipment Handlers	4,265	.79	Food service	3,691	.56
Machine operators	4,198	.65	Management-related occupations	3,015	.58
Motor vehicle operators	3,940	.88	Secretaries, stenographers, and typists	2,947	.98
Other equipment handlers	3,219	.75	Professional specialty occupations (e.g., paralegal)	2,842	.54
Food service	2,923	.44	Health assess. & treatment (includes nursing)	2,822	.86
Supervisors and proprietors	2,916	.60	Personal service	2,649	.81
63% of all men work in these 10 occupations			64% of all women work in these 10 occupations; 18% work in clerical work		

Note: Data from U.S. Department of Labor Bureau of Labor Statistics (2002) categories based on census bureau information.

* Numbers are in thousands – so each number would be multiplied by 1000 to reflect the actual number of people. The total shown for this table is 136,485 - actually representing 136,485,000 individuals.

Work Over the Lifespan

For many decades the traditional work trajectory for men would involve early entry into the workforce, relatively few changes of employers or job types, and a consistent work pattern until retirements (McCanna, Pearse, & Zrebiec, 1994). In addition, in many companies, promotions were accompanied with a move to another city or market. Women, on the other hand, have traditionally shown a different pattern. Women are more likely to come in and out of the labor force and tend to show more job shifts (Blau, 1998; Hoffman & Averett, 2005: Key, 1999; Krecker, 1993). Why might that be? As you might expect, women are likely to drop out of the market to care for children and elders. In addition, they are more likely to be the "trailing spouse" and quit work to move for their husbands' careers. However, researchers have also established that women are more likely to make "lateral" shifts – shifts in jobs at the same level of prestige that do not involve a promotion or change in income or duties (Krecker). Researchers argue that women change jobs more often precisely because there are fewer advancement opportunities. So, instead of moving up, they may move "over" just to have a different working experience.

Currently, the comparison of men's and women's workforce pattern yield many fewer differences than in the past. In fact, although, as we have established, women have a lower labor force participation rate than do men, those who enter the workforce, show a similar pattern as men.

The Wage Gap

The wage gap has improved in the past several decades. In 1980 the wage gap comparing annual salaries for men and women was 60.2 cents to the dollar. Currently, it is 74 cents to the dollar (U.S. Census Bureau, 2002). Of course, there are racial variations within the wage gap too. Table 13.4 shows the wage gap in 2002 by race and gender.

Table 13.4
Gender and racial comparisons of the wage gap in 2002

European American Men	African American Men	Hispanic Men	European American Women	African American Women	Hispanic Women
100	78.2	63.3	75.6	65.4	54.3

Note: Statistics based on median annual earnings as a percentage of European American men's annual earnings (National Committee on Pay Equity, 2004).

WOMEN
Like men,
only cheaper.

IF YOU DON'T LIKE IT,
HELP US RIGHT IT.

Why Do We Have The Wage Gap? In some ways the wage gap makes sense given what we have already learned in this chapter. We know that women have historically been less educated and completed fewer years in the workforce. In addition, women tend to cluster in lower paying fields. However, traditional variables that might affect the wage gap – such as experience, seniority, and education – do not fully account for the wage gap. Experts estimate that approximately 50% of the wage gap can be attributed to known reasons such as educational attainment and education (e.g., Levine, 2003). In addition, the wage gap appears in the same occupational field. Figure 13.3 shows a comparison of men's and women's salaries in the top income jobs for men. Note that the percentage ranges from 62% to 77% even in these high paying fields.

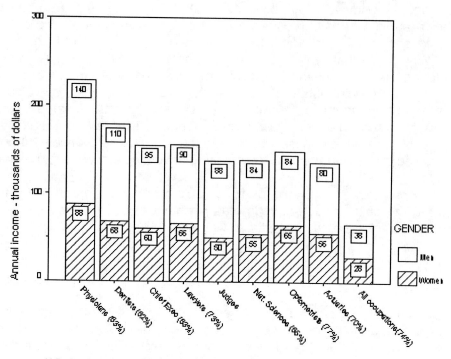

U.S. Census Bureau 2000 - Top Paying Jobs for Men

Source: (Weinberg, 2004).

Recall that one of the arguments about why the wage gap exists is due to education and experience. One way to get a better sense of why researchers are concerned about variables beyond education and experience is to compare recent college graduates. By comparing college graduates, you are largely holding experience and education steady. Figure 13.3 shows the gender wage gap by discipline for recent college graduates.

Figure 13.3
Gender wage gap by discipline for recent college graduates
(Horn & Zahn, 2001) Permission obtained.

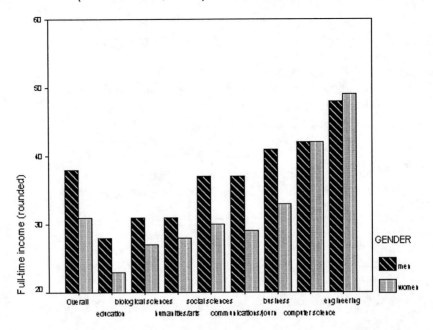

1997 College Graduates by Field and Gender

How does gender play into the earnings of newly graduated individuals? Let's take the example of dentistry. If a female and male dentist were to graduate from the same professional school and open their own private practice, why might their incomes be different? It is actually easier to understand in a situation like this where they set their own rates because it is clearer how a difference could occur. Many scenarios can be spun but here are a few: perhaps she feels that she will be less likely to attract clients because she is female so she sets her rates lower, perhaps she feels sorry for her clients because of the high costs and sets her rates lower, perhaps she has a family and is only able to put in 50 billable hours a week compared to his 70, perhaps he has a senior relative who is in the business so his overhead costs are lower and/or perhaps he

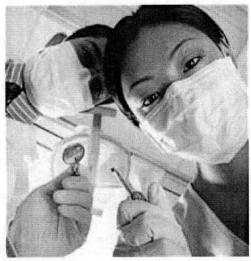

specialized in dental school while she stayed in general dentistry. These would all be fairly subtle reasons why a wage gap would exist between two people in an occupation that appears to have a fairly level playing field.

Another variable that influences the wage gap is the negotiation of the starting salary and subsequent request for raises or promotions. Women are much less likely to try to negotiate their salaries then are men (Babcock & Laschever, 2003). Raises tend to be based as a percentage of the base salary, so women can lose ground quickly over the lifetime of their careers. In fact, Babock and Laschever estimate that a woman who routinely negotiates her salary increases will earn over one million dollars more by the time she retires than a woman who accepts what she's offered every time without asking for more. Naturally, she would need to be in a good paying position at the beginning. Interestingly, although there are several practice guides to negotiating salaries (e.g., Pinkley & Northcraft, 2000), the simple act of asking is the biggest key to gaining a higher salary.

What Will Improve The Wage Gap? Some things are slow to change – let's take a look at college graduates as an example. Earlier we saw a figure looking at the wage gap in specific fields in which college graduates work. However, we also know that part of the wage gap contributor is the fact that women are clustered in lower paying jobs. Let's look again at college graduates, but this time look at the gender differences in some of the fields. Figure 13.4 shows the majors most likely to yield large gender differences.

Figure 13.4
Majors most likely to yield large gender differences
(Horn & Zahn, 2001). Permission obtained.

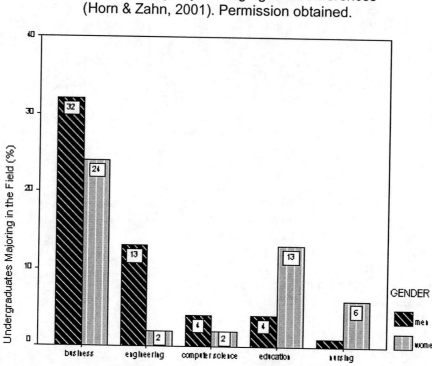

Top majors showing gender differences

These data tell us that that part of the puzzle will be slow to change. On the other hand, some fields have seen huge changes. Figure 13.5 shows the increase in the number of bachelor's degrees in engineering being earned by women (National Science Foundation and census data compiled by the Society of Women Engineers, 2004).

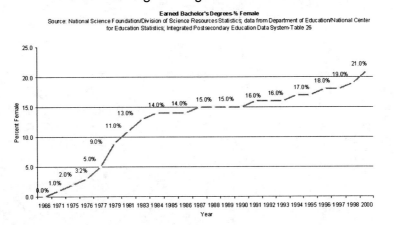

Figure 13.5
Percent of engineering students who are female

Earned Bachelor's Degrees-% Female
Source: National Science Foundation/Division of Science Resources Statistics, data from Department of Education/National Center for Education Statistics, Integrated Postsecondary Education Data System-Table 26

Professional schools have also seen a large increase in the number of women in their incoming classes. For instance, women comprise 50% or more of both law school and medical school incoming classes (Zhao, 2004). In addition, women comprise 40% of MBA graduates (Zhao). Interestingly, these fields are beginning to pay attention to the potential drop in salary when a field becomes more "**feminized**." The American Psychological Association has already initiated a task force to look at the potential impact of the feminization of psychology on the discipline and on earning potential (Street, 1994).

What do observers make of these gains for women in labor force participation? Some of the response to these numbers is based on an individual's world view. One can see the glass as both half empty and half full. In terms of a positive view, some of the change has been dramatic. So, as shown earlier for engineer degrees, it is positive to see a doubling of the percentage of engineers who are female in the past 30 years. However, one could also take a negative view and see 21% overall rate as a very low percentage. In addition, the women gaining engineering degrees still appear to face job opportunities with fewer long term prospects. In addition, some occupations have shown much better strides than others. Some fields are much more resistant to change. Women are still less than 1% of auto mechanics (Wooton, 1997).

Overall, one of the positive outcomes of the changes in **gender equity** in occupations is better research on the kinds of interventions that actually improve occupational opportunities. In a summary report, the Women's Educational Equality Act Equity Resource Center (2002) suggests that several interventions have been shown to help increase women's participation in non-traditional fields: collaborations between K-12 schools and employers, technical schools and colleges, the important role of teachers, providing accurate and current information about careers and career preparations and training, helping students identify discrimination and strategies for dealing with it, providing role models and mentors, and, starting occupational education earlier in the schools.

Finally, we must revisit the question about why gender equity is important. Gender equity is important because individuals deserve equal opportunities to individuals. However, more centrally, individual deserve equal earning opportunities. We will close out this discussion of the engendered labor force with a discussion of some pay equity interventions that have been established.

Wage Gap "Fixing". Some of the more interesting work on the wage gap comes from government and political groups intent on reducing the wage gap through pay equity plans. In general, these plans attempt to reduce gender-based wage inequities by analyzing jobs by their duties rather than their titles. The best examples of this work come from federal, state and local governments who have been mandated to work against pay inequity. Pay equity adjustments look at the important variables that "should" affect pay rates including skill, effort, responsibility, complexity, supervisory responsibility, education/training and working conditions. Oftentimes, risk is included in job ratings such as police officers and fire fighters. Most of the data on this type of reclassifying find that women have been underpaid given the conditions and duties of their jobs rather than men being overpaid. A job like "warehouse manager" may actually not be much difference than a school office manager. Both jobs involve a lot of paperwork. However, one is male dominated and other female dominated. Reclassifying jobs helps take the "gender" out of the job and reduce pay equity.

What if an employer were to oversee both nursing assistants (female-dominated) and plumbers (male-dominated), what might she/he see? When compared on responsibility, supervisory, and training dimensions, which job "deserves" more pay? In a hospital in Ontario, Canada, the comparison of these two jobs resulted in a 17% increase adjustment for the nursing assistants (National Committee on Pay Equity, 2004). In Hawaii in 1995, a comparison of nurses and corrections officers yielded a correction of a monthly pay gap of almost $1000 (National Committee on Pay Equity, 2004).

Overall, we have seen that women and men still face different occupational opportunities that are directly linked to earning opportunities.

Do Men And Women Differ At Work?

We have seen that the labor market is engendered and affords different opportunities to men and women. However, it is also important to ask whether men and women differ at work? Do they have different values? Expectations? Behaviors? Early research on men and women and work focused on different motivations for work. The research often outlined a difference between extrinsic and intrinsic rewards. **Extrinsic rewards** are external rewards such as pay or awards. **Intrinsic rewards** are internal rewards such as a sense of satisfaction. Intrinsic rewards can be from the person or from the job and they are related to positive well-being, work satisfaction and work performance (Ryan & Deci, 2001). Most workers have a combination of both types of motivations toward work. Individuals, regardless of gender, drawn to the same type of work, tend to have the same types of motivation structures. Dubinsky, Jolson, Michaels, Kotabe, and Lim (1993) found that male and female salespersons had no significant differences on work motivation.

Early research on gender and motivation suggested that women were more motivated by social rewards (such as relationships with coworkers) whereas men were more motivated by external outcomes such as pay (as reviewed by Maccoby, 1995; Sansone, & Harackiewicz, 2000). There is some evidence of these types of orientations today. For instance, Tang and Talpade (1999) found that males leaned toward a higher satisfaction with salary/pay than females, and females had a higher satisfaction rating with co-workers than males and that these factors were associated with overall job satisfaction. However, in general, gender differences in motivations toward work, particularly those in the same fields, have largely disappeared and some commentators indicate that the distinction is really one that characterizes the older generation (Maccoby) and that currently younger men and women have a fuller sense of expectations for their work situations that do not yield gender differences (Browne, 1997). Even in the study by Tang and Talpade discussed above, the authors conclude that employers should emphasize salary and/or benefits when hiring but realize that job satisfaction will be of greater importance in regards to retention of employees. In chapter 5 on expectations we discussed leadership and gender, now we will now turn to another workplace issues that has distinctive gender implications – sexual harassment.

Sexual Harassment

Since the 1980s, America has seen a rising level of attention paid to **sexual harassment** in the workplace by corporations and researchers. Definitions of sexual harassment vary. The legal definition of sexual harassment tends to be narrow and will yield smaller incidence rates than more psychological definitions (Gutek & Done, 2001; Lengnick-Hall, 1995). Legal definitions of sexual harassment center on two broad categories. **Quid pro quo** sexual harassment occurs when a co-worker (normally a supervisor) implies that sexual interaction is needed in order for the employee to advance or keep his/her job (Equal Employment Opportunity Commission (EEOC), 1980). **Hostile working environment** occurs co-worker(s) create an environment that is negative to an employee's professional or personal well-being by making sexual comments and/or negative comments regarding that individual's sex (EEOC, 1980). A working environment will only be deemed hostile if a pattern can be shown and if it passes the "reasonable" person standard (Paetzold & O'Leary-Kelly, 1996). Rotundo, Nguyen, and Sackett (2001) conducted a meta-analysis on a gender differences in the perception of sexual harassment. Several scholars have suggested sexual harassment should be based on a "reasonable woman" standard rather than person (Blumenthal JA., 1998). The meta-analysis yielded a small to medium effect size of .30 suggesting that women perceive a broader range of social-sexual behaviors as harassing (Rotundo, Nguyen, & Sackett, 2001). The female-male difference was greater for social-sexual behaviors (such as hostile environment) and lesser for more overt behaviors such as sexual propositions and sexual coercion. Future research will be faced with disentangling the role of sexual socialization (such as the sexual script) and its interaction with the real and perceived power of male and female co-workers. Interestingly, both men and women who have experienced sexual harassment attribute the harassment to power, not sex (Berdahl, Magley, & Waldo, 1996).

"Sexual Harassment"

Not surprisingly, incidence rates of sexual harassment depend on how the researchers measured harassment and vary based on type of survey used, sampling technique, and the type of work environment in which the study was conducted (Ilies, Hauserman, Schwochau, & Stibal, 2003). Ilies, Hauserman, Schwochau and Stibal found that 24% of women from an aggregated sample of 86,000 women reported experiencing sexual harassment at work. Almost 60% of women reported have experienced potentially harassing behavior at work. The researchers also established that sexual harassment is more prevalent in organizations characterized by relatively large power differentials between organizational levels (such as the military). Research on male victims of harassment yields lower rates (less than 10%) but men are both less likely to report and less likely to perceive various scenarios as harassment (Berdahl, Magley, & Waldo, 1996; Waldo, Berdahl, & Fitzgerald, 1998). Additionally, men report less anxiety in response to sexual harassment scenarios (Berdahl, Magley, & Waldo).

The consequences of sexual harassment for the individual being harassed are varied. However, whether or not a woman labels an event as "harassment" the experiencing of harassment is associated with negative (Gutek & Done, 2001: Schneider, Swan, & Fitzgerald, 1997). Women who experience harassment are more likely to quit a job, be transferred or be fired. In addition, researcher have linked psychological disorders such as depression and decreased life satisfaction to harassment (Lenhart, 2004).

Employers ought to be motivated to reduce sexual harassment for several reasons including the potential psychological and financial costs to the organization. One study found that over two-years the cost to federal government resulting from sexual harassment in terms of lost productivity, as well as use of sick leave and job turnover, was $267.3 million (Levinson, Johnson, & Devaney, 1988). In addition, sexual harassment lawsuits result in additional financial and time costs. In 2003, more than 25,000 lawsuits related to workplace sexual harassment were brought to the Equal Employment Opportunity Commission (EEOC). Regardless of the motive for harassment, research across many employment settings indicates that sexual harassment can be reduced by vigilant supervisors who actively denounce sexual harassment in behavior and tone (Pryor, La Vite, & Stroller, 1993).

Stringer, Remick, Salisbury, and Ginorio (1990) recommend that employers have multiple strategies to respond and prevent sexual harassment that are linked directly to the several reasons behind the harassment. For instance, they recommend that for harassment that is due to a personal crisis in the life of the harasser the employer's responsibility to tell the harasser to discontinue the harassment; secondly, the employer should suggest an employee assistance program or appropriate counseling to help the harasser resolve the personal crisis. Harassment is clearly a complex and multi-level situation. Our "a closer look" study focuses on a model of sexual harassment that measures several levels of analysis.

Box 13.1 A closer look at an interesting study...

Who did the study?

> Cortina & Wasti (2005)

What did they study?

> Women's coping in response to sexual harassment with an interest in "whole patterns" of experience by examining multiple levels of variables including, individual, organizational, and cultural.

Who did they study?

> Four separate samples of women. 447 working class Anglo Americans (mostly food manufacturing employees), 476 working class Hispanic Americans (mostly unskilled labor and service delivery jobs), 240 professional Anglo Americans (university staff and faculty), and a sample of 355 professional women in Turkey (professional and office jobs).

How did they do the study?

> The authors conceptualized coping in response to sexual harassment as a multi-level experience (often referred to as ecological models). They identified four levels. 1) *The individual level* (social power) measured by a composite categorization based on education levels and age and marital status. 2) *Microcontext* (stressor severity) measured by respondents' report of the frequency and type of sexual harassment. 3) *Mesocontext* (social support) measured by a composite of the respondents' view of the organizational support and the gender composition of the workplace. 4) *Macrocontext* (culture) measured by the categories of Anglo, Hispanic or Turkish. The outcome of "harassment coping" was divided into categories of denial, avoidance, negotiation, and social coping (involving coworkers or bosses).

What did they find?

They summarized their results in terms of each of the ecological levels. *Individual* – older women more likely to avoid confrontation than younger women. *Micro* – the more severe the harassment the broader the coping response (e.g. negotiation or social coping). *Meso* – findings indicate that a no tolerance policy toward sexual harassment from organizational leaders reduced women's need for coping behaviors. *Macro* – across occupational classes, women in collectivist, patriarchal cultures (Hispanic and Turkish) reported more avoidance and denial without seeking social support or advocacy responses.

What is so interesting about it?

Although psychologists recognize that behavior is contextual and occurs within the boundaries of larger systems, it is difficult to design research that attempts to get at the complexity of the behavior. In this case, the authors use the results to indicate to organizations that due to variations in individual, organizational and cultural experiences, formal grievances should not be the only mechanism offered. Informal third-party intervention may be appropriate in many cases.

Work/Life Balance

The high overall level of women's labor force participation has now existed long enough for scholars to have conducted high quality research on work/life concerns. Interestingly, very little research existed on men and work/life balance or concern until women's rates began to change. Several issues relate to the relative balance of work and family life in the United States. Namely, researchers have explored the impact of parents' (namely mothers') employment on children, the impact of wives' employment on husbands, the impact of wives' employment on the women's mental and physical health, and the impact and role of policy on work/life balance.

Several excellent sources exist that summarize decades of work with several key points of consensus (Applebaum, 2001; Folbre, 2001; Gornick & Meyers, 2003; Jacobs & Gerson, 2004; Smolensky & Gootman, 2003; Williams, 2000). These researchers appear to agree on ten major points regarding work in the United States. First, the United States' workforce has become more diverse in terms of gender, ethnicity, race, social class and age. Second, the United States workforce is comprised of many more "atypical arrangements" than in the past (changes in number of hours, times of day, shared work, etc.). Third, most of the responsibility for balancing employment and children's needs falls on individuals. Parents in the U.S. invent a patchwork a variety of creative arrangements to allow

work/family to coexist. Fourth, a large percentage of children live in families where all available parents are employed (single parents or dual income). Fifth, a large percentage of children spend a significant amount of time in nonparental care. Sixth, quality nonparental care leads to positive cognitive and social outcomes for children. Seventh, much nonparental care is not of high quality, including opportunities for adolescents after school. Seventh, access to parental leave and other key work/life balance policies is limited. Eighth, the problems associated with work/family coexistence appear to be more acute in the U.S. than in other western industrialized countries. Finally, although researchers speak of work/life balance, the reality is much closer to imbalance or co-existence for many families and individuals who do not experience the situation as balanced nor positive for themselves or their children. In this next section, we will look at the impact on parents and their children. We will conclude by looking at work/life policy and how the United States compares to other western industrialized countries.

Impact on the Parents. Due to their multiple roles, college students rarely need to have role strain and role conflict explained in much depth. **Role strain** refers to a single role (e.g., student or employee) being too much to handle; whereas, **role conflict** refers to two roles being in conflict with one another (e.g., partner and employee or employee and student). Most of the early research on individuals with multiple roles assumed a type of "**role scarcity**" theory where there an individual is portrayed as a pie that can only be sliced up in so many ways. More recent research has focused on "**role enhancement**" or "expantionist" theories where holding multiple roles can actually enhance the well-being of the whole individual or individual roles (Barnett & Hyde, 2001). Many of us can relate to a situation where it was "nice" to be in class because we didn't have to be dealing with a loved one – or, when it was nice to be with ones friends to work off a bad day at the office. Researchers refer to both "positive" and "negative" **spillover** from work to family and vice versa. A good day at the office can bring a good mood home just as a bad day at home can make the work day difficult on your coworkers. While there is evidence to support some components of scarcity theory "there is only so much to go around," when it comes to overall well-being, the evidence strongly supports the concept that multiple roles are beneficial (Barnett & Hyde).

"The Stress of Balancing Work and Family"

Role theory is an important background to understanding the implications of the research on the balance of work and family for parents. For both men and women multiple roles are positive. Interestingly, for men, family involvement is particularly associated with well-being; whereas, for women, employment is particularly associated with well-being (Barnett & Hyde, 2001). Multiple roles appear to be of benefit for several reasons including: the buffering effect as described above where one role can provide support for another, added income helps the family unit, social support is increased because of networks associated with each role, and multiple roles also give increased opportunities to experience success. Of course, there is an upper limit and there can be too many roles and the quality of roles is more important than the quantity. In particular, for parents, long work hours are associated with poor outcomes (Voydanoff & Donnelly, 1999).

This discussion of role theory does not negate the stress that employed parents feel when balancing work and family. Ample evidence exists to support the fact that women feel the brunt more acutely than men. Hochschild (1989) coined the phrase "**the second shift**" to describe the fact that employed women tend to complete a shift at work and then a second shift of being the primary care giver and home manger when they are home. Recent data suggest that the average employed mother spends twice as much time as the average employed father on household chores and the care of children (Andrews, 2004). In addition, two-thirds of the working mothers reported doing housework and preparing meals on an "average" day; whereas, only 19% of men reported doing housework and 34% reported helping with meals or clean-up. A recent study used beeper technology where participants are beeped and then report what they are doing – a technology that tends to yield more exact results than retrospective reporting or daily logs. Husbands' estimated that they did 42% of the housework; wives' estimated that husbands did about 33% of the housework and the reality was 38% (Lee & Waite, 2005). Interestingly, longitudinal studies suggest that egalitarian behaviors (such as equal division of home labor) for boys in later life are predicted by parents who shared care when children are young; whereas girls' later behaviors are better predicted by education and adulthood experiences (Myers & Booth, 2002).

Despite this second shift, when women are assessed in the aggregate there are essentially no predictable differences in well-being between employed mothers and stay-at-home mothers (Mccarten, 2004). Employed mothers have been found to have some tendency toward higher anxiety and higher self esteem; whereas, higher depression is sometimes seen stay-at-home mothers (Mccarten). In addition, larger numbers of children are associated with more work-family stress, lower well-being, and lower marital satisfaction (Matthews & Power, 2002; Twenge, Campbell & Foster, 2003). Most importantly, the research suggests that women's attitudes toward their employment plays an important role (Chang, 2004; O'Keeffe, 2002). Women who work because "they want to" versus "they have to" have better well-being.

Single mothers tend to have lower well being than married mothers (Cairney, Boyle, Offord, & Racine, 2003). However, it is important for both research and policy to note that the key issues for single mothers are financial resources, stress, and social support. Single mothers with strong social support and good resources have less stress and better mental health outcomes (Cairney, Boyle, Offord, & Racine). Finally, although single fathers tend to have better economic resources than single mothers, when they have similar economic circumstances, they have similar well-being, regardless of the gender of their children (Downey, Ainsworth-Darnell, & Dufur, 1998).

For men, the findings support the concept that men with higher involvement with their children have higher well-being (Barnett, Marshall, & Pleck, 1992; Veroff, Douvan, & Kolka,

1981). In addition, men who provide more child and household care tend to have wives who report higher marital satisfaction and higher well-being (Ozer, Barnett, Brennan, & Sperling, 1998).

Impact on the Children

Early research in this field was limited by overly simplistic comparisons between the children of women who "worked" vs. those who were stay-at-home moms. Scholars in the field are now aware of a myriad of variables that affect children's outcomes including the family's economic level, the perception of choice by the mother, the child's age, the child's personality, the quality of the parents' relationship, etc. One genuine misnomer of arguments against women's labor force participation is the idea that home environments are always best (e.g., Gelernter, 1996). In fact, the research suggests that it is the quality of the care that matters more than who is giving the care (National Institute of Child Health and Human Development, NICHD, 2003). Overall, quality day care is associated with positive outcomes (Duncan, 2003; HICHD, 2004; HICHD, 2003; Love, Harrison, Sagi-Schwartz, 2003). Table 13.5 provides a list of indicators of quality day care generated by research and often used in licensing decisions.

Table 13.5 Indicators of Quality Day Care

Staffing
- o Low child to staff ratio (most states have standards that licensed centers must adhere to such as 3 to 1 for infants, 7 to 1 for 4 year olds)
- o Smaller numbers of children overall
- o Trained staff
- o Low turn-over in staff
- o Age-appropriate supervision (no child left alone)
- o Safe and effective discipline practices

Safety & Health
- o Children and staff properly immunized
- o Regular hand washing
- o Practiced fire drills
- o Emergency plans in place
- o Toxic substances removed or locked up
- o Access to safe outdoor play area
- o Medications handled properly

Fiene (2002)

One area that appears to be hotly contested currently in the literature is the impact of longer numbers of hours in day care on infants. There are children who are better off spending more time out of their home environments than in them if the non-home environment is stimulating and caring (Smolensky & Gootman, 2003). In addition, studies on the impact of parents' employment on children are confounded by the fact that the additional income associated with employment can lead to positive outcomes such as the provision of adequate food, clothing, housing, health care, and stimulating environments (such as books in the home or stimulating outings) (Smolensky & Gootman). One of the most hotly debated topics in this category is the impact of child care on children under the age of one.

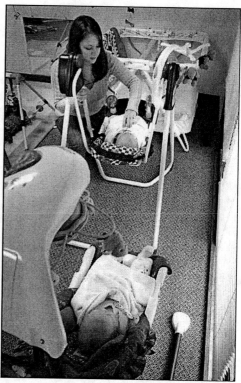

The children of single mothers tend to be at increased risk for poor behavioral outcomes (e.g., academic achievement). However, just as single mothers' well-being is mediated by social support and financial resources, children of single mothers with support also appear to be at no greater risk than children from two-parent families (Lipman, Boyle, Dooley, & Offord, 2002).

Overall, we have seen that multiple roles are generally positive for both men and women and that good quality child care is associated with positive outcomes for children. While these are positive findings, the reality is that 45% of employed parents still report feeling "some or "a lot" of interference between their jobs and their families lives (and that number is up from a similar study 25 years ago) (Bond, Thompson, Galinsky & Prottas, 2002). For infants, it appears that both the mother and the child are better off physically and emotionally if the mother is able to take longer than the "traditional" 6-week leave and/or work fewer hours (Smolensky & Gootman, 2003). Most employed pregnant women in the U.S. use a combination of short-term disability, sick leave, vacation, personal days, and unpaid family leave to comprise their maternity leaves. Consequently, the last segment of this chapter is on work/life policies.

Work/Life Policies

Scholars generally assert that high rates of women's labor force participation are here to stay. Slowly corporations and organizations have responded to develop for a workplace that responds better to the needs of a workforce that no longer fits the "traditional" mode of employed male with stay-at-home wife. Originally, these policies and options were called "family-friendly" to reflect the idea that work and family could be more effectively balanced. Currently, the standard term in the field is **"work/life" balance**. This newer term reflects the fact that all workers have lives outside of the workplace. In addition, the term allows the discussion

to focus on life situations that particularly appear to create more stress between work and life such as raising children, caring for aging parents, and illness. Although some of us may consider such policies both humane and necessary on a basic level, research clearly supports the fact that organizations with good work/life policy show economic advantages (Burud & Tumolo, 2004; Jacobs & Gerson, 2004). Work-to-family conflict negatively affects work performance (e.g., Kinnunen, Geurts, & Mauno 2004). Effective work/life policies lead to increased retention of employees, increased employee satisfaction, organizational commitment, self-reported productivity, and increased recruitment of employees (Bond, Thompson, Galinsky, & Prottas, 2002; Burud & Tumolo, 2004; Eaton, 2003).

Many types of work/life policies exist. Table 13.6 provides examples of several. However, one of the more hotly contested issues in work/life policy is the role of government policy. After nine years of concerted lobbying, the **Family Medical Leave Act** (FMLA) was established in 1993. The FMLA (provides 12 of job-protected leave for family and medical issues (U.S. Department of Labor, 1993). FMLA allows for unpaid leave and the promise of job security. FMLA indicates that the employer must provide a similar job to the employee rather than the "exact" job, or, as it often used to happen, a demoted job.

"BMCC – Helping Women Find Their Balance"

One drawback of the FMLA is that in only applies to companies with 50 employees or more. Approximately 40% of private employees work for companies with less than 50 employees (National Partnership for Women and Families, n.a.); and, therefore, do not have these opportunities protected. Smaller companies were exempted because legislators and lobbyists felt that it may be an economic burden to smaller companies. However, the other problem with exemption for small companies is the fact that low-wage workers are disproportionately employees in smaller businesses (Newman, 2000).

Overall, the United States Government (through FMLA) provides for unpaid leave for many employees. As noted in Table 13.6 there are several options that employers can offer their employees. A survey conducted by the Society for Human Resource Management (2003) indicated that 57% of the companies surveyed provided a type of leave that exceed FMLA obligations such as paid leave or leave for parent-teacher conferences or for employees who have been employed for less than 13 months. To give you another sense of how available these work/life policies are for employees, a study of over 300 companies in Michigan found that 75% of all employers offered some from work/life benefits or policies (Community Research Institute, 2002). However, these policies included options that generally benefit employees rather than focusing more directly on mothers and fathers (e.g., retirement plans and professional development opportunities). Approximately 50% of the employers offered more traditional work/life policies such as flexible work schedules and maternity leave. However, the most utilized policies such as health benefits for part-time staff and/or job sharing were the least likely to be available (e.g., only 1 out of 4 employers).

Table 12.5
Types of Work/Life Policies in the United States

National Policy & Procedures
• Tax credit (e.g., child care credit – a percentage of child care expenses up to a set level).
• Childcare subsidies for low-income parents, subsidies for meals at schools or day care
• Family Medical Leave Act (FMLA) allows for 12 weeks of unpaid leave and job security for full-time employees of companies with 50 or more employees.
Corporate Work/Life Policies
• Maternity/Paternity leave.
o Some companies build on FMLA and offer longer leaves and/or paid leaves for their employees

- Dependent Care Assistance Programs
  - Permit employees to put aside a set amount of pre-tax income annually for care of dependents
- Family Leave
  - Corporations can add benefits to FMLA such as "personal leave days" where employees use a pool of days for selves or kids
- Child Care
  - On-site child care (infants, toddlers, pre-school, school age), kindergartens & schools; before and after school care
  - "Sick child" child care
  - Referrals for child care
  - Lactation rooms (for nursing mothers)
  - Parenting seminars and newsletters
- Elder Care
  - Referral services
  - Plans that allow pre-payment for coverage of nursing home costs for self, spouse, parents or in-laws
- Flex-time (non-traditional hours or job-sharing)
  - Compressed work- week: e.g., 4 10-hour days or 80 hours over 9 work days to give every other Friday off.
  - Telecommuting: employee works at home or in satellite office close to home
  - Cross functional teams (cross train so that when a worker is unavailable, another can step in)
- Financial Arrangements
  - Financial help such as subsidized childcare or direct reimbursements
  - Flexible benefit plans where employees can choose among benefits such as health insurance and the dependent care assistance program.

Other Innovations
- On-site personal services such as dry-cleaning, shoe repair, pharmacy delivery, and access to take home dinners.
- Health insurance and other benefits to domestic partners (especially important to gay and lesbian employees)
- Adoption Assistance and Benefits
- Low Cost education loans for employees and dependents, tuition reimbursement- policies
- Convenient parking for expectant mothers
- Employee Assistance Programs (EAP)
  - Confidential and free access to psychological and professional help (e.g., to discuss child care, parenting and adult care concerns)
- Spouse Relocation Assistance for dual career couples
- Encouraging parents to take children on business trips by adding extra weekend day for sightseeing
- Extension of "probationary period" for tenure and partnership -decisions where childbirth adoption, elder care, etc. can delay employee's progress
- Responding to needs of family without affecting work
  - Providing pagers to parents with sick children
  - Scheduling meetings at manageable times (e.g., at noon, rather than early am or evening)
  - Make phones accessible to employees to monitor elderly dependents,

latch-key kids
- Consultants within or from without the company to monitor and adapt work/life policies to better meet the needs of workforce

Note: Susan Willy and Donna Anderson helped in the compiling of these policies.

One policy that gains much attention is the option of **paid leave** for maternity or paternity. As you can imagine, paid *paternity* leave is even rarer than paid maternity leave. One study showed a rate of fewer than 7% of employers offered paid paternity leave (U.S. Office of Personnel Management, 2001). One of the reasons that paid leave garners attention is that the U.S. is one of only two industrialized nations not to have *paid* leave. In fact, until 1993, The U.S. was the only industrialized nation not to have unpaid leave. Indeed, the U.S., in comparison to other western industrialized countries, provides substantially fewer options. Table 13.7 compares the government provided policies in 19 industrialized countries that were chosen due to their high volume of business with one another. In most of these countries, paid leave is a mandated by law to be provided by the government or the business.

Not only are the U.S. and Australia the only two countries out of these 19 industrialized nations without paid maternity leave, they are, in fact, the only two without paid maternity leave out of the 175 countries who are members of the International Labor Organization (International Labor Organization, 2004). The ILO is a component of the United Nations devoted to minimum basic labor rights.

Table 13.7
Comparison of Maternity Leave Benefits across Developed Countries

Country or area	Length of maternity leave	Percentage of wages paid in covered period	Provider of coverage
Developed countries [a] without paid leave			
United States	12 weeks	0	--
Australia	1 year	0	--
Developed countries with paid leave			
Canada	17-18 weeks	55 for 15 weeks	Government
China	90 days	100	Employer
France	16-26 weeks	100	Government

Germany	14 weeks	100	Government to ceiling; employer pays difference
India	12 weeks	100	Employer/ Government
Indonesia	3 months	100	Employer
Italy	5 months	80	Government
Japan	14 weeks	60	Health insurance
Malaysia	60 days	100	Employer
Netherlands	16 weeks	100	Government
New Zealand	12 weeks	Up to a set amount that approximates 55% of women's average wages	Government
Republic of Korea	60 days	100	Employer
Saudi Arabia	10 weeks	50 or 100	Employer
Singapore	8 weeks	100	Employer
Thailand	90 days	100 for 45 days then 50% for 15 days	Employer for 45 days, then Government.
United Kingdom	14-18 weeks	90 for 6 weeks, flat rate after	Government
Vietnam	4-6 months	100	Government

[a] Countries represent Australia and its top trading partners.
Human Rights and Equal Opportunity Commission (2002).

Although this book has chosen to focus on the U.S. and not international comparisons, in the case of work/life policy, it is important to see that the U.S. is the outlier and that more thorough policies are working for other industrialized nations. *(Note: As of September 2008 – the Australian Prime Minister introduced a bill for paid maternity leave for consideration by the government – a decision is expected in 2009).*

Does everyone embrace the idea of work/life policies? Not necessarily. When individuals criticize work/life policies, they focus namely on the fact that the policies are not merit-based (e.g., Zaleska, 2004). In other words, the policies focus on those in need, rather than those who may "deserve" benefits. How fair is it that some employees have access to special non-work related benefits whereas others do not? Of course, health insurance is a similar metaphor. All of us pay into a system that will differentially benefit those who get very sick. However, a particular employee may compare him/herself to another employee and see an injustice. Like many policies, it depends on who is doing the comparisons. A corporation may see work/life policies as benefiting the company at-large. In addition, very few work/life policies are limited to parents except maternity/paternity leaves, the others can usually be categorized as allowing for more flexibility. Finally, Hegtvedt, Clay-Warner, and Ferrigno (2002) found that parents and non parents employed by companies perceived as supportive of their employees were likely to feel resentment about specific policies.

Gornick and Meyers (2003) conclude their analysis of families that work by outlining three "transformations" that would allow a society to realize dual earner families. First, the gendered division of the care of children and household obligations need to shift such that men need to shift to more housework and women to more wage earning hours at work. Second, the labor market would need to be more family-friendly in terms of policies and flexibility. Finally, government policies would need to be expanded to support the emotional and economic costs of raising society's children. As you think about these recommendations and the findings from this chapter, think about the number of personal and political assumptions and beliefs that go into any individuals' views about work, family and the role of government.

Additional ways to think about the material in this chapter

- ❖ Implicit Attitudes Test (IAT) –
  https://implicit.harvard.edu/implicit/demo/
  - o Visit this site and complete the measure on "gender & career".
- ❖ Sloan Work & Family Research Network –
  http://wfnetwork.bc.edu/
  - o The network has a collection of activities associate with work/life balance at http://wfnetwork.bc.edu/activities.php

Global Connection Opportunities

- ❖ http://www.ilo.org/ International Labour Organization
  - o Click on the "themes" tab in the upper right
  - o Comparisons of maternity leave
    - ▪ http://www.ilo.org/global/About_the_ILO/Media_and_public_information/Press_releases/lang–en/WCMS_008009/index.htm
  - o Comparisons of paternity leave
    - ▪ http://www.emplaw.co.uk/researchfree-redirector.aspx?StartPage=data%2f20033221.htm

Chapter 14
Conclusions

A. *What have we learned?*
B   *What does the future bring?*
C. *Where Are the Men in Gender?*
D. *The End?*

> One night we had friends over with their then 10-year old boy, Jake, and 12-year old daughter, Audrey. I promised Audrey that we could rent a "chick flick." Jake asked what a "chick flick" was and I answered "Princesses, Ponies, Pink and Kisses." Jake smirked and asked "wouldn't it be cool if the pink blinded the princesses and the kisses made the ponies explode?" His immediate ability to be playful about the exaggerated silliness of the chick/dude distinction made me feel hopeful about the future.

What Have We Learned?

This book started with the analogy that humans relate to gender the way that fish relate to water. I argued that gender is all around us, moves through us, and serves as the defining force behind some of our social systems – often without us even being aware of it. This final chapter serves to pose more questions than assertions. I hope that this textbook deepened your understanding of the roles of sex and gender in American society and provided you both intellectual and personal insights.

Several overarching themes arise from gender psychology research and a reminder. Let's first consider the issue of research on gender "differences." Research has established that men and women are overwhelmingly more similar than different (Hyde, 2005). We also know that people tend to overestimate the differences between men and women. Anselmi and Law (2007) impart six important caveats associated with analyzing sex and gender (italicized below and originally introduced in Chapter 2) that provide an excellent framework for continuing to think about the key issues.

1. *Sex/Gender differences attract attention.* In other words, the public as well as researchers are interested in them. In Tavris' (1998) review for *Scientific American* of a Maccoby's (1998) book *The Two Sexes: Growing up Apart, Coming Together*, she humorously started her review with the comment "Talking about sex differences is America's second favorite indoor sport" and concludes her review with the assertion that the discussion of sex and gender differences will continue for many years to come.

2. ***Scientific research is the only way to dispel myths and break stereotypes.*** In Chapter 2 (see Table 2.1), we reviewed the results of from Maccoby and Jacklin's (1974) groundbreaking tally of scientific research on sex/gender difference research. If you review the table, the findings hold up remarkably well to current findings generated from more extensive research.

3. ***Too much focus on similarity can create norms based on one gender or one way of doing things.*** In other words, as with work on ethnicity or race, the goal is not to erase difference or argue that one way of doing things is better than another. The applied goal for research on gender is to appreciate any real differences that are can be determined. In addition, the scientific goal also aims at the uncovering the interplay of nature/nurture in affecting gender similarities and differences.

4. ***Small differences can be overblown.*** Not only do individuals overemphasize difference, the practice in the social sciences of prioritizing the publishing of studies that find differences over those that do not establish a difference also exacerbates the view of the existence of differences.

5. ***Descriptions can become prescriptions*** – for instance, if men are supposed to like sports, does a man have to like sports to be a real man?

6. ***Gender research has revealed that the study of gender is much more complex than expected, and complexity suggests a need for more research and fewer global differences statements.*** As we have seen throughout this book, the interpretations of gendered attitudes and behaviors have to consider the **context** of the individuals involved and each layer of the situational context. The complicated nature of gender studies results in many questions being answered with the phrase "well, it depends..." While it may be frustrating for to receive that answer, it actually reflects a more sophisticated and complex understanding of the sophisticated and complex experience of gender. Most of the interesting findings are in the area of "it depends," because then we can begin to understand under what conditions we would be most likely to see predicted sets of outcomes.

"Sex, Gender, Gender Identity and Gender Roles"

The study of gender also indicates some additional overarching themes important to future study. The analysis of surface difference/similarities often obscures a more insidious result of beliefs about gender differences – the fact that our individual beliefs about gender affect our own behaviors and our interpretations of others. The impact of our beliefs is also a "context of gender" analysis because our beliefs influence our display of gender attitudes and behaviors.

The relationship and intersection of ethnicity, race, and social class with gender reflects an additional overarching theme regarding the context of gender issues. As we have seen throughout this book, basic demographic distinctions between individuals and their associated cultures provide some of the most salient situational contexts of importance. Additional research is needed to better understand the interplay and intersectionality of these important issues

(Hurtado, 1996). One key area of psychological research in this field argues that a variety of gender-linked and other demographically linked behavior (such as ethnicity) depend heavily on self identification processes such as self categorization and social comparison (Deaux, 1999; Jones, 2006) as well as more external experiences such as sexism and racism.

Internal processes such as identification are also related to another key contextual aspect – power. Given that most societies reflect situations where men have the sanctioned power ("patriarchy"), it is often easy to overemphasize the role of "gender" rather than "power." Power may ultimately be the more useful explanatory tool in gender-related attitude/behaviors; however, it is difficult to tease apart gender and power and gender plays its own distinctive role in individuals' lives. Power need not be recognized by any of the individuals involved, it can be imagined, perceived, or implied and still have consequences (Rosenblum & Travis, 2002). Understanding power can help us comprehend how men and women can experience the world differently even if they do not fundamentally differ from one another on many psychological attributes (Stewart & McDermott, 2004).

Finally, the last overarching theme to emphasize is the interdisciplinary nature of gender studies. Understanding sex and gender requires the insights and methodologies of many fields including biology, sociology, political science, etc. Gender and women's studies programs throughout colleges and universities are by necessity interdisciplinary. This book focused on the psychological perspective and reflected work from other disciplines, but I encourage you to read widely in many fields to develop a fuller sense of gender studies.

What Does the Future Bring?

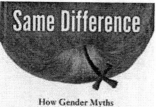

As we have seen, the study of gender is an exciting field that generates much public and scientific interest. Recently a popular press book on gender garnered good reviews and strong sales (Barnett & Rivers, 2005). Barnett and Rivers drew from the research to argue that several gender myths such as "men are better at math" continue to affect how we interact with one another. The authors further argue that beliefs in innate gender differences serve to "rationalize" gender discrimination patterns still prevalent in modern societies. The book reflects the evolution in the study of gender in psychology from a direct comparison of men and women to one where we try to more fully understand the context of the behavior.

Current academic examinations of the future of gender pose a variety of intense questions. For instance, the introduction to an edited collection entitled *The Future of Gender,* Browne poses the following questions:

> *...how useful is the concept of gender in social analysis? To what degree does gender relate to sex? How does gender feature in shifts in familial structures and demography? How should gender be conceived in terms of contemporary inequality and injustice, and what is gender's function in the design and pursuit of political objectives? (p. 3; 2007)*

Another interesting insight into current gender-related debates is a book series called *opposing viewpoints.* The series tackles many hot topics, but has published several volumes on men's and women's roles. Keeping in mind that the series exaggerates difference to allow for interesting debate, I believe the titles of the current match-ups give an interesting view into current gender discussions (Miller, 2009).

1. Men Are Becoming More Like Women (*Chris Nutter) "versus"* Women Are Becoming More Like Men (*Boyé Lafayette De Mente*)

2. Gender Equity Is Increasing (*Marilyn Gardner) "versus"* The Future of Gender Roles Is Uncertain (*Alexandra Montgomery)*

3. "Gender Will Become a Choice (*Karen Moloney) "versus"* Gender Will Become Obsolete (*George Dvorsky)*

I encourage you and your classmates to generate a list of the types of gender discussions that will persist into the future.

Where Are The Men In Gender?

Studies of gender have often resulted in focusing on women's experience. Given that many accepted "truths" of human behavior were originally based on male models and theories and tended to result in a focus that could be interpreted as "male=normal and female=other", it is not surprising that some gender research was "corrective" and some transformative. However, both men's and women's experience comprise a genuine understanding of gender. In the past several decades, psychology has seen an important and useful rise in scholarship on masculine experience. For instance, the American Psychological Association has a division of *The Society for the Psychological Study of Men and Masculinity* (Div. 51) that was founded in 1995. In contrast, Division 35, *The Society for the Psychology of Women* was founded in 1974. In addition, several textbooks now exist devoted to men and masculinity (e.g., Kilmartin, 2007; Kimmel & Messner, 2009). The text that you are reading was written to address gender psychology and therefore addresses research on men, women and individuals who prefer not to categorize as either.

In less academic, more popular press, discussions there are examples of male perspectives on issues previously seen as women's issues – such as violence against women. Although many writers have pointed to the role of men in defining a masculine culture that is positive for both men and women, a book such as Katz' (2006) reiterates the fact that men should be the centers of the discussion of behavior like violence because men are the more likely perpetrators. He makes the argument that violence such as rape, battering, sexual abuse and harassment are so widespread that have to be seen as a social problem not the problem of individual troubled men. As we have already seen, this argument is not new – however, it is relatively new to have a male on the forefront of encouraging men to take an active role in challenging the societal norms in this area (http://www.jacksonkatz.com/).

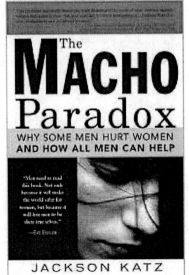

In a similar vein, the "old" question of the relationship of men to feminist thought and activism continues to be addressed in new and more current ways (e.g., Tarrant, 2009). Tarrant's book *Men and Feminism* argues that men are the "key" to feminism's continuing relevance and importance. It is recommended that you discuss this assertion with your classmates and friends, even if you do not consider yourself to be a feminist. The question is not as simple as it might originally seem: it reflects many of the facets of gender experience discussed in this book. You many also find this short essay written by a young woman for a men's magazine where she outlines ways for men to be feminist intriguing (http://www.mademan.com/manly-ways-be-feminist/).

Another interesting trend in the field of gender psychology is continued attention to expanding view of the categories "male" and "female." As we saw in chapter 4 on the biological basis of sex and gender, evidence continues to grow regarding the concept that these categories are more fluid than originally expected. Several current books exist where individuals describe their experiences as both genders or some category of sexual ambiguity. As mentioned previously in Chapter 4, there are books such *As Nature Made Him: The Boy Who Was Raised as a Girl* that profile individuals who have lived both as a biological woman and biological man; however, other interesting books focus on the choices surrounding gender such as *Self-Made Man* that accounts the life of a woman who chooses to "pass" as a male for a year (Vincent, 2006).

Why is gender psychology political? Discussions of gender often quickly become political. Fundamental beliefs about men and women fuel beliefs about our current society and our individual place in our changing society. In writings on gender, you will find a full spectrum of political beliefs. However, generally speaking, when individuals learn more about the current status of men and women in our society and internationally, it often leads to an increased desire for more gender equity (e.g. Katz, Swindell, & Farrow, 2004).) The question of how to bring about more gender equity is a very political question. Box 14.1 provides some links to several websites that you may wish to peruse to get a fuller sense of the blogosphere regarding feminism. This text does not endorse these sites, but provides an insight into a larger number of perspectives on gender issues.

Box 14.1:
Edgier feminist sites
- http://bitchmagazine.org/
- http://www.feministing.com/
- http://theangryblackwoman.com/
- http://blog.iblamethepatriarchy.com/
- http://www.reappropriate.com/
- http://www.offourbacks.org/

and a good resource to these and other sites:
- http://www.thefword.org.uk/resources/websites/

Less edgy feminist sites:
- http://www.now.org/
- http://www.feminist.org/
- http://www.feminist.com/

GLBT and gender-bending sites:
- http://www.curvemag.com/
- http://www.out.com/
- http://etransgender.com/
- http://www.eric-jost.com/
- http://www.thegirlinside.com/

Anti-feminist sites
- http://www.angryharry.com/
- http://ladiesagainstfeminism.com/

This book started and ended with the metaphor of gender culture being to humans as water is to fish. The argument that gender functions as a type of "cultural upbringing" is not original and variations on the general theory have been nicely illuminated in several academic works (e.g., Bem, 1993; Fiske & Stevens, 1993; Maccoby, 1998; Stewart & McDermott, 2004). However, it is a powerful theory with strong explanatory power. This book will close with another metaphor that my students and I both find to be helpful. It is a metaphor I learned at a workshop and it is helpful for people who want change. If you stand on an escalator, you will go the direction the escalator is heading even if you don't actively step in that direction. The only way to keep from going with the mainstream is to actively turnaround and walk the other way. Even if you have no interest in walking the other way – I encourage you to think about what kinds of behaviors in terms of gender in our society "count" as walking the other way?

References

Abramson, L. Y., Metalsky, G. I., & Alloy, L. B. (1989). Hopelessness depression: A theory-based subtype of depression. *Psychological Review, 96(2),* 358-372.

Ackerman, E. (2002, November 25). *Students lobby for new diversity requirement.* The Cavalier Daily. Retrieved on October 6, 2006 http://www.cavalierdaily.com/CVArticle.asp?ID=14324&pid=942

ACT. (2003, September 29). *ACT scores steady despite record number of test-takers.* Retrieved from. http://www.act.org/news/releases/2003/8-20-03.html

Adahere (2003, August 3). *Exceptionally offensive anti-white male ad* [Msg. 1]. Message posted to uspoliticsonline.com/forums/

Adrian M. (2002). A critical perspective on cross-cultural contexts for addiction and multiculturalism: Their meanings and implications in the substance use field. *Substance Use& Misuse, 37(8-10),* 853-900.

Adrian, M., Dini, C. M., MacGregor, L.G. Stoduto, G. (1995). Substance use as a measure of social integration for women of different ethno-cultural groups into mainstream culture in a pluralist society: The example of Canada. *International Journal of Addictions, 30*(6), 699-734.

Adult Video News (1998). *Survey of adult video stores.* Retrieved November 21, 2003 at http://www.adultvideonews.com/charts/pro0903.html

Alan Guttmacher Institute (2003). *Facts in brief: Induced Abortion.* New York: Author.

Albert, A. A. & Porter, J. R. (1986). Children's gender role stereotypes: A comparison of the United States and South Africa. *Journal of Cross-Cultural Psychology, 17,* 45-65.

Alexander, G. M. & Hines, M. (1994). Gender labels and play styles: Their relative contribution to children's selection of playmates. *Child Development, 65,* 869-879.

Ali, S. R., Liu, W. M. & Humedian, M. (2004). Islam 101: Understanding the religion and therapy implications. *Professional Psychology: Research and Practice, 35,* 635-642.

Allen, B. P. (1995). Gender stereotypes are not accurate: A replication of Martin (1987) using diagnostic vs. self-report and behavioral criteria. *Sex Roles, 32(9-10),* 583-600.

Allgeier, E. R. & Allgeier, R. E. (2000). *Sexual interactions* (5th ed). New York: Houghton Mifflin.

Alsaker, F. D. (1996). Annotation: The impact of puberty. *Journal of Child Psychology & Psychiatry & Allied Disciplines, 37*(3), 249-258.

Amer, M. (2008). *Membership of the 110th Congress: A profile.* CRS Report for Congress. Washington D.C.: CRS.

American Association of University Women (AAUW) (1992). *How Schools Shortchange Girls.* NY: Marlowe & Co.

American Lung Association. (2003, June). *Trends in tobacco use 2003.* Washington DC: Author.

American Psychiatric Association. (2000). *Diagnostic and statistical manual of mental disorder* (DSM IV – text revision). Washington DC: Author.

American Psychological Association (2001). *Publication manual of the American Psychological Association* (5th Ed). Washington D.C.: Author.

American Psychological Association (APA) (1998, December). Researcher finds gender stereotypes to be accurate, part of nature, *APA Monitor, 29(12),* 23.

American Urological Association (2003). *Normal and abnormal sexual differentiation.* Retrieved November 11, 2003 at http://www.urologyhealth.org/pediatric/index.cfm?cat=01&topic=110.

Anderson, J. C., Martin, J. L., Mullen, P. E., Romans, S. E., & Herbison, P. (1993).The prevalence of childhood sexual abuse experiences in a community sample of women. *Journal of the American Academy of Child and Adolescent Psychiatry, 32,* 911-919.

Andres, L. & Adamuti-Trache, M. (2008). Life-course transitions, social class, and gender: A 15-year perspective of the lived lives of Canadian young adults. *Journal of Youth Studies, 11(2),* 115-145.

Andrews, E. L. (2004, September 14). Survey confirms it: Women outjuggle men. *New York Times.* C12.

Andsager, J. L. & Roe, K. (1999). Country music video in country's year of the woman. *Journal of Communication, 49(1),* 69-82

Angier, N. (1999, February 21). Men, women, sex, and Darwin. *New York Times Magazine.* p. 92.

Ano, G., & Vasconcelles, E. (2005). Religious Coping and Psychological Adjustment to Stress: A Meta-Analysis. *Journal of Clinical Psychology, 61(4),* 461-480.

Anonymous (n.d.). Retrieved January 8, 2004 from http://www.mental-health-today.com/ptsd/domestic/stories.htm

Anselmi, D. & Law, A. L. (2007). *Questions of gender: Perspectives and paradoxes (*2nd Ed.*).* New York: McGraw Hill.

Applebaum, E. (Ed.). (2001). *Balancing acts: Easing the burdens and improving the options for working families.* Washington, DC: Economic Policy Institute.

Archer, J. (2002). Sex differences in physically aggressive acts between heterosexual partners: A meta analytic review. *Aggression and Violent Behavior. 7(4),* 313 –351.

Archer, J., Pearson, N. A., & Westeman, K. E. (1988). Aggressive behaviour of children aged 6-11: Gender differences and their magnitude. *British Journal of Social Psychology, 27(4),* 371-384.

Archibald, A. B., Graber, J. A., & Brooks-Gunn, J. (1999). Associations among parent-adolescent relationships, pubertal growth, dieting, and body image in young adolescent girls: A short-term longitudinal study. *Journal of Research on Adolescence, 9(4),* 395-415.

Argyle, M. (1994). *The psychology of social class.* New York: Routledge.

Arias, E. & Smith, B. L. (2003). *Deaths: Preliminary Data for 2001. National vital statistics reports, 51(5).* Hyattsville, Maryland: National Center for Health Statistics.

Aries, E. (1996). *Men and women in interaction: Reconsidering the differences.* New York: Oxford University Press.

Armstrong, M. J. (2000). Older women's organization of friendship support networks: An African American-White American comparison. *Journal of Women & Aging, 12(1-2),* 93-108.

Ashmore, R. D. & del Boca, F. K. (1981). Conceptual approaches to stereotypes and stereotyping. In D. L. Hamilton (Ed.) *Cognitive Processes in stereotyping and intergroup behavior* (pp. 1-35). Hillsdale, NJ: Erlbaum.

Atkeson, L. R. & Rapoport, R. B. (2003). The more things change the more they stay the same: Examining gender differences in political attitude expression, 1952-2000. *Public Opinion Quarterly, 67,* 495-521

Babcock, L. & Laschever, S. (2003). *Women don't ask: Negotiation and the gender divide.* Princeton, NJ: Princeton University Press.

Bandura, A. (1977) Self-efficacy: Toward a unifying theory of behavioral change. *Psychological Review, 84,* 191–215.

Banich, M. T. & Heller, W. (1998). Evolving perspectives on lateralization of function. *Current Directions in Psychological Science, 7(1),* 1-2.

Barber, N. (2003). Divorce and reduced economic and emotional interdependence: A cross-national study. *Journal of* Divorce *& Remarriage, 39*(3-4), 113-124.

Bargh, J A.; Chen, M; & Burrows, L. (1996). Automaticity of social behavior: Direct effects of trait construct and stereotype activation on action. *Journal of Personality & Social Psychology, 71(2),* 230-244.

Barker, L., Edwards, R., Gaines, C., Gladney, K., & Holley, F. (1980). An investigation of proportional time spent in various communication activities by college students. *Journal of Applied Communication Research, 8,* 101-109.

Barnett, L. B., & Corazza, L. (1998). Identification of mathematical talent and programmatic efforts to facilitate development of talent. *European Journal for High Ability, 9(1),* 48-61.

Barnett, R. C. & Hyde, J. S. (2001). Women, men, work, and family. *American Psychologist, 56*(10), 781-796

Barnett, R. C., Gareis, K. C., James, J. B., & Steele, J. (2003). Planning ahead: College seniors' concerns about career-marriage conflict. *Journal of Vocational Behavior, 62*(2), 305-319.

Barnett, R. C., Marshall, N. L. & Pleck, J. H. (1992). Men's multiple roles and their relationship women's psychological distress. *Journal of Marriage and the Family, 54,* 358-367.

Barnett, R., & Rivers, C. (2005). *Same difference: How gender myths are hurting our relationships, our children, and our jobs.* New York: Basic Books.

Baron, L., Straus, M. S., & Jaffee, D. (1987). Legitimate violence, violent attitudes, and rape: A test of the cultural spillover theory. In R. A. Prentky & V. L. Quinsey (Eds.), *Annals of the New York Academy of Sciences* (pp. 78-110). New York: New York Academy of Sciences.

Baron, R. A. & Byrne, D. (2003). *Social Psychology* (10th Ed). Boston, MA: Allyn & Bacon.

Baron, R. A. (1993). Reducing aggression and conflict: The incompatible response approach, or why people who feel good usually won't be bad. In G. C. Brannigan & M. R. Merrens (Eds.), *The undaunted psychologist* (pp. 203-218). Philadelphia: Temple University Press.

Barry, D. (1995). *Dave Barry's complete guide to guys: A fairly short book.* New York: Fawcett Columbine.

Barry, D. T., & Grilo, C. M. (2002). Eating and body image disturbances in adolescent psychiatric inpatients: Gender and ethnicity patterns. *International Journal of Eating Disorders, 32(3),* 335-343.

Barnett, R., & Rivers, C. (2005). *Same difference: How gender myths are hurting our relationships, our children, and our jobs.* New York: Basic Books.

Bart, J. (1998). *Feminist theories of knowledge: The good, the bad and the ugly.* Retrieved November 5, 2003 from http://www.dean.sbc.edu/ bart.html

Basile, K. C..*(1995). Gender differences in K-12 Education: What indicators are important?* Atlanta: Georgia: Georgia State University Applied Research Center.

Baudouin, J., & Humphreys, G. (2006). Configural information in gender categorisation. *Perception, 35*(4), 531-540.

Baumeister, R. F., Catanese, K. R., & Vohs, K. (2001). Is there a gender difference in strength of sex drive? Theoretical views, conceptual distinctions, and a review of relevant evidence. Personality & *Social Psychology Review, 5*(3), 242-273.

Baxandall, R. F., Gordon, L. & Reverby, S. (1995). *America's Working Women: A Documentary History 1600 to the Present.* New York: W. W. Norton.

Baxter, L.C., Saykin, A. J., Flashman, L. A., Johnson, S.C., Guerin, S. J., Babcock, D. R., & Wishart, H.A. (2003). Sex differences in semantic language processing: A functional MRI study. *Brain and Language, 84,* 264-272.

Beasley, B., & Standley, T. C. (2002). Shirts vs. skins: Clothing as an indicator of gender role stereotyping in video games. *Mass Communication & Society, 5(3),* 279-293.

Becker, D., Kenrick, D., Neuberg, S., Blackwell, K., & Smith, D. (2007). The confounded nature of angry men and happy women. *Journal of Personality and Social Psychology, 92*(2), 179-190.

Becker, S. W. & Eagly, A. H. (2004). The heroism of women and men. *American Psychologist, 59* (3), 163-178.

Beckwith, J. & King, J. (1974) The XYY syndrome: a dangerous myth. *New Scientist, 64*(923), 744-476.

Bee, H. L. (2001). *Lifespan development (3rd Ed.)* Boston, MA: Allyn & Bacon.

Beitchman, J. H., Zucker, K. J., & Hood, J. E. (1992*). A review of the long-term effects of child sexual abuse. Child Abuse & Neglect, 16*(1), 101-118.

Belansky, E. S. & Boggiano, A. K. (1994). Predicting helping behaviors: The role of gender and instrumental/expressive self-schemata. *Sex Roles, 30*(9-10), 647-661.

Belenky, M. F., Clinchy, B. M., Goldgerger, N. R., & Tarule, J. M. (1986). *Women's Way of Knowing: The Development of Self, Voice, and Mind.* Basic Books.

Bem, S. L. (1974). The measurement of psychological androgyny. *Journal of Consulting and Clinical Psychology, 42,* 155-162.

Bem, S. (1981) Gender schema theory: A cognitive account of sex typing. *Psychological Review, 88,* 354-364.

Bem, S. L. (1983) Gender schema theory and its implications for child development: Raising gender-aschematic children in a gender-schematic society. *Signs: Journal of Women in Culture and Society, 8,* 598-616.

Bem, S. L. (1989). Genital knowledge and gender constancy in preschool children. *Child_Development, 60(3),* 649-662.

Bem, S. L. (1993). The lenses of gender: Transforming the debate on sexual inequality*.* New Haven: Yale University Press.

Bem, S. L. (1998). *An unconventional family.* New Haven: Yale University Press.

Benbow, C. P. (1988). Sex differences in mathematical reasoning ability in intellectually talented preadolescents: Their nature, effects, and possible causes. *Behavioral and Brain Sciences, 11,* 169-232.

Benin, M. H., & Edwards, D.A. (1990). Adolescents' chores: The difference between dual- and single-earner families. *Journal of Marriage & the Family, 52(2),* 361-373.

Berdahl, J. L., Magley, V. J. & Waldo, C. R. (1996). The sexual harassment of men? *Psychology of Women Quarterly, 20(4),* 527-547.

Berman, P. W. (1976). Social context as a determinant of sex differences, in adults' attraction to infants. *Developmental Psychology, 12(4),* 365-366.

Berman, P. W. (1981). Are women more responsive than men to the young? A review of developmental and situational variables. *Annual Progress in Child Psychiatry & Child Development,* 321-361.

Bernstein, J. (2004). The low-wage labor market: Trends and policy implications. In A. C. Crouter & A. Booth (Eds.), *Work-family challenges for low-income parents and their children* (pp. 3-34). Mahwah, NJ: Lawrence Erlbaum.

Besharov, D. J., & West, A. (2001). African American marriage patterns. In A. Thernstrom & S. Thernstrom (Eds.), *Beyond the color line* (pp. 95-113). Stanford: Hoover Press.

Bettencourt, B. A. & Miller, N. (1996). Gender differences in aggression as a function of provocation: A meta-analysis. *Psychological Bulletin, 119*(3), 422-447.

Beyer, S. (1990). Gender differences in the accuracy of self-evaluations of performance. *Journal of Personality & Social Psychology, 59(5),* 960-970.

Bickham, D. S., Vandewater, E. A., Huston, A. C., Lee, J. H., Caplovitz, A. G., & Wright, J.C. (2003). Predictors of children's electronic media use: An examination of three ethnic groups. *Media Psychology, 5(2),*107-137.

Biernat, M. & Kobrynowicz, D. (1999). A shifting standards perspective on the complexity of gender stereotypes and gender stereotyping. In W. B. Swann, Jr., J. H. Langlois, & L. A. Gilbert (Eds). *Sexism and stereotypes in modern society: The gender science of Janet Taylor Spence.* (pp. 75-106). Washington DC: American Psychological Association.

Bjorkqvist, Lagerspetz, & Kaukiainen, (1992). Do girls manipulate and boys fight? Developmental trends in regard to direct and indirect aggression. *Aggressive Behavior, 18,* 117-127.

Black, D. (1999). *Bad boys, bad men: Confronting antisocial personality disorder.* Oxford: Oxford University Press.

Blakemore, J. E. & Centers, R. E (2005). Characteristics of boys' and girls' toys. *Sex Roles, 53,* 619-633.

Blau, F. (1998). Trends in the well-being of American women, 1970-1995. *Journal of Economic Literature, 36,* 112-165.

Blumenthal JA. (1998). The reasonable woman standard: A meta-analytic review of gender differences in perceptions of sexual harassment. *Law and Human Behavior, 22,* 33-57.

Bock, R. (1993). *A Guide for XXY Males and Their Families* (NIH Pub. No. 93-3202). Washington DC: U.S. Department of Health and Human Services.

Bodenhausen, G. V. (1988). Stereotypic biases in social decision making and memory: Testing process models of stereotype use. *Journal of Personality & Social Psychology, 55(5),* 726-737.

Boehm, H. (1986). *The official guide to the right toys.* New York: Bantam.

Bogaert, A. F. (2001). Personality, individual differences, and preferences for the sexual media. *Archives of Sexual Behavior, 30,* 29-53.

Boldt, D. (1998, November 22). Keeping the faith may keep mind, body going. *Champaign News-Gazette,* pp. B-1, B-5.

Boles, J. & Elifson, K. W. (1994). Sexual identity and HIV: The male prostitute. *Journal of Sex Research, 31*(1), 39-46.

Boman, U. W., Bryman, I., & Möller, A. (2004). Psychological well-being in women with Turner syndrome: Somatic and social correlates. *Journal of Psychosomatic Obstetrics & Gynecology, 25(3-4),* 211-219.

Bond, J. T., Thompson, C. Galinsky, E. & Prottas, D. (2002). *Highlights of the national study of the changing workforce: Executive Study.* New York: Families and Work Institute.

Bonds-Raacke, J. M., Bearden, E. S., Carriere, N. J., Anderson, E. M., & Nicks, S. D. (2001). Engaging distortions: Are we idealizing marriage. *Journal of Psychology, 135*(2), 179-184.

Book, A. S., Starzyk, K. B., & Quinsey, V. L. (2001). The relationship between testosterone and aggression: A meta-analysis. *Aggression & Violent Behavior, 6*(6), 579-599

Booth, A., Shelley, G., Mazur, A., Tharp, G., & Kittok, R. (1989). Testosterone, and winning and losing in human competition. *Hormones and Behavior, 23,* 556-771.

Borkowski, J. & Ramey, S. (2001). *Parenting and the child's world: Influences on academic, intellectual and socioemotional development.* New York: Erlbaum.

Botkin, D. R., Weeks, M. O. & Morris, J. E. (2000). Changing marriage role expectations: 1961-1996. *Sex Roles, 42*(9-10), 933-942.

Boyarin, D. (1997). *Unheroic conduct: The rise of heterosexuality and the invention of the Jewish man.* Berkeley, CA: University of California Press

Boyes, M. C., & Walker, L J. (1988). Implications of cultural diversity for the universality claims of Kohlberg's theory of *moral* reasoning. *Human Development, 31(1),* 44-59.

Brabant, S. & Mooney, L. A. (1997). Sex role stereotyping in the Sunday comics: A twenty-year update. *Sex Roles, 37,* 269-281.

Bradley, E. & Stahl, L. (1999, September 12). *Harry Potter book sales skyrocket around the world.* CBS News: 60 Minutes. Retrieved November 9, 2003 at http://www.the-leaky-cauldron.org/quickquotes/articles/1999/0999-cbsnews-stahl.html

Bradshaw, Z. & Slade, P. (2003). The effects of included abortion on emotional experiences and relationships: A critical review of the literature. *Clinical Psychology Review, 23*(7), 929-958.

Braver, S. L. & O'Connell, D. (1999). *Divorced dads: Shattering the myths.* New York: J. P. Tarcher.

Bridges, J. S. (1993). Pink or blue: Gender-stereotypic perceptions of infants as conveyed by birth congratulations cards. *Psychology of Women Quarterly, 17(2),* 193-205.

Brinkman, K. G. (2000). Religious affiliation, spirituality and gender identity. *Dissertation Abstracts International Section A: Humanities & Social Sciences, 61(2-A),* 781.

Bronstein, P. (2006). The family environment: where gender role socialization begins. In J. Worell & C. Goodheart (Eds.), *Handbook of girls' and women's psychological health: Gender and well-being across the lifespan* (pp. 262-271). New York: Oxford University Press.

Brooks-Gunn, J., Schley, S., & Hardy, J. (2000). Marriage and the baby carriage: Historical change and intergenerational continuity in early parenthood. In L. J. Crockett & R. Silbereisen (Eds.), *Negotiating adolescence in times of social change* (pp. 36-57). New York: Cambridge University Press.

Brown, K. R. (2005; Feb 18). Different opinions on gender differences. [Letter to the editor]. *The Chronicle of Higher Education, 51 (24).* A47.

Browne, B. A. (1997); Gender and preferences for job attributes: A cross cultural comparison. *Sex Roles, 37*(1-2), 61-71.

Browne, J. (Ed.) (2007). *The future of gender.* New York: Cambridge Press.

Bullough, B. & Bullough, V. L. (1996). Female prostitution: Current research and changing interpretations. *Annual Review of Sex Research, 41,* 158-180.

Burdman, P. (2005, Spring). Scholarship sweepstakes: National merit program offers millions in scholarship dollars without regard to financial need. *National Crosstalk, 13* (2), 1-5.

Bureau of Justice Statistics (2003). *Crime and victims statistics.* Retrieved January 3, 2004 from http://www.ojp.usdoj.gov/bjs/cvict.htm.

Burns, D. D. (1999). *Feeling good: The new mood therapy.* (2nd Ed.). New York: New American Library.

Burud, S. & Tumolo, M. (2004). Leveraging the new human capital: Adaptive strategies, results achieved, and stories of transformation. Mountain View, CA: Davies-Black.

Buss, D. M. (1998). *Evolutionary psychology: The new science of the mind* Boston, MA: Allyn & Bacon.

Buss, D. M. (Ed.). (2005). *The handbook of evolutionary psychology.* New York: Wiley.

Buss, D. M., Larsen, R., Westen, D., & Semmelroth, J. (1992). Sex differences in jealousy: Evolution, physiology, and psychology. *Psychological Science, 3,* 251-255.

Buss, D. M., Shackelford, T. K. & LeBlanc, G. J. (2000). Number of children desired and preferred spousal age difference: Context-specific mate preference patterns across 37 cultures. *Evolution & Human Behavior, 21(5),* 323-331.

Bussey, K., & Bandura, A. (1992). Self-regulatory mechanisms governing gender development. *Child Development, 63,* 1236-1250.

Bussey, K., & Bandura, A. (1999). Social cognitive theory of gender development and differentiation. *Psychological Review, 106,* 676-713.

Byrd-Craven, J., Geary, D., Rose, A., & Ponzi, D. (2008). Co-ruminating increases stress hormone levels in women. *Hormones and Behavior, 53*(3), 489-492.

Cafferata, G. L., & Meyers, S. M. (1990). Pathways to psychotropic drugs: Understanding the basis of gender differences. *Medical Care, 28*(4), 285-300.

Calavita, M. (2005). *Apprehending politics: News media and individual political development.* Albany, NY: State University of New York Press.

Caldera, Y. M. Huston, A. C. & O'Brien, M . (1989). Social interaction and play patterns of parents and toddlers with feminine, masculine, and neutral toys. *Child Development, 60,* 70-76.

Calmes, C., & Roberts, J. (2008, August). Rumination in interpersonal relationships: Does Co-rumination explain gender differences in emotional distress and relationship satisfaction among college students?. *Cognitive Therapy and Research, 32*(4), 577-590.

Cameron, D. (1990). *The Feminist critique of language: A reader.* New York: Routledge

Cameron, D. (1997). Performing gender identity: Young men's talk and the construction of heterosexual masculinity. In S. Johnson and U. H. Meinhoff, *Language and Masculinity* (pp. 47-64). Oxford: Blackwell.

Campbell, A. (1993). *Out of control: Men, women and aggression.* London: Pandora.

Campbell, J. C. (2002). Health consequences of intimate partner violence. *Lancet, 359(9314),* 1331-1336.

Campbell, J. C.; Oliver, C. E., & Bullock, L. F. C. (1998). The dynamics of battering during pregnancy: Women's explanations of why. In J. C. Campbell (Ed), *Empowering survivors of abuse: Health care for battered women and their children* (pp. 81-89). Thousand Oaks, CA: Sage Publications.

Campbell, R. (2008) The psychological impact of rape victims. *American Psychologist, 63*(8), 702-717.

Canli, T. Desmond, J. E. Zhao, Z., & Gabrieli, J. D. E. (2002, May 22) Sex differences in the neural basis of emotional memories. *Proceedings of the National Academy of Sciences. 99,* 10789-10794.

Cann, A., Mangum, J. L., & Wells, M. (2001). Distress in response to relationship infidelity: The roles of gender and attitudes about relationships. *Journal of Sex Research, 38(3),* 185-190.

Capaldi, D. M. & Gorman-Smith, D. (2003). The development of aggression in young male/female couples. In P. Florsheim (Ed.), *Adolescent romantic relations and sexual behavior: Theory, research, and practical implications* (pp. 243-278). Mahwah, New Jersey: Lawrence Erlbaum.

Caplan, P. J., Crawford, M., Hyde, J. S., & Richardson, J. T. E. (1997). *Gender differences in human cognition.* NY: Oxford.

Carli, L. L., LaFleur, S. J,. & Loeber, C. C. (1995). Nonverbal behavior, gender and influence. *Journal of Personality and Social Psychology, 68(6),* 1030-1041.

Carpenter, C. J., Huston, A.C., & Holt, W. (1986). Modification of preschool *sex*-typed behaviors by participation in adult-structured activities. *Sex Roles, 14(11-12),* 603-615.

Carroll, J. (2006. September 1). Americans Prefer Male Boss to a Female Boss. Retrieved January 10, 2009 from http://www.gallup.com/poll/24346/Americans-Prefer-Male-Boss-Female-Boss.aspx

Casey, M. B., Pezaris, E. & Nuttall, R. L. (1992). Spatial ability as a predictor of math achievement: The importance of sex and handedness patterns. *Neuropsychologia, 30,* 35-45.

Cattaneo, L. B. & Goodman, L. A. (2003). Victim-reported risk factors for continued abusive behavior: Assessing the dangerousness of arrested batterers. *Journal of Community Psychology, 31(4),* 349-369.

Ceci, S. J. & Williams, W. M. (Eds). (2007) *Why aren't more women in science: Top researchers debate the evidence.* Washington, DC: American Psychological Association.

Center for American Women and Politics (2005). *The gender gap: Voting choices in presidential elections.* New Bruswick, NJ: Author.

Center for Women in Government (1999). *Appointed policy makers in state government: A trend analysis, 1997, 1998, 1999.* Albany, NY: Author.

Centers for Disease Control (2001). *Women and smoking: A report of the Surgeon General - 2001.* Washington DC: Author.

Centers for Disease Control and Prevention (2002). *National center for health statistics.* Retrieved May 1, 2002, from www.cdc.gov/nchs/fastats

Central Intelligence Agency (2008). *The world factbook.* Washington DC: Author.

Chao, R. & Tseng, V. (2002). Parenting of Asians. In M. H. Bornstein (Ed). *Handbook of parenting: Vol. 4: Social conditions and applied parenting* (2nd ed.) (pp. 59-93). Mahwah, NJ: Lawrence Erlbaum.

Chavous, T. M., Harris, A., Rivas, D., Helaire, L., & Green, L. (2004). Racial stereotypes and gender in context: African Americans at predominantly Black and predominantly White Colleges. *Sex Roles, 51(1-2),* 1-16.

Cherpital, C. & Borgers, G. (2002). Substance use among emergency room patients: An exploratory analysis by ethnicity and acculturation. *American Journal of Drug and Alcohol Abuse, 28(2),* 287-305.

Chodorow, N. (1978). *The reproduction of mothering: Psychoanalysis and the sociology of gender.* Berkeley, CA: University of California Press.

Christopher, F. S. & Sprecher, S. (2000) Sexuality in marriage, dating and other relationships: A decade review. *Journal of Marriage and the Family, 62,* 999-1017.

Chumlea W. C., Schubert C. M., Roche A. F., Kulin H. E., Lee P. A., Himes J. H., & Sun S. S. (2003). Age at menarche and racial comparisons in US girls. *Pediatrics, 111*(1), 110-113.

Chung, R. H. G. (2001). Gender, ethnicity, and acculturation in intergenerational conflict of Asian American college students. *Cultural Diversity & Ethnic Minority Psychology, 7*(4), 376-386.

Ciarrochi, J. V., & Deane, F. P. (2001). Emotional competence and willingness to seek help from professional and nonprofessional sources. *British Journal of Guidance & Counseling, 29*(2), 233-246.

Clark, M. (1988, November 28). Cherchez la Difference. *Newsweek.* 61.

Clark, R. A. (1998). A comparison of topics and objectives in a cross section of young men's and women's everyday conversations. In D. J. Canary, & K. Dindia (Eds.), *Sex differences and similarities in communication: Critical essays and empirical investigations of sex and gender in interaction.* Mahwah, NJ: Lawrence Erlbaum Associates.

Cloitre, M. (1998). Sexual revictimization: Risk factors and prevention. In V. M. Follette & J. I. Ruzek (Eds.) *Cognitive-behavioral therapies for trauma* (pp. 278-304). New York, NY: Guilford Press.

Cohen, J. (1988). *Statistical power analysis for the behavioral sciences* (2nd Ed.) Hillsdale, NJ; Erlbaum.

Coker, D. R. (1984). The relationships among gender concepts and cognitive maturity in preschool children. *Sex Roles, 10*, 19-31.

Colapinto, J. (2000). *As nature made him: The boy who was raised as a girl.* NY: HarperCollins.

Cole, E. R. & Stewart, A. J. (1999). Meanings of political participation among Black and White women: Political identity and social responsibility. In L. A. Peplau, S. C., DeBro, R. C. Veniegas, & P. L. Taylor (Eds.), *Gender, culture, and ethnicity: Current research about women and men* (pp. 153-172). Mountain View, CA: Mayfield Publishing.

Cole, J. B. & Guy-Sheftall, B. (2003). *Gender talk: The struggle for women's equity in African-American communities.* New York: Ballantine.

Coleman, P. K. & Nelson, E. S. (1998). The quality of abortion decisions and college students' reports of post-abortion emotional sequelae and abortion attitudes. *Journal of Social & Clinical Psychology, 17*(4), 425-442.

Coley, R. L. & Chase-Lansdale, P. L. (1998). Adolescent pregnancy and parenthood: Recent evidence and future directions. *American Psychologist, 53*(2), 152-166

College Entrance Examination Board (2007). *2007 College-bound seniors: A profile of SAT program test-takers.* New York: Author.

Colley, A., & Todd, Z. (2002). Gender-linked differences in the style and content of e-mails to friends. *Journal of Language and Social Psychology, 21(4),* 380-392.

Collins, P. H. (1997). The meaning of motherhood in Black culture and Black mother/daughter relationships. In M. M. Gergen & S. N. Davis (Eds.), *Toward a new psychology of gender* (pp. 325-340). Florence, KY: Routledge.

Comedy Central. (1999, January 22). *Comedy Central and Stone Stanley Productions join to produce 22 episodes of testosterone-powered weekly series.* Retrieved August 25, 2003, from http://www.geocities.com/HotSprings/.

Congenital Adrenal hyperplasia Research, Education and Support Foundation, Inc.(n.d.) http://www.caresfoundation.com/

Connidis, I. A. & McMullin, J. A. (1999). Permanent childlessness: Perceived advantages and disadvantages among older persons. *Canadian Journal on Aging, 18*(4), 447-465.

Conway, M. M, Ahern, D. W. & Steuernagel, G. A. (2005). *Women and public policy: A revolution in progress.* Washington D. C.: CQ Press.

Conway, M. M, Steuernagel, G. A. & Ahern, D. W. (2005). *Women and political participation: Cultural change in the political arena.* Washington D. C.: CQ Press.

Copenhaver, M. M., Lash, S. J., & Eisler, R. M. (2000). Masculine gender-role stress, anger, and male intimate abusiveness: Implications for men's relationships. *Sex Roles, 42*(5-6), 405-414.

Cortina, L. M. & Wasti, S. A. (2005). Profiles in coping: responses to sexual harassment across persons, organizations, and cultures. *Journal of Applied Psychology, 90*(1), 182-192.

Cosgrove, G. R., Buchbinder B. R., & Hong J. H. (2000). *Functional magnetic resonance imaging for intracranial navigation.* Retrieved November 11, 2003 at http://neurosurgery.mgh.harvard.edu/Functional/fmrimage.htm.

Cott, N. F. (1997). *The bonds of womanhood: "Woman's sphere" in New England, 1780-1835* (2nd ed.). New Haven, CT: Yale University Press.

Cott, N. F. (2002). *Public vows: A history of marriage and the nation.* Cambridge: Harvard University Press.

Cott, N. F. (2004). *No Small Courage: A History of Women in the United States.* Oxford, England: Oxford University Press.

Crabb, P. B., & Bielawski, D. (1994). The social representation of material culture and gender in children's books. *Sex Roles, 30(1-2),* 69-79.

Crawford, M. & Unger. R. (2004). *Women and gender: A feminist psychology* (4th Ed). Boston, MA: McGraw Hill.

Crews, F.(1995). *The memory wars: Freud's legacy in dispute.* New York: New York Review of Books.

Cromie,W. J. (1997, September 11). Researchers discover how hormone thwarts heart disease. *The Harvard University Gazette.* Retrieved December 17, 2003 from http://www.news.harvard.edu/gazette/1997/09.11/ResearchersDisc.html

Culley, M. R. & Angelique, H. L. (2003). Women's gendered experiences as long-term three mile island activitists. *Gender & Society, 17,* 445-461.

D'Emilio, J. (2003). *Lost prophet: The life and times of Bayard Rustin.* New York: Free Press.

Dabbs, J. M., Chan, E. L. Strong, R. A., & Milun, R. (1998). Spatial-ability, navigation strategy, and geographic knowledge among women and men. *Evolution and Human Behavior 19,* 89-98.

Daly, M. & Wilson, M. (1988). *Homicide.* New York: A. de Gruyter.

Darwin, C. (1871). *The Descent of Man.* London, John Murray .

Darwin, C. 1968 (1859) *Origin of the Species,* London, Penguin.

Das, M. (2001) Business students' perceptions of best university professors: Does gender role matter? *Sex Roles, 45(9-10),* 665-676.

Deaux, K. (1999) An overview of research on gender: Four themes from 3 decades. In W. B. Swann, Jr., J. H. Langlois, & L. A. Gilbert (Eds). *Sexism and stereotypes in modern society: The gender science of Janet Taylor Spence* (pp. 11-34). Washington DC: American Psychological Association.

Deaux, K.; Emswiller, T. (1974). Explanations of successful performance on sex-linked tasks: What is skill for the male is luck for the female. *Journal of Personality & Social Psychology, 29(1),* 80-85.

Deaux, K.; White, L. & Farris, E. (1975). Skill versus luck: Field and laboratory studies of male and female preferences. *Journal of Personality & Social Psychology, 32(4),* 629-636.

Deaux, K; Winton, W., & Crowley, M. (1985). Level of categorization and content of gender stereotypes. *Social Cognition, 3(2),*145-167.

Dell, P., & Korotana, O. (2000). Accounting for domestic violence: A Q methodological study. *Violence Against Women, 6*(3), 286-310.

DeMaris, A. (1997). Elevated sexual activity in violent marriages: Hypersexuality or sexual extortion? The *Journal of Sex Research, 34,* 361-373.

Deveny, K. (1994) Chart of Kindergarten Awards. *Wall Street Journal,* B1.

Diamond, L. M. (2003). What does sexual orientation orient? A biobehavioral model distinguishing romantic love and sexual desire. *Psychological Review, 110*(1), 173-192.

Dickerson, B. J. (1995).Centering studies of African American single mothers and their families In: Dickerson, Bette J. (Ed). *African American* single mothers: Understanding their lives and families (pp. 1-20). Thousand Oaks, CA: Sage.

Dietz, T. L. (1998). An examination of violence and gender role portrayals in video games: Implications for gender socialization and aggressive behavior. *Sex Roles, 38(5-6), 425-442.*

Dill, B. T. (1994). *Across the boundaries of race & class: an exploration of work & family among black female domestic servants.* New York: Garland.

DiPietro, J. A. (1981). Rough and tumble play: A function of gender. *Developmental Psychology, 17*(1), 50-58.

Dixson, A. D. (2003). 'Let's do this!' Black women teachers' politics and pedagogy. *Urban Education, 38,* 217-235.

Dolin, D. J., & Booth-Butterfield, M. (1993). Reach out and touch someone: Analysis of nonverbal comforting responses. *Communication Quarterly 41,* 383-393.

Donelson, E. (1999) Psychology of religion and adolescents in the United States: Past to present. *Journal of Adolescence, 22(2),* 187-204.

Donley, R. & Vachon, D. (2001). *Eating concerns survey 2000: How did Notre Dame students respond?* Retrieved December 11, 2003 from http://www.nd.edu/~ucc/ucc_ed_survey_2000.html.

Downey, D. B.; Ainsworth-Darnell, J. W.; & Dufur, M. J. (1998) Sex of parent and children's well-being in single-parent households. *Journal of Marriage & the Family, 60*(4), 878-893.

Downs, B. (2003, October). *Fertility of American women: June 2002.* Washington DC: U.S. Census Bureau.

Dubinsky, A. J., Jolson, M. A., Michaels, R. E., Kotabe, M. & Lim, C. U. (1993). Perceptions of motivational components: Salesmen and saleswomen revisited. *Journal of Personal Selling & Sales Management, 13*(4), 16-37.

Dudden, F. E. (1983). *Serving women: Household service in nineteenth-century America.* Scranton, PA: Wesleyan University Press.

Duerst-Lahti, G. (2007, May). *Reflection on studying public leadership. Leading The Future of the Public Sector: The Third Transatlantic Dialogue.* University of Delaware, Newark, Delaware.

Duncan, G. J. (2003 Sep-Oct). Modeling the impacts of child care quality on children's preschool cognitive development. *Child Development, 74*(5), 1454-1475.

Eagly, A. (1995). The science and politics of comparing women and men. *American Psychologist, 145,* 145-158.

Eagly, A. H, & Crowley, M. (1986). Gender and helping behavior: A meta-analytic review of the social psychological literature. *Psychological Bulletin, 100(3),* 283-308.

Eagly, A. H. & Carli, L. L. (2007). *Women and the labyrinth. The truth about how women become leaders.* Boston, MA: Harvard Business School Press.

Eagly, A. H. & Crowley, M. (1986). Gender and helping behavior: A meta-analytic review of the social psychological literature. *Psychological Bulletin, 100(3),* 283-308.

Eagly, A. H. & Johnson, B. T. (1990). Gender and leadership style: A meta-analysis. *Psychological Bulletin, 108,* 233-256.

Eagly, A. H. & Karau, S. J. (1991). Gender and the emergence of leaders: A meta-analysis. *Journal of Personality and Social Psychology, 60,* 685-710.

Eagly, A. H. & Karau, S. J. (2002). Role congruity theory of prejudice toward female leaders *Psychological* Review, *109*(3), 573-598.

Eagly, A. H. &; Carli, L. L.(1981). Sex of researchers and sex-typed communications as determinants of sex differences in influenceability: A meta-analysis of social influence studies. *Psychological Bulletin, 90(1),* 1-20.

Eagly, A. H. (2007). Female leadership advantage and disadvantage: Resolving the contradictions. *Psychology of Women Quarterly, 31,* 1-12.

Eagly, A. H. Johannesen-Schmidt, M. C., & van Engen, M. L. (2003). Transformational, transactional, and laissez-faire leadership styles: A meta-analysis comparing women and men. *Psychological Bulletin, 129,* 4, 603-614.

Eagly, A. H., Karau, S. J. & Makhijani, M. G. (1995). Gender and the effectiveness of leaders: A meta-analysis. *Psychological Bulletin, 117,* 125-145.

Eagly, A. H., Makhijani, M. G. & Klonsky, B. G. (1992). Gender and the evaluation of leaders: A meta-analysis. *Psychological Bulletin, 111,* 3-22

Eaton, S. C. (2003). If you can use them: Flexibility policies, organizational commitment, and perceived performance. Industrial Relations: *A Journal of Economy & Society, 42*(2), 145-167.

Eaton, W. O. & Enns, L. R. (1986). Sex differences in human motor activity level. *Psychological Bulletin, 100(1),* 19-28.

Eckert, P., & McConnell-Ginet, S. (2003). *Language and gender.* Cambridge: Cambridge University Press.

Ecuyer-Dab, I. & Robert, M. Have sex differences in spatial ability evolved from male competition for mating and female concern for survival? *Cognition, 91(3),* 221-257.

Edelman, M. W. (2000). *Lanterns: A memoir of mentors.* New York: Harper.

Edelsky, C., & Adams, K. (1990). Creating inequity: Breaking the rules of debates. *Journal of Language and Social Psychology, 9,* 171-190.

Ehrhardt, A. A. (1984). Gender differences: A biosocial perspective. *Nebraska Symposium on Motivation, 33,* 37-57.

Eisenberg, N. &, Lennon, R. (1983). Sex differences in empathy and related capacities. *Psychological Bulletin, 94*(1), 100-131.

Ellenson, D. (2004, March 12). *Same-sex marriage, in the Jewish tradition.* Retrieved October 12, 2006 http://www.thejewishweek.com/top/editletcontent.php3?artid=3323

Elshtain, J. B. (1981). *Public man and private woman: Women in social and political thought .* Princeton: Princeton University Press.

Elze, D. E. (2002). Against all odds: The dating experiences of adolescent lesbian and bisexual women. *Journal of Lesbian Studies, 6*(1), 17-29.

England, J. C. (2004). *Asian Christian theologies.* Maryknoll, NY: Orbis Books

Equal Employment Opportunity Commission. (1980). Guidelines on discrimination because of sex (Sect. 1604. 11). *Federal Register, 45,* 74676-74677.

Etaugh, C. & Liss, M. B. (1992) Home, school, and playroom: Training grounds for adult gender roles. *Sex Roles, 26,* 129-147.

Evans, S. M. (1990). *Born for liberty: A history of women in America.* New York: Free Press.

Evans, T. (1994) (Ed.) *Seven promises of a promise keeper.* Colorado Springs, CO: Focus on the Family.

Fagot, B. (1995). Psychosocial and cognitive determinants of early gender role development. *Annual Review of Sex Research, 6.* 1-31.

Fairtest Examiner. (1998, Winter) *Gender gap narrows on revised PSAT.* Retrieved from http://www.fairtest.org/examarts/winter98/psat.htm.

Farrar, K. M., Krcmar, M. & Nowak, K. L., (2006). Contextual features of violent video games, mental models, and aggression. *Journal of Communication, 56*(2), 387-405.

Fausto-Sterling, A. (1992). *Myths of gender: Biological theories about women and men.* New York: Basic Books.

Fausto-Sterling, A. (2001). *Sexing the body: Gender politics and the construction of sexuality.* New York: Basic Books.

Dudden, F. E. (1983). *Serving women: Household service in nineteenth-century America.* Scranton, PA: Wesleyan University Press.

Feingold, A. (1988).Cognitive gender differences are disappearing. *American Psychologist, 43(2),* 95-103.

Fernando, S. (2002). *Mental health, race and culture (2nd ed.).* Basingstoke, England: Palgrave.

Fiene, R. (2002). *13 indicators of quality child care: Research update.* Denver, CO: National Resource Center for Health and Safety in Child Care.

Finkelhor, D., Hotaling, G., Lewis, I. A., & Smith, C. (1990). Sexual abuse in a national survey of adult men and women: Prevalence, characteristics, and risk factors. *Child Abuse and Neglect, 14,* 19-28.

Fischer, A. (1993). Sex differences in emotionality: Fact or stereotype? *Feminism & Psychology, 3*(3), 303-318.

Fischer, A. H. (2000). (Ed.) *Gender and emotion: Social psychological perspectives.* New York: Cambridge University Press.

Fish, S. (2005, March 4). Clueless in academe. The *Chronicle of Higher Education, 51 (26).* C1.

Fisher, B. & Akman, J. S. (2002). Normal development in sexual minority youth. In Billy E. Jones & M. J. Hill (Eds.) *Mental health issues in lesbian, gay, bisexual, and transgender communities.* (pp. 1-16.) Washington, DC: American Psychiatric Publishing.

Fisher, W. A. & Barak, A. (2002). Internet pornography: A social psychological perspective on Internet sexuality. *Journal of Sex Research, 38*(4), 312-323.

Fishman, P. M. (1978). Interaction: The work women do. *Social Problems, 25,* 397-406.

Fiske S. T., & Stevens, L. E. (1993). What's so special about sex? Gender stereotyping and discrimination. In S. Oskamp & M. Costanzo (Eds.) *Gender Issues in Contemporary Society*, pp. 173–96. Thousand Oaks, CA: Sage.

Flagler, S. (2003). *Women smoking: Fact Sheet for providers.* Retrieved December 13, 2003 from http://depts.washington.edu/uwcoe/

Floyd, K. (1995). Gender and closeness among friends and siblings. *Journal of Psychology, 129,* 193-202.

Foertsch, J. & Gernsbacher, M. A. (1997). In search of gender neutrality: Is singular they a cognitively efficient substitute for generic he? *Psychological Science, 8(2),* 106-111.

Fogg, P. (2005, March 4). Women and science: The debate goes on. The *Chronicle of Higher Education, 51 (26).* A1, 8.

Folbre, N. (2001). *The invisible heart: Economics and family values.* New York: New Press.

Fong, V. (2004) *Only hope: Coming of age under China's one-child policy.* Menlo Park, CA: Stanford University Press.

Foreman, J. (1998, September 21). Health equity?: The other ways the sexes differ. *Boston Globe.* C1.

Frances, L. J. (2005). Gender role orientation and attitude toward Christianity: A study among older men and women in the United Kingdom. *Journal of Psychology and Theology, 33,* 179-186.

Francoeur, R. T. (1991). (Ed.) *A descriptive dictionary and atlas of sexology.* Westport, CT: Greenwood Press.

Franklin, C. W. (1992). "Hey, home--Yo, bro": Friendship among black men. In P. M. Nardi (Ed.), *Men's friendships* (pp. 201-214).Thousand Oaks, CA: Sage.

Frazier, P. A., Tix, A. P., Klein, D. D. & Arikian, J. J. (2000). Testing theoretical models of the relations between social support, coping, and adjustments to stressful life events. *Journal of Social and Clinical Psychology, 19,* 341-335.

Freedman, D. H. (1992, June). The aggressive egg. *Discover.* 61-65.

Freud, S. (1960). *A general introduction to psychoanalysis* (J. Riviere, Tras.). New York: Washington Square Press. (Original work published 1924).

Freud, S. (1974). Some physical consequences of the anatomical distinction between the sexes. In J. Strachey (Ed. and Trans.) *The complete standard edition of the complete psychological works of Sigmund Freud* (Vol. 19, pp. 241-260). London: Hogarth. (Original work published 1925).

Freud, S. (1980). *Interpretation of dreams.* New York: Avon. (Original work published 1899).

Freund, M., Lee, N., & Leonard, T. L. (1991). Sexual behavior of clients with street prostitutes in Camden, NJ. *Journal of Sex Research, 28(4),* 579-591.

Frieze, I. H., Olson, J. E., & Good, D. C. (1990). Perceived and actual discrimination in the salaries of male and female managers. *Journal of Applied Social Psychology, 20,* 46-67.

Frieze, I.H., Whitley, B. E., Hanusa, B. H. & McHugh, M. C. (1982). Assessing the theoretical models for sex differences in causal attributions for success and failure. *Sex Roles, 8(4),* 333-343.

Frisby, C. M. (1999). Building theoretical insights to explain differences in remote control use between males and females: A meta-analysis. *Journal of Current Issues and Research in Advertising, 21 (2),* 59-76.

Fullerton, H. N. (1999, December). Labor force participation: 75 years of change, 1950-98 and 1998-2025. *Monthly Labor Review,* 3-12.

Futuyma, D. J. (1998). *Evolutionary biology.* (3rd Ed.). Sunderland, MA: Sinauer Associates Inc.

Galliano, G. (2003). *Gender: Crossing Boundaries.* Belmont, CA: Wadsworth.

Gamble, W. C. & Dalla, R. L. (1997). Young children's perceptions of their social worlds in single- and two-parent Euro- and Mexican American families. *Journal of Social and Personal Relationships, 14,* 357-372.

Ganster, D. C., Fox, M. L., & Dwyer, D. J. (2001). Explaining employees' health care costs: A prospective examination of stressful job demands, personal control, and physiological reactivity. *Journal of Applied Psychology, 86*(5), 954-964.

Gardner, H. (1983). *Frames of mind: The theory of multiple intelligences.* New York: Basic Books.

Garrod, A. C. Smulyan, L., Powers, S. I. & Kilkenny, R. (2004). *Adolescent portraits: Identity, relationships, and challenges* (5th Ed.). Boston, MA: Allyn & Bacon.

Gater, R., Tansella, M., Korten, A., Tiemens, B. G., Mavreas, V. G.,Olatawura, M. O.(1998). Sex differences in the prevalence and detection of depressive and anxiety disorders in general health care settings: Report from the World Health Organization collaborative study on psychological problems in general health care. *Archives of General Psychiatry, 55(5),* 405-413.

Gaulin, S.J., FitzGerald, R.W. & Wartell, M.S. (1990). Sex differences in spatial ability and activity in two vole species (Microtus ochrogaster and M. pennsylvanicus). *Journal of Comparative Psychology, 104,* 88-93.

Gay, D. A. Ellison, C. G. & Powers, D. A (1996). In search of denominational subcultures: Religious pro-family issues revisited. *Review of Religious Research 38,* 3- 17.

Gayle, B. M., Preiss, R. W..Burrell, N. (2006). *Classroom communication and instructional processes: Advances through meta-analysis.* Mahwah, NJ: Lawrence Erlbaum Associates Publishers.

Gazzaniga, M. S., Ivry, R. B., & Mangun, G. R. (1998), *Cognitive neuroscience: The biology of the mind.* New York: Norton.

Geary, D. C. (1998). *Male, female: The evolution of human sex differences.* Washington DC: APA.

Gelernter, D. (1996, February) Why mothers should stay home. *Commentary, 101* (2).

George, D. M., Carroll, P., Kersnick, R., & Calderon, K. (1998). Gender-related patterns of helping among friends. *Psychology of Women Quarterly, 22*(4), 685-704.

Gergen, K. J. (1999). *An invitation to social construction.* Thousand Oaks, CA: Sage.

Geschwind, N. & Galaburda, A. M. (1987). *Cerebral lateralization: Biological mechanisms, associations and pathology.* Cambridge, MA: MIT Press.

Gettings, J., Johnson, D., Brunner, B. & Frantz, C. ((2007). *Wonder women: Profiles of leading female CEOs and business executives.* Retrieved August 8, 2008 from http://www.infoplease.com/spot/womenceo1.html

Gilligan, C. (1982). *In a different voice: Psychological theory and women's development.* Cambridge, MA: Harvard University Press.

Girshick, L. B. (2002). *Woman-to-woman sexual violence: Does she call it rape?* Boston: Northeastern University Press.

Gladstone, T. R. G., Kaslow, N. J.; Seeley, J. R., & Lewinsohn, P. M. (1997). Sex differences, attributional style, and depressive symptoms among adolescents. *Journal of Abnormal Child Psychology, 25(4),* 297-305.

Glover, G. (2001). Parenting in Native American families. In N.B. Webb (Ed) *Culturally diverse parent-child and family relationships: A guide for social workers and other practitioners.* (pp. 205-231) New York: Columbia University Press.

Goldman J. D. G. & Padayachi, U. K. (2000). Some methodological problems in estimating incidence and prevalence in child sexual abuse research. *Journal of Sex Research, 37*(4), 305-314.

Goldstein, J. (1998). Immortal Kombat: War toys and violent video games. In J. H. Goldstein *Why we watch: The attractions of violent entertainment.* (pp. 53-68).London: Oxford University Press.

Goleman, D. (1997). *Emotional intelligence.* New York: Bantam Books.

Gordon, D. (2005, December 13). *Transforming the world view of minority cultures.* Retrieved October 6, 2006 http://www.international.ucla.edu/article.asp?parentid=35562

Gornick, J. C. & Meyers, M. K. (2003). *Families that work: Policies for reconciling parenthood and employment.* New York: Russell Sage.

Gossett, J. L. & Byrne, S. (2002). "Click Here": A content analysis of Internet rape sites. *Gender & Society, 16*(5), 689-709.

Gottman, J. (1994). *What predicts divorce? The relationship between processes and marital outcomes.* Mahwah, NJ: Erlbaum.

Gottman, J. M. (1994). *Why marriages succeed or fail: What you can learn from the breakthrough research to make your marriage last.* New York: Simon & Schuster.

Gould, S. J. (2002). *The Structure of Evolutionary Theory.* Cambridge, MA: Harvard Press.

Gouldner, H. & Strong, M. S. (1987). *Speaking of friendship: Middle-class women and their friends.* New York: Greenwood Press.

Grall, T. S. (2003, October). Custodial mothers and fathers and their child support: 2001. Washington DC: U.S. Department of Commerce.

Grant et al. (2004). Prevalence, correlates, and disability of personality disorders in the United States: Results from the national epidemiologic survey on alcohol and related conditions. *Journal of Clinical Psychiatry, 65,* 948-958.

Graves, K. (1998). *Girl's schooling during the progressive era: From female scholar to domesticated citizen.* New York: Garland Press.

Gray, J. (1993). *Men are from Mars, women are from Venus: A practical guide for improving communication and getting what you want in your relationships.* New York: HarperCollins.

Green, R. J., Sandall, J. C., & Phelps, C. (2005). Effect of *experimenter* attire and *sex* on participant productivity. *Social Behavior & Personality, 33,* 125-132.

Greene, B. (1994). African American women. In I. Comas-Diaz & B. Greene, Beverly (Eds.), *Women of color: Integrating ethnic and gender identities in psychotherapy* (pp. 10-29). New York: Guilford Press.

Greenwald, A. G., & Banaji, M. R. (1995). Implicit social cognition: Attitudes, self-esteem, and stereotypes. *Psychological Review,102*(1), 4-27.

Griffiths, J. A., & McCabe, M. P. (2000). The influence of significant others on disordered eating and body dissatisfaction among early adolescent girls. *European Eating Disorders Review*, 8(4), 301-314.

Grigorenko, E. (2005). Behavior genetics principles: Perspectives in development, personality, and psychopathology. *Journal of the American Academy of Child & Adolescent Psychiatry, 44*(2), 202-203.

Gross, R. M. (1996). *Feminism and religion: An introduction*. Boston, MA: Beacon Press.

Groth, A. N. (2001). *Men who rape: The psychology of the offender*. Cambridge, MA: Da Capo Press.

Groth, A. N. & Hobson, W. F. (1997).The dynamics of sexual assault. In L. B. Schlesinger & E. Revitch, (Eds.),*Sexual dynamics of anti-social behavior* ((2nd ed, pp. 158-170), Springfield, IL: Charles C. Thomas.

Grusec, J. E., Davidov, M., & Lundell, L. (2002). Prosocial and helping behavior. In P. K. Smith, & C. H. Hart (Eds.), *Blackwell handbook of childhood social development* (pp. 457-474). Malden, MA: Blackwell Publishers.

Gur, R. C., Turetsky, B. I., Matsui, M., Yan, M., Bilker, W., Hughett, P., & Gur R. E. (1999) .Sex differences in brain gray and white matter in healthy young adults: correlations with cognitive performance. *Journal of Neuroscience, 19,* 4065-4072.

Gutek, B. A., & Done, R. S. (2001). Sexual harassment. In Rhoda Unger (Ed.), *Handbook of the psychology of women and gender* (pp. 367-387). New York: John Wiley & Sons.

Guttman, D. L. (1994). *Reclaiming powers: Toward a new psychology of men and women in later life.* Evanston, IL; Northwestern University Press.

Hackney, C., & Sanders, G. (2003). Religiosity and mental health: A meta-analysis of recent studies. *Journal for the Scientific Study of Religion, 42(1),* 43-55.

Hadley, M. E. (1996). *Endocrinology.* (4th Ed.) Upper Saddle River, NJ: Prentice-Hall.

Hajnal, Z. L. (2007). *Changing white attitudes toward black political leadership.* New York: Cambridge University Press.

Hall, J. A. (1978). Gender effects in decoding nonverbal cues. *Psychological Bulletin, 85,* 845-857.

Hall, J. A. (1984). *Nonverbal sex differences: Communication accuracy and expressive style.* Baltimore, MD: John Hopkins.

Hall, K. & Bucholtz, M. (1995). *Gender articulated: Language and the socially constructed self.* New York: Routledge.

Hall, K. (1995). Lip service on the fantasy line. In K. Hall & M. Buckholtz (Eds.), *Gender articulated: Language and the socially constructed self* (pp. 183-216.). New York: Oxford University Press.

Halpern, D. F. & LaMay, M. L. (2000). The smarter sex: A critical review of sex differences in intelligence. *Educational Psychology Review, 12(2),* 229-246.

Halpern, D. F. (2000). *Sex differences in cognitive abilities.* (3rd Ed). Mahwah, N. J.: Lawrence Erlbaum.

Hamilton, D. L. &; Rose, T. L (1980). Illusory correlation and the maintenance of stereotypic beliefs. *Journal of Personality & Social Psychology, 39(5),* 832-845.

Hampson, E. & Kimura, D. (1988). Reciprocal effects of hormonal fluctuations on human motor and perceptual-spatial skills. *Behavioral Neuroscience, 102,* 456-459.

Hampson, E. (1990). Influence of gonadal hormones on cognitive function in women. *Clinical Neuropharmacology, 13* (Suppl. 2), 522-523.

Hampson, E. (1990). Variations in sex-related cognitive abilities across the menstrual cycle. *Brain and Cognition, 14,* 26-43.

Hannah, A., & Murachver, T. (1999). Gender and conversational style as predictors of conversational behavior. *Journal of Language & Social Psychology, 18(2),* 153-174.

Hare-Mustin, R. T., & Broderick, P. C. (1979). The myth of motherhood: A study of attitudes toward motherhood. *Psychology of Women Quarterly, 4,* 114-128.

Harper, L V., & Sanders, K. M. (1975). Preschool children's use of space: Sex differences in outdoor play. *Developmental Psychology, 11(1),* 119.

Harris, J. A. (1999). Review and methodological considerations in research on testosterone and aggression. *Aggression & Violent Behavior, 4*(3), 273-291.

Harris, J. R. (1998). *The nurture assumption.* New York: Free Press.

Hartog, H. (2000). *Man and wife in America: A history.* Cambridge: Harvard University Press.

Hassouneh-Phillips, D. (2003). Strength and vulnerability: Spirituality in abused American Muslim Women's lives. *Issues in Mental Health Nursing,* 24(6), 681-694.

Hawley, J. S. (1994). *Fundamentalism and gender.* New York: Oxford University Press.

Hedges, L. V. & Nowell, A. (1995). Sex differences in mental test scores, variability, and numbers of high-scoring individuals. *Science, 269,* 41-45

Hegtvedt, K. A., Clay-Warner, J., & Ferrigno, E. D. (2002). Reactions to injustice: Factors affecting workers' resentment toward family-friendly policies. *Social Psychology Quarterly, 65*(4), 386-400.

Helgeson, V. S. & Fritz, H. L. (2000). The implications for unmitigated agency and unmitigated communion for domains of problem behavior. *Journal of Personality, 68,* 1032-1057.

Hendrick, C. & Hendrick, S. S. (1995). Gender differences and similarities in sex and love. *Personal Relationships, 2,* 5-65.

Henley, N. M. (1977). *Body politics: Power, sex and nonverbal communication.* Englewood Cliffs, N.J.: Prentice-Hall.

Hensley, W. E. (1993). Height as a measure of success in academe. *Psychology, 30,* 40-46.

Hequembourg, A. L. & Farrell, M. P. (1999). Lesbian motherhood: Negotiating marginal-mainstream identities. *Gender & Society, 13*(4), 540-557.

Herd, P., Meyer, A., & Harrington, M. (2002). Care work Invisible civic engagement. *Gender & Society, 16,* 665-688.

Hermes, S. F., & Keel, P.K. (2003).The influence of puberty and ethnicity on awareness and internalization of the thin ideal. *International Journal of Eating Disorders, 33(4),* 465-467.

Hertel, B. R. & Hughes, M. (1987). Religious affiliation, attendance, and support for 'Pro-Family' issues in the U.S. *Social Forces 65,* 858-82.

Hess, U., Senécal, S. Kirouac, *G.,* Herrera, P.; Philippot, P., & Kleck, R. E. (2000). Emotional expressivity in men and women: Stereotypes and self-perceptions, *Cognition & Emotion, 14 (5),* 609-642.

Hill, J. P., & Lynch, M. E. (1983). The intensification of gender-related role expectations during early adolescence. In J. Brooks-Gunn & A. Petersen (Eds.), Girls at puberty: Biological and psychosocial perspectives (pp. 201-208). New York: Springer.

Hill, S. A. (2002). Teaching and doing gender in African American families. *Sex Roles, 47(11-12),* 493-506.

Hilton, N. Z., Harris, G. T. & Rice, M. E. (2000). The functions of aggression by male teenagers. *Journal of Personality & Social Psychology, 79*(6), 988-994.

Hines, M. & Collaer, M. L. (1993). Gonadal hormones and sexual differentiation of human behavior: Developments from research on endocrine syndromes and studies of brain structure. *Annual review of sex research. 4,* 1-48.

Hochschild, A. R. (1989). *The second shift: Working parents and the revolution at home.* New York: Viking.

Hoelter, L. F. (2002). Fair is fair---or is it? Perceptions of fairness in the household division of labor. *Dissertation Abstracts International Section A: Humanities & Social Sciences, 62,* 7A.

Hoffman, J. P. & Miller, A. S. (1997). Social and political attitudes among religious groups: Convergence and divergence over time." *Journal for the Scientific Study of Religion, 36, 52-70.*

Hoffman, R. M. & Borders, L. D. (2001). Twenty-five years after the Bem Sex-Role Inventory: A reassessment and new issues regarding classification variability. *Measurement & Evaluation in Counseling & Development, 34(1*), 39-55.

Hoffman, S. D. &. Averett, S. L. (2005). *Women and the economy.* New York: Pearson Education.

Hogben, M, Byrne, D., Hamburger, M. E., & Osland, J. (2001). Legitimized aggression and sexual coercion: Individual differences in cultural spillover. *Aggressive Behavior, 27,* 26-43.

Holmes, B. (1999, February).*Betty's Thought Bullets: The Barbie™ Fantasy.* Wellness IN Wyoming. University of Wyoming Cooperative Extension Service. Retrieved May 15 2002. www.uwyo.edu/winwyoming/.

Holmes, J. (1982). The functions of tag questions. *English Language Research Journal, 3,* 40-65.

Holt, C. L. & Ellis, J. B. (1998). Assessing the current validity of the Bem Sex-Role Inventory. *Sex Roles, 39 (11-12),* 929-941.

Honey, M. (1985). *Creating Rosie the Riveter: Class, gender, and propaganda during World War II.* Amherst, MA: University of Massachusetts Press.

Horgan, D. M. (1975). *Language development.* Ann Arbor: University of Michigan

Horn, L. J. & Zahn, L. (2001). *From bachelor's degree to work: Major field of study and employment outcomes of 1992-1993 bachelor's degree recipients who did not enroll in graduate education by 1997* (NCES 2001-165).

Horney, K. (1942). *The collected works of Karen Horney (Volume II).* New York: W.W. Norton Company.

Hort, B. E., Fagot, B. I. & Leinbach, M.D. (1990). Are people's notions of maleness more stereotypically framed than their notions of femaleness? *Sex Roles, 23 (3-4),* 197-212.

Houppert, K. (2006, June 12). Cindy Sheehan: Mother of a movement? *The Nation,* 3-15.

Houston Stanback, M. (1985). Language and black women's place: Evidence from the black middle class. In P. A. Treichler, C. Kramarai, & B. Stafford (Eds.), *For Alma Mater: Theory and Practice in Feminist Scholarship* (pp. 177-193). Urbana, IL: University of Illinois Press.

Hrdy, S. B. (1999). *Mother Nature: A history of mothers, infants, and natural selection.* New York: Pantheon Books.

Huba, M. E. & Freed, J. E. (2000). *Learner-centered assessment on college campuses: Shifting the focus from teaching to learning.* Boston, MA: Allyn & Bacon.

Hudak, Mary A., (1993). Gender schema theory revisited: Men's stereotypes of American women. *Sex Roles, 28(5-6),* 279-293.

Hughes, T. L. (2003). Lesbians' Drinking Patterns: Beyond the Data. *Substance Use & Misuse, 38*(11-13), 1739-1758.

Hukill, T. (1999, January 21-27). Getting nailed. *Metro.* Retrieved November 12, 2003 from http://www.metroactive.com/papers/metro/01.21.99/nails-9903.html.

Human Rights and Equal Opportunity Commission (2002). *Valuing Parenthood: Options for Paid Maternity Leave: Interim Paper 2002.* Sydney, Australia: Author. Retrieved August 12, 2004. http://www.ilo.org/

Hunsberger, B. & Jackson, L. M. (2005). Religion, meaning, and prejudice. *Journal of Social Issues, 61*(4), 807-826.

Hurtado A. (1996). *The color of privilege: Three blasphemies on race and feminism.* Ann Arbor: University Michigan Press

Huston, A. C. (1985). The development of sex typing: Themes from recent research. *Developmental Review, 5,(1)* 1-27.

Hutson-Comeaux, S. L., & Kelly, J. R. (2002). Gender stereotypes of emotional reactions: How we judge an emotion as valid. *Sex Roles, 47*(1-2), 1-10.

Hyde, J, S,, Fennema, E., & Lamon, S. J. (1990). Gender differences in mathematics performance: A meta-analysis. *Psychological Bulletin, 107(2),* 139-155.

Hyde, J. (1984). How large are gender differences in aggression? A developmental meta -analysis. *Developmental Psychology, 20(4),* 722-736.

Hyde, J. (2005). The gender similarities hypothesis. *American Psychologist, 60,* 581-592.

Hyde, J. S. & Oliver, M. B. (2000). Gender comparisons in sexuality: Results from a meta-analysis. In C. B. Travis & J. W. White (Eds.), *Sexuality, society, and feminism* (pp. 57-77). Washington, DC: American Psychological Association.

Hyde, J. S. & Plant, E. A. (1995). Magnitude of psychological gender differences. *American Psychologist, 145,* 145-158.

Hyde, J. S. (1981). How large are cognitive gender differences? A meta-analysis using ω and d.

Hyde, J. S. (1984). How large are gender differences in aggression? A developmental meta-analysis. *Developmental Psychology, 20(4),* 722-736.

Hyde, J. S. (2005). The gender similarities hypothesis. *American Psychologist, 60*(6), 581-592.

Hyde, J. S., Fennema, E., & Ryan, M. (1990). Gender comparisons of mathematics attitudes and affect: A meta-analysis. *Psychology of Women Quarterly. 14(3),* 299-324.

Hyde, J., Mezulis, A., & Abramson, L. (2008). The ABCs of depression: Integrating affective, biological, and cognitive models to explain the emergence of the gender difference in depression. *Psychological Review, 115*(2), 291-313.

Hyman, P. (1995). *Gender and assimilation in modern Jewish history: The roles and representation of women.* Seattle, WA: University of Washington Press.

Hymowitz, C., & Weissman, M. (1984). *A history of women in America.* New York: Bantam.

Ilies, R., Hauserman, N., Schwochau, S., & Stibal, J. (2003). Reported incidence rates of work-related sexual harassment in the United States: Using meta-analysis to explain reported rate disparities. *Personnel Psychology, 569*(3), 607-632.

Imperato-McGinley, J., Guerrero, L., Gautier, T. & Peterson, R. E. (1974). Steroid 5 alpha-reductase deficiency in men: An inherited form of male psueudohermaphroditism. *Science, 186,* 1213-1215.

Ingall, M. (2004, May 28). *Why 'Free to Be...' still kicks butt.* Retrieved June 25, 2005 http://www.mayan.org/category.aspx?catid=1795.

Ito, T., & Urland, G. (2003). Race and gender on the brain: Electrocortical measures of attention to the race and gender of multiply categorizable individuals. *Journal of Personality and Social Psychology, 85*(4), 616-626.

Jackson, L. A., (1983). The perception of androgyny and physical attractiveness: Two is better than one. *Personality & Social Psychology Bulletin, 9(3),* 405-413.

Jacobs, J. A. & Gerson, K. (2004). *The time divide: Work, family and gender inequality.* Cambridge, MA: Harvard University Press.

James, D., & Clarke, S. (1993). Women, men, and interruptions: A critical review. In D. Tannen (Ed.), *Gender and conversational interaction* (pp. 231-280). New York: Oxford University Press.

James, D., & Drakich, J. (1993). Understanding gender differences in amount of talking: A critical review of research. In D. Tannen (Ed.) *Gender and conversational interaction* (pp. 281-312). New York: Oxford University Press.

Jansz, J. (2000). Masculine identity and restrictive emotionality, in A. Fischer (Ed.) *Gender and emotion: Social psychological perspectives. Studies in emotion and social interaction* (pp. 166-186). New York: Cambridge University Press.

Janus, S. S. & Janus, C. L. (1993). *The Janus report on sexual behavior.* New York: Wiley.

Jeffries, S. & Konnert, C. (2002). Regret and psychological well-being among voluntarily and involuntarily childless women and mothers. *International Journal of Aging & Human Development, 54(2),* 89-106.

Jenson, L. & Slack. T. (2004). Beyond low wages: Underemployment in America. In A. C. Crouter & A. Booth (Eds.), *Work-family challenges for low-income parents and their children* (pp. 45-53). Mahwah, NJ: Lawrence Erlbaum.

Job Outlook (2004). *Recreate yourself: From student to the perfect job candidate.* Retrieved October 6, 2006 http://www.jobweb.com/joboutlook/2004outlook/outlook5.htm

Johnson, J. T., & Shulman, G. A. (1988). More alike than meets the eye: Perceived gender differences in subjective experience and its display, *Sex Roles, 19*(1-2), 67-79.

Johnson-Mondragón, K. (2005). *Youth ministry and the socioreligious lives of Hispanic and White Catholic teens in the U.S.* Stockton, CA: Institute Fe y Vida.

Jones, C. M., Braithwaite, V. A. & Healy, S. D. (2003). The evolution of sex differences in spatial ability. *Behavioral Neuroscience,117,* 403-411.

Jones, J. M. (2006) Introduction to Kay Deaux's SPSSI Presidential Address. *Journal of Social Issues, 62*(3), 629-631.

Jose, P., & Brown, I. (2008). When does the gender difference in rumination begin? Gender and age differences in the use of rumination by adolescents. *Journal of Youth and Adolescence, 37*(2), 180-192.

Julian, T. W. et al. (1994). Cultural variations in parenting: Perceptions of Caucasian, African-American, Hispanic, and Asian-American parents. *Family Relations, 43,* 30-37.

Kafai, Y. B. (1999). Elementary school students' computer and Internet use at home: Current trends and issues. *Journal of Educational Computing Research, 21(3),* 345-362.

Kagan, J. (1989). *Unstable ideas: Temperament, cognition, and self.* Cambridge, MA: Harvard University Press.

Kaiser Family Foundation (2003). *National survey of adolescents and young Adults: Sexual health knowledge, attitudes and experiences.* Menlo Park, CA: Author.

Katharine Dexter McCormick Library (2001, November). *The emotional effects of induced abortion.* Retrieved March 3, 2004 from www.plannedparenthood.org/files/PPFA/fact-induced-abortion.pdf

Katz, J. (2006). The macho paradox: Why some men hurt women and how all men can help. New York: Sourcebooks.

Katz, J., Swindell, S., & Farrow, S. J. (2004). Effects of participation in a first women's studies course on collective self-esteem, gender-related attitudes, and emotional well-being. *Journal of Applied Social Psychology,* 34(10), 2179-2199.

Keitt, S. K. (2003). Sex and gender: The politics, policy, and practice of medical research. *Yale Journal of Health Policy, Law, and Ethics, 3*(2), 253-278.

Kelly, H. A. (1994). Rule of thumb and the folklaw of the husband's stick. *Journal of Legal Education, 44,* 341-365.

Kelly, J. R. & Hutson-Comeaux, S. (1999). Gender-emotion stereotypes are context specific. *Sex Roles, 40*(1-2), 107-120.

Kent, R. L., & Moss, S.E. (1994). Effects of sex and gender role on leader emergence. *Academy of Management Journal, 37(5),* 1335-1346.

Kersting, K. (2005, June). Men and depression: Battling stigma through public education. *Monitor on Psychology,* 66-68.

Kessler, R. C. (1997). The effects of stressful life events on depression. *Annual Review of Psychology, 48,* 191-214.

Kessler, R. C., McGonagle, K. A., Zhao, S., Nelson, C. B., Hughes, M., Eshleman, S., Wittchen, J. & Kendler, K. S. (1994). Lifetime and 12-month prevalence of DSM-III-R psychiatric disorders in the United States. Results for the National Comorbidity Survey. *Archives of General Psychiatry, 51,* 8-19.

Kessler-Harris, A. (1982). *Out to work: A history of wage-earning women in the United States.* Oxford, England: Oxford University Press.

Kessler-Harris, A. (2003). *In pursuit of equity: Women, men, and the quest for economic citizenship in 20th-century America.* Oxford, England: Oxford University Press.

Key, J. A. (1999). *An Empirical Study of Gender and Racial Differences in Quits and Layoffs of Young Workers* Ph.D. Dissertation, University of Colorado at Boulder.

Khosroshahi, F. (1989). Penguins don't care, but women do: A social identity analysis of a Whorfian problem. *Language in Society, 18,* 505-525.

Kidd, S. A. & Kral, M. J. (2002). Suicide and prostitution among street youth: A qualitative analysis. *Adolescence, 37*(146), 411-430.

Kilbourne, J. (1999). *Deadly persuasion: Why women and girls must fight the addictive power of advertising.* New York: Free Press.

Kilbourne, J. (2003). Advertising and disconnection. In T. Reichert & J. Lambaise (Eds.), *Sex in advertising: Perspectives on the erotic appeal* (pp. 173-180). Mahwah, New Jersey: Lawrence Erlbaum.

Killen, M. & Turiel, E. (1998). Adolescents' and young adults' evaluations of helping and sacrificing for others. *Journal of Research on Adolescence, 8*(3), 355-375.

Kilmartin, C. (2007). *The masculine self (3rd Ed.).* Boston, MA: McGraw Hill.

Kimmel, M. & Messner, M. A. (2009). *Men's lives* (8th Ed.) Boston, MA: Allyn & Bacon.

Kimmel, M, & Mosmiller, T. (1992). *Against the Tide: Pro-feminist Men in the United States, 1776-1990.* Boston: Beacon Press.

Kimura, D. & Hampson, E. (1994). Cognitive pattern in men and women is influences by fluctuations in sex hormones. *Current directions in psychological science. 3(2),* 57-61.

Kimura, D. (1992). Sex differences in the brain. *Scientific American. 267,* 118-126.

King, J. (2006). *Gender equity in higher education: 2006.* Washington D. C.: American Council on Education.

Kinnunen, U., Geurts, S., & Mauno, S. (2004). Work-to-family conflict and its relationship with satisfaction and well-being: A one-year longitudinal study on gender differences. *Work & Stress, 18*(1), 1-22.

Kirby, J. (1999, January). Excerpts from *Dieting For Dummies® . American Dietetic Association.* Accessed 15 May 2002. www.eatright.org/dieting.html

Kite, M. E. & Deaux, Kay (1987). Gender belief systems: Homosexuality and the implicit inversion theory. *Psychology of Women Quarterly, 11(1),* 83-96.

Kleinke, C. L., Desautels, M. S., & Knapp, B. E. (1977). Adult gaze and affective and visual responses of preschool children. *Journal of Genetic Psychology, 131(2),* 321-322.

Klemmer, E. T., & Snyder, F. W. (1972). Measurement of time spent communicating. *Journal of Communication, 22(2),* 142-158.

Kling, K. C., Hyde, J. S., Showers, C.J., & Buswell, B. (1999). Gender differences in self-esteem: A meta-analysis. *Psychological Bulletin, 125(4),* 470-500.

Klohnen, E. C. & Luo, S. (2003). Interpersonal attraction and personality: What is attractive--self similarity, ideal similarity, complementarity or attachment security? *Journal of Personality & Social Psychology, 85(4),* 709-722.

Knox, B. (1994). *Oedipus the king.* New York: Pocket Books.

Kochman, T. (1981). *Black and white styles in conflict.* Chicago: University of Chicago Press.

Kogan, N. & Mills, M. (1992). Gender influences on age cognitions and preferences: Sociocultural or sociobiological? *Psychology & Aging, 7*(1), 98-106.

Kohlberg, L. (1966). A cognitive developmental analysis of children's sex-role concepts and attitudes. In E. E. Maccoby (Ed.), *The development of sex differences* (pp. 82-173). Stanford, CA: Stanford University Press.

Kohlberg, L. (1973). *Collected Papers on Moral Development and Moral Education.* Cambridge: Harvard.

Kolbe, R. & LaVoie, J. C. (1981). Sex-role stereotyping in preschool children's picture books. *Social Psychology Quarterly, 44(4),* 369-374.

Koss, M. P. & Kilpatrick, D. G. (2001). Rape and sexual assault. In E. Gerrity & T. M. Keane (Eds.), *The mental health consequences of torture* (pp. 177-193). Dordrecht, Netherlands: Kluwer Academic Publishers.

Koss, M. P., Bachar, K. J., & Hopkins, C. Q. (2003). Restorative justice for sexual violence: Repairing victims, building community, and holding offenders accountable In R. A. Prentky & E. S. Janus (Eds.) *Sexually coercive behavior: Understanding and management* (pp. 384-396). New York, NY: New York Academy of Sciences.

Koss, M. P., Bailey, J. A., Yuan, N. P., Herrera, V. M., & Lichter, E. L. (2003). Depression and PTSD in survivors of male violence: Research and training initiatives to facilitate recovery. *Psychology of Women Quarterly, 27(2),* 130-142.

Koss, M. P., Gidycz, C. A., & Wisniewski, N. (1987). The scope of rape: Incidence and prevalence of sexual aggression and victimization in a national sample of higher education students. *Journal of Consulting & Clinical Psychology, 55(2),* 162-170.

Kost, K. A. (2001). The function of fathers: What poor men say about fatherhood. *Families in Society, 82(5),* 499-508

Krecker, M. L. (1993). *Work history data in the national survey of families and households: An overview and preliminary assessment.* NSFH Working Paper No. 56.

Krupnick, C. G. (1984). Sex differences in college teachers' classroom talk. *Dissertation Abstracts International, 45,* 1657-1658.

Kunkel, A. W. & Burleson, B. R. (1998). Social support and the emotional lives of men and women: An assessment of the different cultures perspective. In D. J. Canary & K. Dindia (Eds.), *Sex differences and similarities in communication: Critical essays and empirical investigations of sex and gender in interaction* (pp. 101-125). Mahwah, NJ: Lawrence Erlbaum.

Kurdek, L. A. (1991). Sexuality in homosexual and heterosexual couples. In K. McKinney & S. Sprecher (Eds.), *Sexuality in close relationships* (pp. 177-191). Hillsdale, NJ: Erlbaum.

Kurdek, L. A. (1993). Predicting marital dissolution: A 5-year prospective longitudinal study of newlywed couples. *Journal of Personality and Social Psychology, 64,* 221-242.

Labov, W. (2001). *Principles of linguistic change: Social factors.* Oxford: Blackwell.

Lachman, M. E. & James, J. B. (1997). Charting the course of midlife development: An overview. In M.E. Lachman & J. B. James (Eds.), *Multiple paths of midlife development* (pp.1-17). Chicago: University of Chicago Press.

Lakoff, R. (1973). Language and woman's place. *Language in Society, 1(2),* 45-80.

Laland, K. N. & Brown, G. R. (2002). *Sense & Nonsense: Evolutionary Perspectives on Human Behaviour.* Oxford, England: Oxford University Press.

Lamb, M. E., & Roopnarine, J. L. (1979). Peer influences on sex-role development in preschoolers. *Child Development, 50(4),* 1219-1222.

Landrine, H. (1985). Race and class stereotypes of women. *Sex Roles, 13(1-2),* 65-75.

Larson, J. (1988). The marriage quiz: College students' beliefs in selected beliefs about marriage. *Family Relations, 37,* 3-11.

Lau, A. S., McCabe, K. M., Yeh, M., Garland, A. F., Hough, R. L., & Landsverk, J., (2003). Race/ethnicity and rates of self-reported maltreatment among high-risk youth in public sectors of care. *Child Maltreatment: Journal of the American Professional Society on the Abuse of Children, 8(3)*, 183-194.

Laumann, E. O, Gagnon, J. H., Michael, R. T. & Michaels, S. (1994). *The social organization of sexuality: Sexual practices in the United States.* Chicago: University of Chicago Press,

Lauterbach, K. E. & Weiner, B. J. (1996). Dynamics of upward influence: How male and female managers get their way. *Leadership Quarterly, 7,* 87-107.

Law, D., Pellegrino, J. W., & Hunt, E. G. (1993). Comparing the tortoise and the hare: Gender differences and experience in dynamic spatial reasoning tasks. *Psychological Science, 4*, 35-41.

Lawless, J. L. & Fox, R. L. (2004). *Why don't women run for office?* Brown Policy Report. Providence, RI: Brown University.

Le Vay, S. (1996). *Queer science: The use and abuse of research into homosexuality.* Cambridge, MA: MIT Press.

Leaper, C. (2000). Gender, affiliation, assertion, and the interactive context of parent-child play. *Developmental Psychology, 36 (3),* 381-393.

Leaper, C. (2002). Parenting girls and boys. In M. H. Bornstein (Ed). *Handbook of parenting: Vol. 1: Children and parenting* (2nd ed.) (pp. 189-225). Mahwah, NJ: Lawrence Erlbaum.

Leaper, C., Leve, L., Strasser, T, & Schwartz, R. (1995). Mother-child communication sequences: Play activity, child gender, and marital status effects. *Merrill-Palmer Quarterly, 41,* 307-327.

Lee, Y. & Waite, L (2005). Husbands' and wives' time spent on housework: A comparison of measures. *Journal of Marriage and the Family, 67(2),* 328-336.

Leinbach, M. D., Hort, B. E., & Fagot, B. (1997). Bears are for boys: Metaphorical associations in young children's gender stereotypes. *Cognitive Development,12,*107-130.

Leitenberg, H., Detzer, M.J., Srebnik, D. (1993). Gender differences in masturbation and the relation of masturbation experience in preadolescence and/or early adolescence to sexual behavior and sexual adjustment in young adulthood. *Archives of Sexual Behavior, 22(2),* 87-98.

Lengnick-Hall, M. L. (1995) Sexual harassment research: A methodological critique. *Personnel Psychology, 48,* 841-864.

Lenhart, S. A. (2004). *Clinical aspects of sexual harassment and gender discrimination: Psychological consequences and treatment interventions.* New York: Brunner-Routledge.

Lerner, G. (2005). *Majority finds its past: Placing women in history.* Durham, NC: North Carolina Press.

Lerner, R. M. (2002). *Concepts and theories of human development.* Mahwah, NJ: Lawrence Erlbaum.

Levine, L. (2003). *The gender wage gap and pay equity: Is comparable worth the next step?* Washington D.C.: Congressional Research Service.

Levinson, D. R., Johnson, M. L.,& Devaney, D. M. (1988). *Sexual harassment in the federal government: An update* (Report to Congress and the President No. 1988-220-085/ 90132). Washington, DC: U.S. Merit Systems Protection Board.

Levy, B. R., Slade, M. D., Kunkel, S. R. & Kasl, S.V. (2002). Longevity increased by positive self-perceptions of aging. *Journal of Personality & Social Psychology, 83(2),* 261-270.

Lewin, K. (1951) *Field theory in social science; selected theoretical papers.* D. Cartwright (Ed.). New York: Harper & Row.

Lewis, R. (2003). *Human genetics: Concepts and applications.* (5th Ed.) Boston, MA: McGraw Hill.

Lewko, J. H., & Ewing, M. E. (1980). Differences and parental influence in sport involvement of children. *Journal of Sport Psychology, 2(1),* 62-68.

Lin, E., Goering, P., & Offord, D. R. (1996). The use of mental health services in Ontario: Epidemiologic findings. *Canadian Journal of Psychiatry, 41(9),* 572-577.

Lips, H.M. (2000). *Sex & Gender: An Introduction* (4th Edition). Mountain View, CA: Mayfield.

Lo, V. & Wei, R. (2002). Third-person effect, gender, and pornography on the Internet. *Journal of Broadcasting & Electronic Media, 46*(1), 13-33.

Long, C. D. (1958). *The labor force under changing income and employment.* Princeton: Princeton University Press.

Loring, M., & Powell, B. (1988). Gender, race, and DSM-III: A study of the objectivity of psychiatric diagnostic behavior. *Journal of Health & Social Behavior, 29*(1), 1-22.

Losey, K. M. (2002). Gender and ethnicity as factors in the development of verbal skills in bilingual Mexican American women. In V. Zacmel, & R. Spack (Eds.), *Enriching ERSO pedagogy: Reading and activities for engagement, reflection, and inquiry.* Mahwah, NJ: Lawrence Erlbaum.

Love, J. M., Harrison, L., & Sagi-Schwartz, A. (2003); Child care quality matters: How conclusions may vary with context. *Child Development, 74*(4), 1021-1033.

Lytton, H. & Romney, D. M. (1991). Parents' differential socialization of boys and girls: A meta-analysis. *Psychological Bulletin, 109(2),* 267-296.

Maccoby, E. E. & Jacklin, C. N. (1974). *Psychology of sex differences.* Stanford, CA: Stanford Press.

Maccoby, E. E. (1980). *Social development: Psychological growth and the parent-child relationship.* New York: Harcourt, Brace, and Jovanovich.

Maccoby, E. E. (1998). *The two sexes: Growing up apart, coming together.* Cambridge, MA: Harvard University Press.

Maccoby, E. E., (1988). Gender as a social category. *Developmental Psychology, 24(6),* 755-765.

Maccoby, M (1995). *Why work?: Motivating the new workforce* (2nd ed). Alexandria, VA: Miles River Press.

Macrae, C. N., Bodenhausen, G. V., Milne, A. B., Thorn, T. M. J., & Castelli, L. (1997). On the activation of social stereotypes: The moderating role of processing objectives. *Journal of Experimental Social Psychology 33(5),* 471-489.

Maddox, T. (Ed.) (2002). *Tests: A Comprehensive Reference for Assessments in Psychology, Education, and Business. (5th Ed.)* Austin, TX: Pro-ed.

Madson, L. (2001). A classroom activity exploring the complexity of sexual orientation. *Teaching of Psychology, 28*, 32-35.

Major, B., Carnevale, P. J., & Deaux, K. (1981). A different perspective on androgyny: evaluation of masculine and feminine characteristics. *Journal of Personality and Social Psychology, 41,* 988-101.

Major, B., Cozzarelli, C., Cooper, M. L., Zubek, J., Richards, C., Wilhite, M. & Gramzow, R. H. (2000). Psychological responses of women after first-trimester abortion. *Archives of General Psychiatry, 57*(8), 777-784.

Major, B., Schmidlin, A. M., & Williams, L. (1990). Gender patterns in social touch: The impact of setting and age. *Journal of Personality & Social Psychology, 58(4),* 634-643.

Malamuth, N. M. & Donnerstein, E. (Eds.), (1984). *Pornography and sexual aggression.* Orlando FL: Academic Press.

Markos, A. R., Wade, A. A. H.; Walzman, M. (1994). The adolescent male prostitute and sexually transmitted diseases, HIV and AIDS. *Journal of Adolescence, 17(2),* 123-130.

Marleau, J. D., & Saucier, J. (2002). Preference for a first-born boy in Western societies. *Journal of Biosocial Science, 34(1),* 13-27.

Marshall, S. J., Gorely, T. & Biddle, S. J. (2006). A descriptive epidemiology of screen-based media use in youth: A review and critique. *Journal of Adolescence, 29*(3), 333-349.

Marsiglio, W. & Diekow, D. (1998). Men and abortion: The gender politics of pregnancy resolution. In L. J. Beckman & S. M. Harvey (Eds.), *The new civil war: The psychology, culture, and politics of abortion.* Psychology of women book series (pp. 269-287). Washington, DC: American Psychological Association.

Martin, C. L. & Fabes, R. A. (2001). The stability and consequences of young children's same-sex peer interactions. *Developmental Psychology, 37(3),* 431-446.

Martin, C. L. Ruble, D. N. and Szkrybalo, J. (2002). Cognitive theories of early gender development. *Psychological Bulletin, 128 (6),* 903-933.

Martin, C. L., & Dinella, L. M. (2002). Children's gender cognitions, the social environment, and sex differences in cognitive domains. In A. McGillicuddy-De Lisi & Richard De Lisi (Eds.), *Biology, society, and behavior: The development of sex differences in cognition* (pp. 207-239). Westport, CT: Ablex.

Martin, C. L., Eisenbud, L.& Rose, H. (1995). Children's gender-based reasoning about toys. *Child Development, 66(5),* 1453-1471.

Martin, C. L., Wood, C. H., & Little, J. K. (1990). The development of gender stereotype components. *Child Development, 61,* 1891-1904.

Martin, C. L., Wood, C. H., & Little, J. K. (1990). The relation of gender understanding to children's sex-typed preferences and gender stereotypes. *Child Development, 61,* 1427-1439.

Martin, E. (1991). The egg and the sperm: How science has constructed a romance based on stereotypical male-female roles. *Signs, 16(3),* 485-501.

Martin, W. (1996). *With God on our side: The rise of the religious right in America.* New York: Broadway Books.

Maselko, J. & Kubzansky, L. D. (2006). Gender differences in religious practices, spiritual experiences and health: Results from the US General Social Survey. *Social Science & Medicine, 62,* 2848-2860.

Masson, J. M. (1984). *The Assault on Truth: Freud's Suppression of the Seduction Theory.* New York: Farrar Straus & Giroux.

Mastroianni, A. C., Faden, R. & Federman, D. (Eds.) (1994). *Women and health research: Ethical and legal issues of including women in clinical studies.* Washington DC: National Academy Press.

Mathews, T. J. & Hamilton, B. E. (2002, December 11). Mean age of mother, 1970-2000. *National Vital Statistics Reports, 51*(1).1-14.

Matthews, S. & Power, C. (2002). Socio-economic gradients in psychological distress: A focus on women, social roles and work-home characteristics. *Social Science & Medicine, 54(5),* 799-810.

Mayell, H. (2003, January 28). Fossil tusks indicate earliest sexual differentiation, *National Geographic News* retrieved10/10/03 from http://news.nationalgeographic.com/news/2003/01/0128_030128_diictodon.htm.

Mayer, E., Kosmin, B. A. & Keysar, A. (2001) *American Religious Identification Survey.* Retrieved October 9, 2006 http://www.gc.cuny.edu/faculty/research_briefs/aris/religion_ethnicity.htm

Mazure, C. M., Keita, G. P. & Blehar, M. C. (2002). *Summit on women and depression.* Washington DC: American Psychological Association.

McCabe, A., & Lipscomb, T. J. (1988). Sex differences in children's verbal aggression. *Merrill-Palmer Quarterly, 34*(4), 389-401.

McCabe, Marita P.; Vincent, M. A. (2003). The role of biodevelopmental and psychological factors in disordered eating among adolescent males and females. *European Eating Disorders Review, 11*(4), 315-328.

McCanna, W. F., Pearse, R. F., & Zrebiec, D. A. (1994, May-June). Career strategies for the 1990s manager. *Business Horizons, 37(3),* 27-31.

McCarthy, B. W. (1998). Commentary: Effects of sexual trauma on adult sexuality. *Journal of Sex & Marital Therapy, 24*(2), 91-92.

McClone, J. (1978). Sex differences in functional brain asymmetry. *Cortex, 14,* 122-128.

McCullough, M., Hoyt, W., Larson, D., Koenig, H., & Thoresen, C. (2000). Religious involvement and mortality: A meta-analytic review. *Health Psychology, 19*(3), 211-222.

McDonald, S. M. (1989). Sex bias in the representation of male and female characters in children's picture books. *Journal of Genetic Psychology, 150*(4), 389-401.

McDoo, H. P. (2002). African American parenting. In M. H. Bornstein (Ed). *Handbook of parenting: Vol. 4: Social conditions and applied parenting* (2nd ed.) (pp.47-58). Mahwah, NJ: Lawrence Erlbaum

McFarlane, J. M. & Williams, T. M. (1994) Placing premenstrual syndrome in perspective. *Psychology of Women Quarterly, 18(3),* 339-373.

McFarlane, J.; Martin, C. L.; & Williams, T. M. (1988). Mood fluctuations: Women versus men and menstrual versus other cycles. *Psychology of Women Quarterly, 12(2),* 201-223.

McGee, S. G., (1999). *Why Some Battered Women Sometimes Stay.* The Domestic Violence Project Inc. Retrieved January 12, 2004: http://comnet.org/dvp/prof1.html.

McGivern, R.F., Huston, J.P., Byrd, D., King, T., Siegle, G.J., & Reilly, J. (1997). Sex differences in visual recognition memory: support for sex-related difference in attention in adults and children. *Brain and Cognition, 34,* 323 - 336.

McIlwain, C. D. (2007) Perceptions of leadership and the challenge of Obama's blackness. *Journal of Black Studies, 38,* 64-74.,

McIntyre, T. & Tong, V. (1998). Where the boys are: Do cross-gender misunderstandings of language use and behavior patterns contribute to the overrepresentation of males in programs for students with emotional and behavioral disorders? *Education & Treatment of Children, 21(3),* 321-332.

McLaughlin, J. E.(2002). Reducing diagnostic bias. *Journal of Mental Health Counseling, 24(3),* 256-269.

McPherson, M., Smith-Lovin, L. & Cook, J. M. (2001). Birds of a feather: Homophily in social networks. *Annual Review of Sociology, 27,* 415-444.

Mechikoff, R., & Estes, S. (1998). *A history and philosophy of sport and physical education: From the ancient Greeks to the present* (2nd ed.). Madison, WI: Brown & Benchmark.

Media Awareness Network (2003). *Talking to kids about gender stereotypes.* Retrieved October 20, 2003 from http://www.media-awareness.ca/english/resources/tip_sheets/gender_tip.cfm

Media Education Foundation (1997). *Media Gender and diversity: Dreamworlds II.* Retrieved November 12, 2003 from http://www.mediaed.org/videos/MediaGenderAndDiversity/Dreamworlds2/studyguid e/Dreamworlds2.pdf

Mehta, M. D. & Plaza, D. E. (1997). Pornography in cyberspace: an exploration of what's in Usenet" In S. Kiesler (ed.), *Culture of the internet* (pp. 53-67). Mayway, NJ: Lawrence Earlbaum.

Mehta, M. D.(2001). Pornography in Usenet: A study of 9,800 randomly selected images. *CyberPsychology & Behavior, 4*(6), 695-703.

Meinz, E. J., & Salthouse, T. A. (1998). Is age kinder to females than males? *Psychonomic Bulletin and Review, 5,* 56-70.

Menon., U. (2002). Middle adulthood in cultural perspective: The imagined and the experienced in three cultures. In M.E. Lachman (Ed), *Handbook of midlife development* (pp. 40-74). New York: Wiley.

Mezulis, A., Abramson, L., Hyde, J., & Hankin, B. (2004). Is there a universal positivity bias in attributions? A meta-analytic review of individual, developmental, and cultural differences in the self-Serving attributional bias. *Psychological Bulletin, 130*(5), 711-747.

Millard, L. (1996). Differences in coaching behaviors of male and female high school soccer coaches. *Journal of Sport Behavior, 19(1),* 19-31.

Miller, B. C., Christopherson, C. R. & King, P. K. (1993). Sexual behavior in adolescence. In T. S. Gullotta, G. R. Adams, & R. Montemayor (Eds.), *Adolescent Sexuality* (pp. 57-76). Newbury Park, CA: Sage.

Miller, K. (Ed.) (2009). *Male/female roles: Opposing viewpoints.* San Diego, CA: Greenhaven Press.

Miller, K. (2002, May). Part-time. *Lifeblood, 1 (40).* p. 3.

Millon, T. (2004). *Personality disorders in modern life* (2nd ed). New York: Wiley.

"Miss America pageant needs to rethink purpose" (1995, September 18). The *Daily Beacon*. Retrieved October 1, 2003, from http://dailybeacon.utk.edu/issues/v70/m18/wim.18v.html.

Mitchell,, J. (2000). *Psychoanalysis and feminism: A radical reassessment of Freudian psychoanalysis*. New York: Basic Books.

Moeller-Leimkuehler, A. M. (2002) Barriers to help-seeking by men: A review of sociocultural and clinical literature with particular reference to depression. *Journal of Affective Disorders, 71(1-3)*, 1-9.

Monastersky, R. (2005, March 4). Women and science: The debate goes on. *The Chronicle of Higher Education, 51 (26)*. A1, 12.

Mondimore, F. M. (1996). *A natural history of homosexuality*. Baltimore, MD: Johns Hopkins University Press.

Money, J. W. & Ehrhardt, A. A. (1972). *Man and woman, boy and girl: Differentiation and dimorphism of gender identity from conception.* Baltimore, MD: Johns Hopkins University Press.

Monsour. M. (2002). *Women and men as friends: Relationships across the lifespan in the 21st century.* NJ: Lawrence Erlbaum.

Montepare, J. M. & Lachman, M. E. (1989). You're only as old as you feel": Self-perceptions of age, fears of aging, and life satisfaction from adolescence to old age. *Psychology & Aging, 4*(1), 73-78.

Moore, L. & Vanneman, R. (2003). Context matters: Effects of the proportion of fundamentalists on gender attitudes. *Social Forces, 82*(1), 115-139.

Moos, J. (1997, April, 17). High-kicking hopefuls put it all on the line for Rockette dream. *CNN news*. Retrieved October 3, 2003 from http://edition.cnn.com/SHOWBIZ/9704/17/rockettes/

Morgan, B. L. (1998). A three generational study of tomboy behavior. *Sex Roles, 39*(9-10), 787-800.

Mott, F. L., Fondell, M. M., Hu, P.N., Kowaleski-Jones, L. & Menagahn, E. G. (1996). The determinants of first sex by age 14 in a high risk adolescent population. *Family Planning Perspectives, 28,* 13-18.

Mulac, A., Studley, L. B., Wiemann, J. M., & Bradac, J. J. (1987). Male/female gaze in same-sex and mixed-sex dyads: Gender-linked differences and mutual influence. *Human Communication Research, 13(3),* 323-343.

Muller, C. B., Ride, S. K., & Fouke, J. M. (2005; Feb 18). Different opinions on gender differences. [Letter to the editor]. *The Chronicle of Higher Education, 51(24)*. A47.

Murnen, S. K., Wright, C., Kaluzny, G. (2002). If "boys will be boys," then girls will be victims? A meta-analytic review of the research that relates masculine ideology to sexual aggression. *Sex Roles, 46*(11-12), 359-375.

Murnen, S. K., & Stockton, M. (1997). Gender and self-reported sexual arousal in response to sexual stimuli: A meta-analytic review. *Sex Roles*, 37(3-4),135-153.

Murnen, S. K., Wright, C., Kaluzny, G. (2002). If "boys will be boys," then girls will be victims? A meta-analytic review of the research that relates masculine ideology to sexual aggression. *Sex Roles, 46*(11-12), 359-375.

Murnen, S. K.; Smolak, L. & Mills, J. A. (2003). Thin, Sexy Women and Strong, Muscular Men: Grade-School Children's Responses to Objectified Images of Women and Men. *Sex Roles, 49*(9-10), 427-437.

Murray, C. B. (1996). Estimating achievement performance: A confirmation bias. *Journal of Black Psychology, 22(1),* 67-85.

Museum of Menstruation and Women's Health (n.d.). Retrieved February 12, 2004 from http://www.mum.org/

Myers, D. G. (2004). *Psychology* (7th Ed), New York: Worth Publishers.

Myers, S. M., & Booth, A. (2002). Forerunners of change in nontraditional gender ideology. *Social Psychology Quarterly,* 65(1),18-37.

Nanay, B. (2002). Evolutionary psychology and the selectionist model of neural development: A combined approach. *Evolution and Cognition, 8, 2,* 200-205.

Nasaw, D. (1981). *Schooled to order: A social history of public schooling in the United States.* Cambridge, MA: Oxford University Press.

Nason-Clark, N. (1995, Summer). [Review of the book *Fundamentalism and Gender*]. *Sociology of Religion,* 219-220.

National Center for Health Statistics (2000) *Vital Statistics of the United States, 1997.* Retrieved February 28, 2004 from http://www.cdc.gov/nchs/datawh/statab/unpubd/natality/natab97.htm

National Center for Health Statistics (2002). *Divorce Fast Stats.* Retrieved February 28, 2004 from http://www.cdc.gov/nchs/fastats/divorce.htm

National Center for Injury Prevention and Control (2005). *WISQARS Leading Causes of Death Reports, 2005.* Retrieved August 8, 2008 http://webapp.cdc.gov/sasweb/ncipc/leadcaus10.html.

National Center of Health Statistics (2002). *Mean Age of Mother, 1970-2000.* NVSR Vol. 51, No. 1. 14 pp. (PHS) 2003-1120.

National Committee on Pay Equity (2004). *Real life examples of equivalent jobs.* Retrieved September 14, 2004. http://www.pay-equity.org/info.html.

National Health and Nutrition Examination Survey (HANES)(1996). *The Third National Health and Nutrition Examination Survey (NHANES III, 1988-94) Reference Manuals and Reports.* Retrieved on 9/23/03 http://www.cdc.gov/nchs/nhanes.htm.

National Institute of Child Health, Human Development Early Child Care Research Network (2003). Does amount of time spent in child care predict socioemotional adjustment during the transition to kindergarten? *Child Development, 74(4),* 976-1005.

National Institute of Health (2000). *Depression* (NIH Publication No. 02-3561). Bethesda, Maryland: Author.

National Institute of Health (2001). *Eating disorders.* (NIH Publication No. 01-4901). Bethesda, Maryland: Author.

National Institute of Mental Health (1995). *Depression: What every woman should know* (No. 95-3871). Washington D.C.: Author.

National Partnership for Women & Families (n.d.). Retrieved June 15, 2004 http://www.nationalpartnership.org/

National Retail Federation (2007, November 17). *Transformers top must-have toys for boys while Barbie still on top of list for girls .* Retrieved August 9, 2008, http://www.nrf.com/modules.php?name=News&op=viewlive&sp_id=413.

Nelson, T. D. (2002). *The psychology of prejudice.* Boston MA: Allyn & Bacon.

Newcombe, N. S. (2006, August). Uses and abuses of evolutionary psychology. American Psychological Association, New Orleans, LA.

Newcombe, N. S. (2007). Taking science seriously: Straight thinking about spatial sex differences. In S. J. Ceci & W. Williams (Eds.), *Why Aren't More Women in Science? Top Researchers Debate the Evidence* (pp. 79-100). Washington, DC: American Psychological Association.

Newman, K. (2000). On the hire wire: How the working poor juggle job and family responsibilities. In E. Appelbaum (Ed.) *Balancing acts: Easing the burdens and improving the options for working families* (pp. 85-94). Washington, DC: Economic Policy Institute.

NICHD Early Child Care Research Network, CRMC (2004)., Type of child care and children's development at 54 months. *Early Childhood Research Quarterly, 19*(2), 203-230.

Nicotera, A. M., & Rancer, A. S. (1994). The influence of sex on self-perceptions and social stereotyping of aggressive communication predispositions. *Western Journal of Communication, 58,* 283-307.

Nolen-Hoeksema S. (1995). Gender differences in coping with depression across the lifespan. *Depression, 3,* 81-90.

Nolen-Hoeksema, S. & Girgus, J. S. (1994). The emergence of gender differences in depression during adolescence. *Psychological Bulletin, 115*(3), 424-443

Nolen-Hoeksema, S. (1987). Sex differences in unipolar depression: Evidence and theory. *Psychological Bulletin, 101(2),* 259-282.

Nolen-Hoeksema, S. (2000). The role of rumination in depression disorders in depression and mixed anxiety/depressive symptoms. *Psychological Bulletin, 109,* 504-511.

Nolen-Hoeksema, S. (2008). It is not what you have; it is what you do with it: Support for Addis's gendered responding framework. *Clinical Psychology: Science and Practice, 15*(3), 178-181.

"Now" (n.d.) Retrieved February 19, 2004 from ttp://www.gomilpitas.com/homeschooling/humor/012.htm.

Oesterman, K., Bjoerkqvist, K., Lagerspetz, K. M. J., Kaukiainen, A. Landau, S. F., Fraczek, A., Caprara, G. V., 1998. Cross-cultural evidence of female indirect aggression. *Aggressive Behavior, 24*(1),1-8.

Office of Child Support Enforcement (1998). *The Child Support Enforcement Program: An Overview.* Retrieved March 3, 2004 from http://www.acf.dhhs.gov/programs/cse/rpt/21t/annrpt21.htm

Office of Research on Women's Health (2003). *Inclusion of women.* Retrieved December 17, 2003 at http://www4.od.nih.gov/orwh/.

O'Hara, S., & Biesecker. A. (2003).Globalization: Homogenization or newfound diversity? *Review of Social Economy, 61,* 281-294.

Okamoto, D., & England, P. (1999). Is there a supply side to occupational sex segregation? *Sociological Perspectives, 42(4),* 557-582.

Olatawura, M. O.(1998). Sex differences in the prevalence and detection of depressive and anxiety disorders in general health care settings: Report from the World Health Organization collaborative study on psychological problems in general health care. *Archives of General Psychiatry, 55(5),* 405-413.

Ortner, S. B. (1996). *Making gender: The politics and erotics of culture*. Boston: Beacon Press.

Oskamp, S., Kaufman, K., & Wolterbeek, L. A. (1996). Gender role portrayals in preschool picture books. *Journal of Social Behavior & Personality,11(5)*, 27-39.

Oswald, P. A. (2000). Subtle sex bias in empathy and helping behavior. *Psychological Reports, 87(2)*, 545-551.

O'Toole, L. L., & Schiffman, J. R. (1997). *Gender violence: Interdisciplinary perspectives*. New York: New York University Press.

Ozer, E. M., Barnett, R. C., Brennan, R. T., & Sperling, J. (1998). Does child care involvement increase or decrease distress among dual-earner couples? *Women's Health: Research on Gender, Behavior, and Policy, 4*, 285-311.

Paetzold, R. L., & O'Leary-Kelly, A. M. (1996). In M.S. Stockdale (Ed.), *Sexual Harassment in the Workplace: Perspectives, Frontiers, and Response Strategies* (pp. 85-104). Thousand Oaks, CA: Sage.

Palmer, P. (1989). *Domesticity and dirt: Housewives and domestic servants in the United States, 1920-1945*. Philadelphia: Temple University Press.

Panter-Brick, C., Layton, R. H., & Rowley-Conwy, P. (2001) *Hunter-gatherers: An interdisciplinary perspective*. Boston, MA: Cambridge University Press.

Paquette, D., Carbonneau, R., Dubeau, D., Bigras, M., & Tremblay, R. E. (2003). Prevalence of father-child rough-and-tumble play and physical aggression in preschool children. *European Journal of Psychology of Education, 18(2)*, 171-189.

Paris, R., & Helson, R. (2002). Early mothering experience and personality change. *Journal of Family Psychology, 16(2)*, 172-185.

Park, M. Y. (2002, May 25). *Women: Let's talk about sex*. Fox News. Retrieved December 17, 2003 from http://www.foxnews.com/story/0,2933,53696,00.html.

Parrot, A., & Cummings, N. (2006). *Forsaken females:Tthe global brutalization of women*. Lanham, MD: Rowman & Littlefield.

Paterson, W.A . (2001). *Unbroken homes: Single parent mothers tell their stories*. Binghamton, NY: Haworth Press.

Peabody, J. (1991, June). The turning point. *Prenatal Care Matters*. Loma Linda, CA: Loma Linda Medical Center.

Pennell, G. E. (1999). Doing gender with Santa: Gender-typing in children's toy preferences. *Dissertation Abstracts International: Section B: The Sciences & Engineering, 59,* 8-B.

Perez, M., & Joiner, T. E. Jr. (2003). Body image dissatisfaction and disordered eating in black and white women. *International Journal of Eating Disorders, 33(3),* 342-350.

Perry, W. G., Jr. (1970), *Forms of Intellectual and Ethical Development in the College Years: A Scheme*. New York: Holt, Rinehart, and Winston.

Peterson, R. (1996). A re-evaluation of the economic consequences of divorce, *American Sociological Review, 61 (2)*, 528-536.

Piaget, J. (1929). *The child's conception of the world*. NY: Harcourt, Brace Jovanovich.

Piel, J. (1990). Unmasking sex and social class differences in childhood aggression: The case for language maturity. *Journal of Educational Research, 84(2)*,100-106.

Pigott, T. A. (1999). Gender differences in the epidemiology and treatment of anxiety disorders. *Journal of Clinical Psychiatry, 60 (18),* 4-15.

Pinkley, R. L., & Northcraft, G. B. (2000). Get paid what you're worth: The expert negotiator's guide to salary and compensation. New York: St. Martin's Press.

Plous, S., & Neptune, D. (1997). Racial and gender biases in magazine advertising: A content-analytic study. *Psychology of Women Quarterly, 21,* 627-644.

Polivy, J., & Herman, C. P. (2002). Causes of eating disorders. *Annual Review of Psychology, 53(1),* 187-213.

Pollack, W. (1999). *Real boys: Rescuing our sons from the myths of boyhood.* Bellingham, WA : Owl Books.

Pomerleau, A., Bolduc, D., & Malcuit, G. (1990). Pink or blue: Environmental gender stereotypes in the first two years of life. *Sex Roles, 22(5-6),* 359-367.

Pomfret, J. (2001, May 29). In China's Countryside, 'It's a Boy!' Too Often. *Washington Post Foreign Service,* p. A01.

Pope Paul VI *(*1968, July 25). Humanae Vitae: Encyclical of Pope Paul VI on the regulation of birth. Retrieved October 4, 2006 http://www.vatican.va/holy_father/paul_vi/encyclicals/documents/hf_p-vi_enc_25071968_humanae-vitae_en.html.

Pope, G. H., Olivardia, R., Gruber, A., & Borowiecki, J. (1999). "Evolving Ideals of Male Body Image as Seen Through Action Toys." *International Journal of Eating Disorders* 26, 65-72.

Porter, L. S., Marko, C. A., Schwartz. E., Neale, J. M., Shiffman, S., & Stone, A. A. (2000). Gender differences in coping: A comparison of trait and momentary assessments. *Journal of Social and Clinical Psychology, 19,* 480-498.

Potts, M. K., Burnam, M. A., & Wells, K. B. (1991). Gender differences in depression detection: A comparison of clinician diagnosis and standardized assessment. *Psychological Assessment, 3(4),* 609-615.

Poulin-Dubois, D., Serbin, L. A., Eichstedt, J. A., Sen, M. G., & Bissel, C. F. (2002). Men don't put on make-up: Toddlers' knowledge of the gender stereotyping of household activities. *Social Development, 11,* 166-181.

Presnell, K., Bearman, S. K., & Stice, E. (2004). Risk factors for body dissatisfaction in adolescent boys and girls: a prospective study. *International Journal of* Eating Disorders, *36*(4), 389-401.

Purves, D., Augustine, G. J., Fitzpatrick, D., Katz, L. C., LaMantia, A, Mcnamara, J. O., & Williams, S. M. (2001). *Neuroscience* (2nd Ed.) Sunderland, MA: Sinauer.

Putnam, F. W. (2003). Ten-year research update review: Child sexual abuse. *Journal of the American Academy of Child & Adolescent Psychiatry, 42*(3), 269-278.

Pyke, S. W., (1985). Androgyny: An integration. *International Journal of Women's Studies, 8(5),* 529-539.

Raber, J. (1998) Detrimental effects of chronic hypothalamic-pituitary-adrenal axis activation. From obesity to memory deficits. *Molecular Neurobiology,* 18(1), 1-22

Ramirez, J. M. (2003) Hormones and aggression in childhood and adolescence. *Aggression & Violent Behavior, 8*(6), 621-644.

Rane, T. R., & Draper, T. W. (1995). Negative evaluations of men's nuturant touching of young children. *Psychological Reports, 76*(3), 811-818.

Rank, M. R. (2000). Socialization of socioeconomic status *In W. C.* Nichols, & M. A. Pace-Nichols (Eds.), *Handbook of family development and intervention.* (pp. 129-142) New York: John Wiley & Sons.

Reichert. T., & Lambaise, J. (2003). *Sex in advertising: Perspectives on the erotic appeal.* Mahwah, New Jersey: Lawrence Erlbaum.

Reid, I.(1989). *Social class differences in Britain* (3rd ed). London: Fontana.

Richardson, D. R., Green, L. R., & Lago, T. (1998). The relationship between perspective-taking and nonaggressive responding in the face of an attack. *Journal of Personality, 66*(2), 235-256

Richardson, D. S., & Green, L. R. (2000). Aggression among older adults: The relationship of interaction networks and gender role to direct and indirect responses. *Aggressive Behavior, 26*(2), 145-154.

Richardson, J. T. E. (1997). Conclusions from the study of gender differences in cognition. In P.J. Caplan, M. Crawford, J. S. Hyde & J. T. E. Richardson (Eds.), *Gender differences in human cognition.* (pp. 131-169). New York: Oxford University Press.

Rickwood, D. J. & Braithwaite, V. A. (1994) Social-psychological factors affecting help-seeking for emotional problems. *Social Science & Medicine, 39(4),* 563-572.

Ridgeway, C. L. (2001). Gender, status, and leadership. *Journal of Social Issues, 57(4)*, 637-655.

Ridker,P. M., Cook, N. R., Lee, I. M., Gordon, D., Gaziano, J. M., Manson, J. E. Hennekens, C. H.,& Buring, J.. E. (2005). A randomized trial of low-dose aspirin in the primary prevention of cardiovascular disease in women. *New England Journal of Medicine, 352* (13), 1293-1304.

Riggs, D. S., & O'Leary, K. D (1996). Aggression between heterosexual dating partners: An examination of a causal model of courtship aggression. *Journal of Interpersonal Violence, 11*(4), 519-540.

Riggs, D. S., O'Leary, K. D., & Breslin, F. C.. (1990). Multiple correlates of physical aggression in dating couples. *Journal of Interpersonal Violence, 5*(1), 61-73.

Rimm, M. (1995). Marketing pornography on the information superhighway: A survey of 917,410 images, descri0ptions, short stories, and animations downloaded 8.5 million times by consumer in over 2000 cities in 40 countries, provinces and territories. *The Georgetown Law Journal, 83*(5), 1849-1934.

Roberts, C. (2000). Biological Behavior? Hormones, Psychology, and Sex. *National Women's Studies Association Journal, 12 (3),* 1-20.

Rodriquez, J. (1996, March 25). *Broadened diversity requirement misses the point.* The University of Washington Student Newspaper. Retrieved October 6, 2006. http://archives.thedaily.washington.edu/1996/032596/cedagain.html

Rogers, S. J., & DeBoer, D. D.; (2001). Changes in wives' income: Effects on marital happiness, psychological well-being, and the risk of divorce. *Journal of Marriage & the Family, 63*(2), 458-472.

Rohde, D. (2003, October 26), India Steps Up Effort to Halt Abortions of Female Fetuses, *New York Times.* p. A3, A5.

Roschelle, A. R. (1997). *No more kin.* Thousand Oaks, CA: Sage.

Rose, A. J., & Montemayor, R. (1994). The relationship between gender role orientation and perceived self-competency in male and female adolescents. *Sex Roles, 31(9-10)*, 579-595.

Rosenbaum, A., & Leisring, P. A, (2003). Beyond power and control: Towards an understanding of partner abusive men. *Journal of Comparative Family Studies, 34(1)*, 7-22.

Rosenblum, K. E., & Travis, T. C. (2002). *The meaning of difference: American constructions of race, sex and gender, social class, and sexual orientation* (3rd ed). New York: McGraw-Hill.

Rosenthal, R,. & Rubin, D. B., (1982). Further meta-analytic procedures for assessing cognitive gender differences. *Journal of Educational Psychology, 74(5)*, 708-712.

Rossi, A. S., & Rossi, P.E. (1977). Body time and social time: Mood patterns by menstrual cycle phase and day of week. *Social Science Research, 6*, 273-308.

Rotundo, E. A. (1985). American fatherhood: A historical perspective. *American Behavioral Scientist, 29(1)*, 7-23.

Rotundo, M., Nguyen, D., & Sackett, P. R. (2001). A meta-analytic review of gender differences in perceptions of sexual harassment, *Journal of Applied Psychology, 86*(5), 14-26.

Rowling, J. K. (2003). Harry Potter and the order of the phoenix. New York: Scholastic.

Rozee, P. D. & Koss, .M. P. (2001). Rape: A century of resistance. *Psychology of Women Quarterly, 25(4)*, 295-311.

Rubin, L. B. (1976). *Worlds of pain: Life in the working-class family.* New York: Basic Books.

Rubin, L. B. (1985). *Just friends: The role of friendship in our lives.* New York: HarperCollins.

Ruble, D. N., Taylor, L. J., Cyphers, L., Greulich, F. K., Lurye, L. E., & Shrout, P. E.; (2007). The role of gender constancy in early gender development. *Child Development, 78(4)*, 1121-1136.

Rusbult, C. E., Zembrodt, I. M., & Iwaniszek, J. (1986). The impact of gender and sex-role orientation on responses to dissatisfaction in close relationships. *Sex Roles, 15(1-2)*, 1-20.

Russo, N. F. (1976). The motherhood mandate. *Journal of Social Issues, 32*, 143-153

Sadker, M,. & Sadker, D. M. (1994). *Failing at fairness: How America's schools cheat girls.* New York: C. Scribner's Sons.

Sala,S. D. (Ed). (2007). *Tall tales about the mind and brain: Separating fact from fiction.* Oxford: Oxford Press.

Salmivalli, C., Kaukiainen, A., & Lagerspetz, K. (2000). Aggression and sociometric status among peers: Do gender and type of aggression matter? *Scandinavian Journal of Psychology, 41*, 17-24.

Samter, W., Whaley, B. B., & Mortenson, S. T. (1997). Ethnicity and emotional support in same-sex friendship: A comparison of Asian-Americans, African-Americans, and Euro-Americans. *Personal Relationships, 4(4)*, 413-430.

Sansone, C., & Harackiewicz, J.M. (Eds.), (2000). *Intrinsic and extrinsic motivation: The search for optimal motivation and performance.* San Diego, CA: Academic Press.

Sarkisian, N., Gerena, M., & Gerstel, N. (2007). Extended family integration among Euro and Mexican Americans: Ethnicity, gender, and class *Journal of Marriage and Family, 69(1)*, 40-54.

Savin-Williams, R. C., & Esterberg, K. G. (2000). Lesbian, gay, and bisexual families. *In W. C.* Nichols, & M. A. Pace-Nichols (Eds.), *Handbook of family development and intervention.* (pp. 197-215.) New York: John Wiley & Sons.

Sawatzky, R., Ratner, P., & Chiu, L. (2005). A meta-analysis of the relationship between spirituality and quality of life. *Social Indicators Research*, 72(2), 153-188.

Schiefelbein, V. L. (2002). Rape and sexual assault. In J. Sandoval (Ed) *Handbook of crisis counseling, intervention, and prevention in the schools* (2nd ed.) (pp. 359-392). Mahwah, NJ: Lawrence Erlbaum Associates.

Schneider, K. T., Swan, S., & Fitzgerald, L. F. (1997). Job-related and psychological effects of sexual harassment in the workplace: Empirical evidence from two organizations. *Journal of Applied Psychology, 82(3),* 401-415.

Scully, D., & Marolla, J. (1985), Interviewing in a difficult situation: 'Riding the bull at Gilley's": Convicted rapists describe the rewards of rape. *Social Problems, 32(3),* 251-263.

Seidman, S. N., Mosher, W. D., & Aral, S. O. (1992). Women with multiple sexual partners: United States, 1988. *American Journal of Public Health, 82,* 1388-1394.

Sell, R. L., Wells, J. A., & Wypij, D. (1995). The prevalence of homosexual behavior and attraction in the United States, the United kingdom, and France: Results of national population-based samples. *Archives of Sexual Behavior, 24,* 235-248.

Selman, R. (1980). *The Growth of Interpersonal Understanding.* New York: Academic Press.

Selye, H. (1956). *The stress of life.* New York: McGraw-Hill.

Sen, B. (2002). Does married women's market work affect marital stability adversely? An intercohort analysis using NLS data. *Review of Social Economy, 60(1),* 71-92.

Senay, E. (2004, January 13). *Deadliest cancer for women.* CBSNews.com. Retrieved January 15, 2003 at http://www.cbsnews.com/stories/2004/01/12/earlyshow/contributors/emilysenay/main592834.html

Serbin, L. A., Powlishta, K. K. & Gulko, J. (1993). The development of sex typing in middle childhood. *Monographs of the society for research in child development, 58 (2).* v-74.

Serbin, L.A., Poulin-Dubois, D., & Eichstedt, J.A. (2002).Infants' response to gender-inconsistent events. *Infancy, 3(4),* 531-542.

Seto, M. C., Maric, A., & Barbaree, H. E. (2001). The role of pornography in the etiology of sexual aggression. *Aggression & Violent Behavior, 6(1),* 35-53.

Shakin, M., & Sternglanz, S. H. (1985). Infant clothing: Sex labeling for strangers. *Sex Roles, 12(9-10),* 955-964.

Shapiro, J. L., Diamond, M. J., & Greenberg, M. (Eds.), (1995). *Becoming a father: Contemporary, social, developmental, and clinical perspectives.* New York: Springer Publishing.

Sharp, E. A., & Ganong, L. H. (2000). Raising awareness about marital expectations: Are unrealistic beliefs changed by integrative teaching? *Family Relations: Interdisciplinary Journal of Applied Family Studies, 49(1),* 71-76.

Sheets, V. L., & Wolfe, M. D. (2001). Sexual jealousy in heterosexuals, lesbians, and gays. *Sex Roles, 44.* 255-276.

Shields, C. (1976). *Small ceremonies.* New York: Penguin Press.

Shields, S. A. (2002). *Speaking from the heart: Gender and the social meaning of emotion.* New York: Cambridge University Press.

Shih, M., Pittinsky, T. & Ambady, N. (1999). Stereotype susceptibility: Identity salience and shifts in quantitative performance. *Psychological Science, 10(1),* 80-83.

Signorella, M. L., Bigler, R. S., & Liben, L. S. (1997). A meta-analysis of children's memories for own-sex and other-sex information. *Journal of Applied Developmental Psychology, 18(3),* 429-445.

Signorella, M., Bigler, R. S., & Liben, L. (1994). Gender stereotypes in MTV commercials: The beat goes on. *Journal of Broadcasting and Electronic Media, 38(1),* 91-101.

Sines, M. C. (2003). A comparison of the psychological functioning of sexually abused Mexican-American and non-Hispanic White children and adolescents. Dissertation Abstracts International, 63(8-B), 3939.

Singer, L. T., Barkley, M., & Taylor, C. (2005; Feb 18). Different opinions on gender differences. [Letter to the editor]. *The Chronicle of Higher Education, 51 (24).* A47.

Sinnott, J. D., & Shifren, K. (2001). Gender and aging: Gender differences and gender roles. In J. E. Birren, (Ed). *Handbook of the psychology of aging* (5th ed.) (pp. 454-476). San Diego, CA: Academic Press.

Slaby, R. G., & Frey, K. S. (1975). Development of gender constancy and selective attention to same-sex models. *Child Development, 46,* 849-856.

Slusher, M. P., & Anderson, C. A. (1989). Belief perseverance and self-defeating behavior. In R. C. Curtis (Ed), *Self-defeating behaviors: Experimental research, clinical impressions, and practical implications* (pp. 11-40). New York: Plenum Press.

Smith, C. A., & Stillman, S. (2002). What do women want? The effects of gender and sexual orientation on the desirability of physical attributes in the personal ads of women, *Sex Roles, 46*(9-10), 337-342.

Smith, D., Kyle, S., Forty, L., Cooper, C., Walters, J., Russell, E., et al. (2008). Differences in depressive symptom profile between males and females. *Journal of Affective Disorders, 108*(3), 279-284.

Smith, T. W. (1991). Adult sexual behavior in 1989: Number of partners, frequency of intercourse, and risk of AIDS. *Family Planning Perspectives, 23,* 102-107.

Smith-Lovin, L., & Robinson, D. T. (1992). Gender and conversational dynamics. In C. L. Ridgeway (Ed.). *Gender, interaction and inequality* (pp. 122-156). New York: Springer-Verlag.

Smith-Lovin, L., Skvoretz, J. V., & Hudson, C. G. (1986). Status and participation in six-person groups: A test of Skvoretz's comparative status model. *Social Forces, 64(4),* 992-1005.

Smolensky, E., & Gootman, J. A.. (2003). *Working families and growing kids: Caring for children and adolescents.* Washington, DC: National Academies Press.

Snyder, M., Tanke, E. D., & Berscheid, E. (1977). Social perception and interpersonal behavior: On the self-fulfilling nature of social stereotypes. *Journal of Personality & Social Psychology, 35(9),* 656-666.

Sobek, M. J. (1997). A century of work, gender, labor force participation and occupational attainment in the United States 1880-1990. PhD dissertation. University of Minnesota.

Society of Women Engineers (2004). *Education statistics about women in engineering in the USA.* Retrieved January 15, 2004 http://www.swe.org/stellent/idcplg?IdcService=SS_GET_PAGE&nodeId=98&ssSourceNodeId=5.

Somers, M. D. (1993). A comparison of voluntarily childfree adults and parents. *Journal of Marriage & the Family, 55*(3), 643-650.

Sommer, B. (1992). Cognitive performance and the menstrual cycle. In J.T.E. Richardson (Ed.), *Cognition and the Menstrual Cycle.* (pp. 39 – 66). New York: Springer-Verlag.

Sommers, C. H. (2000). *The war against boys: How misguided feminism is harming our young men.* New York: Simon & Schuster.

Sorbara, M., & Geliebter, A. (2002). Body image disturbance in obese outpatients before and after weight loss in relation to race, gender, binge eating, and age of onset of obesity. *International Journal of Eating Disorders, 31*(4), 416-423.

Souad with Cuny, M. (2004). *Burned alive: A survivor of an 'honor killing" speaks out.* New York: Warner Books.

Spence, J. T., & Helmreich, R. L. (1978). *Masculinity and femininity: Their psychological dimensions, correlates, and antecedents.* Austin, TX: University of Texas Press.

Spicer, P., Beals J., Croy, C. D., Mitchell, C. M., Novins, D. K., Moore, L & Spero M. M. (2003). The Prevalence of DSM-III-R Alcohol Dependence in Two American Indian Populations Alcoholism: *Clinical and Experimental Research*, 27(11), 1785-1797.

Sprecher, S., & Toro-Morn, M. (2002). A study of men and women from different sides of earth to determine if men are from Mars and women are from Venus in their beliefs about love and romantic relationships. *Sex Roles, 46(5-6)*, 131-147.

Sprock, J., Crosby, J., P., & Nielsen, B. A. (2001). Effects of sex and sex roles on the perceived maladaptiveness of DSM-IV personality disorder symptoms. *Journal of Personality Disorders, 5*(1), 41-59.

Sprock, J., Crosby, J., P., & Nielsen, B. A. (2001). Effects of sex and sex roles on the perceived maladaptiveness of DSM-IV personality disorder symptoms. *Journal of Personality Disorders, 5(1)*, 41-59.

Stanley, D. R. (1988). Sexual dimorphism of pelvic fin shapes in four species of catostomidae. *Transactions of the American Fisheries Society, 117*, 600-602.

Stark, R. (2002). Physiology and faith: Addressing the "universal" gender differences in religious commitment. *Journal for the Scientific Study of Religion, 41,* 495-507.

Steil, J. M. (2000). Contemporary marriage: Still an unequal partnership. In C. Hendrick & S. Hendrick (Eds.), *Close relationships: A sourcebook* (pp. 125-136). Thousand Oaks, CA: Sage Publications

Steil, J. M. (2001). Family forms and member well-being: A research agenda for the Decade of Behavior. *Psychology of Women Quarterly, 25*(4), 344-363.

Steinberg, L. (2004) *Adolescence* (7th Ed.). New York: McGraw-Hill.

Stern, B. B. (2003). Masculinism(s) and the male image: What does it mean to be a man? In T. Reichert & J. Lambaise, (Eds.), *Sex in advertising: Perspectives on the erotic appeal* (pp. 215-228). Mahwah, New Jersey: Lawrence Erlbaum.

Sternberg, R. J. & Zhang, L. (Eds.) (2001). *Perspectives on thinking, learning, and cognitive styles.* Mahwah, NJ: Lawrence Erlbaum Associates.

Stewart, A. J. & McDermott, C. (2004). Gender in psychology. *Annual Review of Psychology, 55*, 519-544.

Stewart, L. P., Cooper, P. J., & Stewart, A. D. (2003). *Gender and communication* (4th Ed). Boston, MA: Allyn & Bacon.

Stoops, N. (2004, June). Educational attainment in the United States: 2003. *Current Population Reports*. Washington DC: U.S. Census Bureau.

Stoppard, J. M., & Gruchy, C. G. (1993). Gender, context, and expression of positive emotion. *Personality & Social Psychology Bulletin, 19*(2), 143-150.

Street, W. R. (1994). *A chronology of noteworthy events in American psychology*. Washington, DC: American Psychological Association.

Stringer, D. M., Remick, H., Salisbury, J., & Ginorio, A. B. (1990). The power and reasons behind sexual harassment: An employer's guide to solutions. *Public Personnel Management, 19*(1), 43-52.

Strouse, J. S. Buerkel-Rothfuss, N., & Long, E. C. J. (1995). Gender and family as moderators of the relationship between music video exposure and adolescent sexual permissiveness. *Adolescence, 30*, 505-521.

Strube, M., Turner, C.W., Cerro, D., Stevens, J., & Hinchey, F. (1984). Interpersonal aggression and the Type A coronary-prone behavior pattern: A theoretical distinction and practical implications. *Journal of Personality and Social Psychology, 47*, 839-847.

Stukas, A. A. Jr., Switzer, G. E., Dew, M. A., Goycoolea, J. M., & Simmons, R. G. (1999). Parental helping models, gender, and service-learning. In J. G. Chapman & J. R. Ferrari (Eds.), *Educating Students to make a difference: Community based service learning* (pp 5-18). New York: Hawthorne.

Subrahmanyam, K., & Greenfield, Patricia M. (1998). Computer games for girls: What makes them play? In J. Cassell, & H. Jenkins,(Eds.), *From Barbie to Mortal Kombat: Gender and computer games.* (pp. 46-71) Cambridge, MA: MIT Press.

Summers, L. H. (2005, Jan, 14.) *Remarks at NBER conference on diversifying the science & engineering workforce.* Retrieved July 21, 2005 from http://www.president.harvard.edu/speeches/2005/nber.htm

Suskind, R. (1999). *A Hope in the Unseen: An American Odyssey from the Inner City to the Ivy League.* New York: Broadway Books.

Sutaria, S. D. (1985). *Specific learning disabilities: Natures and needs.* Springfield, IL: Thomas.

Suzuki, D., & Knudtson, P. (1990). *Genethics: The clash between the new genetics and human values.* Cambridge, MA: Harvard Press.

Svartberg, J., Jorde, R., Sundsfjord, J., Bønaa, J. H. & Barrett-Connor, E. (2003). Seasonal Variation of Testosterone and Waist to Hip Ratio in Men: The Tromsø Study. *The Journal of Clinical Endocrinology & Metabolism, 88,* 3099-3104.

Swain, S. (1989). Covert intimacy: Closeness in men's friendships. In B. Risman & P. Schwartz (Eds.), *Gender in intimate relationships: A microstructural approach* (pp. 71-86). Belmont, CA: Wadsworth.

Sweeney, J., & Bradbard, M. R. (1988). Mothers' and fathers' changing perceptions of their male and female infants over the course of pregnancy. *Journal of Genetic Psychology, 149(3),* 393-404.

Swenson, J., & Casmir, F. L. (1998). The impact of culture-sameness, gender, foreign travel, and academic background on the ability to interpret facial expression of emotion in others. *Communication Quarterly, 46,* 214-230.

Swim, J. K., & Sanna, L. J. (1996) He's skilled, she's lucky: A meta-analysis of observers' attributions for women's and men's successes and failures. *Personality & Social Psychology Bulletin, 22(5),* 507-519.

Tamres, L. K., Janicki, D, & Helgeson, V. S. (2002). Sex differences in coping behavior: A meta analytic review and an examination of relative coping. *Personality and Social Psychology Review. 6(1):* 2-30.

Tang, T., & Talpade, M. (1999) Sex differences in satisfaction with pay and co-workers. *Public Personnel Management, 28*(3). 345-352.

Tannen, D .(1994). *Gender and discourse.* New York: Oxford University Press.

Tannen. D. (1990). *You just don't understand: Women and men in conversation.* New York: William Morrow.

Tarrant, S. (2009). *Men and feminism.* Berkeley, CA: Seal Press.

Tatham, M., & Morton, K. (2006). *Expression in speech: Analysis and synthesis.* New York: Oxford University Press.

Tatum, B. D. (1997). *Why are all the Black kids sitting together in the cafeteria?" and other conversations about race.* New York: Basic Books.

Tavris, C. (1998). The paradox of gender. *Scientific American, 279* (4), 126-129.

Taylor S. E., Klein L. C., Lewis B. P., Gruenewald T. L., Gurung, R. A., & Updegraff, J.A. (2000). Biobehavioral responses to stress in females: tend-and-befriend, not fight-or-flight. *Psychological Review,107(3),* 411-29.

Taylor, R. J., Tucker, M. B., & Chatters, L. M. (1997). Recent demographic trends in African American family structure. In R. J. Taylor & J. S. Jackson (Eds.), *Family life in Black America.* (pp. 14-62). Thousand Oaks, CA: Sage Publications.

Taylor, S. E. (2003). *Health psychology* (5th Ed.) New York: McGraw Hill.

The Financial Express. (2008, May 13). *Male bosses preferred.* Retrieved January 10, 2009 from http://www.financialexpress.com/news/male-bosses-preferred-says-assocham-industry-survey/309030/#

The Kinsey Institute for Research in Sex, Gender and Reproduction (2003). *The Kinsey continuum.* Retrieved December 15, 2003 at http://www.indiana.edu/~kinsey/.

Tjaden, P. ,& Thoennes, N. (2000). *Extent, nature and consequences of intimate partner violence.* (NIJ 181867). Washington DC: National Institute of Justice .

Trollvik, M. (2005). *Final report: Women to the top.* Retrieved July 27, 2005 http://www.women2top.net/uk/facts/final_report.htm.

Trudel, G. (2002). Sexuality and marital life: Results of a survey. *Journal of Sex and Marital Therapy, 28,* 229-249.

Tucker, M. B., & Mitchell-Kernan, C. (Eds.) (1995). *The decline in marriage Among African Americans: Causes, consequences, and policy implications.* New York: Russell Sage Foundation.

Turner Syndrome Society (n.d.). Retrieved October 13, 2003, from http://www.turner-syndrome-us.org/

Twenge, J. M., & Nolen-Hoeksema, S. (2002). Age, gender, race, socioeconomic status, and birth cohort difference on the children's depression inventory: A meta-analysis. *Journal of Abnormal Psychology, 111(4),* 578-588.

Twenge, J. M., Campbell, W. K., & Foster, C. A. (2003). Parenthood and marital satisfaction: A meta-analytic review. *Journal of Marriage & Family, 65*(3), 574-583.

Twitchell, J. B. (1996). *AdCult USA: The triumph of advertising in American culture.* New York: Columbia University Press.

Twitchell, J. B. (2003). Adcult and gender. In T. Reichert & J. Lambaise, (Eds). *Sex in advertising: Perspectives on the erotic appeal* (pp. 181-194). Mahwah, New Jersey: Lawrence Erlbaum.

U. S. Department of Labor (1993). *Family medical leave act.* Retrieved June 12, 2004 http://www.dol.gov/esa/whd/fmla/.

U.S. Census Bureau (1942, April 23). *Educational attainment of the population 25 years old and over in the United States:1940.*

U.S. Census Bureau (2001). *Statistics of U.S. Businesses: 2001: All industries United States.* Retrieved August 12, 2004 http://www.census.gov/epcd/susb/2001/us/US--.HTM.

U.S. Department of Health and Human Services. (2001). *Mental Health: Culture, Race, Ethnicity – A Supplement to Mental Health: Report of the Surgeon General* (SMA Publication No. 01-3613). Rockville, MD: Author.

U.S. Department of Labor (1993, June). *Facts on working women.* No. 93-2.

U.S. Department of Labor (2000, June). *A Nation of Opportunity: Building America's 21st Century Workforce.* Washington DC: 21st Century Workforce Commission.

U.S. Department of Labor (2004). *Women in the labor force: A databook.* Report 973. Washington DC: Author.

Ullman, S. E., (2004). Sexual assault victimization and suicidal behavior in women: A review of the literature. *Aggression & Violent Behavior, 9(4),* 331-351.

Ullman, S. E., Karabatsos, G., & Koss, M. P. (1999). Alcohol and sexual aggression in a national sample of college men. *Psychology of Women Quarterly, 23*(4), 673-689.

UNESCO (2000). *Illiteracy world maps and graphs.* United Nations Educational, Scientific and Cultural Organization. Retrieved November 20, 2003 http://www.uis.unesco.org/en/stats/statistics/literacy2000.htm

Unger, R. K. (1979). Toward a redefinition of sex and gender. *American Psychologist,* 34(11), 1085-1094

Ungerleider, L. G. (1995). Functional brain imaging studies of cortical mechanisms for memory. *Science, 270,* 769-75.

US Bureau of the Census (2003a). *Median age at first marriage.* Retrieved March 3, 2004 from http://www.infoplease.com/ipa/A0005061.html.

US Bureau of the Census (2003b). *Percent never married.* Retrieved March 3, 2004 from http://www.infoplease.com/ipa/A0763219.html.

US Bureau of the Census (2003c). *Marriages and divorces, 1900–2001.* Retrieved March 3, 2004 from http://www.infoplease.com/ipa/A0005044.html.

US Department of Transportation, (2002.) *Traffic safety facts 2001.* Washington DC: Author.

Van Leeuwen, M. S. (2002). *My brother's keeper: what the social sciences do (and don't) tell us about masculinity.* Downers Grove, IL: Inter-Varsity Press.

van Poppel, F., Monden, C.; Mandemakers, K. (2008) Marriage timing over the generations. *Human Nature, 19*(1), 7-22.

Van Volkom, M. (2001). The relationships between childhood tomboyism, siblings' activities, and adult gender roles, *Sex Roles, 49*, 609-618.

Vanzetti, N. & Duck, S. (1996). *A lifetime of relationships.* Pacific Grove, CA: Brooks/Cole.

Vincent, N. (2006). *Self-made man: My year disguised as a man.* New York: Atlantic.

Veroff, J., Douvan, E. & Kolka, R. A. (1981). *The inner American: A self portrait from 1957-1976.* New York: Basic Books.

Voydanoff, P., & Donnelly, B. W. (1999) Multiple roles and psychological distress: The intersection of the paid worker, spouse, and parent roles with the role of the adult child. *Journal of Marriage & the Family, 61*(3), 725-738.

Wagner, H. L., Buck, R., & Winterbotham, M. (1993). Communication of specific emotions: Gender differences in sending accuracy and communication measures. *Journal of Nonverbal Behavior*, 17(1), 29-53.

Wagner, T. D., Phan, K. L., Liberzon, I., & Taylor, S. (2003). Valence, gender, and lateralization of functional brain anatomy in emotion: A meta-analysis of findings from neuroimaging. *NeuroImage, 19,* 513-531.

Walcott, D. D., Pratt, H. D., & Patel, D. R. (2003). Adolescents and eating disorders: Gender, racial, ethnic, sociocultural and socioeconomic issues *Journal of Adolescent Research, 18(3),* 223-243.

Waldner-Haugrud, L. K., & Magruder, B. (1995). Male and female sexual victimization in dating relationships: Gender differences in coercion techniques and outcomes. *Violence & Victims, 10*(3), 203-215.

Waldo, C.R., Berdahl, J. L., & Fitzgerald, L. F. (1998). Are men sexually harassed? If so, by whom. Law & *Human Behavior, 22*(1), 59-79.

Walker Bynum. C. W. (1986) (Ed.) *Gender and Religion: On the Complexity of Symbols.* Boston: Beacon Press.

Walker, K. E. (1994). Between friends: Class, gender, and friendship. Dissertation Abstracts International, 54(12-A), 4593.

Walker, L. E. (1984). *The battered woman syndrome.* New York: Springer.

Walker, L. J. (1984). *Sex* differences in the development of moral reasoning: A critical review. *Child Development, 55(3),* 677-691.

Walker, L. J. (1986). A longitudinal study of moral reasoning. *Child Development, 60,* 157-166.

Walker, S. (1999). Parental helping models, gender, and service-learning. *Journal of Prevention & Intervention in the Community, 18*(1-2), 5-18.

Ward, M. (1995). Talking about sex: Common themes about sexuality in the prime time television programs children and adolescents view most. *Adolescence, 24,* 595-615.

Wardlaw. M. K. (2002). As if. *WIN Kids Lesson*, Wellness IN the Rockies, Retrieved November 11, 2003, http://crhreweb.uwyo.edu/WinTheRockies/WIN%20Kids%20Lessons/as%20if/As_If _Lesson.pdf

Waschbusch, D. A., Sellers, D. P., LeBlanc, M., & Kelley, M. L. (2003). Helpless attributions and depression in adolescents: The roles of anxiety, event valence and demographics. *Journal of Adolescence 26(2),* 169-183.

Wassenaar, D., le Grange, D., Winship, J., & <u>Lachenicht, L.</u> (2000). The prevalence of eating disorder pathology in a cross-ethnic population of female students in South Africa. *European Eating Disorders Review, 8*(3), 225-236.

Waters, J. (1992). *On gender and sexual orientation.* Retrieved September 15, 2003 from http://songweaver.com/writing/article1.html.

Watkins, P. L. & Lee, J. (1997). A feminist perspective on panic disorder and agoraphobia: Etiology and treatment. *Journal of Gender, Culture, & Health, 2,* 65-87

Waugh, I.M., & Rienzi, B. M. (1998). Gender portrayals in telephone books for gay community versus Pacific-Bell yellow pages. *Psychological Reports, 83(3),* 751.

Websdale, N., & Chesney-Lind, M. (1998). Masculinities and violence. In L. Bowker (Ed.) *Doing violence to women: Research synthesis on the victimization of women* (pp. 51-81). Thousand Oaks, CA: Sage Publications.

Webster, R. (1996). *Why Freud was wrong: Sin, science and psychoanalysis.* New York: Basic Books.

Weichold, K., Silbereisen, R. K., & Schmitt-Rodermund, E. (2003). Short-term and long-term consequences of early versus late physical maturation in adolescents. In C. Hayward (Ed.), *Gender differences at* puberty (pp. 241-276). New York: Cambridge University Press.

Weinberg, D. H. (2004). *Evidence from census 2000 about earning by detailed occupation for men and women.* U. S. Census Bureau CENSR-15.

Weiner, B. (1974). *Achievement motivation and attribution theory.* Morristown, N.J.: General Learning Press.

Weinstock, J. S. (1998). Lesbian, gay, bisexual, and transgender friendships in adulthood. In C. J. Patterson & A. R. D'Augelli, (Eds), Lesbian, *gay, and bisexual identities in families: Psychological perspectives* (pp. 122-153). London: Oxford University Press.

Weisenfeld, A. R. (1985). Psychophysiological response of breast- and bottle-feeding mothers to their infants' signals. *Psychophysiology, 22*(1), 79-86.

Weiss, E. L., Longhurst, J. G. & Mazure, C. M. (1999). Childhood sexual abuse as a risk factor for depression in women: Psychosocial and neurobiological correlates. *American Journal of Psychiatry, 156,* 816-828.

Welter, B. (1966, Summer). The cult of true womanhood: 1820-1860. *American Quarterly, 18,* 151-174.

Werner-Wilson, R. J. (1998). Gender differences in adolescent sexual attitudes: The influence of individual and family factors. *Adolescence, 33*(131), 519-531.

West, C. M. (1998). Leaving a second closet: Outing partner violence in same-sex couples. In J. L. Jasinski & L. M. Williams (Eds.), *Partner violence: A comprehensive review of 20 years of research* (pp. 163-183). Thousand Oaks, CA: Sage.

West, P. (1999). Boys' underachievement in school: Some persistent problems and some current research. *Issues in Educational Research, 9*(1), 33-54.

Westen, D. (1988). The scientific legacy of Sigmund Freud: Toward a psychodynamically informed psychological science. *Psychological Bulletin, 124(3),* 333-371.

What is AIS?", (2002, September, 26). Retrieved October 13, 2003 from http://www.medhelp.org/www/ais/

White, J. W., Smith, P. H., & Koss, M. P. (2000). Intimate partner aggression--what have we learned? Comment on Archer. *Psychological Bulletin, 126*(5), 690-696.

White, L., & Rogers, S. J. (2000). Economic circumstances and family outcomes: A review of the 1990s. *Journal of Marriage & the Family, 62(4)*, 1035-1051

Wiehe, V. R., & Richards, A. L. (1995). *Intimate* betrayal*: Understanding and responding to the trauma of acquaintance* rape. Thousand Oaks, CA: Sage Publications.

Wiesner, M.,& Ittel, A. (2002). Relations of pubertal timing and depressive symptoms to substance use in early adolescence. *Journal of* Early *Adolescence, 22(*1), 5-23.

Wilcox, S., Evenson, K. R., Aragaki, A., Wassertheil-Smoller, S., Mouton, C. P., Loevinger, B. L. (2003). The effects of widowhood on physical and mental health, health behaviors, and health outcomes: The Women's Health Initiative. *Health Psychology, 22*(5), 513-522.

Williams, (2000). *Unbending gender: Why family and work conflict and what to do about it.* Oxford, England: Oxford University Press.

Williams, B., & Williams, D. P. (2003). *How to be a good wife.* Retrieved February 26, 2004 at http://www.snopes.com/language/document/goodwife.htm

Williams, J. E., & Best, D. L. (1982). *Measuring sex stereotypes: A thirty nation study.* Beverly Hills: Sage.

Willis, F. N., & Carlson, R. A. (1993). Singles ads: Gender, social class, and time. *Sex Roles, 29*(5-6), 387-404.

Willis, F. N. Jr., & Dodds, R A. (1998). Age, relationship, and touch initiation. *Journal of Social Psychology*, 138(1), 115-123.

Wilsnack, S. C., Wilsnack, R. W., & Kristjanson, A. F. (2004). Child sexual abuse and alcohol use among women: Setting the stage for risky sexual behavior. In L. J. Koenig, & L. S. Doll (Eds.) *From child sexual abuse to adult sexual risk: Trauma, revictimization, and intervention* (pp. 181-200). Washington, DC: American Psychological Association.

Wilson, C. C. II., & Gutierrez, F. (2003). Advertising and people of color. In G. Dines & J. M. Humez (Eds.) *Gender, race and class in media: A text reader* (2nd Ed). (pp. 283-292). Thousand Oaks, CA: Sage.

Wilson, F. L. (1995). The effects of age, gender, and ethnic/cultural background on *moral* reasoning. *Journal of Social Behavior & Personality, 10(1),* 67-78.

Winkielman, P., Halberstadt, J., Fazendeiro, T., & Catty, S. (2006). Prototypes Are Attractive Because They Are Easy on the Mind. *Psychological Science, 17*(9), 799-806.

Winsler, A., Caverly, S. L., Willson-Quayle, A., Carlton, M. P., Howell, C., & Long, G. N., (2002). The social and behavioral ecology of mixed-age and same-age preschool classrooms: A natural experiment. *Journal of Applied Developmental Psychology, 23(3)*, 305-330.

Witkin, H. A., Mednick, S. A., Schulsinger, F., Bakkestrom, E., Christiansen, K. O., Goodenough, D. R., et al. (1976). Criminality in XYY and XXY men: The elevated crime rate of XYY males is not related to aggression. It may be related to low intelligence *Science,193*, 547-55.

Witt, S. D., (2000). The influence of peers on children's socialization to gender roles. *Early Child Development & Care, 62*, 1-7.

Wolffers, I., & van Beelen, N. (2003). Public health and the human rights of sex workers. *Lancet, 361* (9373), 1981.

Women's Educational Equality Act Equity Resource Center (2002, September). Equity and Careers: Progress and Promise. WEEA Equity Resource Center Digest. Newton, MA: Author.

Women's Health Interactive (2001). How heart disease differs in women. Retrieved December 18, 2003 from http://www2.womens-health.com/health_center/cardio/wcvd_women.html

Wong, P., Lai, C. F., Nagasawa, R., & Lin, T. (1998). Asian Americans as a model minority: Self-perceptions and perceptions by other racial groups. Sociological Perspectives, 41, 95-118.

Wood, E., Desmarais, S., & Gugula, S. (2002). The impact of parenting experience on gender stereotyped toy play of children. *Sex Roles, 47(1-2),* 39-49.

Wood, J. T. (1994). *Gendered relationships..* Mountain View, CA: Mayfield.

Wood, J. T. (1999). *Relational Communication: Continuity and Change in Personal Relationships* (2nd Ed). New York: Wadsworth Publishing.

Wood, J. T. (2000). Gender and personal relationships. In C. Hendrick & S. S. Hendrick. *Close relationships: A sourcebook* (pp. 301-313). Thousand Oakes: Sage.

Wood, J.T., & Inman, C. C. (1993). In a different mode: Masculine styles of communicating closeness. *Journal of Applied Communication Research, 21(3),* 279-295.

Woods, C. J. P. (1996). Gender differences in moral development and acquisition: A review of Kohlberg's and Gilligan's models of justice and care. *Social Behavior & Personality, 24(4),* 375-384.

Wooton, B. H. (1997, April). Gender differences in occupational employment, *Monthly Labor Review,* 15-22.

World Health Organization (1999). *Female genital mutilation.* Geneva, Switzerland: World Health Organization.

World Health Organization (2000). WHO Issues New Healthy Life Expectancy Rankings. Retrieved December 12, 2003 http://www.who.int/inf-pr-2000/en/pr2000-life.html

Wright, J. C., Huston, A. C., Vandewater, E. A., Bickham, D. S., Scantlin, R. M., Kotler, J. A., Caplovitz, A. G., Lee, J. H., Hofferth, S. & Finkelstein, J. (2001). American children's use of electronic media in 1997: A national survey. *Journal of Applied Developmental Psychology, 22(1),* 31-47.

Wright, J. V., & Morgenthaler, J. (1997). *Natural hormone replacement for women over 45.* New York: Smart Publications.

Wurzel, J. S. (Ed.). (2004). *Toward multiculturalism: A reader in multicultural education* (2nd Ed.) Newberry, MA: Intercultural Resource Corporation.

Yapko, M. D. (1998). *Breaking the patterns of depression.* New York: Doubleday.

Yee, J. L., & Schulz, R. (2000). Gender differences in psychiatric morbidity among family caregivers: A review and analysis. *Gerontologist, 40(2),* 147-164.

Young-Bruehl, E. (1990). (Ed.) *Freud on women: A reader.* New York: Norton, W. W. & Company, Inc.

Zaleska, J. (2004). Pay and rewards. Retrieved June 15, 2004, http://www.cass.city.ac.uk/faculty/j.zaleska/files/Management_of_HRM.session7.ppt #6.

Zebrowitz, L. A. (1997). *Reading faces: Window to the soul?* Boulder, CO: Westview Press,

Zhao, G. M. (2003). Trafficking of women for marriage in China: Policy and practice. *Criminal Justice, 3,* 83-102.

Zhao, Y. (2004, November 7). Beyond 'Sweetie': Women's place in professional schools: More is merrier. Education Life. *New York Times.* 20-22.

Zillmann, D., & Bryant, J. (1988). Pornography's impact on sexual satisfaction. *Journal of Applied Social Psychology, 18,* 438-453.

Zimmerman, D., & West, C. (1975). Sex roles, interruptions and silences in conversations. In B. Thorne & N. Henley (Eds.), *Language and sex: Difference and Dominance* (pp. 105-129). Rowley, MA: Newbury House.

Zucker, A. N. (1999). The psychological impact of reproductive difficulties on women's lives. *Sex Roles, 40*(9-10), 767-786.